T0307192

THE EMBASSY

A STORY OF WAR AND DIPLOMACY

DANTE PARADISO

BEAUFORT
BOOKS

THE EMBASSY

Greene, Graham. Lawless Roads. 1960

Library of Congress Cataloging-in-Publication Data On File

ISBN: 9780825308253

For inquiries about volume orders, please contact:

Beaufort Books
27 West 20th Street, Suite 1102
New York, NY 10011
sales@beaufortbooks.com

Published in the United States by Beaufort Books
www.beaufortbooks.com

Distributed by Midpoint Trade Books
www.midpointtrade.com

Printed in the United States of America

Interior design by Mark Karis
Cover Design by Michael Short
Jacket Design by Mark Karis

Cover Images from Getty Images:
Top Image U.S. Air Force / Handout
Bottom Image Chris Hondros / Staff

For

ACCP

"…it must be difficult to shoot a laughing man:
you have to feel important to kill."

— GRAHAM GREENE

In Memoriam

CHARLES SAYPAN

JAMES KORYON

SAMUEL KARTEE

CHRIS HONDROS

TIM HETHERINGTON

NABIL HAGE

JOSEPH ELLINGSON

ARTHUR A. DELA CRUZ

JOHN AUFFREY

AUTHOR'S NOTE

This book is a work of narrative non-fiction designed to place readers as much as possible alongside the actors in the incredible drama that occurred in Liberia in 2003. It has been written by stitching together the recollected experiences of those who were there based on interviews, conversations and other exchanges after the fact, as well as the author's own memories. The author was a political officer at U.S. Embassy Monrovia in 2003. A full list of persons interviewed is provided at the end of the text. The book also draws inspiration from the ample film, photographic and written record produced by the many news agencies and filmmakers who were in Liberia at that time. The text hews as closely as possible to the major facts and timelines of the war, but in reconstructing the thoughts, dialogue, and experiences of the actors, spoken language and descriptions have been shaped for clarity and narrative cohesion.

This book does not make use of cables or email traffic, or any other official, recorded nonpublic communications of the United States government. To the extent that such material may come to light and be at variance with what is presented here, it would be because memories or perceptions of events are different than whatever may have been recorded in official channels at the time. Of course, if any significant, material factual inaccuracies should be revealed, they should be brought to the attention of the author and/or the publisher so that appropriate corrections can be made in later editions.

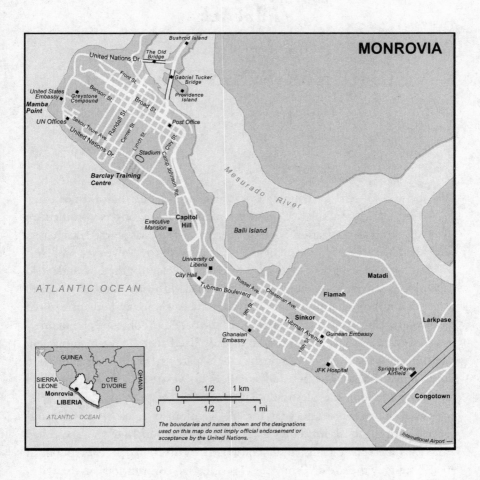

MONROVIA

Bushrod Island

The Old
Bridge

United Nations Dr.

Front St.

Gabriel Tucker
Bridge

United States
Embassy

Greystone
Compound

Benson St.

Broad St.

Providence
Island

Mamba
Point

Randall St.

Post Office

UN Offices

Sekou Toure Ave.

Center St.

United Nations Dr.

Lynch St.

Stadium

Camp Johnson Rd.

1st St.

Barclay Training
Centre

Mesurado River

Executive
Mansion

Capitol
Hill

Balli Island

University of
Liberia

City Hall

Russel Ave.

Matadi

Tubman Boulevard

Chessman Ave.

Fiamah

ATLANTIC OCEAN

9th St.

Sinkor

Larkpase

Tubman Avenue

Ghanaian
Embassy

Guinean Embassy

10th St.

JFK Hospital

Spriggs-Payne
Airfield

Congotown

International Airport

GUINEA

SIERRA
LEONE

CTE
D'IVOIRE

GHANA

Monrovia
LIBERIA

ATLANTIC OCEAN

0   1/2   1 km

0   1/2   1 mi

The boundaries and names shown and the designations
used on this map do not imply official endorsement or
acceptance by the United Nations.

PREFACE

LIBERIA SCENESETTER

Liberia is an African country that started as an idea that did not come from Africa. In the 1820s, the United States Congress funded an "American Colonization Society" to return freed slaves to Africa, either as a philanthropic venture or as a facile attempt to resolve race problems by sending blacks "back" to Africa. The lands selected for the new state held much promise: rivers and coastal shoals teemed with fish; veins of gold and minerals ran through hills; and forests yielded teak, ebony, and other treasured hardwoods. Unfortunately, the riches also belonged to someone else, namely the sixteen tribes, give or take, who already lived there. This inconvenient fact did not deter the sponsors or the emancipated African-Americans, who sailed across the Atlantic in wooden galleys to West Africa and set up camp on a small island in the Mesurado River delta.

Over the next two decades the black colonists coaxed, cajoled, and clashed with the locals until they had their patch, and in 1847 these so-called "Americo-Liberians" established Liberia as Africa's first independent republic in an area roughly the size of Tennessee. The Liberian constitution was drafted at Harvard, the Liberian flag patterned after Old Glory, and the Liberian capital named for U.S. President James Monroe, to honor his support for "repatriation" efforts. The Americos anointed themselves the governing class, though they were never more than a fraction of the country's population and their numbers were bolstered only modestly over time through intermarriage with locals and by the embrace of various waves of "Congo" people, former slaves from European colonies and territories who had escaped or been liberated by the British navy. The new elites deeded themselves the best lands, wrote the laws favorable to their interests, and erected manses along the shore that, for many of the first settlers, recalled antebellum plantation houses they had left behind. They ruled Liberia from the comfortable shade of their verandahs and employed their African countrymen, the original tribes of Liberia, as cheap labor, sometimes as forced labor, while largely excluding them from politics and civic life. Liberia was even rebuked by the League of Nations for its labor practices, which in some cases were slave-like, and it took the government until the mid-nineteen thirties to codify some basic protections that ought to have been in place from the start for a country with its particular origins.

Although the United States established its first diplomatic mission in Africa in Monrovia, transatlantic communication in the nineteenth century was, as one might imagine, as slow as the sailing ships and steamers of the time, so for more than fifty years Liberia developed in relative isolation from the country that had birthed it. At the start of the new century, however, coincident with the rise of U.S. power, Liberian elites called upon their ties across the Atlantic to attract investment, which mostly took the form of concessional arrangements in rubber and mining. The most visible symbol of Liberia's emergence as a U.S. trade partner was the Firestone Corporation's sprawling rubber plantation, opened to support the rapid growth of the automotive industry.

With Liberian-American joint ventures as the core of its economy, Liberia over time came to be counted upon as a dependable U.S. ally and was called upon during World War II to support the fight against the Axis powers. U.S. engineers built Robertsfield, the national airport, as a refuel stop and depot for military planes headed to North Africa, and they later supervised the construction of the Free Port of Monrovia, financed through the Lend-Lease program, to ensure Liberia's iron-ore could be brought to market. During the Cold War, the United States trained the Armed Forces of Liberia as a bulwark against the Reds and Liberia hosted a Voice of America complex, whose broadcasts from a network of towers north of the capital were intended to counter Soviet propaganda across much of Africa.

By the mid-1970s, the outsized U.S. diplomatic mission comprised multiple agencies, more than eight hundred officials, and family members. Monrovia became a most sought-after Foreign Service posting, known for pleasant beachfront housing, pools and lawn sports, somewhat reliable electricity and running water, and friendly locals who, for the most part, adored the United States. Liberian elites, in turn, embraced the relationship as never before. They traveled frequently back and forth to the United States and their children attended American colleges and professional schools. Family trees filled with dual-nationals and the notion of a special bond between the two countries, even if not fully reciprocated, was more or less taken as gospel. It was even built into school curricula. For Liberians of all stripes, the United States was forever patron and partner, known colloquially to those with means enough to visit as the "Second Heaven" and to everyone else as the "Great United States" or Liberia's "Big Brother Country." From time to time some even suggested, only half in jest, that the republic apply for statehood.

In the late 1970s, though, the polity changed. Liberia's presidents had always been elected by the dominant True Whig Party through opaque and insular processes designed to maintain the status quo. Swept up in the academic bent of the era, some students at Liberia's best institutions leaned left and decried big business capitalism, called for more equitable distribution of wealth and even, at times, agitated for the rights of "indigenous" Liberians, who, for the most part, lived on concessions or in squalid conditions in the interior of the country. President William Tolbert started down the path of reform, but his halting measures either came too late or backfired. Riots erupted when he authorized a one-third increase in the price of rice in a misguided attempt to relieve inflationary pressures on the state budget. "If you haven't taken rice today," it was said in Liberia, "you haven't eaten." The sleepy, tree-lined streets of the capital for the first time were strewn with broken glass and debris, and the effects were palpable and immediate. A notion spread, in the classrooms and in the streets, in the villages and on the concessions, that the state was vulnerable and that Liberia's long-ignored internal splits were now manifest.

The coup started, as most do, in the barracks. In 1980, Armed Forces of Liberia Master Sergeant Samuel Kanyon Doe, and a few cohorts, stormed the Executive Mansion. They burst into the president's office and disemboweled Tolbert at his desk. Nobody had seen it coming, but some in the streets cheered, little aware of what lay ahead. Shocked into paralysis, or silent in tacit complicity, the elites allowed the coup to stand. Doe, then just twenty-eight years old and semi-literate, of ethnic Krahn descent, became Liberia's first head of state without a colonial pedigree. He wasted no time with reforms of his own.

Thirteen prominent Liberians were lashed to telephone poles hastily raised on the beach and executed by firing squad in front of a startled press corps. The grainy black and white images that circled the globe dismayed Liberia's many friends, yet Cold War dynamics were at play and nothing was done. Coups were all too common at the time and the U.S. government had no intention of abandoning its main toehold in West Africa over this one. A few years on, President Ronald Reagan invited Doe to the White House to highlight the importance of the alliance, though he famously called him "Chairman Moe." Over the next decade, U.S. assistance to Liberia totaled more than 800 million dollars, much more than the usual bilateral assistance to African countries and big money at the time.

Flush with cash, Samuel Doe appointed family and ethnic Krahn allies to key posts. Contracts were voided and rewritten to accommodate the personal equities of Liberia's new rulers, while talent bled from the country and civil servants complained privately about a marked decline in professionalism in government. A joke circulated that corruption in the old days wore a morning coat, then in Tolbert's time underclothes, but now, under Doe, it pranced around butt naked. Just as concerning, Doe meddled with the Armed Forces of Liberia, seeding the ranks with ill-trained acolytes. In 1985, Thomas Quiwonkpa, Doe's former top lieutenant, failed at his own coup. In response, Doe dispatched the army to Nimba County to pacify the Gio and Mano peoples, traditional enemies of the Krahn. Villages were torched, families were killed. As news of massacres drifted through the jungle and into the capital, Doe stood accused of "tribalizing" Liberia.

By the late 1980s, as the Cold War receded, the United States government awoke to the mounting record of human rights abuses and distanced itself from Doe and his cronies. Embassy staffing was cut, military training and economic assistance reduced, and the Peace Corps sent packing. As Liberia's economy spiraled into decline, an overmatched Doe could do little to stem the erosion of the state. On Christmas Eve, 1989, a local braggadocio named Charles Taylor led a band of roughly eighty rebels into Liberia from the north, and Doe's army could not muster a coherent defense. The president did not last the next year, his ears sliced off, on video, by Prince Yormie Johnson, a Taylor ally-turned-rival. Liberia quickly fell into vicious factional fighting.

From that point on, Charles Taylor became the story in Liberia, synonymous with its new era, though little in his background had forecast him as a generational figure. Born of mixed heritage, Taylor grew up in the seventies as

Liberian elite and attended the same parties as everyone else. He had his first brush with minor celebrity when, according to the Apocrypha, he was expelled from a missionary school for pissing in a well. He recovered well enough to attend Bentley College in Massachusetts, but latent ambition bloomed somewhere along the way and he returned to Liberia in the early 1980s to serve under President Doe as Director of the General Services Agency, which handled government contracting and procurement. Charged with embezzlement not long after, he fled to the United States, only to be arrested and jailed in Massachusetts pending an extradition request. The record shows he escaped prison, although how is entirely unclear, and somehow made his way back to West Africa to plot a grab for power.

Doe's coup could be in some sense characterized as a visceral rejection of the politics of exclusion. Taylor's movement, though the faithful might deny it, was fueled by personal ambition, opportunism, and the desire, among certain quarters of the old guard, to restore the status quo ante. Charisma and energy helped Taylor win early support and he picked up the backing of some of Doe's old enemies in Nimba County, in the northeast. His forces quickly claimed a large swath of the countryside. The Liberian government broke apart under the pressure and Taylor might easily have stormed the capital but for rifts within his movement. West African peacekeepers were hastily deployed to separate the warring parties, but the poorly planned and under-equipped mission went awry from the start, and the peacekeepers were drawn into the combat. They held their own: even Charles Taylor, clearly the strongest warlord, could not displace them.

Instead, he laid siege to Monrovia for six years.

The war brought Taylor, and Liberia, international notoriety. Taylor financed his campaign with "blood diamonds" and cash from timber concessions under his control, and, early on, children were integrated into the ranks of his fighters through the infamous "Small Boys Unit." Liberia was always a land under the spell of the fantastic, where many of the vibrant animist traditions were shrouded in secrecy, at least to outsiders. Deep in the bush, *poro* and *sande* societies initiated members with piercing, scarring, and mutilation, while bush devils, strange, masked, and stilted creatures, still haunted the villages and much happened under cover of darkness, when shape-shifters, believers said, walked in their natural forms. Liberian fighters cannibalized these traditions. The world press, which otherwise ignored the country, was quick to run images of child fighters dressed in lurid wigs and wedding dresses, wearing necklaces of human fingers. For those predisposed to see Africa as the Dark Continent, Liberia became a place that, as Graham Greene once put it, "acted strongly on the unconscious mind, with a quality of darkness, and the inexplicable, and an unexplained brutality." Exiled Liberian elites lamented the collapse of civility and the civil order, while Taylor's apologists and those inclined to defend Liberian honor decried what they called the dehumanization of their nation by the (racist) media.

In the first six years of the nineties, the peak of the civil war, tens of thousands of Liberians died and hundreds of thousands were driven from their homes. The country lay in ruins, its roads torn up, its water and electrical systems destroyed. Nearly every bilateral mission closed save the U.S., the Lebanese, and a few African embassies. Liberia was left in the hands of churches, mosques, local self-help groups, and international humanitarian organizations. A series of transitional governing arrangements failed and the "international community," such as it was, finally in 1997 organized an election as face-saving way to cut bait. To no one's surprise, Charles Taylor at long last captured high office, elected with the campaign slogan, "You killed my ma, you killed my pa, I'll vote for you." The newly-elected president swapped his trademark fatigues for immaculate white suits and presided over a nationwide disarmament campaign that disarmed only his rivals, who, within a few years, had mostly been killed or driven from the country.

It is unlikely Washington would have ever embraced Charles Taylor, as his warlord image and track record as a rebel were hard to overlook, but he squandered any chance to mend fences by opting to run Liberia as a personal fiefdom. His defenders, and he had some, would argue he had never been given a chance, that he always faced pressure from the United States and its allies, who could not accept the results of the election, but by all accounts he ran a cash and carry economy that could not be sustained in the long run. He doled out timber and mining concessions and pocketed the cash or used it to arm militia and new paramilitary forces. Random violence and torture were common, and, perhaps worse, he exported his brand to neighboring states, most damning to Sierra Leone. A Global Witness report, the accuracy of which Liberian officials vigorously protested, documented how profits from timber flowed to the fight.

Washington policymakers had seen enough and systematically, over a three-year period at the turn of the new century, coordinated with allies to place sanctions on the Liberian government and travel bans on its top officials, in an attempt to cut off Taylor's money supply and, eventually, force him from power. At the same time, a new armed faction appeared in the forests in northwestern Liberia, along the border with Guinea and Sierra Leone, funded, it was rumored, by a loose coalition of Taylor's old adversaries. Initially the fighting occurred far from the capital, in the bush, and many observers at first did not believe the war had resumed, but, as camps of displaced people swelled on the outskirts of Monrovia, it became apparent that, indeed, the violence was real.

The United States urged the Liberian government to talk to the rebels, but Liberian officials dismissed the calls, bitter that, as an elected government, anyone would ask them to validate an insurgency and extra-constitutional pressures. Taylor did sometimes hold talks in Monrovia with Liberian political parties and civil society activists, which the U.S. ambassador derided as "peace jamborees" that would have little effect without the participation of the armed opposition. But, by late 2002, the nature of the conflict changed and Taylor began to lose territory. In early 2003, a second rebel group appeared on the border with the Ivory Coast, to the southeast, and the government found itself fighting on two fronts. Slowly, inexorably it seemed, Taylor's forces fell back.

Presidential elections were slated for 2003, but the government had not announced a date and the Liberian street, from all that could be told, assumed that Taylor would simply rig them if he felt that he could not win at the ballot box, but the shadow of war that crept across the map convinced many that elections could not be held in any event. Squeezed by sanctions and losing territory, Taylor finally agreed to sit down with the rebels and negotiate. After several false starts, the talks were set to begin in early June in Accra, Ghana. The new parlay did not stop the rebel advance on either front. The rebels claimed that Taylor would not be serious and that he was playing for time. The government, in turn, countered that the rebels did not want peace, only power that they could not otherwise win.

Complicating the picture were wars in Sierra Leone and the Ivory Coast, in which Liberian money and fighters were involved. A British intervention brought Sierra Leone a fragile peace following years of medieval violence, and the new government and the United Nations jointly established a Special Court for Sierra Leone, based in Freetown, to prosecute individuals for the horrors that had been committed. The Court received funding from the

United States Congress and its chief prosecutor was an American lawyer. In the region, many believed the Special Court was set up specifically to nab Taylor for his support for the Revolutionary United Front, the baddest of the bad in the Sierra Leone war. The Court had issued several indictments under seal and Taylor was rumored to have been named, but no one could confirm. The prospect of indictment, though, overshadowed the peace talks: Taylor knew that if he ever ceded power, he could be prosecuted. Those who knew him well often said that he feared no man, but he would not submit to a court or go to prison. Given the choice, they said, he would fight to the death.

PART ONE

THE FIRST ATTACK

Charles Taylor speaks at opening of peace talks in Accra

1

THE INDICTMENT

The Liberian civil war had lasted three years, or thirteen, or twenty-three, depending on how you counted, yet as in most enduring conflicts, the violence was episodic. Disquiet was the persistent condition and your mind sought relief where it could. On the morning of the latest round of peace talks, the last chance to save what was left of the state, Senior Master Sergeant Robert Ferguson lingered on the balcony of his embassy-furnished flat, lit a hand-rolled cigarette and allowed a moment of seduction.

Dawn broke low and grey over the coast. The first rains of the season drifted from the sky in gossamer strands and settled lightly on the leaves of the mango and breadfruit trees across the way. The air bore a sweet, vaguely post-coital smell, of sea salt and fruit pulp and damp linens. In the alley below, red soil softened underfoot as the harlots and handmaids jogged to shelter in their calico skirts and flip-flops, laughing, holding scraps of cardboard to cover their beads and braids. The generators were off, spent after a long night of huff and shudder, and a cool veil of rain tamped down the din of the waking city on the narrow cape between the jungle, the river, and the sea.

Fergy, as he called himself, took a pensive drag and exhaled slowly. The Operations Coordinator cut a rugged figure against the block and plaster high-rise as he leant on the rail in a bath towel, with his broad chest and softening waist exposed, his yeoman's shoulders and muscular arms drawn in like an aging contender. Over the past few months, the rebels in the southeast had advanced to River Cess, while the rebels in the northwest had captured Bomi Hills, not fifty miles off, but from the remove of a few stories, in the half-light, you could fool yourself that this could be anywhere in the tropics with tolerated disparities, that the war and privation could be walled off by white-washed masonry and bougainvillea, and that the day ahead held promise of parasols and frosted drinks. Fergy had half a notion to grab his golf clubs and drive out to the old Firestone plantation for a quick round on the rambling fairways and oil sand greens, but he had just enough doubts about what could happen in the next several hours that he thought better of it.

Charles Taylor, Liberia's president and West Africa's bogeyman, had flown last night to Ghana to attend the peace talks' opening ceremonies, and in the city he left behind his anti-terrorist units and olio of pro-government militia were more restive than usual at the checkpoints. Taylor kept his irregulars off the streets until it was time to fight, but, for most Liberians, they were at least as dangerous as the rebels, their threat distinguishable more by proximity than by affiliation. With their *papay* away and two rebel armies marching on the capital, there was no telling how they would react if negotiations foundered.

Cadence calls burst from the alley, accompanied by the tramp of leather boots. Parallel columns of the embassy's local guards appeared, skirted the high-rise, and crossed a narrow public road to the imposing slate and cinder walls that encircled the nineteen-acre U.S. diplomatic compound. A wiry commander slapped a black club against his palm as he barked out lefts and rights. The guards wore crisp khakis and black baseball caps and, though they were only modestly paid contractors, they were the most disciplined security force of any kind in the country. Fergy watched the trim formation march in place until each guard shuffled through the galvanized steel tubes of the embassy's roto-gate, then flicked away his smoke and quit the balcony. Horacio "Hersh" Hernandez, the local guard force supervisor, had been in Liberia for the worst of the nineties, when hopped-up gangs of child soldiers stalked the streets and corpses littered the curbs. Fergy asked him once if he thought the fighting would reach the capital again anytime soon. "This place," Hersh shrugged, "can turn into a nightmare in the blink of an eye."

Expatriates generally steer clear of war-torn countries, but those who take root, if they are not marginally criminal or outright mercenary, tend to be one of idealist, itinerant, or iconoclast, and Fergy was no exception. He dressed at the leisurely pace of a man who had been ordered to hurry up and wait too often in his career and now kept his own time. He was not an obvious fit for the military, but as a pimpled twenty-year-old he had, for kicks, siphoned fuel from a patrol car while the officers dozed up front. At the arraignment, the county judge told him he could either serve time or serve his country, so he enlisted in the Air Force. Eighteen years on he had become a senior non-commissioned officer and was drifting toward retirement until his squadron slated him for a dead-end job, which irked him enough to wade into the personnel system and secure the billet in Monrovia. No sooner had he landed in country then he shed his jumpsuit and dress blues for tropical shirts, cargo-shorts, and open-toed sandals. If you asked him what he did, he said he was just a secretary, albeit a secretary who got shot frequently: once through the calf in Iraq, during the first Gulf War, and twice in the back with rubber bullets in Indonesia, amid street demonstrations, as he galloped through curtains of tear gas.

On his bureau lay a black Beretta. He slapped in a clip and let the weight of the gun sink briefly in his palm. Guns can change men, unsettle them or pump them with bravado, but Fergy was in a line of work that trained you to kill and he knew well the limitations of a nine-millimeter. The men and children who fought Liberia's war were practiced in the dark arts of the bush and, when they were lathered for blood, would neither fear nor respect a sleek bit of iron, plastic, and brass. They also had more firepower. He tucked the gun at his back so that the folds of his shirt concealed it, hitched a radio handset to his belt, locked up, and left. The echoes of his footsteps in the wide, empty stairwell sounded, almost, as if someone shadowed him as he made his way down to the street.

Outside, the rain had stopped and the dark water stains on the clay started a slow retreat from the whitening sky. On the far curb, his driver waited for him behind the wheel of "Fifty-eight." In every city there are men who are paid to watch things, and the men in Monrovia who loitered at the corners and copped a few Liberian dollars for their marks all knew Fergy's snow white Land Rover by its diplomatic plate number. CD 58 could turn up at any time, in any neighborhood, and the appearance of a Defense Attaché car inevitably sparked a round of hurried, furtive calls on local mobiles.

"The fuck you lookin' at, Jay?" Fergy said with a grin as he slid into his seat and shut the plated door. James Arthur Jimmy had worked for the Defense Attaché Office for almost the entirety of the war. Like most of the embassy's locally employed staff, he encountered a wide variety of personalities and knew well that, for Americans, tone and inflection generally meant more than the words themselves. "Morning, Bob," he replied as he eased away from the curb and slalomed past a series of serpentines painted with red and white candy cane stripes. The veteran driver was the only person who called Fergy "Bob," and, not for the first time, Fergy pointed that out. "Okay Bob," Jay Jay laughed.

Along the road there was little indication that the events unfolding in a conference center several hundred miles down the coast would have any effect on the rhythms of the day. Half-naked men crouched by the gutters to perform their daily ablutions, while stooped grandmothers laid curdled clothes to dry on the basalt that poked through the vines and creepers. Smoked fish was in season and slender women shaped like papayas walked to market with bright plastic buckets of *bony* and *napleh* balanced on their heads. Attacks and counterattacks during the dry months had ruined the harvest, but a few withered farmers unrolled gunny cloth along the curbs and stacked for sale small clutches of okra, tomatoes, and red and yellow scotch bonnet peppers.

Most Westerners see Africa only through the windshield of sports utility vehicles, on safari or brief business trips or charity missions, but, more often than not, Fergy could be found on foot, sweating among the hawkers or day laborers unless, as now, he had reason to canvass the city more broadly. Jay Jay knew his preferences and did not bother to ask for a route. They swung onto Benson Street, past a neo-Greco Masonic temple whose white marble blocks and fluted ionic columns seemed almost a hallucination against the greenery and zinc-roofed shacks clustered on the slopes.

Below, the city center was piled along the cape like an untended graveyard. A decade without a working electric grid or proper sewers left the capital defenseless against the equatorial heat and damp, so that it was now hard to tell if more of the damage had been caused by weather or by war. The low skyline consisted only of several bald towers of distressed concrete, plundered and stripped bare of fixtures in the nineties, or never finished, that overshadowed the city like an homage to Brutalism. A tall crane stood next to the frame of what was to have been the central bank, and from the main jib hung a sling of concrete slabs that had been frozen in place for more than a decade as the cables rusted high above the unwitting street. The rest of the buildings formed a haphazard, fourteen-square block collection of uninspired tin and cinder construction common to African cities, interspersed with churches, mosques, and sausage trees.

Throngs of people drifted past, walking here and there with no evident purpose. Monrovia was a city after the deluge, a kind of hand-to-mouth scrum that modernity was supposed to have resolved. Unemployment was by most counts over eighty percent, but the statistic meant little against the sprawl of the informal sector, where nearly everyone scraped by with remittances from family abroad. Plywood stalls and hole-in-the-wall shops were stocked with the detritus of the global market: obsolete electronics, costume jewelry, plastic bouquets, and various other sundries made halfway around the world. You could find rough analogues for anything you might purchase at a stateside mall, but everything was sold off clotheslines or wooden racks or from piles on the ground.

Fifty-eight stopped after a time on a rise that overlooked the vast Mesurado River. Powerful currents moved in variegated bands westward from an endless swath of mangroves to the sandy, frothing shoals at the mouth. A low, sleek cantilever bridge skimmed across the rough waters to link downtown with Providence Island, a spit of land where colonists first staked their claim to Liberia, and, further on, with Bushrod Island, five-miles of distended neighborhoods that encompassed the port and petroleum depots and the spidery remains of cannibalized industrial complexes. Pirogues sailed into view. In the bows, lithe fisherman swayed silently against the sparkling black waves.

Acrid smoke filled the cab and Fergy cussed at his cigarette. The Lebanese grocers in town could no longer secure regular shipments and the tobacco was stale, wasted by long days on exposed pallets at some port. The many years of conflict and international sanction that isolated Liberia from its neighbors and the wider world had scattered the small business community that once serviced the country's elites. Lebanese traders were now the fixers. Their informal networks crisscrossed the continent like scarab trails and in the usual course they could get their hands on the odd things that people with means sought in ruined countries: cement, chandeliers, and courtesans. When even their couriers could not find their way through customs unmolested, you knew that the war profiteers were circling and that bets had been placed against détente.

In among the crowds that milled by the bridge Fergy spotted Kalashnikovs, slung across wiry backs in a casual manner. He drew a green field pad from his breast pocket and scribbled his notes in ballpoint. The Defense Attaché Office had lead responsibility for liaising with host country military and security forces, but it was not such a straightforward job in Liberia. Order of battle can be difficult to assess anywhere, but in a regime that long ago relegated its proper army to shanties on the outskirts of town, the strength and disposition of government forces was difficult to sort. Arms and munitions were stashed in battered aluminum footlockers in plywood kiosks or in private homes throughout the city, and fighters mustered on promises of cash, or loot, or virgins, but their numbers and enthusiasm seemed to vary with the incentives.

Fergy counted men and counted weapons. It was not something he had been asked to do, not part of his job, but Fergy, who was mechanically inclined, had a restless, relentless curiosity, a desire to know how things fit together, whether parts in an aircraft or men in a military formation. The rifles looked timeworn, like toys left too long in the sandbox, with splintered butts and banana clips held in with blackened and frayed duct tape. A United Nations arms embargo imposed prohibitive costs for refit. Rumor had it that the presidency was short on cash and stopped paying the men and it did not pass unnoticed that a number of alleged "rebel" attacks happened in villages far removed from the front lines, deep in government-held territory. As the countryside smoldered, militia who fought for Charles Taylor turned up at the markets at Waterside or Red Light with enough coin to buy beer, stonewashed denim jackets, and gold pendants for newfound girlfriends, with their names embroidered in glitter and varsity script. Somewhere in their long, benighted history Liberians embraced gallows humor, and, with each new indignity, clever catchphrases popped up and spread like wildfire.

They called the obviously staged attacks "Operation Pay Yourself."

Jay Jay switched on the radio and spun the dial to Veritas, the Catholic station. A sonorous, slightly graveled voice rustled in the speakers and swirled around the cab like wind in the eaves of a country church. In Accra, Charles Taylor was at the rostrum. "Some people," the Liberian president told a packed auditorium of African dignitaries, "believe I am the problem." Fergy nodded as if to mean "more than some."

"They say," Taylor said, "that Liberians are ready to put down their weapons and live together in peace so long as I am gone. I remind you that I didn't start this war and my government is under attack by Islamic fundamentalists. But I say to my fellow Liberians: if I remove myself from Liberia – will that bring peace? If so, I will remove myself."

Applause from the audience in Ghana rained through the speakers, but Taylor's use of the conditional was not lost on his constituents back home. He had said "if" he were to remove himself – and for Liberians that clearly meant he had no intention of quitting office. Fergy had a standing bet with Jay Jay that Taylor would not finish his term, which in theory expired in a few months if he were not reelected in a national vote that he had not yet scheduled and which the state was entirely unprepared to conduct. Jay Jay took the over and fully expected to collect. Charles Taylor had taken the presidency with the campaign slogan, "You killed my ma, you killed my pa, I'll vote for you." The idea that such a man would ever prematurely cede power was laughable to most Liberians, and few believed the rebels had the tactical acumen or logistical support to oust him.

The Operations Coordinator gazed out the window. Militia wandered about like dazed tourists and three or four squatted by a hulking, long dead ironwood tree and smoked spliffs of cartoonish proportions. When the war was last in the city, snipers had favored the tree for its clear sight lines into the neighborhoods of lower Bushrod Island, but now it was better known for a colony of bats that took wing from its hollows at dusk and circled the skies like a dark, whispering cloud. Closer to water's edge, near the footings of the bridge, policemen in threadbare brown uniforms flagged down cars with their truncheons. They pretended to write tickets for this or that until someone passed them a few crumpled bills and then, with a careless motion, they waved the cars on. It looked like any other day, Fergy thought. It was business as usual.

Jenkins Vangehn, U.S. Embassy Monrovia Political Specialist, a local, stopped for lunch at one of the "attae" teashops on Broad Street. An oft-overlooked aspect of embassy work was that, in most cases, much of a mission's routine work was performed by locals from the host country. They expedited immigration and customs processes, drove and serviced the motorpool fleet, maintained the embassy facilities, managed the warehouse and housing inventories, and generally provided all manner of "back office" support, from payroll to human resources to consular services. In short, they did the unheralded things that allowed the diplomats to focus on diplomacy.

Jenkins more directly supported bilateral relations. His job entailed, in the main, helping the political section gauge local socio-political dynamics, tracking breaking news, and arranging meetings between embassy officials and a wide range of contacts in government and civil society. It was not an easy role in a place like Liberia, where the authorities were perpetually aggrieved with the embassy's political censure, as reflected in the annual human rights report, and often fingered him for "allowing" the Americans to criticize the country for its failings. He was still new enough in the role, having been hired a couple of years before, that not every official or policeman recognized him and he could still walk out of the office, stroll the few blocks into town, and disappear into the crowds.

Steam and smoke from the kettles and grills softened the features of the young men who hunched over thermoses and cheap transistors to sip spiced Arabian tea and listen for news from Ghana as they sat beneath faded four-color prints of past World Cups that buckled with condensation. Taylor's latest gambit, his conditional offer to resign, sparked a raucous debate and the rafters echoed with the staccato rap of Liberian English, the local patois. Jenkins found a seat by the door.

The radio at his table buzzed with static. He toyed with the wire antennae without success, then lifted the little black box, peeled the masking tape from the back, and pressed the Double A's hard into the plastic tray with his thumb. BBC came through again just as a correspondent delivered, in the neutral cadence of a weather forecast or a market update, the kind of news that jolts a nation. "Liberian President Charles Taylor," he said, "has just been indicted for war crimes by a United Nations-backed court in Sierra Leone."

The collective gasp in the teashop was audible.

"Mister Taylor is currently in neighboring Ghana," the BBC continued, "where he opened peace talks with rebels by offering to stand down. A warrant for his arrest has been served on the Ghanaian authorities and sent to Interpol." Jenkins, like everyone else in the place, was caught by surprise. The Sierra Leone tribunal had issued sealed indictments several months ago, and Charles Taylor was presumed to have been named, but this was the first public confirmation. That the announcement had been made while the Liberian president was on foreign soil raised the possibility that Taylor would be rendered on the spot and not return. The ship of state was for the moment rudderless. In an instant chairs and tables were shoved aside, thermoses overturned, and gruff voices raised in exuberance or outrage. Someone shouted: "The Papay finished!"

Outside, the news that an international criminal court made a grab for Liberia's sitting president exploded across the city with the violence of an unexpected thunderclap that sent cracks along the rim of the sky. Everyone started to run. The street filled with a dizzying spectrum of headscarves, blouses, tee shirts, sateen gowns, and tie-dyed *lappas* that blurred together in continuous motion like streams of color in time-lapse film. No place was safe, so there was no reason to run, but if President Taylor was in trouble the militia would surely be let loose and it was hard not to want to run somewhere.

The air filled with the torrential sound of rubber soles and calloused feet against the hard earth. Men and women ran down sun-splashed avenues and through narrow alleys piled with garbage. They ran across fields and causeways and vacant lots edged with *poo poo* grass. They ran with wailing children cupped against their backs and ran behind medieval wooden carts listing with storm lanterns. They ran and stumbled and plowed into one another as they ran in opposite directions. When Jenkins tried to stop anyone, to ask where they were headed, or why, urgent voices shot back "I beg you leave us! You can't hear the news? The Papay arrested!"

CD 58 drove past him, headed uphill.

He called his boss then left the street.

Gunfire overhead scattered the crowds and the street emptied. Within minutes only the militia boys were left. Fergy and Jay Jay were on foot when the wayward kids Fergy had seen by the bridge morphed into menacing, spectral figures that grouped in far greater numbers in the arcades and on the roofs. As they reached Fifty-eight, a Toyota flatbed bulled around the corner, backend fishtailing as it cut the turn. Juju dolls swung from the grill, misshapen plastic heads and appendages of different playthings spliced together with twine and barbed wire. Halos of dust across the cracked windshield obscured the driver, but crouched in the back were a band of feral young men who wore wraparound shades and Liberian flag bandanas and brandished automatic weapons.

The moment guns are drawn danger spikes like upbeats on an electrocardiogram. Fergy felt the blood surge in his veins as the flatbed slowed and the crooked shadows of the rifles passed over him. Never one for prudence, he stared down the kids like he was fixing for a schoolyard brawl, but Jay Jay, whose eldest son had been killed by Taylor's men, hog-tied naked and dragged through the streets, ducked into the Land Rover, reached across and tugged at Fergy's shirt. Fergy relented and slipped into the car. Bullet resistant glass provided illusory distance, as if an electrical current were snapped, but as soon as they pulled away, a chant from the battlewagon lapped against the windows: "No Papay, no Monrovia! No Papay, no Monrovia. If Papay ain't come, blood will waste!"

Jay Jay tapped the gas and drove off at a pace calibrated not to spark a chase. In silence they passed a flotsam of cars and lorries that pulled off the road, their drivers fled on foot. The end game had begun. The tribunal's stunt dimmed chances that the palaver in Ghana could stop the war. If he were not already arrested, Charles Taylor now had every incentive to stay in office, while the rebel cause seemed to have gained color of law. At the embassy, the Marines would be opening the armory and the guards unspooling concertina wire by the gates. As the city receded in the rear-view mirror, more shots rang out, and Fergy knew that the militia had already started to kick down doors.

Operation Pay Yourself was in full effect.

2

THE RETURN

Hands pressed against blistered black paint, the guards grimaced and bent against the rising grade like old-time porters until wheels churned in rusted tracks and, little by little, the sheet metal gate slid open to reveal a white sports utility vehicle. Fifty-eight rolled several yards into the embassy compound and stopped, idling heavily, while a hydraulic ramp barrier sank into its concrete bed. A wizened gardener with a hose coiled over his shoulder and green plastic watering jug in hand saluted as the Land Rover lurched forward and made a sharp right turn onto a short, steep access road that plateaued at a concrete plaza with a circular panterre at the center, in which stood a thirty-foot flagpole of brushed steel. The Land Rover passed in a broad arc around the lavender irises and low hedges and stopped again in the shadow of the chancery, where the passenger side door swung wide and a pair of sandaled feet stepped out.

Fergy did not enter the chancery immediately. After Fifty-eight left, he stayed for a few moments on the front steps, his head tilted ever so slightly as he listened to the ringing silence. The consular outbuilding was closed and Gate One sealed and he heard no sounds from the street or the city beyond. No running, no gunshots, only the trills of weaverbirds high up in the coconut palms as they darted in and out of their round nests of twigs and grass. He felt brief disorientation, akin to the first lightheaded steps outside after an illness, where there is often some elusive divide between your senses and the things that happen around you. Six months into his tour, Fergy had seen more than once the febrile tendencies of the Liberian crowds, in fisticuffs outside the clubs or in the pitched anger and theatrics of labor strikes that always ended abruptly after a few tires were set afire and kiosks sacked. Outrage, or nearly any other impulse to act, took effort to sustain in the thick and watery air along the coast, yet he was still stunned at how quickly Liberians had gone to ground.

It was a "what the fuck" moment.

He turned and headed in. It was said that the condition of an embassy told the state of relations between two countries. Even in naked sun, the chancery had the forlorn mien of a shopping mall that had lost its anchor tenant. It was a non-descript rectangular structure fronted by a series of grim concrete sun louvers that stood just far enough from the exterior walls to form a covered arcade. The louvers blocked the view and created the inescapable impression of a poorly conceived military pillbox. Inside, the lobby whispered of deferred maintenance in its stained acoustic tile and chipped linoleum. Leaves pooled around the bases of several potted figs. Guests who waited for official escort could stare at an elaborate teak carving of the embassy seal and jungle motifs, gifted long ago by a forgotten community group in the days when ambassadors still traveled upcountry, or they could recline on a vinyl divan near Post One, where a Marine stood guard behind dark glass and a bank of electronic switches and blinking video screens.

Crisis imposes a certain discipline for those who can handle it: the nonsense falls away and you are left with the clarity of the tasks at hand. As Fergy crossed behind the hard line and mounted the narrow, dog-legged staircase to the executive suites, he rifled through a mental checklist: account for personnel, secure classified materials, check message traffic, report to higher headquarters, stand by for orders. He had been through the drill dozens of times before, only it was always different at embassies, as opposed to military bases, because he had to deal with the State Department. Other than the Ambassador, he still did not know what Foreign Service officers did, other than volley emails back and forth, or hold talk shops that never ended with decisions. Now they called another meeting.

Fergy entered a barren, windowless room scented with camphor and settled dust and shut the door as carefully as he could. Swag valances, faded yellow and draped from an iron rod, concealed the far wall for no reason and lent the solemnity of a funeral parlor to the briefing. Chargé d'Affaires Christopher Datta sat alone at the head of a boardroom table, while the rest of the winnowed country team filled out the sides. Fergy slid roughly into a mesh seat beside the Defense Attaché, his boss, a reservist on temporary assignment who had papers in hand for departure in the next seventy-two hours and wore the harried expression of a man in a cab stuck in traffic. Bowed heads and frowns suggested that a fair number of the others at the table were irritated to be there and would rather have been back in their offices, waiting for close of business so they could drive off to the Anchor Club and down a few beers on the pier as the tides crept against the pilings.

Datta stared intently at a black console in the middle of the table. A dry, tinny voice could be heard on the speakers, patched in via a feeble satellite uplink from Accra, where the United States' ambassador to Liberia talked to a blinking red light on a similar console in a hotel room several hundred miles away. John Blaney had been on hand for the debut of the Liberian peace talks and had been in the street waiting for an embassy car when the BBC broke the news that the Special Court for Sierra Leone indicted Charles Taylor. The usually deliberative ambassador did not bother to hide his disgust with the timing of the announcement. Static peaked at his harsher inflections, as though synchronized.

"For the court to pull a stunt like that without warning us was irresponsible," he said. "Everybody knows we fund the court, so they put your lives at risk in Monrovia. You could have been grabbed at any checkpoint. And they jeopardized the peace talks and didn't even get their man. There's no way the Ghanaians, as hosts, were going to arrest the head of state of a country in the region. You can't simply shame them into action. They invited him to Accra to try to end the war. The court had no plan!"

Fingers pressed to brow, Datta frowned in agreement. Fergy had so far had little contact with the Chargé, but he was not unsympathetic. The guy was not permanently assigned to Monrovia. Washington sent him to post as the number two for several weeks to fill a gap in staffing and cover the embassy while the Chief of Mission was on travel, but command responsibility had fallen to him at a bad time. At least he knew the stakes: Datta had recent experience as Chargé in Sierra Leone, where the very groups that the Special Court accused Taylor of directing had moved from village to village hacking off children's arms and tossing them in piles. They even named the cuts: "short sleeve," if they hewed at the shoulder, and "long sleeve" if they severed only the wrists.

"How many Americans are still in country?" Blaney asked.

Papers rustled in the soft hands of the Consular Officer, a mild, retiring sort averse to direct questions. Months ago the Ambassador directed him to scrub the F-77, the list of U.S. citizens who registered with the embassy at one point or another and the only way to estimate how many Americans might need assistance if things got out of hand. Verifications and updates were admittedly difficult in a country with no postal system, no landlines, and spotty cellular coverage. Ghost names were still on the list and unregistered Americans were surely still in country. If the embassy had no clear headcount, Fergy knew, some Major in a J-5 plans cell up at European Command would be hard pressed to find a number to fill in a briefing slide when the general staff inevitably asked the same question.

"You know how it is here, sir," the Consular Officer said.

"I need a number."

"Maybe, uh, five hundred."

Fergy was taken aback that an official would toss a number on the wall like wet pasta to see if it stuck, but he could not argue with the guess. A couple weeks back, when rebels reached the Bong Mines, close enough to strike the capitol, the Chargé convened a town hall to urge Americans to leave the country before it was too late. About fifty turned up, mostly dual nationals, missionaries, and relief workers. If you added families and other staff you could justify a ten multiple on the crowd, but it was a hell of a way to try to match needs to resources. At least it was not Fergy's fight.

"Tell them again to leave," the Ambassador said.

Datta nodded.

"And tell the government we expect them to protect our people."

Still nodding, Datta leaned toward the microphone, his thin, angular frame bent low across the edge of the table so that his clasped hands nearly touched his chest. He asked if the peace talks were dead on arrival, which, as Fergy saw it, was another way of asking when the Ambassador would return. Blaney demurred. "We met with Taylor's team in Brussels just before I came down here to Accra," the Ambassador said. "Taylor's people asked for the meeting. They insisted that Taylor told them that everything is on the table, all of what they called the 'superfluous' issues"—he laughed—"you know, like working with the rebels, elections, freedom of the press, and human rights. Everything. But they wanted a transition period before elections. And Taylor gets to stay in office for the transition."

"How long?" Datta said.

"Two to three years. They call it a 'soft landing.'"

Even in the best of times, Liberia was a country of constant irritants, sand and sweat and bugs and musky smells. Close-cropped hair and airy cottons did not help enough, and if Fergy found himself seated for any length of time, he reflexively scratched his wrists or the back of his neck. The tiny prickles started as he listened to the call. Diplomacy was not his trade, but he knew that if Charles Taylor wanted three more years, the rebels had little reason to stay at the table. Of course, that did not mean that the negotiations would end. African peace talks generally lasted at least as long as someone was willing to foot the bill for rooms and per diem at comfortable resorts. It was how things fell apart. Gin and tonics in hand at poolside bars, discredited ministers and their shadow counterparts berated the wait staff and made preposterous demands through the press, while, back home, their boozy henchmen raped women and trashed the countryside.

"I told them the rebels would never go for it," the Ambassador said, "and then for the first time I told Taylor's people what I really thought. First, I told them we can't help them out of this mess as long as Charles Taylor stays in power. Second, I had always said I didn't think they could win this war. This time I told them I thought they were going to lose." Datta rocked far back, hands locked behind his head, until the leather chair engulfed him. An audible puff pushed through his lips.

"Liberia stands at the edge of a precipice," the Ambassador said. "It's clear to me that Charles Taylor has to step down and leave altogether. Not in two years or three years, not even later this year—but now." The connection cut in and out. Datta looked at his technician, who shrugged and smiled apologetically. The Ambassador's voice returned mid-sentence after another brief static wrinkle.

"—to prevent chaos and wider bloodshed."

As the meeting broke, the Defense Attaché tugged Fergy's elbow and asked him to join a follow-on huddle with the Chargé. The light fixtures in the hall that led to the front office flickered and buzzed as if flies were trapped in the tubes. Rosewood plaques and certificates in dollar store frames lined the walls. The United States had never completely shut its oldest diplomatic mission on the continent, but over the past two decades, U.S. Embassy Monrovia had conducted more drawdowns than any other post in the world. In the wake of each, the troops that had dropped in to secure the compound and evacuate civilians left behind mementos with their operation code names and unit insignias, all variations of knives and snakes and scorpions, carved by local artisans or, in one case, self-made with aid of a felt tipped pen, photocopy paper and a few colored pencils. The Marine detachment assigned to the embassy hung them in the haphazard way of eighteen year-olds who understandably had more experience with barracks than with office corridors.

"Who's running the country right now?" Datta asked.

Five pairs of eyes found boot tips and worn beige carpet. Each of the Regional Security Officer, the Defense Attaché, the USAID Country Director, the Political Officer, and the Operations Coordinator knew the Liberian constitution provided that the vice president took charge if the president were incapacitated. Charles Taylor, they also knew, was still the commander in chief, but he was far away in Ghana, maybe in detention. It was unclear who would pass orders to the boys at the checkpoints.

"You heard the Ambassador, I need a contact."

Someone nudged Fergy.

"I can probably track down Yeaten," Fergy said.

General Benjamin Yeaten was Taylor's hatchet man.

"What about the vice president?" Datta asked.

Fergy arched his eyebrows. The Liberian vice president was a senior political contact and it made no sense to him why anyone would think that an E-8 would have his number. But everyone was looking at him, so he cussed in silence and flipped open his small grey mobile. The best he could do was to call people who could call people. "The vice president doesn't control the militia," he felt compelled to say.

The custom ringtone on Fergy's Nokia was the lowing of a cow. He claimed, somewhat implausibly, that he had not selected it but could not figure out how to change it. Outside the office, whenever his phone rang, anyone nearby would cast him a sidelong glance and, if he knew the person well enough, he would deadpan "shut up." Now, after ten uncomfortable minutes working the lines, the inane digital "moooo" belted from his breast pocket. Datta looked at him, puzzled.

"Fergy, is that your phone?"

"Yessir."

The Chargé took the phone in one hand and cupped the other against his ear. He moved to the window where, hunched into the call, he peered absently through the clouded panes at the grey backsides of the sun louvers. "This is the Chargé d'Affaires of the United States embassy," Datta said. "Yes—Mr. Vice President I know the current situation is very tense—yes, I understand—yes—yes—I'm calling to urge you to ensure the security forces respect the rights of American citizens. They should protect private property. Yes. Look, I want to be clear, we're going to hold your government responsible if any American citizens are injured or killed. Thank you, Mister Vice President—thanks—"

Datta passed a dark screen back to Fergy.

"I think I was clear," he said uncertainly.

He folded his arms and thought a moment.

"We should talk to someone in the military."

A number was found for General Yeaten. Nobody knew him well and Datta had never spoken with him before. It was terse. "We have been receiving reports of looting," the Chargé said. "We would like assurances that someone will calm the situation, no matter what happens in Accra." Again he listened, nodded, and hung up. Next to him, the Regional Security Officer frowned. "Ironic, isn't it?" Ted Collins said. "Charles Taylor might be a war criminal but right now everyone out there is praying like hell that he gets back as quickly as possible to get his men under control."

It was not just Liberians "out there," Fergy thought, but the team at the embassy too. If there were a breakdown in command and control, things in the streets could turn ugly fast. Of course if he were so disposed, if he believed that the embassy had something to do with the theater of the unsealed indictment, President Taylor could order a reprisal attack on the compound at any time; but unless and until he did so, the U.S. mission and its facilities stayed under the nominal protection of his government.

Poverty, violence, and wilderness are the archetypal constructs of sub-Saharan Africa. Each is reductive by definition, racist even, but the last is the most deceptive as it is portrayed through images of solitude: a sole flat-topped acacia silhouetted against the horizon; a lone black-mane lion hunting in the dried grasses; an isolated white mountain that wavers on bands of heat above the plains. In truth, the lands below the Sahara have scant few ascetic traditions. Everything is done together, in pairs, or groups. Fergy was mildly amused, then, when the smack of the steel door to the Defense Attaché suite signaled that his boss had left, and that, for the first time since he woke that morning, save a couple minutes out front, he was alone. The ambient hum of electronics and murmur of a shortwave radio masked the other sounds of the building. He glanced away from the stream of data on his monitor, pushed back from his desk and tucked a wedge of tobacco under his lip.

Outside the streets had quieted. General Yeaten had gone on DC-101 radio and announced that members of the military were expected to protect civilians and property and those who did not would face "military vibrations." Idly Fergy picked up the jewel case that contained the disc of a bootleg film that he meant to watch for some time, and spotted his own image in the glossy surface. Dim light and the distortion of the plastic accentuated his rogue Scots-Irish features: the round dome of his head and black hair; the low, lined forehead; the dark brow that concealed his eyes in shadow; the straight nose oddly lit, bright as though touched with gesso; the small comma cleft in his chin; the bow of his mouth that curled impishly at the corners. Age had yet to soften the strong line of his jaw, which he rubbed absently and absent any vanity. "What am I doing here?" he thought.

For several days there had been talk in the halls that the State Department wanted to pare down the embassy roster even more to keep it as lean as possible in case the post had to be abandoned, but he had paid no mind until his boss mentioned off-hand that afternoon that the Defense Attaché's Office might be closed. It made little sense to Fergy that a post rated "critical threat" for security would let any military assets leave, but he shrugged it off as he started to disable sensitive equipment and reduce his burn pile.

Fergy had reached the age when even the most resolute men begin to cast about, and though he little doubted that, if he were ordered out of Monrovia, the Air Force would keep him in the ranks for several more tours, a manila folder of blank retirement papers lay in plain sight in a black plastic tray on his desk, fixed by a globe paperweight. Military careers often ended at a point where everyone else is still climbing the corporate ladder, but none of the Defense Department's cheerful websites or colorful trifold brochures that touted transition services could resolve the dissonance for early pensioners. Over nearly two decades, Fergy had been deployed at least as often as he had been home and, on his last trip to the States, his wife told him that she wanted him back in her bed. Their daughters had just left the house and he felt a vague unease at the thought of Stacie dusting the empty bedrooms or washing the car in the lonely desert light that drew everything in sharp angles.

And yet. Something was happening in Liberia, something that hooked him in the way we are entranced by dust devils and flames and storm fronts, something big and strange and terrible, something he wanted to be part of. He had never really understood the ethic of the armed services, the idea that so many would sign up for life under orders, where you volunteered to be told what to do and how to do it, but it also never occurred to him that he could be sent *away* from conflict. To that point he had never taken himself or his career too seriously, but no soldier—or sailor or airman—wants to miss a war.

Charles Taylor's voice came to his ears and he raised the volume on the radio. "It's nonsense," the Liberian president intoned, "to think I have been arrested. I want to assure my fellow countrymen that I am fine. I am okay and I am returning to you tonight." Fergy glanced at his watch. The hours had passed in a fog of electronic mail and he had not been outside since midday. By now the sun stumbled off the ledge of the Atlantic and the colored sky bled out into the slate black sea. Liberia in war was a land of lies and deceit as much as any country in war, and a man indicted for crimes against humanity had every reason to mislead over his whereabouts. There was only one way to find out if Taylor was on his way back. Fergy jumped up, grabbed his keys, and headed out.

Thick clouds pressed down on the city like an attempted suffocation. Through wire screens at the counters of shanty bars lit by paraffin lamps, sloe-eyed women watched Fifty-eight pitch and heave across the furrowed blacktop on the far side of the ruined barracks of the old Barclay's Training Center, a ruined American-built military camp that served as a den and killing ground for armed factions during the nineties. For the most part the streets were abandoned, but at choke points here and there moth-like faces fluttered in the white dust of the headlights as the careless and the desperate used cover of night to scrap for food or drink or sex in the cesspool alleys. At the Buzzi Quarter petrol station, at the corner of the cursed Camp Johnson Road, a two-by-four on stacked cinderblocks barred the way and an awkward kid with razor bumps and an assault rifle flagged down the Land Rover. Twenty paces behind him, on a concrete island strewn with rubble that once housed gas pumps, half-dressed soldiers listed on plastic patio chairs.

Rituals at the makeshift checkpoints were usually just nuisances for cars with diplomatic plates, but could not been taken for granted. Earlier in the year, in the southeast, a van that carried payroll for an aid group lost contact a short time after it passed a police barrier on the outskirts of a remote town. Body parts had to be picked out of the bush when the van was found a mile or two on, burnt, its frame crippled like a dead sunflower with the fingerlike petals bent inward. Nobody ever claimed responsibility.

The Operations Coordinator crossed his wrists atop his steering wheel and waited. In an unpracticed move, the tip of a rifle tapped the windshield. Slowly, Fergy reached up and switched on the overhead so that the pale luster of his face was visible through the dark glass. Revealing himself as a white man was a trick that would only work if a semblance of command and control were still in place. Lips pursed, the boy lowered his weapon, then, hand to mouth, mimed a tippling motion. Fergy shook his head. Hoots from the pump station distracted the boy as his seniors pointed to the "CD" plates and waved the car on. Plywood clattered to the ground and Fergy toed the accelerator.

The parliament and the executive mansion were blacked out, and the wide artery that took you through the Paynesville and Congotown quarters was dark and empty save the light cast by security lamps on the wholesaler shops. The skies gave way somewhere around the Spriggs-Payne airfield. Angry drops smacked against the roof and windshield with the force of hailstones and then, like a river gathers before the falls, rushed down so furiously that Fergy slowed to a crawl. Tires strained to find traction as he ascended a long hill where pepper trees wept over the road and the few buildings along the way staggered off into the darkness. Thin trails of light appeared on his left, illuminating a stretch of unmarked grey wall that resembled a body shop, with two carports and an external metal staircase that might have been a fire escape. Charles Taylor called his home "White Flower" and though he had never been inside, Fergy could not square the name with the austere frontage. He swerved off road and parked on a low rise across the street, under the partial shelter of an enormous tree that sagged with mangos.

He drew a cigarette from the glove compartment and struck a match. Gaunt figures in ponchos appeared in the road like a stand of scarecrows and shouted and flung mud at the car through the folds of rain. They gestured that they would slash his throat, but stood just far enough from the car that it was clear they had no remit to attack. Fergy kept the key in the ignition just the same and blew smoke rings.

Sirens knifed through the rain. Moments later, half a dozen black sedans charged up the hill and blocked the road. The flashing lights that whipped red dye across the rain and the coded chatter from radio sets evoked a crime scene more than a protective detail. Men shouted, chains rattled, and steel curtains were lifted. A black Hummer roared into view and cut the corner into one of the cavernous carports. Aides in suits and slickers bolted from the other cars, ducking as if the rain could be avoided, and dashed after their president. So the Liberian head of state was not in detention and had not followed common practice on the continent to run to another country and spend the rest of his days as a fugitive in some well-appointed villa. Charles Taylor was no coward and he no doubt came back full of fight. Fergy stubbed out his cigarette, plucked his mobile from the cup holder and keyed in a short message: "The Papay is back."

3

THE ATTACK

"Everybody knows everybody," Liberians liked to say. Circles of power constrict in wartime and, in Liberia, once vibrant market towns far from the capital dropped away like so many dead limbs, ceded to the rebels or to the jungle. Monrovia itself more closely resembled Chicago under prohibition than a proper seat of government, a liminal world of brothels and nightclubs filled with fixers and heavies and bagmen. It was easy to track someone. At La Pointe, or Musu's, or the Porch, the few serviceable eateries could be counted on one hand and inside, in frail natural light, a host of fading businessmen and former officials hunched over steaming bowls of *dumboy*, marooned in Liberia for want of a visa or means enough for exile. Dressed in the threadbare suits they once wore to their ministry, they bent your ear about how, back in the day, they were great friends with the American Ambassador. Only those few players who could still make good on their threats held sway over anyone, over the blurred masses in the shacks and tenements that crowded the markets on market days and the churches and mosques on days of worship.

Diplomatic contact work and certain aspects of operations coordination shared this in common: they were best conducted over a drink or a meal. It was Fergy's job to know how to get done whatever the U.S. military might need to get done in Liberia, things like flight clearances or military assistance programs or logistical support for visiting officials. To be most effective, he needed to know the people, or the people who knew the people, that made things happen. La Pointe was Fergy's preferred lunch spot because it was a half-mile from the embassy, it had a reliable buffet and you could relax on a bamboo veranda that overlooked the waves and the shaggy green bluffs of Mamba Point.

When he arrived just past noon, Fergy found an empty dining room, unusual but not surprising given the events of the past day, and there was only one other customer, another white man seated outside at one of the cast aluminum bistro tables. The barmaid told him in a timid voice that the place might shut down for a few months, but the buffet was already prepared. Chafing dishes set on white cloth on a small wooden table offered red *jollof* rice, steaming fish soup, and cassava leaf stewed in palm oil with chicken, onions, and *bitter ball*—Liberian eggplant.

Two beers in, Guus Kouwenhoven smiled broadly and made a show of standing up when Fergy stepped through the sliding glass doors, sweeping his hand forward, and guiding the Operations Coordinator to his seat as if it were a family table. The large Dutchman was a front man for the Oriental Timber Company, a firm run by Fergy's old pal Joseph Wong, whom he knew from the golf courses in Jakarta. A month ago the United Nations Security Council banned the purchase of Liberian timber everywhere in the world, as it had done several years before with Liberian diamonds, in order to cut off blood money with which Charles Taylor could prosecute a war. Guus met expectations as an unapologetic confidant and business partner of a West African warlord, right down to the gold-framed tinted aviators, the gold chains and the black satin shirtsleeves open at the chest in a manner that could only be purposefully low-brow.

"What's happening?" Fergy asked.

Guus shook his head, took a smoldering cigarette from a clamshell, and pressed it to his lips. The land dropped away precipitously on the other side of the rail, and he looked past the decorative ivy draped from the eaves out over marshy flats at the base of the bluffs that marked the site of an abandoned quarry that once yielded stones for the breakwaters. You could see a strip of sand, a few curved palms and, here and there, fishermen drying their nets. The Dutchman spoke with a bitter edge in his voice. "It's a bloody mess out there," he said. "Rebels overran eight of our logging camps in two months. The savages burned everything. But we're just about done moving the equipment. We closed the sawmill this week and our warehouses are empty. After we're gone, everything will be looted. That's always how it happens here. You try to add value and then the war comes and they destroy it all. They'll even peel off the roofs."

The great mystery was where it all went, all the copper wire and corrugated sheets and myriad spare parts for engines and generators. Local markets were moribund. Sierra Leone lay in ruins to the north, Guinea suffered from enduring malaise, and Cote d'Ivoire was being torn asunder by its own civil war, a recent accord notwithstanding. Throughout the Mano River Basin, anything of value had been spirited away, maybe to Nigeria and Burkina Faso and other points east. West Africa, it seemed, was some great circulatory system for scrap metal, with loot flowing from market to market just ahead of the violence. In the end, everything was diminished.

"Where to next?" Fergy asked.

"Maybe Congo for a spell. Maybe France, to get away from all this."

Logging rigs and other heavy equipment floated on a steamer somewhere off the coast, on vicious currents on the edge of the rains, and Guus needed to find a port soon or his burn rate would take him into the red. Liberians called it "get, grab, and go"—you have to make cash fast in war-torn countries, and hand over fist, because wind-downs are always a mess and you need to be able to buy your exit when the knives come out, as they inevitably do when any criminal venture ends. It would have been impolitic to ask Guus about Taylor's indictment, and Fergy did not, since it stood to reason that if the tribunal would go after a sitting head of state, his partners and financiers would be targeted as well. Both men knew that Guus could at any moment be reeled in with the likes of Viktor Bout, the legendary "Merchant of Death," a Russian arms dealer with alleged Kremlin ties who was wanted on at least three continents. Fergy had no problems himself with Guus, but he suspected this would be the last time they met for a while.

"You don't put much stock in the peace talks?"

Guus dismissed the idea with a two fingers and a zig-zag of smoke.

"You Americans want to get rid of Taylor. He said he is willing to go but you have to give the man his dignity. Be careful what you ask for. The rebels are going to be worse. They don't know the game. They don't respect anybody. If you ask me, Liberia's in for another bloodbath. This place is finished, unless you do something about it."

The waitress brought a Club, a ubiquitous local beer produced and bottled at a brewery on Bushrod Island that used European equipment and, after the timber ban, was now the last gasp of Liberian manufacturing. As she poured the beer, she stood close enough that Fergy winced at the sharp perfume of her body, and her bosom brushed softly against his shoulder when she reached over him to place the wet glass on a coaster. Flat on the table, his mobile vibrated across the metal surface and then the familiar moo escaped. Fergy glanced at the number, which he did not recognize, and pressed mute. Moments later, feedback screeched from the handset at his hip and he keyed in to the voice of a Marine elevated with excitement.

"Birdy, Amityville, do you copy?"

The Marines took their call sign from the horror film.

"Amityville, Birdy, Lima Charlie."

"There's fighting at Kle Junction."

That was thirty-six miles from where they sat. Fergy cussed that he would miss the meal. Guus slapped his back in sympathy and they parted at the bar in the small rotunda at the entrance that was meant to evoke a traditional hut. Outside in the gravel lot, Jay Jay was smoking, propped against the car like a cardboard cutout. As they rolled away, Fergy tried to sort the story. To his mind, even if the rebels had the weapons to make a serious push for the capital, they would have to wait until the next dry season, five months off. Rains already started in earnest in the southeast and the laterite roads cut by the timber companies would be soup by now, especially with no one left to maintain them, which would foul up the rat lines from Cote d'Ivoire. The rebels to the northwest admittedly made rapid gains in the last month, but they could be stopped with a simple point defense on the sole paved road into the capital, since the bush on either side was an impassable maze of jungle and swamp at any time of year. The timber ban no doubt hit the regime's cash flow, but the rebels did not have artillery or any serious hardware, as far as anyone knew, and Taylor should have had more than enough resources to parry the thrusts.

Kle Junction was the first real line of defense, though it was nothing more than a fork in the road that took you six miles further on to Bomi Hills, where the paved road tapered off, or shot you straight out to Sierra Leone. Rebels encamped at Bomi would be crazy to chance a direct assault on the Kle checkpoint, a high white wall that flanked the road on either side like the wings of a non-existent building. The last time Fergy drove out, a month ago, several hundred militia boys were visible in and around the pink guardhouse. There were enough guns trained on the bush to hit anything that moved. If the rebels could not attack, Fergy told himself, the reports were just another round of "Operation Pay Yourself," cooked up to divert attention from the indictment.

Cellular towers were few and far between in Liberia, though they were the only commercial structures untouched by theft or mischief, presumably because even the hooligans wanted to call and text. Whenever something was amiss in town, the network swayed and strained to meet a surge in demand like a rope footbridge over a deep chasm. Fergy fielded calls the length of the city and onto Bushrod Island before service crashed and he was cut off from the news, left to parse the bits of rumor that had already fallen to him. Under disapproving skies Fifty-eight pushed north past the landmarks of Bushrod: the Free Port, Bong Mines Bridge, Duala Market, and the New Kru Town slums. At the northern tip of the island, a split lane bridge crossed over the Saint Paul, a brackish river that ran dark with tannins, the old blood of the forests. On the far side, the last buildings fell away and the land opened into a patchwork quilt of grasslands and swamps.

The car paused atop the buckle of a freeway overpass, an incongruously modern loop designed to ease traffic westward toward the grounds of Hotel Africa, where a simple left turn would have sufficed. Africa was littered with decaying vanity projects, palaces and hotels and stadiums erected to showcase wealth and power but which, in their neglect and disrepair, told of impotence and incompetence. For Liberia, Hotel Africa was among the most visible symbols of the collapse of the state. Before the succession of coups and insurrections and child soldiers, a former administration spared no expense to build the lavish complex to host heads of state that came to Monrovia for an Organization of African Unity conference. The pièce de résistance was a grand swimming pool in the shape of the continent, but, when factional fighting swept through the country in the nineties, the vacated resort became a playground for misbegotten youth. Anything of value had been smashed or torn out and the violated six-story edifice now stood in shame by the beach, exposed to the elements like a carcass left by poachers. Anyone who did not know the history and saw the debris heaped in the corners or strewn across the floors, or the excrement in the empty pool, might have guessed it was the work of an epic flood or a tempest, and it told of the singular violence and depravities of men that this was not so.

Fergy scanned the horizon with binoculars. The road ahead was a brush-stroke of gray ink and on either side soft breezes moved across the grasses in silvery swishes. Hidden from view a few miles to the north, he knew, were huge tent cities for people who escaped the fighting in the countryside. They had fled a year ago, a month ago, a week ago, and trekked through forest and overgrown plantations until they reached the outskirts of the capital, where they were permitted to set down the few things they carried on head and back in the shadow of an abandoned Voice of America radio tower.

Over the past decade roughly half of Liberia's population left the country and survived in refugee camps in nearby states, but the two hundred thousand men, women, and children who now sheltered under blue and white tarpaulin within earshot of where CD 58 now sat did not enjoy the thin protections afforded by refugee status. The degradations of modern conflict reach into law and semantics: they were not refugees since they had not crossed an international border. Instead, they were considered "internally displaced people," an inartful term most often shortened to the featureless acronym "IDP." To be an IDP was to have lost your home and become a mark on a statistical roll, reliant on the largesse of the very regime that let you be chased away, or chased you away.

Fergy fiddled with the radio. Charles Taylor was on the air again, his voice hoarse and defiant, tinged with anger. "To call the President of Liberia a war criminal?" he said, "God himself will not permit it." The few stations left relied on generators, and fuel and cash for fuel were hard to come by. One by one they shut down over the past few months. Veritas could broadcast because the Church had money, and DC 101, Taylor's preferred stop on the dial was still up and running, at least for a few hours a day, if only to spin some rhythm and blues and transmit the president's speeches.

"While this was going on in Accra," Taylor said darkly, "certain actions were being perpetrated in Liberia. Contacts were made by certain Western Embassies accredited near the capital, to senior armed forces of Liberia personnel. The attempt was foiled because a general in the army refused." Everyone tuned in at that moment knew that Taylor spoke of only one embassy, and Fergy cringed as the thought of the effect the accusation would have on the scared and jumpy militia. The calls to the Vice President and Taylor's commanders had been necessary and appropriate, but someone must have pulled the records and whispered coup d'etat when Taylor came back.

"This particular time, as in every organization, there are weaklings," the Liberian president continued. "Some succumbed. As a result, we have received and accepted the resignation of the Vice President. He will be explaining in the next few days to the nation and the world what prompted actions on his part and I am sure he will issue an apology for the Liberian people." Too bad for him, Fergy thought. Paranoia and palace intrigue are hallmarks of regimes near the end. If Liberia's number two was not already face down in the swamp rice, a bullet through his skull, it only would be because he was an elder from Nimba and enjoyed the fealty of a number of shooters in the ranks. But the word on the street that morning was that two other civil servants, John Yormie and Isaac Vaye, were also missing. Fergy did not know them, but in Liberia missing and dead were synonymous.

"As I am talking to you," Taylor concluded, almost as an afterthought, "there's massive fighting going on, with units trying to enter Monrovia." When Fergy looked up, strange rafts of hats, headscarves, bedrolls, and plastic tubs bobbed on the surface of the grasses. Moments later, heads sprouted beneath the rafts, then shoulders, then fully clad torsos and arms, until whole people clambered from the low-lying fields. They filtered out along the route as far as the eye could see, walking at pace on the hot and tenderizing tarmac, with children and the infirm in tow, headed south toward the Saint Paul. Spooked enough to quit the grid of tents, trenches, and pit latrines in the same hurried way they quit their upcountry villages, their numbers swelled quickly to the thousands. It looked like ants coming down, Fergy thought.

"Turn the car around, Jay," the Operations Coordinator said. Gray gauze settled over the land as they drove in parallel to the exodus back to the river, where a stiff breeze wrestled leaves from stands of cottonwood and ironwood at the bend in the watercourse. Anti-terrorist units in black berets and forest camouflage kept the restive crowds off the bridge by shooting in the air and, like water spreads along a curb from a clogged sewer, haggard families wandered along the banks until they found a spot to drop their bundles of clothes and bedding. The ATU were Taylor's most elite paramilitary forces, a praetorian guard of sorts trained by mercenaries and foreign agents who chose not to publicize their services to African warlords. Taylor had forced his way into power by waging a long bush war against Liberia's constitutional army, the remnants of which he relegated to squalid, crumbling barracks while he surrounded himself with a coterie of specialized troops that answered directly to him. To see ATU at the municipal limits meant that Fergy had to re-think his thesis: something was amiss at Kle Junction.

Fifty-eight doubled back a mile or two and rambled up a barren knoll where the crabgrass had been stamped out by goats and herdsmen. In the embassy's armored fleet, windows were sealed shut, so Fergy cracked the door to catch the breeze, a hollow sound like the echo of waves in a conch shell. Rain started to fall and the air was fresh and clean. After a time he heard a low crackle, like wax paper unwrapped in a cafeteria. The noise came in fits and starts, then grew louder until he was certain it was gunfire. Mile markers flashed through his memory as he calculated distance. Fighting, if that was what it was, had to be near Iron Gate, under fifteen miles away, the last permanent checkpoint before the lonely stretch to Kle. Amoebic black forms broke loose from the green smear of the horizon and grew until they became pick-up trucks scarred with rust and spray paint, hammering their shocks as they approached. Militia were fleeing the front. Jay Jay gunned the engine, but the Operations Coordinator stayed him with a hand.

"Pretty cool, huh, Jay?"

"We should go, Bob."

Fergy grinned, but then came an ominous new sound, a series of thumps as if someone beat a pillow against a wall over and over until the feathers bunched at one end. You do not hear mortars until they hit, but when they do, the sound is blinding. BOOM. Fergy felt the concussive force of the blast, like an unexpected gust that knocks you off-balance, and everywhere around the car loose topsoil kicked into the air. The shell landed close enough to kill but the shrapnel somehow missed them. He didn't have time to thank God. Legs flailing and fists clenched around his seatbelt, Fergy yanked himself back into the cab in time to see Jay Jay throw his entire weight into the power steering. Arcs of dirt spit from the back tires as Fifty-eight jerked over to the tarmac.

"Go, go, go" Fergy yelled.

Jay Jay shouted at him incoherent with fear and anger. He had no need to prove his courage. He had taken Fergy close to the frontlines before, but this was too much even for him. "You're trying to get us ki-ki-killed, Bob," he blurted out. Fergy's head throbbed with adrenaline and the echo of the blast but he could not help but stifle a laugh as he stared at the driver staring wild-eyed back at him. Hot damn, he thought.

Ahead, the ATU had fallen back. The Saint Paul River Bridge was open. Packs of people three or four abreast moved, as if in a processional, south toward the heart of Bushrod Island. Jay Jay nosed cautiously through crowds so fixated on their own progress that they hardly seemed to notice the shining white Land Rover in their midst. The rain stopped again. Maybe a hundred yards in, Fifty-eight passed a rundown petrol station, in the parking lot of which stood a pick-up with an anti-aircraft gun mounted jauntily in back. The rebels had no airlift, so the gun could only have been forward deployed to hold the bridge, which in turn meant that Kle Junction was breached and Charles Taylor did not expect his men even to hold Iron Gate. Nonsensical as it seemed, Fergy realized, the only conclusion that could be drawn was that a full-scale attack on Monrovia was underway.

A mountainous man in olive battle dress waved a crudely bandaged forearm at Fifty-eight and Jay Jay cut the engine and rolled roughly onto the shoulder. Lieutenant General Macsfarian "Momo" Jibba, once of the infamous "small boy's unit," pounded the glass with his giant fist. "Fifty-eight, Fifty-eight, you're not supposed to be here." Pushing his door wide enough to speak without strain, Fergy pointed out that they were en route to Mamba Point until the general stopped them. He knew Jibba and wanted to ask about the bandage, as a wound to one of Taylor's most trusted deputies indicated that things were not going well, but Jibba stepped back and shouted invectives.

Markets in poor, heated climes are loud with diesel engines, bartering, fast-talking hawkers, and foul-mouthed touts who herd passengers into over-full vans and taxis, and in all the noise and bumping about it takes little to set off the crowds: an accident, an argument, or a theft can spark a riot. Fergy feared the worst as Fifty-eight followed the tide of displaced people as they swept toward Duala, the largest market on the island and usual flashpoint for murders and mob justice. The walls of the brewery passed on the left and the outlying kiosks of Duala came into view. As the first wave of displaced surged into the fractious crowds, bundles fell from heads, slings of housewares were flung to the ground, and everyone sank to the mud like pilgrims at the end of their way. But there was no shrine, no place for respite, only muddy tracks and a churning, indifferent wall of their countrymen. Fergy had never seen anything like it. It was, he thought, like they had done this all before: ten thousand people, maybe more, just sat down.

Men in danger instinctively gather in circles, and Christopher Datta and the five members of his core security team stood in a small circle as they recon-vened in the embassy's executive suite. Shades were drawn. Datta stood beside a particleboard bookcase, eyeing the curious assortment of publications lined on the shelves like brooding patrons at a local coffee shop. Pamphlets written by obscure Liberian politicians from the sixties and typewritten surveys conducted by defunct engineering firms shouldered against glossy, bound volumes like *The Birds of Liberia* and *Biodiversity of West African Forests.* Datta held up a spent round, the tip of the bullet blunted and chalked.

"Stay away from windows," he said with a wry smile.

The door opened and in walked Ed Birgells, the Country Director for the United States Agency for International Development, or USAID, as it was known. At six foot six and sixty years old, from Chicago, Ed defined "old school." He had the testiness of a veteran basketball player not ready to quit the roster: all elbows. Before Liberia, he spent over half a decade in Mongolia, where his booming voice maybe dissipated a bit across the steppes. Fergy called him "Big Bird" and looked at him like that uncle you saw at holidays a few times a year who embarrassed the rest of the family but, when he pulled you aside, spirits on his breath, told you that you better learn to take a punch and hit back if you ever wanted to amount to anything.

"Fergy, what the hell is going on out there?" Birgells said.

"Fighting at Iron Gate and thousands of IDPs on Bushrod."

Birgells turned to Datta and spoke louder than the close environs warranted and Fergy was impressed the Chargé held his ground. "If the camps north of the city emptied," Birgells said, "we got two hundred thousand new neighbors and nothing to offer them. No food, no water, no shelter. That's a problem that you don't want to have."

"If I may sir," Ted Collins said, "in the past, whenever there's been trouble, they come here, to the U.S. Embassy." The baby-faced Collins was an Annapolis graduate and former Marine Infantry Officer who transitioned to Diplomatic Security after he completed his service requirements. In his mid-thirties, he was still fairly young to run his own shop. Embassy security was the job. At his disposal were one assistant, several local investigators, the Marine Security Detachment, and Hersh's crew of two hundred unarmed contract guards and maybe some of the local police whom the embassy paid and equipped to patrol the nearby streets. It was enough, Collins said, to secure the mission so long as the local guards and police stayed. If they quit: loony tunes.

Every crisis unfolds in its own way and, as doctors chart familiar maladies in unfamiliar bodies, the security team had to adjust to the new realities. Derailment of the peace talks was not unexpected, but legal action against Charles Taylor so swiftly followed by an assault on the capital served as lighter fluid on slow burning coals. Collins laid it out for the Chargé. There was a spectrum of threats that ran from violence and civil unrest to a properly planned and executed military attack against the embassy compound by the rebels, the government, or even individuals. The Regional Security Officer had to work a number of different equations at the same time, so it was hard to prepare an optimum response for everything. They were decision trees: every moment was A or B, left or right.

There were other issues. Embassies were often assumed to be self-sustaining American islands in foreign places. In fact, most often they relied on the host country for basic services. If there was a fire, they called the local fire department. If someone was badly injured, he or she was sent to a local hospital. Electricity came from the local grid and water was drawn from local aquifers. In Liberia, none of those systems were reliable, if they even existed, and in even a mild crisis they often failed. The capital had no electricity or running water since the hydroelectric dam was ruined during Charles Taylor's own attack on the city thirteen years before. The embassy had some limited redundancies, but if it were under protracted lock-down, sustainability would be at issue. Cisterns would drain, stocks of fuel and food would deplete, and cash to pay the guards and local employees would run low. If the airport closed, they could end up with evacuees on the grounds.

Datta stared at the ridges of the plastic blinds.

"Can we augment embassy security?" he asked.

"We can request a FAST," Collins said. "That's a Marine Fleet Anti-Terrorism Support Team. They're based out of Rota and trained specifically for situations like this. If we think we're looking at evacuations, we can ask European Command to send a survey and assessment team, what they call an ESAT. We've worked with them on contingencies for a couple years, so they know our post. They'll likely bring Navy SEALs with them. They'll look things over, see what we need if we're going to conduct a full-fledged non-combatant evacuation operation, a NEO, and help us make it work."

Datta keyed on one word and brightened.

"How quickly can we get the SEALs?"

"Yes sir, I'll check on that," Collins said.

Everyone readied to leave, but Datta caught them with a quick clear of the throat. The Chargé was neither a screamer nor particularly soft-spoken, but he lowered his voice enough to make everyone take notice and made eye contact as he talked. He spoke as if he had been holding his breath for a long time and finally decided to exhale.

"I got a call from Washington," he said.

Nobody in the room was surprised. Rebel attacks in Africa were not headline news back home—they did not even merit the crawl most nights—but they caught the attention of the Operations Center, the State Department's 24-7 monitoring team, and other elements in the vast interagency network back in Washington that were paid to track crises. Embassy Monrovia fielded call after call for updates from staffers who twenty-four hours ago could not have told you the difference between Libya and Liberia and now needed real-time data on who controlled the Saint Paul River Bridge.

"The good news," he said, turning to Fergy, "is that I told them that I need my Operations Coordinator. Fergy, you're staying." "They" were not identified by the Chargé, and most likely "they" were not in Fergy's chain of command, but Fergy figured that, if State wanted him there, the Defense Intelligence Agency would not object. It was not exactly relief that he felt, though he was glad to stay, but more a mild irritation, because it was so typical of the bureaucracy that the right answer, that someone in his role should stick around a shitty, war-torn country and risk his life to help out, was somehow treated as a reward. It was a no-brainer. Still, Big Bird shook his hand.

"The bad news is," Datta said, "they want me to close the post."

He frowned and looked like he could use one of those stress-relief squeeze balls they used to sell at the counter of five and dimes. He had a wife and a dog back home and was in the process of adopting a child. It was not entirely certain how the African Affairs Bureau convinced him to stand in as Chargé in the first place, but, Fergy laughed to himself, they surely didn't say: in your month in charge, Taylor will be indicted, you'll be accused of a coup plot, rebels will attack and then you will have to pull the plug on the mission.

"Sir," Collins said, "We can hold this place."

Datta nodded, though not in exact concurrence. "I said that's not my call," he said after a pause. "I said that they had to get a hold of the Ambassador in Accra and speak to him directly." He pointed a thumb at the door to the Ambassador's office.

"I told them," he said, "that I'm not going to close John's embassy."

4

THE EVACUATION

Anyone who says a rifle is an impersonal way to kill has not looked through a scope and seen someone in the crosshairs. It is an intimate moment: the balance of a life hinges on your finger, your grip, and the prevailing winds. Fergy knelt in the shade of a rampart of sandbags on the chancery roof and watched as Sergeant Jason Scramlin, a Marine Security Guard, panned his M-14 the length of the public drive, then lifted his head with a slight frown that suggested that he just now grasped the power of his charge. The second most senior Marine on post, after the Gunnery Sergeant, Scramlin was, Fergy thought, the sort of man you wanted on your roof when all hell broke loose, a country strong kid with roots in northern Michigan who wore, in his downtime, a faded green tee shirt stamped "Scramlin Feeds," for the family business. "When you go back home," Fergy said, just to say something, "nobody is going to have any idea about what you saw over here." Twenty yards off, beyond new loops of concertina wire draped along the embassy walls that glittered like tinsel in the morning light, the street was packed with people.

Overnight the rebels had somehow made it onto Bushrod Island and, at daybreak, the families that had stopped so abruptly at Duala market two days ago decamped just as abruptly and trekked with their buckets and bedrolls across the industrial zone, across the old bridge at Waterside, and up the ridge to Mamba Point. Desperation is not something you think to quantify, yet Fergy found himself counting. Someone in his chain of command at some point would ask how large were the crowds. Five thousand men, women, and children already stood in the street, and thousands more were on the way. They milled about in the unremitting heat, gawking at the two men behind the sandbags and the limp flag over the embassy. Fergy knew that Scramlin and Corporal Anthony Adams, who manned the bunker at the south end of the roof, were trained for the crowds that you sometimes saw on the news chanting anti-American slogans, but this was not that: no fists raised in anger, no effigies burnt, no black flags tilted on makeshift lances. The murmurs that drifted up to them were more akin to the ambient noise in an old barn before the auction starts. "America, won't you please come to help us," someone shouted.

"Liberia is your small brother country!"

Gunfire rapped in the distance, up from the flats of Bushrod, little pops like pinched bubble wrap. The crowds packed closer and shifted uneasily. "Moo" rang Fergy's phone, and when he answered he was told that the rebels had reached the beer factory, just north of Duala market. Their target no doubt was the Executive Mansion, but if they were following the IDP's tracks through the city the embassy lay directly in their path. It occurred to him that maybe Charles Taylor wanted it that way, so that the embassy would feel the threat too. More gunfire: rounds winged the palms above with the sound of charcoal on coarse paper, and bits of leaf floated down like green confetti. Then came the mortars, an arrhythmic beat plodding the length of Bushrod. Fergy cussed aloud. He was not a trained analyst, but he could not forgive himself for having missed something. The rebels had come too far, and faster than he imagined possible. The city could fall and the embassy could be overrun. With nods to Scramlin and Adams, he pried open the hatch, stepped in and climbed back down the narrow, rusty ladder into the blinkering lights of the chancery.

Fergy found Christopher Datta in the executive suite huddled at the coffee table with two square-jawed, able-bodied men in plaid flannels and denim jeans. In the predawn hours a pair of blue and white twin-engine Mi-8s chartered out of Sierra Leone had deposited the ESAT, a SEAL team, and a pile of black duffle bags on the helipad, then retreated up the coast with all due haste as the embassy's political office fielded calls from Charles Taylor's National Security Advisor, who decried the breach of protocol and sovereignty. "We would have let them come in if you had asked us," J.T. Richardson complained. "But it's our sovereign air space. You got to ask our permission." In fact, he added, Taylor wanted the U.S. Special Operations Forces to land at Spriggs-Payne, the Liberian military airfield in town, not the embassy. He wanted to welcome them personally. It said something about the Liberian mindset that a president under indictment from a U.S.-backed court would invite U.S. forces onto his turf, but for the moment, it seemed, Charles Taylor bet that Uncle Sam's presence would buy him time against the rebels, and maybe even give him a chance to cut a deal. If things broke wrong, he could always send his boys over the embassy walls. In any event, Datta knew better than to give the Liberian president a photo opportunity, and the ESAT and SEALs had flown in at the earliest waking hour.

The issue at hand was how to evacuate as many as five hundred Americans. Expatriates that only a few weeks before had not heeded the Chargé's plea to leave now called with strained voices to find out about evacuation plans. The embassy had little to work with. There were no U.S. ships afloat off the coast, no cargo planes or helicopters staged in nearby countries, and, contrary to local lore, no submarines docked in vast tidal caves beneath the embassy complex. Although the U.S. mission possessed a vintage boat that the staff took out on weekends to troll for barracuda, it held no more than six persons and had been mothballed after Taylor's men decided to take potshots at it whenever it returned to the docks. Robertsfield, the only commercial airport, lay forty miles to the south. The weekly Sabena flight to Brussels had been suspended and the only other airlines that still came to Liberia were Ghana Airways, which Liberians dubbed "Air Maybe" in a nod to its whimsical schedule, and Weasua, a local carrier that could get you to Abidjan or Freetown with a pair of Soviet-era planes that smelled like the back of an old jalopy, all brittle seat foam and sandy floor mats.

In other words, there was no easy way out.

"Tell me something good Fergy," Datta said.

"The Europeans called for a 'regroupment.'"

Datta cocked his head. Fergy admitted he never heard the term either, but he had just fielded a call from David Parker, an affable British national and long-time Liberia hand, now the European Commission's Aid Coordinator in Liberia, who had been left in charge of the three-person European Union Delegation while the Head of Delegation traveled to the peace talks. Parker had said that all European nationals, plus the Lebanese, had been asked to muster in the next twenty-four hours at the EU compound, which abutted the embassy walls. Apparently the French had sent L'Orage, an amphibious warfare ship, up from Cote d'Ivoire to conduct an evacuation.

"Will they take Americans too?" the Chargé asked.

"Yes, if there's space," Fergy said.

Datta did not hesitate: "Call everyone in."

At the gates you could smell the panic now, all spit and sweat and smoke. Men and women elbowed and bumped into one another like stranded commuters on a subway platform at the height of summer. From time to time the ranks closest to the concertina wire would churn until a gap opened, and a family of four or six or eight would appear with rolling suitcases and half-zipped plaid travel bags. Some of them were obviously foreigners but more often than not they looked little different from anyone else in the street, only their clothes were not tatters or knock-offs. As the crowds looked on in envy, they fished damp blue passports from fanny packs and mashed them against the bars of the consular gate, where they were snatched roughly by the large hand of Hersh Hernandez, who stood guard in an olive helmet and body armor, shotgun over his left shoulder.

Hersh glanced at the photos and handed the passports to a consular officer, who hustled back and forth between the gate and the offices. Roughly two-thirds of those who tried to get through were not Americans, though, Hersh muttered, they all wanted to be. Many were extended family members, but seats on the helicopters, if the French had any at all to spare, were at a premium. Embassy staff could not bump a U.S. passport holder for someone's aunt or nephew or cousin. These were the terrible choices of war, where national boundaries and the vagaries of marriage and place of birth, as annotated in a flimsy booklet or on a laminated card, meant more than kinship or blood. It was unfair, Fergy thought, as he escorted a lucky few to the waiting room where paperwork for the flight manifests and emergency loans was laid out on collapsible tables.

Signatures were dutifully scribbled, then, like visa applicants on a regular business day, the evacuees and their children slumped into rows of plastic bucket seats and looked up at American Forces Network on a small television affixed to the ceiling. Many seemed to know the drill, but a few percolated with nervous energy and wanted to know if they could contact home, when and how would they leave, where they were headed and for how long, and whether there was anything to eat or drink. Embassies, least of all aged facilities in isolated African countries, were not postured to shelter hundreds of people for any length of time, but Fergy prided himself on getting things done and if that meant humping plastic jugs of distilled water up from the warehouse, then he did it. Yet as a man paid to sort logistics, he chafed that he often had no answers for even the simplest queries. He could not even say with assurance that it would all work out. The evacuation was a French military operation and Fergy could do little but wait for updates from David Parker or Francois Prkic, the intense young French military attaché liaising with L'Orage.

As the day wore on, the evacuees were resettled from the consular section to the cafeteria, a drab hall with scuffed linoleum floors and plywood counters that smelled of whatever had been fried and battered for lunch. Chairs and tables were stacked against the walls and families made nests of their suitcases and duffle bags. In muted conversation or silent prayer they grappled with what they had left behind: businesses, homes, families. A few relief workers and journalists smoked together under the tin canopy at the front door, irritated that they had been ordered to leave by their headquarters in Paris or Brussels at a time when their skills were most needed. They wanted to know if the embassy itself would close for good. Nobody could say.

Light rain began to fall and an early dark blacked out the windows. The overhead lamps flickered with the ebb and flow of the generators and small children whimpered and squirmed in their parents' arms. The toilets backed up. And still they came. The first arrivals groused about the petty hassles, but later ones spoke of the fear. En route from Paynesville and points east they encountered checkpoint after checkpoint, and at each one the boys seemed drunker, and angrier, and the threats more wanton. A young woman from Oregon who had volunteered at a local orphanage had tried to get out via Robertsfield the day before, only to be outbid for every seat on every flight. She spent a sleepless night in the ruined terminal, then came all the way back to Monrovia. Tall and lithe, bright-eyed, with brunette hair so long it touched the small of her back, she seemed taken aback by the violence in a land known for violence.

There was always the question of why anyone would travel to such a place, or stay there, but, when he considered it, Fergy could not fault her any more than he could fault himself. Maybe she just wanted to do something good and see the world and took a flyer on a volunteer gig where she knew there were needs, and before long she had made friends and learned the little secrets of how to make things happen. She got to know the militia boys on her block and convinced herself that she could handle whatever went down. Then suddenly the war came and all the rules changed. Tears welled in her eyes as she told anyone who would listen that she had reached the orphanage by mobile, and the news was bad. Soldiers came and rounded up the children and forced them to dig graves. Her last call dropped amid the sound of explosions. She looked around, her clean lines contorted with regret that she had left and guilt at the relief that she now felt.

Near midnight there was a commotion at the gate. A little girl was carried in limp and blanched and soaked in blood, her arm shattered by buckshot. She was rushed to the health unit where Donald "Doc" Lish, the embassy medic, patched her up as best he could with a scalpel and some stitches. The health unit was not meant for surgery, but Médecins Sans Frontieres had pulled back from its clinic on Bushrod and the only other hospital in town was now on the far side of a thicket of checkpoints. John F. Kennedy Hospital was named in honor of the late president, but on the street they joked JFK meant "just for killing." Doc did what he could. Fergy spotted the little girl a short time later, crouched by her mother in a darkened corner of the cafeteria, a handkerchief-sized sling strapped to her shoulder, staring blankly at the cash register on its plywood stand.

The embassy housed its Marine Security Guard detachment in a snow-white Neoclassical mansion with a stately porte-cochere that once served as the Chief of Mission Residence. The reception hall had been converted to a recreation room with a pool table, beaten up leather couches and a wet bar where the Marines hosted happy hours on Friday evenings to raise money for the annual Marine Corps ball. The Marines bunked two to a room and the common areas were marked by glass-topped coffee tables piled high with graphic novels, gun magazines, and video game cartridges. It was not a place you would associate with a war zone, but there it stood, windows trembling, as mortars detonated at daybreak.

Fifty yards further down the slope, under a tin roof and surrounded by plywood walls, roughly one hundred and fifty men, women, and children roused themselves from the floors of the cafeteria, shook the grog from their heads, and peered fretfully through the condensation and the almond trees at an empty helipad, landing lights flashing like red sequins in a light rain. The air pulsated. Palm trees at the seawall danced like Rastafarians and they made out a pair of forest green and sand colored Cougars at the horizon, tilting low against the slate grey waves. The lead helicopter soon lifted over the seawall at the European Union compound and disappeared from view. The evacuation was on.

At the sound of the rotors, Jenkins Vangehn logged off his computer, snatched his Nokia and keys from his desk, and stepped outside. Political and economic specialists, of whom Jenkins was the only one then-employed by the embassy, worked from an office attached to the consular outbuilding, a few steps from the chancery and Gate One. To his left, through the black bars of the roto-gate, he spotted Hersh Hernandez, his deputy Tony Lopez, and the local guards pacing in front of a blurred, murmuring crowd.

Much as he was glad to be on the embassy grounds, Jenkins' mind was afire with thoughts of his own family, whose fortunes were not far removed from the clamor in the street. Nothing he had been told led him to believe the embassy would be abandoned, but even if it closed for a time he was confident he could manage somehow. Diplomatic history was replete with stories of the heroic efforts of local staff members who looked after shuttered properties in places like Kabul or Mogadishu, or kept Washington abreast of local news in the wake of a chaotic evacuation, and Jenkins was prepared to do his part. It helped that he had a fresh visa foil in his passport and a fistful of dollars in his office safe. If it came to it, he could make his way by pirogue or on foot to Sierra Leone, or Senegal, or Ghana, then catch a flight to the United States.

His concern was his mother and five siblings.

In Africa, especially in places where war or disease or bad politics had wrecked the economy, it was common for an entire extended family to rely on a single paycheck. Those with jobs at diplomatic missions, multinational firms, relief agencies, or any other place where the pay was reliable, faced unrelenting demands for cash: for rent, medical bills, school fees, clothes, and even food. Giving was not only expected, it was required. Jenkins was both the primary breadwinner and also the eldest son. He could not let anyone down. He planned to use his savings to send the family to Guinea, where they had lived once before as refugees, and wire them money whenever he could, except even Western Union locked its doors at the news of the attack. He did not know what he would do if the cashier counter were to close indefinitely and he could not send the payments.

Cougars came and went over the treetops. Above him, on the roof of the chancery, Jenkins saw the silhouettes of heavily armed Americans in Kevlar vests and helmets. He had seen them land a few days before. They looked like men with deadly intent and it crossed his mind, perhaps it crossed the mind of every local who saw them, that maybe they had come to take Charles Taylor away. Jenkins made his way to the top of the driveway between the chancery and the Marine house and sat down on the damp, white-painted curb, looking on quietly as embassy officers and other, unfamiliar men in plaid flannels hustled between the chancery, the cafeteria, and the landing pad, and shouted into their Motorola handsets to organize the evacuees into "sticks," or seating groups for the helicopters. Apparitions from his own past drifted through his mind as he watched the small children and suitcases slumped against the wet, rusting rails by the cafeteria doors.

Jenkins had grown up on a Liberian-American Mining Company concession in Yekepa, Nimba county, where his father worked in the mines as a Euclid R60 truck maintenance man. Life in the company town in the hill country was comfortable: wide, paved roads, electricity and running water, and proper sewers. The family lived in LAMCO bungalows and the children attended LAMCO schools. The company ran a modern hospital that also serviced the relatively large American and Swedish expatriate community. The town had a movie theatre, an Olympic-sized swimming pool, a golf course, and an equestrian club. For a boy who knew nothing else, it was a place to attend school and play in the yard free from want and worry, and to dream of a boundless future. Things started to change in the late-eighties, when Jenkins' father was laid off in a mass redundancy caused by a global commodities bust, and the family decamped to a village some miles away. Jenkins stayed behind, in the care of an aunty and uncle, to finish high school.

He had not yet graduated when Charles Taylor brought the war to Nimba. In early 1990, President Doe was still alive and in office and government forces still controlled most of the country. Taylor steered clear of the LAMCO concession at first, but changed tactics when he learned that the Armed Forces of Liberia used it for resupply from Guinea, after the National Patriotic Front of Liberia cut the other major ground lines of communication with the capital. One cool, wet night in April his aunty shook him awake just after midnight and told him that a friend called to tell her that the rebels just telephoned the LAMCO General Manager, an American, and advised him to evacuate the town. Jenkins followed his aunty into the carport and all seven family members squeezed into a small Nissan. Word had spread and the entire town seemed to be up, stumbling around in the dark, crippled shadows passing through the white shafts of torches and headlights. They joined a long train of cars headed toward the border, passing droves of people on foot dragging heavy bags and suitcases through the rolling savannah.

It is hard to know how to pack for an evacuation. You don't assume you will be gone long. You can only carry so much and the instinct is to bring what is necessary, not sentimental, but it is the latter that you most want if you cannot go home again. The family, with Jenkins and his cousins in the back seat, arrived at Thuo just after two in the morning, in heavy rain, and slept leaning on each other in the car. The village was nothing more than a customs outpost, all mud and corrugated tin and thatched roofs, so at dawn they drove on to Bossou, a larger town in Guinea about seven miles from the Liberian border. His aunty and uncle found a house to rent, but those with less means crowded into tents donated by the United Nations or the relief agencies. Heavy rains made it hard on the refugees and Jenkins, still in the first bloom of youth, despaired to know that but for his uncle's salary he could have been where the others were, fetching water from the creek, passing the time by carving circles in the mud with sticks, and waiting for nobody knew what.

Now, as Jenkins watched the Cougars ferry European nationals over the horizon to an unseen battleship, and mortars exploded and small arms fire crackled in the spaces between, the old feelings of fear, and confusion, and sadness flooded back. In the weary, stressed posture of the men and women queued for departure by the cafeteria doors he saw the painful reality of his country: a place you left if you could. He wanted desperately for the bloodletting to end, for people to be able to return to some sort of life. But Liberia was like tower damaged by tremors, walls fractured, foundation cracked, ready to collapse.

It could not bear much more stress.

Midmorning, a blue and white Mi-8 appeared. It floated past the concertina wire at the back wall and shuddered roughly down to the helipad. The door opened and a shortish man in a dark blue suit clambered down, where he was met by the Chargé and the Regional Security Officer. Quick handshakes were exchanged and greetings shouted, then they bent to the hill as the heavy wind from the rotors whipped sand at their backs. They reached a stand of rubber trees as the helicopter lifted off again, and the man in the suit straightened, buttoned his jacket, and tightened his tie. The U.S. Ambassador was back.

An Associated Press reporter intercepted him. John Blaney did not mask his mild surprise that there were members of the press on compound, but he gave Ellen Knickmeyer credit that she would work right up to the moment she boarded the evacuation flight, maybe even after. He knew that the rebels and government alike closely followed the wires and he was not going to miss an opportunity to speak to them directly. Gathering himself, he paused and then said in a resolute tone that the United States called on all sides for an immediate and unconditional ceasefire.

"It's time we become a player," he said afterward, "instead of just taking rounds."

Nokia pressed to his ear, Fergy took a call from his wife. At work twenty-four straight hours already, he realized as soon as he answered that she had already seen the news. Stacie had dealt with deployments before, but it never got easier. He dropped his head at the thought of the jolt she must have felt when she learned that the city was under siege. The rule in any overseas crisis was that if something bad happened you tried to reach your family before the news hit back home, if only to save them a bit of added stress. It was bad enough that you were "over there," but far worse if they saw something on the television and had no way of knowing if you were alive or dead. The first helicopter was three minutes out and he had scant time to explain, only apologize, and tell her he was all right.

She just wanted to know if he would be coming home too.

"No," he said tersely, "We have a small team staying on."

As he clicked off, he realized how finite it sounded and for the first time it hit him the risk they had undertaken. Stacie did not know when she would get him back, or even if she would get him back, and neither did he. But it was "go" time and he had to put it out of mind and focus on the task at hand. ESAT men in plaid and denim appeared alongside him and the embassy consular officers. They spoke to the evacuees in calm, authoritative tones, checked names against the manifests, then handed out white pieces of paper upon which "stick" numbers had been hastily scrawled in blue magic marker. Then the first helicopter bobbed into view, landed heavily on the white H at the center of the concrete slab on the lawn, and spit out French soldiers who jogged to the corners and knelt with rifles to the ground. Fergy raised his forearm to shield his face from the beating wind and led the first stick down to the landing pad.

Ambassador Blaney planted himself by a low hedge of ixoras and offered handshakes and well wishes over the noise and sand kicked up from the nearby beach volleyball court. The eyes of the evacuating people were hard and unfocused, darting between children and embassy officers and soldiers and bags and the dark hold of the helicopter ahead. French soldiers pulled them into the bays, strapped them in, and then, in a blink, the aircraft lifted away and the next one came. The exercise lasted two hours, give or take, then, suddenly, the winds were gone and there were no more hands to shake.

Euphoria came faintly to Fergy in the form of a dry, bittersweet taste in his mouth and he headed to the bar to grab a soda from the cooler. Altogether the French had evacuated more than six hundred people, but fewer than one hundred and fifty Americans. The cafeteria was quiet now, empty save a few lost tee shirts and shoestrings and half-full water bottles. It smelled like fever and stale farts. Manifests, names all ticked off, were stacked haphazardly on the counter like used playbills after a show. Fergy cracked the cap off his bottle and for a few minutes was at a loss.

The Political Officer walked in.

"The rebels retreated," he said.

Fergy stared at him, then went back outside. The mortars and gunfire had stopped and the skies rang with silence. Faint wind was all he heard, and the gentle rustle of almond leaves and the steady push of the tide against the rocks. Shaking his head, he pulled a small green tin from his back pocket, took a pinch of tobacco and jammed the chew between lip and gum. He looked around, as if searching for words.

"You've got to be kidding me," he said.

In the executive suite, the Ambassador and his team took stock. Backlit against the windows, Chris Datta leaned on the convector and jotted some notes. He no longer had command responsibility and looked tired but somehow light, like a hiker who had just set down his rucksack. The Ambassador was focused on discrepancies between the warden lists and those who turned up at the gates. The numbers did not match and he did not like the answers he heard. Not a few Americans simply refused to leave country. They were free to make their own choices, of course. He shifted uncomfortably on his divan.

"You'll always have your Sister Bs," someone said.

"*She's* still here?" the Ambassador huffed.

Sister B ran a Catholic girls school down the road. A regular at the Marine house happy hours, she turned up every Friday evening with her big oval glasses fogged up, ready to laugh and knock back a few beers. She had a well-earned reputation as a pool shark and circled the felt table picking her angles as she cracked wise in her thick Massachusetts accent. She had spent the better part of two decades in Liberia and seen her share of evacuations. Chris Datta had spoken to her in his office and urged her to pack up, but she asked whether the embassy team would leave. When he said no, they had jobs to do, she shot back that so did she. Then she laughed in the patient manner of a survivor and said she would not leave until she saw the flag over the chancery pulled down.

"Well, I want you to try to get everyone else out," he said finally.

"Yessir," Ted Collins replied for the team.

"Whatever it takes. I want you to empty the tub."

"Empty the tub. We got it sir."

"This thing is not over, not by a long shot."

"No sir, not by a long shot."

"We can expect another attack."

The meeting broke up. As Fergy walked out, the Ambassador tapped his shoulder. He asked what the Special Operations Forces had come to do. Fergy said that the Chargé had asked for them in order to help coordinate the evacuations and secure the perimeter. The Ambassador nodded, smiled thinly and said, "That's not the whole picture. I'd still like to know why they're *really* here." Fergy narrowed his eyes, unsure what the boss was driving at. "Well, just let me know what else you hear," the Ambassador said.

PART TWO

PRESSURE

French soldiers evacuate European nationals

5

THE AMBASSADOR TO HELL

The Harry S. Truman building in Washington, D.C., State Department headquarters, was designed in the late nineteen-thirties and expanded in the fifties, a dull period for all but the most gifted prairie school architects, none of whom appear to have worked on the contract. The imposing, featureless limestone exterior is impressive in a city of so many landmarks only in that it is entirely forgettable, like Lego blocks left at the bottom of a bin after all the fun pieces have been used and playtime is over. Inside it was little better. Visitors who passed through security soon found themselves in a maze of drab corridors that amplified the sound of footsteps as they walked beneath low ceilings of abraded acoustic tile with frequent gaps that exposed the ductwork. The corridors were indistinguishable from one another save single, boldly colored horizontal stripes painted along the walls that served as a proverbial trail of breadcrumbs when you inevitably got lost on your way to an appointment. It was a remarkably insular and conformist space for an institution whose mission was premised on creative engagement with diverse cultures.

A few Foreign Service officers, however, who were able to navigate well enough the bureaucratic traps over the course of a career, get some things done and still have the good fortune to be appointed as ambassadors, could look forward to a ceremony on the eighth floor, the top floor, where the eighteenth century décor of the suites and reception halls better reflected the nation's history and ambitions, if not its current tastes. Vaulted ceilings, ornate trim, crystal chandeliers, French doors, terra cotta carpeting, and pink fluted marble columns that served no structural purpose combined to create a throwback gentility for formal occasions. It was nice, everyone agreed.

On September 9, 2002, in the Ben Franklin room, John William Blaney III was sworn in as Ambassador Extraordinary and Plenipotentiary of the United States of America to the Republic of Liberia by Secretary of State Colin Powell in front of a small assembly of family, friends, colleagues, and mentors. As they stepped away from the dais, the Secretary took him firmly by the arm and marched him over to the valances where they ducked into the small space between the white and gold drapery and the French doors. The Ambassador caught a glimpse over his shoulder of the bewildered expressions of the guests queued for the receiving line and he guessed, to the extent he could collect himself, that he would be told that he had a tough assignment ahead. Instead, the Secretary pulled him close and said "Remember, John, you don't work for me anymore." Blaney was taken aback. It was true, because an ambassador was the President's personal representative in the foreign country to which he or she was accredited, but he never imagined he would hear it so plainly from the nation's top diplomat. Then Colin Powell left the reception.

On appearances alone, Blaney would not have seemed the obvious choice for an envoy to deal with a notorious West African warlord. Ruddy and rounded cheeks made him a boyish fifty-three, an impression not offset in the least by his thick glasses, a sparse goatee, and thin, harried hair the color of willow switches. He dressed most often in a faded navy-blue suit, worn at the liner, the cuffs riding up a bit, and whenever he took coffee with staff or guests he resembled a college professor at office hours, kind, attentive, but somewhat distracted by thoughts of his own research. In New York, in a previous assignment, his ability to power through position statements in committee meetings that principals did not wish to attend earned him the moniker "robo-speaker," but he was in some senses what they used to call the retiring sort, though his shier tendencies belied a startling intensity when he spoke to things that mattered. An intellect of the first order, possessed of strategic vision and tactical acumen, Blaney never backed down from a fight.

In many ways the fact that he had reached the apex of a Foreign Service career did not surprise, as he had been the Chargé d'Affaires and Deputy Chief of Mission in South Africa, one of the largest U.S. missions in Africa, and before that had worked directly for former Secretary of State Madeleine Albright when she was the U.S. Ambassador to the United Nations. In other ways he defied convention. In the early nineties, in Moscow, he was a Boris Yeltsin contact and he correctly predicted the collapse of the Soviet Union, which ought to have won him plaudits but, in the inimitable logic of Washington, left him shunted aside by a slew of experts, the largest block in the foreign policy game at the time, who built their careers on Russian studies yet missed the most important call. They resented him for getting it right, but his no-nonsense, call-it-as-you-see-it brand of diplomacy was exactly what the Bush administration wanted in its man in Monrovia.

Success came at a price. At the reception following the swearing-in ceremony, Blaney stood uncomfortably with a glass of champagne in hand on the wide balcony atop the Truman building overlooking the leafy green west end of the Washington Mall and the Lincoln Memorial, as his wife Robin carried the conversation with their guests, her blue-green eyes shining in the afternoon light and her stunning blond hair worn up, stylishly, as in a Sargent painting. She was as brilliant and beautiful as the day he first met her in graduate school, and he owed her an unpayable debt of gratitude that she had set aside her own ambitions to travel the world with him and raise their two daughters, but after everything he would now have to be separated from her.

The Liberia tour was to be three-years "unaccompanied," which meant, in State Department parlance, that his family could not join him at post. They could not even visit. Several other officers had declined the job. When the African Bureau called with news of his nomination, he vacillated. He had never served apart from Robin and could not bear the thought of leaving her alone to guide the girls through high school while he flew off to one of the most violent and chaotic places in the world. She, as ever, saw things more clearly, knew what it meant, and encouraged him. She also told him that if he passed on the chance, he might never get another. He was honest about it: he wanted to be an ambassador.

That made it no less painful.

Then there was this: a few days later, as the new ambassador scurried from office to office to complete the Department's myriad administrative procedures required before he left for assignment, so that he would get paid, he overheard a pair of officers whispering as he passed. "Hey," one of them said, "isn't that the ambassador to Liberia?"

"Yeah," the other said, "there goes the ambassador to Hell."

They laughed.

Embassies under fire as often as U.S. Embassy Monrovia did not get much of a budget for remodeling. Faux wood paneling, vinyl upholstery, and blue-grey carpeting lent the ambassador's office the air of a seventies-era suburban basement, absent only the Farrah Fawcett poster and a couple bean-bag seats, while the bookshelves and the executive desk looked like they had been culled from the aspirational pages of some mid-tier department store catalogue. A philodendron gathered dust in one corner and, by the window, the air-conditioning unit sputtered noisily. The Ambassador did little to personalize the room except hang his own portrait in stick-figure, drawn in crayon by his daughter, alongside a photograph of him with Nelson Mandela from his time in Pretoria, both of them smiling in Madiba shirts. Two cheap clocks showed Washington and local time and the standard portraits of the President and Vice President were paired over the doors that led to the private toilet. The only other decoration, aside from a garish contemporary painting of African dancers placed on the wall by the Art in Embassies program, was a timeworn green, orange, and white concessionaire's map of Liberia, the boundaries of old mining and timber lots drawn by hand, and the day after the evacuations, it was in front of this map that the Ambassador stood, arms akimbo, as he mulled his next move.

Flickering across the television screen in the hutch by the bookshelf, on mute, a montage of the war in Iraq recapped the mission accomplished. Heady days indeed for the Bush administration: "shock and awe" delivered, major combat operations ended, a dictator on the lam, and Paul Bremer nightly on news striding through the dusty souks, a khaki-clad potentate in the hippest desert boots. Looting, lawlessness, and reports of a nascent insurgency, maybe several, were dismissed out of hand by Defense Secretary Donald Rumsfeld, who noted brusquely that free people were free to do bad things. The Middle East was being remade and the scuttlebutt in Washington was Syria was next.

Obscure African wars did not fit into any of this. They were at best distractions and at worst resource siphons. The U.S. European Command, which coordinated U.S. military activities in Africa with the components, no doubt had tasked a handful of planners to draft contingencies and keep the chain of command briefed, while Special Operations Command Europe kept track of its men on the ground, but the United States had no plans to intervene in Liberia. Rather, when Assistant Secretary for African Affairs Walter Kansteiner called Blaney shortly after the last French helicopter dipped over the horizon, he told him that in Washington there was still considerable pressure to close the embassy altogether. Kansteiner did not say who applied it, though he did say that it was well above his pay grade.

The call was not exactly a vote of confidence and the message was clear enough, if unstated: nobody wanted to see another *Black Hawk Down*, a repeat of the Somalia fiasco where the stripped bodies of dead U.S. airmen were dragged through the Mogadishu streets. Blaney knew that the military teams that conducted non-combatant evacuation operations, or NEOs, which sometimes included shuttering the chancery, gamed out scenarios where some half-crazed ambassador refused to quit his post and had to be cuffed and bundled off to the helicopters. He did not want to be that guy.

Still, there were reasons to stay the course. The policy rationale was the easy part. The United States did not cut and run. He knew of course that he perceived U.S. strategic interests differently than some, particularly related to what would happen to U.S. credibility in Africa should it abandon the country it created. European allies already had put modest pressure on Washington to secure their recent investments in neighboring states, as French forces stabilized Cote d'Ivoire and the British intervention in Sierra Leone tamped down the civil war there, because if Liberia were to fail utterly, the whole region would burn. Liberia could become a "Somalia West," the thinking went, a blank spot in the heart of West Africa from which terrorists could stage. Then there was the humanitarian crisis. The United States saved lives by providing critical funds for the few relief organizations in country, many of which would be forced to close shop if the U.S. embassy closed. Widespread ethnic violence would undoubtedly follow any vacuum in international engagement. Many people would die. It was, to him, unthinkable that the United States would again turn its back on African killing fields, as it had in Rwanda, though it had the means to help and, by dint of history, had been implicated in the war from the start.

On the practical side, it was true the compound had taken rounds from small arms fire, but these guys weren't great shots, and no one had yet aimed at the embassy, as far as he could tell. He knew things looked different to decision makers back in Washington, where nobody wanted to stand at a podium and explain why another embassy in Africa was under attack amid a conflict nobody on the home front knew anything about. It did not matter that it would be far costlier in blood and treasure to close and later reopen an embassy than to hang tough, nor did it matter that so many loyal local staff members, the Liberians who had worked at the embassy for so many years, would be abandoned to the violence in the streets. He knew the naysayers would have his scalp if he lost a single American officer or trooper who had deployed to secure the embassy. They would say his judgment was clouded with "clientitis" and he had been a fool to risk the lives of Americans to bring peace to a two-bit country run by warlords. He worried not a lick for his own safety, but he cared deeply about his staff and knew the strain the situation put on families, who would see the images of bloody children on the news. He heard it in Robin's voice over the scratchy, tinny satellite link every time he called home.

The war was going to get worse, he feared. Bureau of African Affairs Director Michael Arietti, who replaced him in Ghana, told him that the peace talks were suspended, not scuttled, as Liberian Minister of State Lewis Brown was still there, along with civil society representatives and the standard-bearers for Liberia's political parties. Although the rebels had walked out, they were still in Accra and it looked to be posturing. These were good signs, but the machinations in the conference halls bore little relation to events in the bush. The Ambassador called Ted Collins to his office.

As soon as the Regional Security Officer appeared, the Ambassador unhooked the concessionaire's map and set it flat on the coffee table. He waved his hand over the entire northwest. "The LURD basically control all this." "LURD" stood for Liberians United for Reconciliation and Democracy, which, when paired with the Movement for Democracy in Liberia, MODEL, the rebels to the south, gave the impression that there might actually be some worldwide registry of insurgent names filled with various combinations of the same words. LURD fighters were based in the dense forests along the border with Guinea and Sierra Leone, their ability to operate freely a predictable consequence of Taylor's regional gamesmanship, which left him without allies in Conakry or Freetown.

The Ambassador's hand gravitated south. "MODEL controls most of this." Towns on the map were marked by small black dots, few and far between, mostly along the coast, with everything else hills and jungle. MODEL drew support from the Krahn community, Samuel Doe's people, and maybe from the Cote d'Ivoire government. The group had appeared earlier in the year, a few months after Liberian fighters were spotted in the Cote d'Ivoire. Taylor had been warned not to get involved, but, as one Liberian Minister put it, morale had ebbed among Taylor's men and it became impossible to stop militia from crossing the border, because the comparatively rich Cote d'Ivoire looked like a cash cow, and "everyone wanted to milk the cow."

Through contacts in Guinea, Cote d'Ivoire, and in Washington, U.S. officials writ large had some sense of the leadership structure of both LURD and MODEL, yet little was known about the actual fighters or their numbers, other than rumor and innuendo. British filmmaker James Brabazon was one of the very few outsiders to have spent time in the bush with the LURD, and, though they treated him well, he had filmed a fighter cut the heart from a man and wave it around shouting "I am a wicked boy." Perhaps the only positive was that the rebels did not appear to have a religious or ideological bent, nor did they have any known anti-American agenda. Still, they offered no vision for Liberia's future, save platitudes about rule of law and prosperity, so their objective, as best anyone could tell, was to overthrow Taylor and rule for themselves.

The Ambassador assessed that LURD would regroup after its retreat and MODEL was still on the move. Neither would likely stop until they ousted Charles Taylor or had enough leverage to dictate the terms of the peace talks. If both reached the capital and Taylor kept fighting, Blaney knew that there would come a point of no return, where his team could not leave the country without taking casualties and any rescue mission would probably have to shoot its way in. Even so, he could not escape the fact that, whether he looked at it from a strategic or a humanitarian point of view, the United States, and the embassy that represented it, was the last safety rod in a nuclear reactor. The United Nations had drawn down its staff and all other embassies had either closed or kept only an officer or two to look after the property.

U.S. Embassy Monrovia was the last diplomatic mission left.

The rebels, the Regional Security Officer agreed, were after Charles Taylor, not the embassy. "The Liberian government has its hands full," Ted Collins said with certitude that put his boss at ease, "so it's unlikely they'd orient themselves against us in any serious way. Now that the embassy has combat reinforcement, even if the Special Operations Forces are lean, seeing the combatants here in town, we can handle those types. Plus we have the advantage. If anyone comes after us they will get tied up in the wire, trying to climb the barriers, and they can be knocked down easily. It might be different if any of these guys had armor or heavy weapons, but they don't."

The Ambassador nodded: it was time to cable Washington.

6

THE OSTRICH AND THE RAT

Catherine, the embassy's local protocol assistant, was on maternity leave, a reminder that Liberians were still trying to live their lives amid the chaos, and Susan, the Ambassador's Office Management Specialist, was not allowed to return from scheduled leave as part of Washington's mandate to pare staff, so the Ambassador often received calls directly from Liberian functionaries. The phone rang. It was Protocol from the Executive Mansion. President Taylor, he was told, demanded to see him.

The first time the Ambassador had met the Liberian head of state in person, for the presentation of credentials, the presidency sent a silver Mercedes and two gentlemen in top hats, white gloves, and taupe morning suits to escort him. Crowds of well-wishers sang and danced the length of the elevated drive that led to the towering front doors of the Executive Mansion, a seven-story post and lintel office building that looked, with its boxlike design and sheet metal sunscreens, part airport terminal, part eighties-style boom-box. The new Ambassador was treated to a full military review while the Armed Forces of Liberia band played a rousing set on dented and scuffed brass instruments that somehow had not been sold for scrap. The Ambassador had not known quite what to expect in meeting someone whose name was associated with the vilest crimes imaginable, but the man he encountered was personable, intelligent, and soft of feature with large, expressive eyes, whose gracious style and manner, if a tad enthusiastic, befit his high office.

The charm offensive was intended to convince John Blaney that President Taylor was misunderstood by Washington, that the strategy to isolate him through sanction and penalty was misapplied. The Ambassador did not take the bait. After they had chance to speak behind closed doors, he stuck to his brief and bluntly warned Taylor to improve human rights and take steps to end the war, then declined any future joint appearances that might lend the embassy's imprimatur to the Taylor administration. Overtures from the government soon stopped.

The last time they met, in May, a few weeks before the peace talks, the Ambassador found himself on the Executive Mansion back lawn in a pagoda known as the Chinese Tea Room, for its Asian décor. Charles Taylor brought a suite of his advisors and offered a spread of soft drinks, peanuts, and cheese puffs. It was an awkward affair. Taylor kept a pair of ostriches on the grounds and Ojukwu, an aggressive male named for a Biafran warlord, spotted the snacks. "Apparently," Minister of State Lewis Brown said later, "the aroma excited Ojukwu, and he decided he would participate. So he came from directly behind Ambassador Blaney with an over-stretched neck." The Ambassador was mildly alarmed. President Taylor grabbed a gold-knobbed cane, the symbol of his traditional authority, and backed the bird down. For his part, the Ambassador was impressed that Taylor was able to thrust and parry without losing his train of thought. Eventually attendants were summoned and Ojukwu was chased off with golf umbrellas, though not before, the Ambassador saw from the corner of his eye, the bird bit one on the backside.

To the Ambassador, it seemed the Liberian side was disappointed with the meeting. They told their contacts at the embassy that they knew their team was behind the eight ball because, as one confidante put it, "Charles Taylor is capable of great good as well as great evil, only every day he wakes up and makes the wrong choice!" Still, they said he was the essential man, the only person who really understood what was going on in the government and the country as a whole. "Here's a guy," Lewis Brown said, "who relied entirely on his own judgment to prosecute a war. He had been able to hold his own and win an election. In that situation, you tend to think something is right just because you thought it. After you've been through that process, you tend to think God speaks to you directly."

Maritime Commissioner Benoni Urey viewed the meeting, and Taylor's green light for the bilateral meeting in Brussels before the Accra talks, as an indication that Taylor realized he needed the United States on board if he were to continue his administration. But, he added, "The overwhelming feeling is that the United States backs the rebels." Lewis Brown agreed, "Our government knows," he said, "that the United States never really accepted the results of the 1997 election. Our mindset is that the long arm of the United States is involved in the war and that the lack of support for us against the insurgency is deliberate. There are two schools of thought. Given our perception that the rebels have support at the highest levels in Washington, one should treat suspiciously any advice from the Americans, to the point where those who advocate trust and faith are considered naïve. The other is, we will embarrass America with friendship and see if we can still work out a political deal. But even then, every bit of advice is treated with high suspicion, as an opportunity to bring the government down, actually. There's a clear wariness of anything Americans might offer, because maybe it's a Trojan Horse."

The Ambassador knew well the Liberian perspective, but Taylor had made no discernable changes in the half-year he had been at post. At the Ambassador's request he released several political prisoners, including well-known editor and journalist Hassan Bility, but he did not help his case by telling Blaney that the grant of clemency was "my biggest mistake," as it made him look soft. The Ambassador again methodically ticked off his concerns about human rights and the peace process. Taylor's advisors were stunned that their man held his tongue during the critique. "We couldn't believe," Urey said, "how relaxed the Ambassador was in the President's presence. He crossed his legs, shook his foot. President Taylor usually scolds anyone who crosses his legs in front of him. It doesn't matter who you are, he'll tell you. When we saw that, we all shook our heads and thought, 'There's Hell on Chief!' He's not even going to say anything!"

The Liberian president let Blaney finish, then patiently replied that he needed time to set things right before new elections could be organized. By the calendar, a national vote would occur that year, but the Ambassador himself had already gone on record saying conditions for free and fair elections did not exist. Much of the country was under rebel control, most of the population had been uprooted, and when the Ambassador visited the provincial offices of the electoral commission, he found what was left of voter registration materials heaped in windowless rooms, mildewing in black pools of water. But he also made it clear that postponed elections did not mean Taylor should stick around. Rapid political transition was, in his view, the only way forward.

"Unfortunately," Lewis Brown conceded, "the tenor of the discussion was that the international community, and the United States, did not want Taylor to run for office again. But there was still the question of, if elections could not be held on time, how to manage a transition. If the government's mandate expired, a vacuum would be created. What would become of the thousands of militia Taylor had recruited for the war effort?" The tête-a-tête did provide Charles Taylor reassurance on a point he had first raised last October. He had just seen a full-scale invasion depose Saddam Hussein and he wanted to know once and for all if America wanted him dead. The Ambassador grinned.

"If that was the case," he replied, "do you think you'd still be here?"

This time there were no cheese puffs. Behind Taylor stood a phalanx of armed guards in shades and black shirts, belts of brass bullets draped on their chests, assault rifles slung over their shoulders. Several of Taylor's advisors were there too, in loose cottons and slacks as though they had just walked in from the country club. Thoughtful, creative, and conversant in business and world affairs, they were of the set you might expect to run into in a first class lounge in one of the Asian or European hubs, sipping macchiato and reading the *Financial Times* while waiting for their connecting flight, only here they stood, relaxed, in the company of scowling men with grenade launchers, as though it were the usual course of things. John Blaney was outmanned and outgunned, accompanied only by Assistant Regional Security Officer Brad Lynn and Political Officer Doug Kent, the former packing a single pistol and the latter only a ballpoint pen and notepad.

He cut to the chase.

"My people tell me the peace process is still on," he said. "Yesterday, when I returned, I called for an immediate unconditional ceasefire by all sides. My government has pressed the rebels to halt the attack. We need international monitoring for the ceasefire, West African and United Nations elements." Eyes wide in mock or genuine surprise, Taylor raised a finger in emphasis and said that, before anything else, the rebels had to quit the city. He dismissed the idea of United Nations monitors out of hand because he said they could turn him over to the Special Court, and to say that Taylor was bitter about his indictment would have been an understatement. It was a war by Sierra Leone against Liberia, he said, and the United States had been ineffective in stopping the rebel attack. He said he would never let anyone arrest him, and anyway the Special Court had no jurisdiction over Liberia, let alone standing to prosecute a sitting head of state. His legitimately elected government, he said, was under attack and he would go down fighting if necessary. Then he leaned forward, brow knotted and fingers steepled.

"Why burn down the house," he asked, "just to get one rat?"

The Ambassador at first demurred. All diplomats needed permission to serve in the host country and it occurred to him that, in retaliation for the indictment, Taylor might declare him "persona non grata," strip him of his accreditation and boot him from Liberia. Probably the only thing that gave Taylor pause was the thought he could still strike a deal that would keep him off the docket. It was clear that the Liberian president had no intention of appearing before the tribunal, and, with Charles Taylor loaded for bear, the war was careening toward a dangerous new phase.

"We've seen the reports of a coup attempt," the Ambassador said, after an awkward silence. "The United States had no involvement whatsoever in any sort of coup here in Liberia, no matter what you have heard. Our embassy did call to urge your government to do everything possible to protect American lives and property." President Taylor stared hard at him, as if in judgment. That he did not fly into a rage the Ambassador took as a sign that he had believed him on the spot. They were not on good terms, but the Ambassador suspected that Taylor knew he had always been straightforward with him. The Liberian Head of State wanted a direct line to Washington, to know clearly the policy. Even though he was angry, he actually seemed glad he could get clear answers.

"You have a humanitarian crisis on your hands," the Ambassador said finally, to change the topic, "and we just evacuated nearly all the relief organizations. You're going to need the fighting to stop to be able to get help—" Taylor cut him off with a wave. The French evacuation was unnecessary, he said. Had his team been consulted, it would have been clear that the government wanted the relief groups to stay, would have protected them, and would have helped evacuate them through either Spriggs-Payne or Robertsfield if necessary. He said he welcomed the U.S. military in Liberia and that his troops would even provide security for the embassy fuel and water trucks, if it came to it.

"We need a ceasefire," Blaney said simply. "You should do your part. There's a draft agreement circulating in Ghana. You should sign it when it comes across your table." Standing to the side, Taylor's National Security Advisor blanched. The Ambassador came across to him as instructing his President what he expected to be done. It took the advisors a little by surprise.

"The Americans," J.T. Richardson said later, "threatened us once more. They were saying, whatever paper comes across the table, sign it, or else we're going to tell these guys across the street." J.T. left the room and called Lewis Brown, who was in Accra. He asked him if he had a copy of an agreement to be signed. "Hell no," Brown told him, "there's a draft that's been floating around that the facilitators brought, but nobody's even read or commented on it."

J.T. returned and slipped his president a note.

President Taylor glared at the Ambassador.

"Well," he said, "I'd appreciate if you would give my team a copy of the agreement. Our delegation has not seen it. And anyway, they don't seem to have access to a fax to get it here." The Ambassador nodded. He did not take the Liberians at their word, but protocols had been known to break down in peace talks and it was quite possible that they really were not in possession of the draft. En route back to the office, he called the U.S. observers in Accra and told them to make sure Lewis Brown had a copy.

After the meeting, President Taylor went to the press.

"I want to prevent a catastrophe in Liberia," he said in his husky baritone. "If I resigned, who will keep the thousands of guerilla fighters, who can hide in the rain forests and hide their guns? Your helicopters, your ships will be useless… The question of this indictment is principal for peace in Liberia. The whole stigma must be removed. How they do it is up to them, but it must be removed…" Taylor paused for emphasis.

"No white boy from Washington can come in and indict a sitting African President."

7

THE AFTERMATH

The rains came at night. Each morning cumulous piled like dirty white plantation cotton atop the hills to the north and east, then tracked the arc of the sun, rolling down the slopes and spreading out over the barbed green canopy all the way down to the coast. At dusk it would start, a stampede across the zinc roofs as the palms and broadleaves in the yards bent and wept like penitents. The rain hit so hard it bled through umbrellas, pried off gutters, beat branches to the ground. Trenches swelled with debris and the rush of water carried the mixed smells of soil and plants and garbage. It gusted through the night then, near dawn, it would let up. For a time, all that could be heard was the murmur of the streams and the drip of the water from the trees. Then the cicadas would start up again, and the birds, while small mists danced across the silt-clouded pools along the street.

It was hot, it was humid, it was uncomfortable, yet the work had to be done. The day after the attack broke off, Fergy slid behind the wheel of Fifty-eight. Jay Jay stayed home, like so many of the local staff, to look after his own family. Fergy brought a political officer along with him and handed him a Baretta. The officer hesitated and Fergy asked if he had ever fired a gun before. "No," came the reply. Fergy tossed it into the backseat with a couple of clips and threw a square of blue terry cloth over it.

"State Department," he said, shaking his head.

Fifty-eight could be moody and the engine spit and coughed before it finally turned over and roared to life. They drove out to empty streets. The crush of people at the gates less than twenty-four hours ago was gone, dispersed, wandered off to who-knew-where with their sacks and bundles. Duff of blackened leaves, fruit rinds and crushed cardboard boxes gummed up the curbs, while shreds of translucent blue plastic bags flapped in the branches of the jacarandas. Downtown, shops were open and people milled in the street. Security forces were noticeably absent, though the few they came across saluted as Fifty-eight rolled past. "Sorry motherfuckers," Fergy said.

The embassy men gleaned little from the expressions of passers-by, the same milieu of blurred faces, eyes lit with cane juice or dim with want and sickness. Fewer cars, perhaps, but larger crowds downtown. If you knew nothing of the past week's events, you would not have known that the city had been attacked so recently. There was a strange elasticity to the place. It was much as before: bright, steaming, and poor.

"I guess they got to be happy for the good days," Fergy said idly.

They crossed the river, its scuffed surface moody with the shadows of the passing clouds. Bushrod Island was eerily quiet, no trucks at all and few taxis. South of the Bong Mines Bridge, an old iron-wrought railroad overpass that bisected the island and linked the port to the inland hills, they came across the Toyota dealership. The bars of the security grates were bent out and gapped, pried open with wire cutters and crowbars, and the plate glass windows lay shattered on the ground, shimmering in the light like melting ice. Divots and scarring from gunfire were obvious on the walls.

"I doubt the rebels made it this far," Fergy said.

He meant: Operation Pay Yourself had visited.

Further on, traffic tailed off to nothing. The steel curtains of the warehouses were all shuttered. There were no vendors on the curbs. Even the kiosks that sold "scratch," the ubiquitous pre-paid calling cards for the lone mobile company, were nailed shut. The U.S. embassy was the largest customer for scratch even though the profits, it was said, were split between Taylor, his crew and Lone Star's Lebanese principals. Further along the island, Duala was barren, the market stalls now a graveyard of broken planks, shredded gunny cloth, and sticks that jutted out menacingly like headhunter spears. Light foot traffic seemed to be mostly displaced people headed back across Saint Paul, back to the camps they just left to see if the relief organizations had returned with food and water bladders.

European Commission Aid Coordinator David Parker told Fergy that the international relief community was down to a handful of expatriates who had started to meet each night on the patio at Malik compound, a staff house for the International Committee of the Red Cross close to the U.S. embassy. Under a single pale light as the mosquitos flitted above, they used a simple chalkboard to divvy up tasks and create a plan to triage an entire country. Monrovia had few services to offer before the attack and now it absorbed more than one hundred thousand new people. What little infrastructure had been built up at the camps, from maternal health clinics to classrooms, had been knocked down. The needs were staggering and logistics for the non-governmental organizations were fouled up with so much uncertainty as to who would stay and who would be forced to evacuate. At least, Parker said, most of the warehouses were still secured.

Fifty-eight rumbled into New Kru Town, the densest, poorest quarter of the island, where houses and shacks stood shoulder to shoulder like passengers on a country bus. The air was thick with the stench of overfull pit latrines. Skinny, sickly women propped elbows on sills and waved listlessly at the bottle flies. At the roadside, the grass was bent, trampled, and muddy, and shade trees so few that you might have thought Liberia was a desert country. In places, plywood was splintered and mesh screens slashed. Corrugated tin roofs were punctured with bullet holes to give them the look of cheese graters. Fergy pointed to a pair of kiosks where cinder block walls lay in rubble.

"Rocket-propelled grenades," he said.

At Redemption Hospital, the only inpatient clinic in New Kru Town, they learned the staff of Médecins Sans Frontières had relocated to Mamba Point. Patient charts littered the floors in the narrow, abandoned corridors and filing cabinets lay on their side, drawers ripped off their tracks, emptied, and cast aside. Rods from intravenous stands were piled in one room like pick-up sticks, their plastic drips wrinkled and drained of fluid and tubing fogged with mold. Mattresses had been ripped from bedframes and soiled sheets tossed carelessly in the corners, while here and there black drag marks of blood could be seen on the floor, evidence of a crime scene with no police to tape it off. Out back, an elderly local staffer in a blue jumper swept caramel colored water into a drain in the courtyard. White, glistening maggots writhed at the edge of the grate and the smell of the sepsis overwhelmed the senses. The man paused at their approach.

"Thirty-six bodies today," he said.

"From the fighting?" Fergy asked.

"They snatched the medicines, kicked them out of bed."

"All the dead were patients here?"

The man shook his head slowly.

"We took many from the streets."

"Who did this?"

"Rebels, militia, nobody can really say."

Nobody could ever say. The only certainty was that gunmen would come again, and nobody could do anything about it. The peace process was remote, an abstraction, no less a fantasy than the diversions that could be watched in the local video shacks. The attendant started to sweep again, the rasp of the bristles across the pavement loud and lonely in the small courtyard. "The Ambassador is right," Fergy said as he started the engine.

Fifty-eight coughed and heaved, then lurched forward.

"This ain't over."

8

THE AFRICANS

Monrovia was the rare war-torn capital where you could get fresh lobster. Before he got to Liberia, Fergy didn't even know they had lobster in Africa, but apparently it was in season and the fishermen who braved the churning currents in their pirogues brought them to town by the bucketful. With the evacuees gone, the cafeteria staff was busier than ever feeding the SEAL contingent and they offered lobster-tail as a cut-rate lunch special. Fergy could count on one hand the times his family could afford lobster growing up and, despite a flash of guilt at dining in a garden compound while so many outside the gates slept under cardboard and leaves, he joined his few colleagues and the various Special Operations Forces and treated himself to a generous helping.

As the melted butter coagulated on his plate among the shells, Fergy watched the Ambassador walk by with a coterie of West African diplomats. They passed quickly through the main hall to the enclosed porch at the back, where a table had been set with tented white napkins, wine glasses, and white starter plates, on which were modest salads of cherry tomato, sliced cucumber, a bit dry, and lettuce, a bit limp. Dr. Mohamed Ibn Chambas, the Executive Secretary of the Economic Community of West African States, or ECOWAS, and Ghanaian Foreign Minister Nana Akufo-Addo, the co-Chair of the International Contact Group for Liberia, were the distinguished guests, tasked with coordinating the actions of a select group of nations trying to rescue Liberia from the brink. Their hastily arranged visit was as welcome as it was unexpected, a reminder that Monrovia was still linked to the outside world, though the air charter company would not let them stay the night.

The Ambassador took his seat at the head of the table, with Chambas at his left in an elegant white robe and Akoufo-Addo to his right in a trim grey business suit that seemed impossibly hot for the climate. Their presence signaled that the countries in the region and the international community more broadly had not yet written off Liberia. The Ambassador saw it as a chance to pitch what he thought needed to happen if the peace talks resumed. You could not just rely on some declaration out of Accra and think it would all work, he knew. Liberians in the nineties alone held thirteen rounds of negotiations. For the country to emerge from its darkest chapter, a sequence of actions was needed in tandem with any political agreement: a ceasefire, a ceasefire verification team, a peacekeeping force, and a comprehensive disarmament, demobilization, rehabilitation, and reintegration program for ex-fighters, coupled with an infusion of aid to help the economy recover. At the same time, there would have to be a transitional government of some sort with a clear timetable and benchmarks for elections. It all required money and resources on a scale that, given the circumstances, could only really come from the international community.

Months before, the Ambassador had spoken with Assistant Secretary Kansteiner, with Director Arietti, with anyone who would listen really, about the need to find funds to support an African-led intervention force, perhaps followed by United Nations "blue hat" peacekeepers. He never mentioned U.S. troops, which Liberians on all sides said they welcomed, because he knew it was not a possibility. Staff poured California wine from the stock of the Chief of Mission Residence and the Ambassador raised a toast.

"To peace in Liberia, and I hope you all like lobster!"

Akufo-Addo spoke in a rich, resonant voice with rhetorical flourishes that suggested his elite education. He said that the delegation met with the Liberian president that morning and informed him that rebel political leaders had promised to stop their military advance and return to the peace talks. Taylor, they said, pledged the government would not counterattack either. The Ambassador clarified this meant that the negotiations would continue in Accra and everyone nodded confidently as could be expected when discussing Liberia.

"We have to separate the factions," the Ambassador said. "Get a ceasefire in place on the ground. We'll need the lines clearly demarcated, or the fighters won't respect them. We'll eventually need a comprehensive disarmament package. Any word on who might contribute?" There was an awkward pause.

"We were hoping you might tell us it would be the United States," Dr. Chambas said, only half in jest. The Ambassador smiled wryly. Washington was still in the business of cutting off resources for Liberia and, other than some travel funds for its observer team in Ghana, had nothing in the pipeline to support stability operations should the respite hold. "You may want to consider UNAMSIL," he said. The United Nations Mission in Sierra Leone, a peacekeeping operation, was winding down. It was conceivable, he thought, they could spare a battalion or two. However, a few days back the United Nations Department of Peacekeeping Operations refused to green-light the use of UNAMSIL helicopters for the evacuation of United Nations staff, because it would have exceeded the contingent's authorities, so he knew that they would need a new mandate, which meant a political tussle in New York and a Security Council vote. That would take time that they did not have. "They could be the lead elements," he suggested, "with United Nations troops later."

Joshua from the cafeteria staff squeezed past the diplomats and whispered something in the Ambassador's ear. From the corner of his eye, Blaney saw other members of his staff in the main dining hall bussing their trays, stacked with bright red shells. He frowned briefly and rose again to address his guests. "Did I say we had lobsters here? I'm sorry to report we're a few lobsters short." He smiled earnestly.

"So can we interest anyone in hamburgers?"

9

THE KEARSARGE

"At the request of the U.S. Ambassador to Liberia," the wire reports from June 12 read, "and at the direction of the Secretary of Defense, the U.S. European Command has sent military support to West Africa to provide the ambassador an enhanced capability to monitor the current situation in Liberia and aid in any evacuation of U.S. citizens." In his office down the hall from Post One, Ted Collins scrolled through his e-mail. Diplomatic Security back in Washington had not yet sent him the operations order, but they confirmed the USS Kearsarge, an 844 foot-long WASP class multipurpose amphibious assault ship, carrying 3000 sailors and Marines and a squadron of Harrier II jet aircraft, was indeed on its way as "Shining Express," a named operation.

Collins noticed the door across the hall was ajar. Through the gap he heard a couple of the ranking ESAT members talking about sticks. They were just doing their job, he thought, no problem, so he tried to not pay attention. Odd phrases floated over to him. They talked about how the embassy was closing the next Monday and how they would handle personnel who refused to leave post. They talked about whether the Ambassador wanted to go or not, which was a serious issue. Then one of them realized Collins was nearby and shut the door, as though he said something he knew he should not have. Collins was a retired Marine Lieutenant Colonel with eighteen combined years of active duty and reserve experience, so he granted them the full professional courtesy of letting them finish, even though it was his building and his offices.

As a Marine, Collins had served in a wide variety of conventional and spe- cial operations/special warfare positions, had received training similar to many

Special Forces units, and had significant operational intelligence collection and collection management experience. During a detail with Special Operations Command Europe, he helped establish the first Diplomatic Security permanent liaison office there. The posting entailed finalizing interagency agreements, clarifying overseas legal protections, determining the propriety of various funding pools and, most importantly, straightening out lines of authority. So he knew exactly the problem with what he had overheard.

Afterward, he caught one of the men in passing. To the man's credit, he was clear. He said the mission was to evacuate the embassy. "This is what we've been told," he said, "this is what's going to happen." Collins gave him the benefit of the doubt. The ESAT had been key to the evacuation efforts to that point and though the embassy team could have handled it without them, it would have been very difficult. To his mind, what they might be doing was leaning forward. The State Department looked at the policy and the long-term effects of actions but Special Operations Forces had to think of the next immediate move. It was what they were paid to do and they were very good at it. Of course preparation was one thing, Collins thought, but driving policy was another. It was possible that somebody in Washington had pre-cooked it. The ESAT could have been told "Look this is what we're working toward, be prepped for next week, we think we can convince someone who can make this decision." Collins understood the thinking out of the Pentagon, if that was where this had come from, which was not to say he agreed with it. It was probably "We've been down to Liberia enough times, fuck this."

Afterward, Collins called Diplomatic Security, his home office.

"What do you think?" they asked. "Do you need to leave?"

"No, bullshit," he said. "We can handle this."

They took it at face value and it did not come up again.

In diplomacy, as in politics, the home front had to be tended, and nearly every ambassador has a wide network in Washington, built over the years, of friends and contacts in other agencies, on Capitol Hill and at Beltway think tanks, who can provide context that he or she cannot always get from counterparts in the regular chain of command. As soon as he heard the news about the Kearsarge and the Regional Security Officer had briefed him on the interaction with the ESAT members, Ambassador Blaney made calls. The backstory he heard was that Secretary Powell and Secretary Rumsfeld were both personally engaged on Liberia, probably the first time in a decade that Liberia was included in the morning briefs of the nation's two most powerful cabinet members. Secretary Rumsfeld, Blaney was told, wanted the embassy shut, and probably had the support of the Vice President.

Nobody knew where the President would come down.

Iraq was the main effort, so much so that even Afghanistan was shunted to the side, even though Osama bin Laden was still at large, and the Pentagon was simply not interested in small but resource-intensive missions, especially unfunded missions, that affected troop rotations and refit cycles. It was not that the Defense Department could not handle it, as it was engaged in operations the world over, but rather that Liberia was simply a nuisance that could easily be taken off the docket. The Kearsarge had been dispatched to West Africa with that aim in mind, he heard, whether it had been stated in any Op-Ord or not. Secretary Powell was livid he had not been consulted, he was also told.

The Ambassador called his security team together. It was the usual group: Collins, Birgells, a political officer and Fergy. Finishing some correspondence at his computer, he kept his back to them until he could tell that they all arrived, but when he finally swiveled round, he struck a light chord, almost cheerful.

"It's nice to have a battleship," he said.

"Yessir."

"But I didn't ask for a battleship."

"Sir?"

"I mean, it's great that they're coming. That's a lot of firepower, terrific capabilities. Both Charles Taylor and the rebel commanders have something to think about now. It will cool things down for a while because nobody knows what it's here to do—" he leaned in for full effect "—except neither do I."

Then he chuckled.

Evacuation, as a rationale, did not quite conform to the ground situation. After the French-led operation ended, the State Department shook loose some funds for additional helicopter flights to help "empty the tub," using contract Mi-8s out of Freetown. A few families that had passed on the Cougars reconsidered their decision to stay and showed up, but, in general, those who made it through the attack said that they had little reason now to leave. Embassy-sponsored radio announcements did not resonate as much without the boom of the mortars and, when embassy staff contacted names on the warden lists, they sounded a bit like discount travel agents hawking a weekend getaway to Sierra Leone. Potential evacuees were also put off by the requisite promissory notes that covered the cost to taxpayers, protesting that they could just as well catch their own flight on Weasua or Ghana Airways, which had resumed the route.

Only eight stragglers boarded the last Mi-8.

"It is no surprise folks in Washington are jittery," the Ambassador said. He hid the stress well enough, except when he took off his glasses to wipe them, revealing skin beneath his eyes white and dark at the same time, like eraser marks, and cheeks dry enough that the frames left red indents. "Or that various people, including some military people, have come to the conclusion that enough is enough. Over the years we've had an expensive pattern of drawdowns and evacuations. This place tends to go nuts fairly frequently."

He looked glanced at the faces of his men.

"Let's just say," he said, "decisions were made and deployments authorized. Now, as a former Army officer, I recognize various types of units, know what their missions are and also the approximate rank of people engaged in those missions. When I got back here, it didn't take me long to figure out that these guys came to close down this embassy. What Ted heard confirmed it. Of course they had other, intermediate tasks, helping our other evacuations, protecting the compound. But that's their objective."

He folds his arms so that his tie buckled.

"The problem is, they forgot to ask me!"

As a veteran, the Ambassador had always been partial to the military, so he was none too pleased to find himself pitted against the Pentagon, even if in the abstract. There is in everyone a continuity of the self, at least in everyone who has not been born-again, and even after twenty-odd years as a Foreign Service Officer, John Blaney still considered himself to be a soldier too. He was the same man who, as a Syracuse University undergraduate, walked into an empty gymnasium and joined the Army while anti-Vietnam protests raged across the campus. He knew what he was getting into: as a freshman he had seen the library burned down by radicals because they mistakenly thought the Reserve Officer Training Corps had an office there.

He had been thirsty. He knew the gym had a Coca-Cola vending machine and walked over from his dormitory. At the steps, protestors grabbed at his shoulders and kicked and punched him, and it was only then he remembered that the recruiting station was inside. He tried to explain that he just wanted a Coke, but they didn't believe him, so he backed away, angry and dry-mouthed and determined to find a way in. At the back, the doors were locked from the inside, but he waited around until someone left, held the door and slipped in. He had never spent much time in the gym and stopped for a moment, lost in the immensity of the space and the dull luster of the overhead lights on the hardwood courts. Across the way the Coke machine glowed red and white, the hum of the coolers audible in the vast quiet. He pulled a few coins and some lint from his pocket, listened as the can clanked into the tray and smiled as he plucked the tab off, raised the can to his lips and felt the tickle of the sweet fizz under his nose as he took a long draught.

He noticed a light on in small office off to the side, where you might expect coaches and trainers to work, and wandered over. Colonel Patten sat there alone in his olive uniform. It was a difficult time to recruit. Students who joined the Reserve Officer Training Corps had to wear a uniform and keep their hair short, and they got jumped and spat on and called motherfuckers and baby killers. It made it nearly impossible to get a date. John Blaney's draft number was quite high, so he knew there was only a slim chance he would be selected, but he liked the idea of being an officer. He was not avidly pro-war or anti-war, he just thought it was a matter of service.

"Sir," he said, "is this what everyone outside is protesting?"

"Yep," Colonel Patten said.

"Well in that case, sign me up."

John Blaney's life turned on the alphabet. At the end of basic training, Lieutenant Sullivan gathered everyone in the mess hall at the camp at Indiantown Gap, stood them at attention and read the first four names off the roster. "Adams, Allen, Baker, Blaney: you guys are going to Korea. The rest of you go to Vietnam." He was disappointed, in a way, because he had trained for it. He guessed from Korea they would send him on to Vietnam anyway, but instead spent thirteen long, cold months in the mountains near Panmunjom as a tactical control officer at a hawk missile battery. He first heard about the Foreign Service when he was laid up in a field hospital and they wheeled in a Foreign Service Officer who had had a heart attack, but lived to spin a few more yarns.

He was inexplicably reassigned to West Point to teach Cadets military heritage, field maneuvers, and how to shoot, and, at the end of the second semester, announced to his classes his intention to drive down to the State Department and enlist. No one had told him there was an exam, so he followed the advice of a receptionist who took kindly to the enthusiastic young officer standing in the lobby, and applied for the graduate program at the Georgetown School of Foreign Service, which is where he met Robin Suppe. He eventually passed the test, joined the Department, and, four years later, was posted to Embassy Lusaka. The Rhodesian war was in its final spasms and the first few nights in their new house he and Robin went to sleep to the sound of firefights in the neighborhood.

The Ambassador plucked a shiny coin from his desk. Often, military commanders handed personalized coins to troopers for jobs well done, and tradition had it that if you were at a bar and slapped one down your colleagues had to pay for your drink, unless they had their own coin from a higher-ranked officer. State Department officials sometimes got them as well, in appreciation for civilian-military cooperation, and the Ambassador always kept a few in a tray on his desk. He turned the enameled coin in his fingers. "I was surprised that obviously there had been advanced thinking and decisions made about closing the post that I was not party to. I started making phone calls and understood that yes, indeed..."

He flipped the coin in the air and snatched it.

"So I've reminded everyone I'm the President's personal representative. My role is fundamental in weighing overall American interests with the pressure and danger on the embassy. I'm not about to allow anyone else to make those determinations for me, absent the President of the United States." He looked at his staff.

"Yes sir," Collins said, to fill the gap.

The Ambassador turned directly to him.

"Ted, you still agree we should not close?"

The Regional Security Officer oversaw all aspects of mission security, including threat assessments, under the guidance of the Ambassador and the Office of Diplomatic Security in Washington. Final responsibility for everything related to the mission was vested in the Ambassador, but he relied on the Regional Security Officer's counsel and Diplomatic Security protocols. If he did not, and something bad went down, there would be no lifeline at the inevitable inquest. If they even made it out alive.

"If we abandon the embassy," Collins replied, "we lose millions of dollars in physical assets almost immediately. Everything on this compound will be stripped bare. It could take us years to get back and a lot of local staff will be killed. We would abandon the local guard force, the police we work with, and all our other friends and contacts. Basically anyone who has repeatedly risked their lives over the years to work with the United States. You just don't do that to your friends."

Collins tugged at his pink polo shirt.

"Sir," he said, "I can tell you that even if we leave Liberia's story won't end, only our ability to influence it. Someday, maybe five years, maybe ten years, but someday, we'd have to come back, roping in from choppers. A nightmare."

The Ambassador raised a hand gently.

They were clearly on the same page.

"We're in a tough spot," he frowned.

"With Washington?" someone asked.

"With Liberia!"

The team laughed uneasily.

"This is the Operations Center," the voice on the other end of the line said, "Please hold for Assistant Secretary Kansteiner." "Ops" was State Department's nerve center, a windowless suite of cramped desks and monitors on the seventh floor staffed around the clock by the some of the most talented up-and-coming Foreign Service Officers, as well as skilled civil servants, who were tasked with, among other things, monitoring events around the globe and instantly routing critical information to principals. The officers worked in shifts and, during a crisis, tended to prepare briefs every few hours, which meant they could not wait for posts to file situation reports, "SITREPs" in the vernacular, and instead reached out to embassies and consulates early and often. U.S. Embassy Monrovia had been hearing from Ops a lot recently, except this was not that type of call.

"John," said the Assistant Secretary, "how you holding up?"

"Fine, Walter."

"Listen, John, you know the Kearsarge is on its way."

"I didn't ask for it, Walter."

"I know, I know. Look, we hear you still have a lot of Americans—"

"We've been emptying the tub."

"I hear you, but it could get worse out there."

"It could. Where are we on the ceasefire?"

"Michael's got that in Accra."

The Ambassador did not reply. He was not sure where this was going. Secretary Powell had a simple, unwritten rule for crisis management: trust the talents of the people in the field unless and until you have cause not to. The Secretary, in other words, would support the call from the ground until mistakes were made, at which point Washington would start to call the shots. Kansteiner's call, he sensed, was a step in that direction. He did not blame him: he liked Kansteiner and knew he was just delivering the message. The Ambassador figured he had done enough over his career to earn the initial trust, but it was clear he had no margin for error. There were other costs for staying the course: Chris Datta was pulled out, the Defense Attaché was long gone and no replacement had been identified, and the State Department wanted three more direct hire bodies sent away. The USAID Country Director, a political officer and a consular officer had to rotate home. For reporting, engagement, and analysis, he was down to one political officer, his operations coordinator, his local political assistant, and himself.

Kansteiner brought it back to the Kearsarge.

"Look, John, they're going to need a formal request for a NEO to be able to help you out." So that was it, the Ambassador thought. The Pentagon wanted *him* to make the call to lower the flag. What it looked like, when he thought about it, was that he had been set up. A ship with massive capabilities had been sent his way, but, if he did not agree to be pulled out, they would probably cut it loose again, leaving the embassy exposed. He did not like the game, and he told Kansteiner so.

"I'll request a NEO," he said, "on the condition we don't close the embassy."

"Transmit it in as soon as you can," Kansteiner replied, ignoring the caveat.

At European Command headquarters, John Blaney's approach raised some eyebrows. Liberia was now on everyone's radar and the Ambassador took a call from General Charles "Chuck" Wald, the EUCOM Deputy Commander and a newly minted four-star. A career Air Force man who had seen combat in Vietnam and Bosnia, Wald came from North Dakota stock and, as expected, did not mince words.

"How's it going down there at 'Fort Blaney?'"

The Ambassador laughed in spite of himself.

"We're doing okay," he said. "We appreciate the support."

"Let me tell it to you straight," the General said, "it might be time for you to think about closing down. You and your team have done a fine job, everyone is impressed with the resolve, but we're going to have some assets parked off your coast shortly. Might want to take advantage of them. No time like the present."

"We'll see how things go in Accra," the Ambassador said.

He thought: I work for the President of the United States.

As he made his rounds, Hersh Hernandez was confused by what he heard. A Navy Commander told him he should pack, that the embassy would close, and that there was nothing that the Ambassador could do about it. Hersh had served twenty years in the Marines and had been in combat, so he knew a little about command authority and knew an O-5 could not close an embassy. "Our man in Liberia," he said, "the Ambassador—he makes that call." The Commander shrugged. Bluntly put, he said, there was nothing in Liberia worth American lives. It gave Hersh pause, to ask whether anything in the country was worth the lives of a platoon or the diplomats or the local guards. He did not have a dog in the fight. As a private contractor, if the embassy closed he would just get sent somewhere else, to manage some other guard force, yet, all in all, it made little sense to him that a mission that survived worse would suddenly close now. Still, Hersh could tell from his expression the officer was thinking, "You guys just don't get it."

In the cafeteria, a self-assured Captain laid it out for the Political Officer over sweet tea and French fries. The Captain had a sharp, angular face, a silver-grey flat top, and distant blue eyes. There was no need, he said, for any American presence in Liberia, diplomatic or otherwise. There were no strategic interests. He would not concede that it could pose much threat as a failed state, that terrorists, pandemics, or transnational crime could metastasize and cause harm elsewhere. He stifled a yawn when it was pointed out that bin Laden staged in Africa before he broke bread with the Taliban, and he waved off the notion that Liberia could have knock-on effects throughout West Africa, though it already had, saying that when he looked at the variables as a planner, at Liberia as it was, not at the potentialities, what he saw was Charles Taylor, two nasty rebel factions and a hopelessly complex crisis. No oil, no terrorists and no obvious geo-strategic considerations. "If al-Qaeda shows up," he said, "just drop a couple Agency guys at the borders. They see something they don't like, they can call in the predators."

He pinched thumb and forefinger together and made a slow arc with his hand in the trajectory of a missile. Inches above the tablecloth, his fingers snapped open, as a burst, and he grinned, no doubt visualizing the smoke in the canopy. As for the humanitarian crisis and the history between the United States and Liberia, he stirred the sugar at the bottom of his glass and grinned again, "African solutions for African problems."

"We'd look weak quitting this place," the Political Officer said.

"I'll give you that one," the Captain winked.

The SEALs looked bored at their posts. Even they were not quite sure where things stood now. The commissary sold out of embassy branded caps and polos, so the Marines called in local vendors. At Gate One, burlap sacks were unfurled on the sidewalk and wooden masks, cockleshell bracelets, and stiff, stinky, sun-dried leopard pelts laid out for sale. Atop the guard booth, the SEALs pointed and bartered as the vendors jumped from item to item, flip-flops snapping against the blacktop, shouting out prices and passing things through the bars of the gate in exchange for damp stacks of Liberian dollars.

Somewhere off the coast, the Kearsarge arrived. Bright blue skies buzzed with the noise of tandem rotors as a Sea Knight helicopter ferried the ship's captain across the winking, white-tipped waves. When the engines were cut and the wind died, the aircraft settled to rest like a great, grey camel, casting two-humped shadows across the tarmac. Ambassador Blaney escorted Captain Terry McKnight back to his office through the back entrance to the chancery, under the shade of the rubber trees.

"You've had a long deployment," the Ambassador said. The ship was en route to Norfolk from the Arabian Gulf, where it had supported Operation Enduring Freedom. The Captain was a trim man of genteel manner and exemplary posture. A touch of grey gave him an appropriately distinguished appearance and he was outfitted in khaki officer's clothes with minimal accouterment. Faint caution in his tone, smile subtly forced, hinted that the Captain did not quite know what to make of the Ambassador and was baffled as to why his ship floated over the horizon, given how quiet and pleasant everything seemed on the embassy grounds. He may also have heard that the Ambassador had requested a NEO but had no plans to close the embassy.

"Yes sir," the Captain replied.

"I don't intend to keep you here any longer than necessary."

"Thank you, sir."

"I'm away from my family too."

The Captain bowed his head in acknowledgement.

"You're here to help with evacuations?"

"We're here to meet your needs."

He had been briefed, the Ambassador thought.

"We've coaxed out just about everyone we can."

"Yes sir, that's what we've heard."

"Now we're working on a cease-fire."

It was not the Captain's concern, but the Ambassador made it a practice to share his vision of the way forward with anyone he encountered, to optimize the chances that it would flow back to influencers. The Captain would likely pass things up his chain of command, although he gave no indication his immediate bosses in the fleet had any appetite for the particularities of the Liberian peace process.

"But we're really happy you dropped by."

Before he flew off, the Captain presented the Ambassador a navy blue cap with the ship's seal. The hat was a snug fit, the brim sitting low and square across the brow, and the Ambassador was visibly delighted. From then on, he wore it any time he left the chancery. After the captain re-boarded the Sea Knight, Blaney told Collins he did not think the ship would not stay long. "Sir," Collins said with a nod, "we just got word the Special Operations Forces will go with them. We lose the SEAL team."

The Ambassador's suspicions were confirmed. If he would not yield, he would lose the extra security. The message from the Pentagon seemed to be: if you say the country is stable enough and you don't need to pull the embassy team, then you don't need the services of one of the most elite units in the military. Perhaps it was not exactly quid pro quo, he allowed, as a fair argument could be made that the SEALs were more urgently needed elsewhere, but the timing was not helpful. The Ambassador turned to Collins.

"We're going to need more shooters, soon."

"The Fleet Anti-Terrorism Support Team."

"We need them in place *before* the Kearsarge sails."

"I'm on it, sir," Collins replied.

10

THE VICE PRESIDENT

Vice President Moses Blah was restored to his high office after eleven days in captivity, and, even well after the incident, neither he nor President Taylor's closest advisors knew quite what to make of the affair. The night the Liberian head of state had returned from Ghana after the unsealing of the indictment, Vice President Blah and Minister of State Jonathan Taylor, among others, drove to the airport to receive him. It was, the Minister recalled, very emotional. A large crowd gathered to welcome their president: militia, cultural groups, and ranking officials. Advisors accompanied the president to the VIP lounge, where they conferred for a few moments. President Taylor was visibly troubled.

It was a low blow, he told everyone, for the Special Court to unseal the indictment at the start of the peace talks. The prosecutors hoped Ghana would be shamed into arresting him and instead the Ghanaians flew him back to Liberia on one of their jets. The advisors shook their heads in sympathy. After a short while, it was decided that General Benjamin Yeaten would ride back to town with the President and update him on the security situation. It was not unusual for the President to receive a brief en route: he was very hands-on in security matters. The Vice President paid his respects then walked to the parking lot to track down his wife, who had been in Accra with the government contingent. He loaded her suitcases into the Mercedes and drove home.

Moses Blah was in his sixties but built like ironwood. Only the grey in his eyebrows, some cloudiness in the eyes, and his slow, stiff gait betrayed his age. He had been with Charles Taylor from the start. Plainspoken and reticent, he often stayed quiet in meetings. Though he considered Taylor a good friend, even by his own account he was not his closest confidante. The Vice President was of Gio descent, from Nimba, and joined the movement because President Doe attacked his people. He still had many supporters in his home region, and, some said, that was why President Taylor appointed him.

The highway was empty and dark, with nothing to see but the sliding wedge of grey pavement and grass in the haze of the headlights. It took more than an hour to reach the house. As he pulled into the driveway, he received a call from General Yeaten, who told him he was at White Flower, the President's private residence. The President, General Yeaten added, wanted to see him. Moses Blah sighed, shrugged, and told his wife he had to go. It was raining now and he said he would offload the suitcases when he returned. She was not pleased, but she agreed. It was only clothes. He turned the car around.

The Vice President arrived at White Flower just after midnight and was admitted by the guards. He walked into the sitting room not knowing what to expect, why he had been summoned, or what the President was going to do. Gathered in the room, he saw colleagues from the Cabinet and a few of the President's relatives. National Security Advisor J.T. Richardson was there, along with General Yeaten. When the President entered, he did not give Moses Blah his hand. The Vice President was taken aback.

"Ha," the President said. "Fine. Well, I called you here. I got the information."

He eyed Moses Blah coolly, as if sizing him up.

"In fact, do you know a telephone number?"

"But which number?" the Vice President asked.

"There was a call from the American Embassy. I have their number."

"Yes," Moses Blah said, "I have their number too. Because they called me."

"Well," the President replied, "then the information is correct. You planned to overthrow my government, with the help of the American government."

Just, Moses Blah thought, because I received a call?

"No," he told the President. "The information is not true." He felt very bad, because when you are accused falsely, you feel very bad. He was not happy. President Taylor was a man he had worked with and always tried to be honest with. It was not fair for the President to call abruptly and accuse him of plotting a coup, of wanting to overthrow the President, of working for the American government. It was not fair at all.

"The Americans," General Yeaten said in the flat, factual tone of an administrative clerk, "called me earlier and said that Moses Blah was no obstacle, that they had contacted the Vice President and he agreed to over-throw the government." Moses Blah could not understand it. Yeaten was his countryman, from Nimba. Maybe, he thought, Yeaten wanted to prove his loyalty to the President, to prove that he was the only loyal guy, that he could protect him better than anyone else. Moses Blah was not scared. He was angry. For such a lie, for General Yeaten to look at him and say that the American people said Moses Blah agreed to overthrow the government…

"No," he said firmly, "that is not so. Your discussion was different from mine. What the Americans asked me was if the situation would be controlled when the President was not in town. They asked what happens if Taylor is not in town and there is a riot. Are you in position to have a control? I said yes. That's what the Americans wanted. Coup was not discussed. They wanted to know if we were in control. We said the soldiers were on the move in case of anything goes wrong. I think that was their concern. They were not after coup. They were not after who becomes president or not."

"O, no," President Taylor said, "that information is not correct."

"But then check," the Vice President said. "Go and find out." Everything that had been said was not true, Moses Blah thought. He did not plan a coup. And anybody that came up to say that he planned a coup should bring the evidence. Because, he insisted, a telephone conversation was not evidence of a coup. Across the room, J.T. Richardson did not know what to make of it. The Americans wanted to know the situation would be controlled? No one at the American Embassy could have believed that Moses Blah had enough influence within the government that he could call the Director of the Police or the Commander of the Anti-Terrorist Unit and tell him to stand down. So why, he wondered as he looked at it, had the Americans gone after Moses? And Moses Blah himself was standing there saying "I don't know what these people wanted from me."

General Yeaten's mobile phone rang. "Ha," the General said, "there's another call from the American people. They are calling me again, to ask what do I have to say about this situation?" He glared accusingly at the Vice President.

"O, do you see that?" Moses Blah heard the President say. "The man is calling." The President turned abruptly to his security. "Y'all take Moses Blah away," he instructed. Then the President confronted his Vice President. "Okay, you are arrested. You must resign tonight. You are no longer Vice President. You wanted to overthrow my government, right? You carry this man." Taylor seemed very angry.

Moses Blah was also mad. This was a friend he had known for years, and for the President to look at him and for such a lie to come from his mouth... And never try to investigate... He had just been sent for and arrested, in the night, as Vice President. The President did not even have the Constitutional right, Moses Blah objected. The Vice President was head of the Senate. Inform the Senate, he wanted to say, and they would set up a committee to investigate if he was guilty. Then the Chief Justice would be informed, and they could strip him of his immunity, and turn him over to a court. Instead, he held his tongue. He did not want to provoke the President. When Charles Taylor was in such a mood, Moses Blah reminded himself, you either died or something else.

The security services grabbed him. They led him downstairs and out of the house. They were afraid of his title, and nobody could just harass him. Before they took his phone, he was permitted to call his wife. "I have been arrested by the President," he said. "For what, for what?" she asked, panicked. "The President," Moses Blah said calmly, "said that I was going to make a coup, that I planned to kill him."

That night, in the darkest hours before dawn, Moses Blah found himself in a cottage just off old SKD Road. He was, he realized, directly behind General Yeaten's house, where the General played sports. There were two bedrooms and a small sitting room. It was clean, at least. He was taken straight into one bedroom. There was a bed, and there was a toilet. It was not bad, he said to himself. It had not been designed as a prison. A lot of armed men, people with Kalashnikovs, milled around out front. Nine or ten, from what he could tell. They had taken his cell phone, so he could not contact anyone. And all of his security men had been arrested and disarmed.

He sat on the bed and cupped his hands. He didn't know where his car was, with his wife's luggage. Then, suddenly, he recognized her voice outside. "You must show me where you have taken my husband," she yelled. "If so necessary, I'll die, we all die tonight, but I must see what you are doing to him." He heard talk, talk, talk, and then the voices ran away. They killed her, he worried, or jailed her. He began to pray in his mind. "God," he said under his breath, "if you know the truth, because what this man is saying, if this is the end of my life, no, you must receive my soul, because I do not know what this man is talking about. I never planned a coup on him. I am a normal person, I am not power-drunk. I don't like power. He knows me for that."

Moses Blah prayed and prayed. Then he fell asleep.

On the fifth day of Moses Blah's captivity, with the city under attack, his oldest daughter was permitted to visit. The rebels, she reported, had been talking on looted radios. "Look," they told government troops, "you better release Moses Blah. We know where you have him. We know you have put him someplace not far from your house. If you don't release him, we will do it ourselves." When Moses Blah's wife heard it, she yelled. "I know," she said, "my husband is finished. If Taylor hears this thing, he will believe it, that my husband is with the rebels, and that the rebels are with the Americans." If you stay until tomorrow, Moses' oldest daughter said to him sadly, it means God is really with you.

The next day came, and the next, and he was still alive.

After ten days, President Taylor finally sent for him. Maritime Commissioner Benoni Urey, for one, thought it was the right decision. He did think there had been a coup plot—he would not say who was involved—but the portion that related to the U.S. Embassy was all rubbish. He had gone to President Taylor and said that disregarding the merits or demerits of the thing with Moses Blah was not expedient. And, he said, one of President Taylor's attributes was that he was always willing to forgive.

When President Taylor finally met his Vice President, Moses Blah heard, "O, this was just for information. I didn't mean to harm you. In fact, we are just investigating." The President didn't, Moses Blah observed, say anything straight. He didn't come out straight and say he was sorry. The President told him he had sent fuel for his generator and given money to his wife. He told him not to worry about his house.

"Okay," Moses Blah said, "thank you very much, Mr. President."

The information, Moses Blah protested again, was not correct. What was said about him was not true. He never planned a coup, and he would never go against his president or friend. The President listened carefully, but took no action. Afterward, Moses Blah was returned to his small, isolated room. If the President would not listen to his words, he was certain that he would be taken away and killed. He wept and prayed.

On his eleventh day in captivity, Moses Blah was awakened by a security guard. "Get dressed," he was told. "You're going to the Executive Mansion." Blah donned a white embroidered African gown, followed security outside, and climbed into a black sedan. At the Executive Mansion he was led into the conference hall, where there was a big crowd, almost three hundred people. They were from Nimba, his home county, except for the Ministers. His wife was there too. President Taylor told him to take a seat.

"Well," the President said, "I have called you here, and the people from Nimba would like to listen to you, to review the facts of the story. You have to explain to the people what happened, your involvement in the coup d'etat." Blah rose up. He never, he told the people, did a coup d'etat. He should apologize, he was told.

"No," he said, he could not apologize. He could not apologize because he never did a coup. He had a call from the American embassy and the man said, "What was the situation in town? Would he, as Vice President, be able to control the soldiers, the looters?" And he said, in reply to that man, "Yes, I am out there, and Benjamin Yeaten, the Chief of Security, is also out there, and we will try to control the situation." They never, Moses Blah said, discussed a coup with him. The Americans called and their concern was the safety of their people in Liberia, and their property. That's all they wanted. That's what they were asking. So if talking to the Americans was wrong, then he must apologize.

"What," the President asked, "do the Nimba people have to say?"

A former Chief Justice stood up. "Mr. President," he said, "there was a chief in a village, and he had a goat, and this goat was running around, running around destroying people's crops. But this goat was a fine goat, and the chief wanted to keep his goat. There was a clay pot by the chief's house. The goat went and put his head in the pot. So the head got stuck in the pot. The chief wanted to save his goat, and the chief wanted to save his pot, because he had to use his pot the next day to cook. What should he do? Kill the goat, or bust the pot open? That, Mr. President, is your guess. You do what you want to do. You either kill the goat and save your pot, or bust your pot and save your goat."

The President paused awhile in thought.

"Sunday," he said. "I will reply to everything you people are saying."

But after a few seconds, he changed his mind.

"In fact," he said, "No. No, not Sunday. Right now, I agree that Moses Blah is free, his immunity is restored, he is Vice President of this country. In fact, I have decided that he will take my place if I resign as President." Tears came to Moses Blah. It had all been a lie, and he was not happy. But he felt life returning to him.

The President smiled, grabbed his hand, and raised it.

"Heeey," he said, "me and my man together again."

11

THE CEASEFIRE

In countries ruined by war, in the days before the mobile revolution, television stations usually got knocked out early and there were only two ways to get news: word of mouth and short-wave. It was by radio that Jenkins Vangehn first heard that a ceasefire had been inked in Accra. The agreement, dated June 17, stated that within thirty days a comprehensive peace agreement would be concluded, leading to the formation of a transitional government that would not include Charles Taylor.

Debate broke out in Monrovia and Accra over whether Taylor had just agreed to step down within thirty days. The Liberian president took to the air to clarify matters. "Anyone who thinks I will resign within a month is holding onto, at best, a dream. The ceasefire agreement calls for a political arrangement to be concluded within thirty days, but that has nothing to do with my tenure." At his desk, Jenkins was impressed that Taylor's defiant voice came in strong as ever despite the weak signal. His words did not inspire optimism that lasting peace was at hand. Taylor said, "Let's not anybody be fooled that our backs are against the wall to the extent that we will accept anything thrown at us. No! Listen, there is a time for everything. There is a time to fight, there is a time to talk peace. We are talking peace, but let nobody believe the fighting spirit is out of us."

Rebel fighters, Jenkins guessed, would take the speech as an affront. The silver lining was that Taylor seemed to offer the United States an olive branch, which likely would keep his fighters away from the embassy for a time. "America is our principal ally," he said, "and relations should be better. I'm seriously anxious to develop a constructive partnership with the United

States, but I don't believe they understand my talents or my connection with the Liberian people." He let his words sink in.

"America can do more," he said, "America should do more."

Once he had briefed his bosses, Jenkins hopped into his blue Daewoo and drove home. He had not been back to Patience Shop, in Gardnersville, on the outskirts of the city, in nearly a fortnight. Erosion in the winding dirt road had left cavities so deep that finger-length minnows appeared in the pools whenever it rained and Jenkins constantly had to repair the battered undercarriage of the sedan. As the concrete walls and tin roof of his white three-bedroom bungalow swung into view through the spots and cracks in his windshield, he felt a sense of release. It was well-appointed by local standards, with a pantry, two baths, and separate kitchen, dining and sitting rooms, and the family owned a small diesel generator to power the lights, television, and ceiling fans, though they had not used it in some time for fear state security would carry it off. They had a well too, a luxury in a town without piped water, a stand of coconut trees, and a swing.

Three large dogs greeted him, tails a-wag, and nipped playfully at his heels as he crossed the yard. Two were golden brown with white patches in the face and legs while the third was dark brown with traces of black and white around the chest and sides. They were good dogs and he had raised them since they were puppies. His mother hugged him tight when he showed up, then he kicked off his leather shoes, went to his room, and sat on the bed. It was a simple pleasure, to smell the sheets and the walls, and he never took it for granted. He remembered the first time he had seen the place, at night, nearly thirteen years ago, when he arrived with his aunty and uncle as the city fell apart. Back then the house was not yet finished and the rooms felt cramped, with seventeen people harbored under the roof, but the high walls gave them a small measure of security, at least for a time, as the din of automatic weapons fire swept through the streets. They had been forced to leave, as they had been forced out of Yekepa, and Bossou, and they fled to exile in Guinea and Ghana. When Jenkins returned to Liberia after nearly ten years, LAMCO had long since folded. The concession he grew up on had fallen into ruin, reclaimed by the forest. The house in Gardnersville, which his aunty still owned, was the only place familiar enough to call home.

Tall, muscular, and ruggedly handsome, Jenkins was a young man who exuded a calm confidence that gave the impression he could carry the world on his shoulders. He spent weekends, when there were weekends, playing football on the regulation-sized pitch at a downtown stadium. It had been his dream to play professionally and he had the skills to do it, but the war derailed his plans. In exile, he played at the University of Ghana, but he put his studies first. When the rebels had attacked the city two weeks ago, Liberia had been hosting Ethiopia for an African Cup of Nations qualifying match, which was played as scheduled, war be damned, because Liberia needed the win. War is a dream-wrecker, but football dreams die hard in those who play. When Jenkins learned that Liberia had fielded a team of semi-professional footballers and refugees, his heart fell that he had not somehow found his way onto the pitch. The Liberian side won by a lone goal after the Ethiopians realized that the bangs they heard were not the crowds stamping in the stands, but the blasts of mortars and rocket-propelled grenades. Nobody went out for football now: the field was a swamp and displaced families sheltered under the bleachers.

Since the attack, Jenkins had done little else but work. At embassies the world over, in countries not at war, local staff jobs were in many respects like any other jobs, with a commute, an office, a routine, and a biweekly paycheck. They differed primarily in that, no matter the title, there was risk in the affiliation with the United States. The embassy was a symbol, with all attendant benefits and drawbacks. Threat of a terrorist attack was ever present and in countries where bilateral ties were tense, such as Liberia, host government authorities often threatened local staff and their families for working with the Americans. Jenkins heard of places where his counterparts sat in jail on trumped up charges for just doing their jobs. In Liberia, in Monrovia, it was no secret that the militia kept an eye on his house. It would only take a word, perhaps not even a word, but a nod, a look, a glance, and he and his family would suffer.

The State Department had ways to recognize local staff contributions, of course, through the grant of awards or even special immigrant visas for those who had served the interests of the United States with distinction over many years, but the incentives did not in and of themselves inspire the tenacious loyalty to mission that so many had shown, in so many countries, for so long. Rather, if asked, many said that they acted out of concern for their colleagues and passion for principle. The United States of America, and the embassy that represented it, stood for liberties that they wanted to enjoy in their own countries, and it was, at times, uniquely positioned to help bring them about.

In Liberia that meant: end the war.

It was why, during the attack on the capital, Jenkins slept on the floor of his office and washed his clothes in the sink while day and night he worked his contacts to keep the Ambassador briefed on news from the front, or from upcountry. It was why he did not look first to his own safety, quit his job, and pack up. It was why now, as the afternoon light faded, he lit the paraffin lamp at his bed stand, picked up his notepad and pen, and parsed the language of the June 17 ceasefire agreement. The Liberian government and the two rebel movements agreed to stop shooting, agreed they wanted international peacekeepers, and agreed they would, within thirty days, seek a final accord on political transition. It all sounded more aspirational than practical. How a peacekeeping mission would stand up, or when, or who would pay for it was not specified.

The Economic Community of West African States, Jenkins read, was to assemble a Joint Verification Team. The team would, in theory, demarcate the frontlines and monitor ceasefire violations, but, when Jenkins made a few calls, he found the initiative was already beset with problems. According to his sources at the peace talks, the rebels claimed that the men tapped to represent them on the team were deep in the bush and needed to be picked up by air, capacity ECOWAS lacked, which led someone to point out that the Joint Verification Team had no exfiltration capabilities. If the team ran into trouble, no one could rescue it, and until that point was resolved, it could not deploy. So it was clear that a ceasefire had been established with no practical way to monitor or enforce it. Fighters, Jenkins knew, could not respect that.

The rebel strike on the capital also gave lie to the idea that Charles Taylor was unbeatable. If the rebels tried again, he thought, Taylor might order his men to do anything. Mayhem would follow. Liberians had not seen much of the rebels, they did not know how they operated, but they knew the militia. Everyone believed that Taylor would use the ceasefire to get rid of as many of his enemies as possible. After the indictment, after the attack, he had been branded a war criminal, so now, it was presumed on the street, he would do whatever he could to hold onto power. The Vice President was already in jail. Everyone figured a counterattack was inevitable, if the rebels did not attack again first.

Jenkins sensed he would not see his own bed again for a while.

The ceasefire triggered the immediate departure of the Kearsarge. The SEALs left with the ship, but, before it sailed, a Brigadier-General, on what he said was his last operation, flew out to take lunch at the cafeteria, which gave the

Ambassador a chance to express his sincere gratitude for the work that the ESAT and SEALs had done. The Brigadier-General helpfully offered some pointers on timelines and tripwires for any future evacuations, should it come to that. The ESAT crew did not say much to anyone on the way out, so it was hard to tell if they were disappointed to leave without seeing the job through, or whether they simply tired of club sandwiches and watered-down pepper soup and were eager for some place more kinetic. The Captain caught the Political Officer in passing and told him with a grin that they would be back, because they always got called back to Liberia.

The intense humidity along the coast soaked dress shirts as soon as you stepped outside, so the Ambassador often saved himself a laundering or two by indulging in a quick air-conditioned drive to his residence over a seven-minute stroll from the chancery. But as the Kearsarge set sail the evening skies were clear and a cool breeze swept off the ocean, evoking those late summer days back home when the season began to turn, and he decided to walk. Mingled scents of leaves and grass and warm asphalt rose up, and he thought of his days as a young Foreign Service Officer in Zambia, when all was possibility and his job was to deliver demarches on esoteric topics to ministry officials who sometimes fell asleep as he read the points. Cracked and stained tennis courts appeared to his left, little used now except at one end where the Marines played basketball with a plywood backboard and metal rim. The cabanas by the swimming pool beyond were empty, like the beach after Labor Day, a few eucalyptus leaves slowly turning in the water.

The Chief of Mission Residence had once been the British chancery and it was said that Graham Greene had stayed there to write. The foyer boasted parquet floors, a high ceiling, and glass chandeliers. Potted zebra plants stood to one side and a striking canvas of a woman and a small child in traditional East African dress, rendered by the Ambassador's sister, graced the back wall. Beneath the painting, a guestbook rested on a small rosewood table beside a glass vase and a bouquet of trumpet lilies, ferns, and ixoras.

The Ambassador noticed the book was open. He flipped the pages out of idle curiosity, smiling at the thought that he had not had many guests of late. At the last marked page, his index finger slid to the latest entry. The date was written small and precise: "6/14/03." The signatory was "ODA 023," and the address listed as Stuttgart, Germany.

"Special Forces," it read, "We're here to get you out!"

PART THREE

THE SECOND ATTACK

12

THE MEZZE HOUSE

The heat stank like a fever. As evening fell, a pall of mist and charcoal smoke settled over the city. Beneath the palm thatch, overlooking the sand and the water, Fergy took a mezze at the open-air Lebanese bar on the sloping grounds of the Mamba Point Hotel, a stone's throw from the southern walls of the embassy. He pressed a wet bottle to his face for a moment's relief. Generators kicked in somewhere out back and the lamps overhead pulsed and brightened. Kamal Ghanem, the manager, appeared in the doorway of a small, well-lit parlor attached to the deck, where the cash register and ice chests were found, and extended a moist hand. His voice was breathy and smelled of garlic and paprika.

"How are you, my friend?"

Fergy was too tired for chit-chat but he was a captive audience. The ceasefire was less than a week old and already he had reports that the kids in the bush had not gotten the word, or ignored it. MODEL took Harper, a port town down south. The Joint Verification Team never showed up and no one could even say at this point if the government still held Kle Junction, but lorry drivers who had been out that way said that militia and the rebels took turns dragging brambles across the road as checkpoints, temporarily staking claim to small stretches of tarmac between Kle and Iron Gate, only fifteen miles off. "Everyone shoots and runs and claims victory," is how it was put to him. With the war so close, Fergy was moored on the deck alone, save a small circle of Lebanese merchants huddled at the far end smoking hookahs. The staff, a pair of drowsy women dolled up in red wigs and black skirts, draped themselves on the rail, and stared at the empty rows of rattan tables and chairs.

Kamal spoke *sotto voce*. "There's a rumor."

"This place is all rumors," Fergy said. Kamal had a thick, black mustache and spoke in heavily accented English. Life must have been pretty bad in Beirut in the early eighties, Fergy considered, that Monrovia was a better place to make your cash for the next twenty years. He had a lot of friends in the Lebanese community, but he knew the game. They all paid something to someone, took care of this guy and that. Now they passed long nights waiting for news from the bush and parsing the tea leaves to see if the Papay would survive the latest mess or end up like his predecessors, disemboweled or on his knees, cut up, and left to bleed out. Kamal stroked his mustache.

"You will send peacekeepers?" he said.

"You think so, huh," Fergy said, reaching for olives.

"The French did for Cote d'Ivoire," Kamal said, "and the British did for Sierra Leone." Fergy spit a couple pits in his hand and dropped them into the scented Kleenex that had been set out as napkins. The town was an echo chamber and Kamal just repeated the mantra of the streets. Only, the United States already had two ground wars on its hands and had gotten out of the African peacekeeping business after Somalia.

"I don't think so, Kamal," he said.

"But these are your people in Africa," Kamal protested.

"You got to ask yourself, Kamal, how's this still on us?"

"If not you, then who?"

Fergy dabbed a wedge of pita in a small dish of baba ghanouj. It was the expatriate parlor game in places like Liberia. With the compulsive logic of addicts, you rehashed the same, timeworn theories and tossed out the same facile answers that reduced the people, the country, and the war to casual shorthand. If the United States just did this, if the Liberians just did that, it could all be fixed so easily. In fairness, Kamal was a little different. He just fished around to find out if he would be able to stay in business. International peacekeeping operations were lucrative for bars and restaurants, but for Kamal, if one did not come to Liberia, and soon, the alternatives were unthinkable.

"Only the Liberians can save this place," Fergy said, but he only half believed it. This was his first time to see diplomacy in action and he was frustrated. His military training and innate competitiveness stopped him from passing off the problem, and experience taught him that solutions could usually be found with persistence and enough elbow grease. Here, there were no easy answers. Superior tactics, technology, and personnel could not eliminate the enemy because it was not America's fight, and anyway between Taylor, LURD, and MODEL there were no good guys. The way forward lay not in military victory, but in buying time and space for those Liberians who sought a better country to make their voices heard. He knew the Ambassador wanted Washington policymakers to back some sort of stabilization force, but even with their buy-in so much more was needed: mandates from multinational organizations, troop contributing countries, and the like. At the same time, Liberian stakeholders in Ghana somehow had to find consensus for a political transition and eventually elections. It was slow, it was maddening. And yet, he thought, all wars end. The country was resource rich. If only…

Fergy caught himself. He peered through the haze past the rail at the stand of candelabra and traveler's palms that separated the hotel from the road and the beach. Half-dressed government soldiers at a checkpoint below crouched on plastic crates and glared at the washerwomen with buckets on their heads sidestepping the planks and the cinderblocks. Staccato gunshots popped through the air, somewhere near. It was not unusual for looters to fire off a few rounds on any given night, but rarely that close to the diplomatic quarter. The soldiers jumped to their feet with rifles poised, mimicking poses they had seen in pirated Hollywood thrillers in the video shacks around town. The Lebanese merchants set aside their water pipes and shifted heavily to pull mobiles from overstretched denim. Kamal smiled grimly and retreated to polish glasses with a grey dishrag.

Fergy keyed Post One on his handset.

"Amityville, Birdy, what you got?"

The voice of Jordan Weeks, on watch, crackled over the receiver.

"Birdy, Amityville. Three Code Deltas. We're calling around."

Static washed across the frequency. Fergy pushed back his chair and made to leave, troubled that the militia would loot with the rebels so close. The capital had not been sacked in many years and the markets were swollen with product, the flood of cheap plastic goods from China and points east. A new joke was already in circulation: "Monrovia is pregnant and will deliver soon." He slipped a twenty under his beer bottle. Tabbouleh and hummus and olive oil glistened in the white porcelain dishes, and a plate of kafta and basmati rice simmered on a black skillet, untouched. A hundred yards up the shore the Chief of Mission Residence was bathed in security lights, visible on the slopes above embassy walls. The Ambassador worked late and a faint glow issued from the arched windows of the old manse. As Fergy walked into the night, the thatch roof behind him shivered in the breeze, rustling like the raffia skirts of the bush devils of old.

13

THE SECOND ATTACK

In the mythologies, oftentimes it was said people were formed from clay, sculpted by the gods, or spontaneously risen from the viscous soils of the early world. In Liberia, if you were Daniel Brown or Brian Stovall, a young Marine assigned to U.S. Embassy Monrovia in the middle of June 2003, your first overseas post of any kind, you might have been forgiven if you started to give some credence to the old beliefs. You would have passed a long night staring at the shadows of the local guards as they walked from time to time beneath the halo of the lamps along the empty street that snaked downhill from Gate One to the entrance at the Chief of Mission Residence. Then, as dawn broke, in the time it took you to hand off your shift, stow your weapon in the armory and hit the head, five hundred people would have appeared at the embassy gates, as if sprung from the soil itself, and a half hour later, five hundred more, and so forth, until there were five thousand.

If there were crowds, the Marines knew, the war was back.

Outside, the morning air filled with the sound of cicadas, boisterous in the branches over the street. High above, cumulous massed mute, white and glaring. Then came a loud crack, like a maul splitting dry pitch. From a plastic garden chair in the arcade in front of the chancery, where he took his morning Red Bull and smoke, Fergy felt a concussive wave blow across his chest. A mortar struck, an 82 millimeter or so he guessed, no more than fifty yards off. Near the flagpole, he saw the Political Officer duck, well after the fact, and hustle to Gate One. For a moment, everything smelled of roots and freshly turned earth. Fergy waved away floaters, stubbed out his cigarette, and jogged after his colleague. As he passed the roto-gates he saw the crowds, heard the whisk of their feet. Inside the guard booth, a ten-foot square control room in a bunker of reinforced concrete and bullet resistant smoked glass, the local guards stood stock still in their starched whites and khakis and stared spell-bound at the street as their Motorola handsets chattered senselessly from black charge stands on the counter. Fergy called around to his contacts on Bushrod Island and found out that yes, indeed, the city was under sustained attack.

Sergeant Scramlin went up on the roof again with Marines Mike Muniz, Jordan Weeks, and Anthony Adams. The streets below were frenzied. Militia in battlewagons swerved wildly though the serpentines with packs of small, spindly legs dangling off the rims of the flatbeds. It was unsettling, Adams said, to look down the rifle and see a child with a gun, knowing that if he fired you might have to eliminate the threat. You couldn't guess at the kids' state of mind, but some were so young they could barely hold their weapons. The idea of firing on anyone beyond the walls played in the back of your head. If you engaged, you knew it could ignite a chain of events that could end really badly, but kneeling on the rooftop gravel, behind a wedge of sandbags, watching the vapor trails of the rocket propelled grenades in the distance and hearing the snap of bullets whip past, it was hard not to want to shoot at something.

It was not like in the movies, Adams realized. The Marines had little control of their tactical environment. Nearby tenements were all taller than the chancery and the Marines were certain some of the rounds that hit the gunnysacks of their bunker were meant for them, but they couldn't spot the shooters. Another crack ripped across the sky and threads of dirt rained down on the Marines as thin black smoke twisted skyward from the trees across the way. Gunnery Sergeant Aldridge's Alabama drawl slipped from the radio. "Hey, can any of you Marines catch a mortar?" Someone answered in the negative.

"Then it's time for y'all to come on down from there."

Ted Collins was not surprised when the grey liquid crystal display on his Nokia lit up with calls. They had drilled for a new attack. Still, it had all happened too fast, a replay of the assault earlier in the month re-cut and re-mixed like a pumped up dance track. From what he could tell, the Liberian government had no stomach for the fight. Rebels blitzed through the so-called point defenses, young soldiers sprinting across the grasslands to the north, their commanders lashing them on with electric cables. Ordinance rapped across the delta and thousands of people on Bushrod again took flight and headed for the red, white, and blue flag flapping at the bluffs. No cover could be found in front of the embassy, but their belief was still that it was best to be close to the Americans. Collins looked on as the roiling crowds reached the embassy, kept back from the walls and gates only by the jumble of razor wire. For a time they were directionless, like waves at the breakwaters.

A third mortar struck, close enough in, Collins guessed, that someone had to have been hit. The collective mind of the crowds suddenly fixated on Greystone, a sprawling adjunct compound fifty yards away across the street, at the end of a narrow tree-covered lane. In better times Greystone was a walled off residential subdivision for U.S. diplomats and their families, nineteen acres of bungalows and carports and tall stands of rubber and ironwood old enough to date to the founding of the country. After years of staff drawdowns the embassy now used it mostly for warehousing and only the Inter-Con team kept an office there. On quiet eves Hersh Hernandez used to stroll alone on the winding flagstone paths between the boarded up houses, as the canopy filled with birdcalls. Now Mamba Point was under attack, maybe the embassy itself, and faces streamed past the embassy guard booth, blurred with fear, and flowed toward Greystone.

Hands by the hundreds thundered against the sheet-iron. Guards grew nervous in the tower posts along the walls that encircled the adjunct compound. From their overlooks they could see the thin divide of razor wire, stone and cement: on one side, the rocks, sand, and greenery of a vacant U.S. plot; on the other, tides of people clamoring to get in. Their orders were clear: protect the American facility. They held firm, all the while hoping the heavy deadbolts at the gates would not fail and they would be overrun.

"Release the teargas!" someone barked over a handset.

Smoke billowed near the main gate, flaring up as if a building had collapsed, the haze whiting out the tumult. For a time all that could be heard were the coughs and shouts of blinded men and women, eyes burning, throats aflame, crashing into one another. Still the crowds pressed forward. Bracing and sheet-iron could only withstand so much and the gates of Greystone gave way. Flat, black sheets bent backward over the bollards behind them. People rushed in, vaulting onto the makeshift ramp, tripping, flailing, crushing others beneath. Cries of terror flew from the mouths of those pushed down by the torrent of bodies, as if caught in an undercurrent, matched by the horrified shouts of those who could not stop themselves as they trampled cotton, flesh, and bone, pressed forward by hands at the back and their own desperate momentum.

"Fall back!" guards shouted at the radio.

Greystone was open. Within minutes everyone who had been in the street in front of the embassy was gone, rushed away to find some patch inside the walls of the other American property, as if it offered any real protection from the arc of the mortars. A middle-aged woman lay dead at the entrance, her body bruised and pulped and cast aside. In front of Gate One, abandoned belongings littered the pavement, sandals and baskets and headscarves pressed flat and somehow drained of color. An eerie silence took hold. The embassy had not opened Greystone during the first attack because the U.S. mission was not set up to run a camp for thousands of displace people. There was no food, no toilets, no potable water, and little cover from the elements. But now it had been done. In the quiet of the booth at Post One, inside the chancery, the Regional Security Officer and Gunnery Sergeant stood behind the Marine on station, and listened to the garbled feed from the radios. Collins scanned the images on the video feed of the gates and the street.

"Well," he said finally, "that was our safety valve."

"How's that, sir?"

"If they don't go to Greystone, they come over our walls."

Ted Collins had the kind of classic untroubled middle-class upbringing, the benefits of which accrued from the hardships born by preceding generations, that instilled within its cohort the sense of possibility. His parents had both been born into the Depression. His father was a former Marine who rose from a rough start in a small railroad town to become a senior executive in several specialty steel corporations, while his mother was a substitute elementary school teacher. Home was caring and rules-based, and it was made clear early on to Ted and his little brother that they had opportunities far beyond what their parents had and, as such, they would be held to the highest standards. They were taught to be well-mannered and polite, and service to the community and broader nation were the ethos.

As a boy in the Pittsburgh area, Ted spent time in the woods, riding bikes, reading history, and playing sports in the street. After the family moved, he attended high school in Cleveland, where he swam and played water polo and made All Conference multiple times in both sports. That he played trumpet in the band and was an Eagle Scout could not have surprised: he also volunteered for Meals on Wheels, served as a counselor at a muscular dystrophy camp, and worked as the senior lifeguard and janitor for an apartment complex on weekends and summers to earn extra money.

Ted applied himself in school, did well, and was offered scholarships and appointments to each of the service academies. Annapolis was the choice both for the education and because, between the Navy and the Marine Corps, it offered the broadest range of career options. The Naval Academy, Ted knew, was very specific preparation to make a difference somewhere, for someone. He would not call it a dream or a vision, or even a premonition, but he sensed that if he pursued a certain path of service, he would someday find himself in a role where the stakes would be high and where he would be relied upon perform some key task with no margin for error, where experience, knowledge, discipline, and sheer force of will would carry the day.

That day, he realized, was at hand.

Standing in the cramped space of Post One with the Marine and Gunnery Sargent Aldridge to one side, Ted Collins felt the weight of his charge. Lives were at stake, nothing less. The Marine Security Guards had been outstanding through the first attack, Gunny had them good to go for a second round, but the new offensive had Collins concerned. After the first attack, he guessed the rebels would strike again. Government forces barely held the line. Seesaw fights out by Kle Junction may have tipped for good in favor of the rebels, which meant that the government could not keep the war away from the city.

At least he had a better grasp now on what the embassy could handle. You never worked with perfect information, you always worked with a percentage, but since the first attack he and his team had filled in a lot of blanks on critical questions about local capabilities and intentions. They could see trends. They were more familiar with the armed knuckleheads running around the streets. Small-arms fire they could manage for sure, and it helped that the two sides did not have heavy armor, but mortars and rocket propelled grenades kept him up at night. They could do damage.

Retaining Greystone through the first attack had been important. In the past, Collins knew, every time that Greystone "opened" it meant, psychologically, to the people in the street, that control of the city was lost. It meant militia fighting block by block. Now the immediate question was whether to send a team over to Greystone to help out Hersh. As Collins stood there in the yellow glow of the recessed lights, it struck him with modest surprise that he could not bring himself to let others take the same risks he had taken as a young officer in places like Algeria and the West Bank and Gaza. It was a whole different ballgame to be responsible for the safety an entire mission, all its personnel, and he found himself sometimes ready to err on the side of safety and caution.

He decided to let Greystone play out. He did not see a better option. They had lost radio contact. The guards were by now overrun and, unless it was worse than he feared, would have fallen back to a bungalow at the center of the compound that Hersh had fortified with sharpened bamboo spikes and punji sticks. If anyone could handle the situation it was the Inter-Con chief, who had seen everything over the years. And Collins also put his faith in the Liberian people. They wanted shelter, not to hurt anyone. Still, he had no idea what was going on over there and in a few minutes he would have to walk up to the front office and brief the Ambassador that they had lost control of the adjunct facility and he could not even say what had happened to his guys.

Another explosion. At Gate One, the thick panes at the guard booth bowed in slightly and the guards on station glanced uneasily at the ceiling, as if they expected it to cave. The air was charged with the shimmer and displacement of a lightning strike. Shrieks, like seagulls at ebb tide. On the radio, a hoarse voice shouted "Greystone's been hit!" Across the way, the adjunct compound regurgitated the crowds. A flying wedge of men burst through the masses still queued to enter. Bodies clashed, shouts of anger and fear could be heard, then the tangled cluster of people uncoiled and everyone ran in different directions. They dashed helter-skelter until many stopped and gave up, turning in slow, confused circles, eyes shut tight, hands viced against their heads. Grimacing, Collins watched things play out across the monitors at Post One.

You saw the blood before you saw the bodies, flung here and there like action painting. A thin, knob-kneed man in a fedora staggered along with a young boy clinging to his back. The boy wore black football shorts, but his legs were gone and arterial spray shot from the rayon flaps in arrhythmic bursts like a broken fountain. When boy's grip failed, the man turned to catch him, then dropped to his knees, and made a cradle of his arms. The eyes of the child rolled white. Another man in a pale yellow shirt made transparent with sweat charged wildly down the lane with an old wheelbarrow. Arms and legs flopped over the sides of the metal bucket, jerking limply with the motion, and at the bottom lay a woman in a fetal pose, or what was once a woman. Linens drenched in blood, limbs at peculiar angles, it was not clear that all the pieces of her body were connected, or that all the pieces in the wheelbarrow were hers. The man ran away, downhill, toward the sea.

The street cleared again. A family of sorts lurched past the embassy gates. An elderly man, the years etched across in his features, raged at the sky and shook his fists impotently. Several young women grabbed at his shoulders, tears streaming down their soft cheeks as they tried to calm him. He stumbled free and left them only with the threads of his shirt, then fell to his knees and beat his head on the curb until it bled.

"O Lord not her! Not her! Not her! O Lord!"

The dirge lingered long after he wandered off.

The Ambassador watched his Regional Security Officer leave his office, then walked to the door and shut it, which he rarely did. Collins had just briefed him that Greystone was overrun with thousands of displaced people and an embassy gardener and one of the Inter-Con contract guards had been killed by shrapnel. There were two hundred guards or so, so the Ambassador did not recognize the name, but he remembered the last time he saw the gardener, between the two attacks, a humble figure in his jumpsuit, trimming the hedges with dull clippers down by the tennis courts. Sorrow settled over him and he felt that pang of helplessness that you feel when you want to claw back time and make things different. This was John Blaney's embassy. These were his people. They did jobs that supported an American diplomacy and that aimed for a better future for their own country. Now they were dead and the fight was on and that future was imperiled.

Viability of the mission was at stake.

The unpalatable truth was that in Washington the report would not count the same as if they had lost an American assigned to post. It would be accepted that Liberians could die in a Liberian war, but if a single American staff member were killed, however random the event, shrapnel, or stray round or otherwise, the decision to keep the embassy open would be taken out of his hands and those that wanted it shut would get their way, with terrible consequences on the ground. It was a perverse way to reach to the right answer, he knew, because in reality, if not in politics, their lives held the same value, but in this case, to make sense of their sacrifice, it needed to be that way. Only peace, an end to the terrible war, could make a difference for their families, and the embassy still had a vital role to play in making that happen. He paid his respects silently.

Then he took a deep breath and opened the door.

Embassies, as might be expected, had crisis management protocols. The State Department required that embassy teams craft "emergency action plans," detailed procedures to respond to bombs, pandemics, civil disorder, and the like. The plans were country-specific and tailored to reasonably foreseeable emergency situations at each locale, so that the plan for Baghdad would certainly be different than that for Bern, presumably as much to get it right as to avoid some eager young officer spending undue time prepping a contingency plan to deploy search and rescue snowmobiles in the alluvial plains of Lower Mesopotamia, as it had been known to snow there, however infrequently.

The Chief of Mission in all cases had to appoint an Emergency Action Committee, made up of key officers and subject matter experts, that maintained the plan and acted on it in the event of a crisis. "Tripwires" were events stipulated in the emergency action plan that, if they occurred, triggered actions, such as the ordered departure of staff, organization of the internal defense of the chancery, or the destruction of sensitive materials, a variation on the old "burn after reading" that was more just "burn it all." Whenever a crisis came, the EAC convened and reviewed the tripwires to find out if they had been tripped, or "crossed," as the Department would have it. In a place like Liberia, or anywhere with a hot war, tripwires might be things like a general breakdown of law and order, a rebel attack on the capital, or an attack on the embassy itself. After an EAC meeting, a telegram would be drafted and sent back to Washington that, generally speaking, would note what the EAC considered, where the tripwires stood, and any actions to be taken.

For U.S. Embassy Monrovia, the problem was that nearly any conceivable tripwire would have been broken or would likely be broken in short order, but staff had been already pared to the marrow, internal defenses fortified to the extent possible, and burn times kept to the bare minimum. Not much was left to be done, short of abandoning the post. Discussion of tripwires under those circumstances was a little like the old Robin Williams skit about Colonel Gaddafi, when he famously drew a line in the sand: "It's a line of death, you cross it, you die! Okay, if you cross this line, you die! Okay, if you cross this line, you die! Okay, you knock on my door I'm not coming out, nyehhh!" Still, Ambassador Blaney and his Regional Security Officer played it by the book, and the EAC was convened, and a cable prepared, and then everyone hurried back to work.

Midday, a Liberian spokesman took to the airwaves and insisted that the government still held the Free Port, only to be contradicted minutes later by a British journalist who spoke to the BBC by satellite phone. "The rebels are firmly in control of the port," James Brabazon said, pointing out that he had marched into Monrovia with the attack and now stood with one of the commanders beneath the green and white arches that marked the entrance. It was a Baghdad Bob moment for the government, the Ambassador thought, but the top Liberian officials were oddly sanguine when his team contacted them. There was a plan, they insisted. The rebels would be lured onto Bushrod (that part had already been a success), then cut off from behind at the Saint Paul River Bridge, and trapped on the island. "It will be like shooting fish in a barrel," they assured their American counterparts, though nobody seemed to care that the barrel was a collection of shantytowns filled with people.

They were also vague on when the counterattack would start.

Florescent lighting in the embassy corridors created a lonely, sterile air, like after-hours in a hospital, even though it was early afternoon. In his office, the Ambassador stared at uninspired wood paneling, the off-white blinds covering the windows, the stack of unread papers in his inbox. It could have been anyone's office anywhere in the world, and sitting there in an ergonomically correct swivel chair you could have no idea what had happened at Greystone only footsteps away. On television, it was Iraq, always Iraq. Traffic moved slowly along Baghdad streets and a CNN reporter talked to a soldier by a new up-armored Humvee about a rise in roadside bombs, which seemed to be killing more soldiers than the invasion. From afar, Iraq seemed to be turning into a strange war, not like the movies where everything was a flashpoint. There would be patrol, a bomb, some shooting, and a mad rush to the field hospital, and then nothing. It was back to daily life for soldiers and the people in the country they occupied. Downtime in the barracks, briefings, maintenance.

Trips to the souk. Extreme violence filled the gaps.

The men and women who read the dispatches from Monrovia in cubicles in bland office complexes in Washington, DC or Northern Virginia would not be interested in the full story of the scenes at the embassy gates. They would expect reports in impersonal Helvetica or Times New Roman that provided facts and figures that they could present easily to principals: the number of dead and injured, the type of ordinance fired (if known), the embassy's latest security posture, who controlled the city. They might want "granularity" on some aspects, like who launched the mortars or what the embassy planned to do about the thousands of displaced people squatting on a spare U.S. government facility, but really everything depended on who asked the questions and why.

The Ambassador was astonished at the volume of requests for information he received. He had been Charge d'Affairés at the very busy mission in South Africa, but it was different even then. The widespread use of email was less than a decade old and the State Department only recently upgraded its systems under Secretary Powell's leadership. John Blaney had come of age in a Foreign Service dependent on well-crafted telegrams for official communications, and he still viewed them as the most reliable means of record traffic, formal statements of the embassy's views and information. Now everything was quick, informal, without edits or context and parsed out in one-off answers. You never had all the right people on the distribution lists, so he found himself answering the same questions phrased differently for different chains.

It was still strange to him that he could hit "send" on a note, half-formed thoughts, or scraps of information, and moments later, thousands of miles across the ocean, in offices lit much like his own, those on the night watch would pull it from the queue. The scribbles would be broken out, reformatted, re-edited, aggregated with other reports and scribbles, then spit back out as briefing notes for principals. The notes would be passed to those who needed to know, who would decide who else needed to know, until someone in the chain gave some guidance about how this agency or that, or the United States as a whole, should respond to someone else's war.

Or until everything was bumped down the queue and forgotten.

14

THE DEAD

The Regional Security Officer reestablished contact with Greystone, where the guards were back at their posts and doing foot patrols through the beleaguered crowds who took shelter on the grounds. Ted Collins had guessed right: Hersh had everything under control again. The good news was that once the displaced people settled inside, they helpfully accepted the authority of Inter-Con to keep order. The bad news was that there were now thousands of people taking refuge on a U.S. facility. The plan now was to let the non-governmental organizations help out, but there were hardly any resources around.

At the Chief of Mission Residence, the Ambassador wandered into the pantry and pulled out a bottle of Buitenverwachting Christine. Ambassadors had representational budgets for receptions, and the staff kept the residence well-stocked with wine and other spirits, but the Ambassador had also brought a case of his own from the celebrated Constantia vineyard, near Cape Town, that he and Robin so often enjoyed when they had been posted to South Africa. He was not particularly in the mood for a red, but it occurred to him that they could wake up to a very different Liberia. He did not want the rebels, or anyone else who came over the wire, to get the good stuff.

He found a corkscrew and a glass and sat down alone at the table.

Darkness came fast and the shooting and shelling stopped. It was as if the fighters from both sides decided to knock off for a few hours and hit the bars, or head out to loot. Or maybe no one wanted to wander through some back alley and accidentally end up in the enemy's camp, which was known to happen since hardly anyone wore uniforms and most of the fighters had cousins on the other side. Jenkins Vangehn called his contacts on Bushrod Island and in neighborhoods north of the city. Few answered, for fear of attracting attention or wasting the battery on their mobiles. Those he reached had little to say. They whiled away the hours by the light of paraffin lamps, they told him, saying their devotions or playing a new card game where you collected an Ace, a King, a four, and a seven.

They called it "AK-47."

It takes a certain type of person to be a relief worker, someone not afraid of filth and affliction, not afraid of the dangers and mysteries of the world, someone who takes people for who they are and as they are. During the war, many Liberians took on that role, aided by only a handful of foreigners who brought resources from abroad that could not be mustered locally. One such foreigner was Merlin Country Director Magnus Wolf-Murray, a rakish young Scot who had only recently arrived in Liberia to direct the efforts of the British health charity, which had received some monies from the Americans for its projects in Liberia. The first night of the second attack, after things had quieted for a spell, he walked down to the beach and grabbed a warm beer at one of the kiosks near the hotel, a short respite from what shaped up to be an epic challenge. It hardly mattered whether the rebels would win or be driven out again. The damage to the humanitarian infrastructure had been done and people could not go back to the camps north of the capital again anytime soon. Estimates put a hundred thousand displaced in the city center and another hundred thousand in the outlying environs, all without services. No food, no water, no latrines.

Halfway into his beer, Magnus heard the heavy breath of a man who had been running, and the sweat stained face of one of his local staffers appeared in the dim light of the kiosk. Someone was sick in front of the U.S. embassy, he was told. Magnus took a last swig of beer, slapped a few soft, worn Liberian dollars on the plastic table and followed the staffer out into night. Ghostly figures of men and women fluttered beneath the yellow embassy security lights that spilled over the walls and onto the streets the length of the winding drive that led to the front gates. Further on, between the serpentines, they found a crowd of people staring piteously at an able-bodied man, perhaps in his late twenties, who had collapsed in the middle of the road.

Magnus called his medical team. Together they dragged the man to the berm and waved away the gawkers. The fellow vomited over and over, and, when there was nothing left in his gut, dry heaved and convulsed so violently it seemed like he would turn himself inside out. He shit his pants. Usually, Magnus thought, you put cholera cases in a sterile ward, so they could not infect others. It was not an option. In Monrovia, with everyone in cramped, wet tents, with no sanitation, they faced an epidemic. Plastic jugs of chlorine were rushed down from the Merlin offices and the medics splashed them in the street where the man had fallen and around the patch of grass and soil where he now lay.

Pulse undetectable, the man's blood pressure hovered at zero. The medics found a vein and jammed in the needle. Two intravenous drips, one on each side, were suspended from nearby branches. Plastic bags were squeezed roughly to force the fluids through the dried veins. Slowly the pulse returned. Suddenly, a pair of mortars struck in quick succession. They had to move, Magnus said, it was too close. They lifted the man as best they could, grabbed the drips and the chlorine jugs, and ran to silence.

After two hours, or what seemed like two hours, the man opened his eyes.

"O thank you, boss," he said to Magnus.

You could, Magnus thought, save someone that easily.

Or they could just be left to die.

In Liberia, they brought the dead to the embassy. During lulls in the fighting, when the sounds of war gave way to the merciful breath of the clouds and the wind, they rolled the bodies up in wheelbarrows and dumped them on the curb, without the dignity of shrouds. Mothers, fathers, and children arrived in the tattered clothes in which they died and were shunted into a pile of tangled limbs on a few sheets of cardboard at the gutter by Gate One. Where fabric had torn, naked breasts and genitals were laid bare. Even the children were treated roughly, lifted by their frail arms and cast atop the others like rag dolls at a tag sale. Wisps of vapor rose from the fluids that leaked out here and there.

At Post One, Corporal Adams watched the disordered images sprawl across the screens. A few months back, when the Iraq war started, he had a gnawing feeling that he had missed out, that he would not get the chance to do what he had trained for as a Marine. Like others in the detachment, he had wished he was there. Now that a war had come to them, he struggled to make sense of it, and of the hollowness he felt as he stood ringside for someone else's fight. The big crowds were gone, either huddled under bivouacs of garbage and sticks at Greystone and the Masonic temple up the street, or sheltering in schoolyards and under the stands at the football stadiums. Those gathered now at the embassy gates stared absently at the bodies of the people they once knew. From time to time they looked to the embassy walls, pale palms up in supplication, and sometimes they ran to the gate and shouted in anger. A man in a threadbare jacket held a sign, the letters handwritten in charcoal: "America, have you seen enough?"

Fergy was outside the gates, standing at the back of the crowd. Nobody took any notice of him. A mobile rang from the pocket of one of the dead. A thin young man elbowed his way to the front, knelt down, and pulled the phone from the body. The man answered and the audio was loud enough that you could hear it was a relative calling from abroad. Wailing. The man hung up, then casually walked off without a word to anyone. No one even tried to stop him. "Son of a bitch," Fergy muttered.

Whoever they once were, they were no longer. Eyes blank, features rigid, clothes bunched and whorled, stiff with rain, sweat and black, caramelized blood, the knot of them on the pavement looked like a pile of discarded plasticene figures backstage of some low-brow slasher production. Logic told Fergy he could have been among them. He too had been outside when the first shell struck. A fractional adjustment to the trajectory and the mortar could have hit the front of the chancery. Yet life carries a certain vanity and the logic could not take. Strangers lay on the ground and his emotions were cauterized. He could not picture himself lying in their midst. It would have been different, he thought, if he knew any of them, if it were his family there in the heap. He felt nothing but a remote, throbbing sadness, like the dull ache beneath an anesthetic. Sad that they lay there obscenely and that he could not fully grieve for them. Sad for the little kids who would never get to grow up. Sad for the families who shamelessly brought their dead to the curb.

He cast his eyes about and wondered where to look.

Who would he remember longer, the living or the dead?

15

THE DEMAND

merican network television did not show the Liberian dead and did not show the relief agencies clear the dead and bury them in mass graves in the beach or in overfull cemeteries downtown. Ted Collins knew they did not show these things because, to the extent he watched any television, he watched Armed Forces Network, which, in the days before streaming services and social media, was how the military and a few other agencies overseas could watch American shows. AFN broadcast news programs from all the major networks, with Fox News dominating the prime time slots, and in return for free content, it aired, in lieu of commercials, public service messages, sophomoric skits in period piece that told the troopers not to gamble, not to beat their spouses, and to see the chaplain. Or else someone dressed as Napoleon dished on how to pack for a permanent change of station: "Don't come up short, make a list." It was weirdly addictive if you were not the target audience.

Inexplicably, Fox News reported that the Ambassador had requested a Fleet Anti-Terrorism Support Team to protect the embassy. Africa, let alone Liberia, was so rarely covered by domestic media it was hard to see how the purported solicitations of a Chief of Mission would merit a story, so it seemed clear to Collins that someone in one of the public affairs shops had gotten ahead of themselves. The U.S. European Command confirmed to Fox that a platoon was ready to deploy if the order came from Washington, which implied that an order had not yet been issued, which in turn meant that, at least to the Regional Security Officer's mind, either someone had failed to run the proper bureaucratic traps or that someone had chosen to slow roll the deployment. At best it was on standby.

It was a bad sign, Collins knew. The FAST was staged out of Rota, Spain, a seven-hour flight direct to Monrovia on the right aircraft, much longer by C-130. Due to the obvious force protection issues for a forty-minute road trip along an unsecured route from Robertsfield to the capital, the Marines would have no choice but to fly directly to the embassy by rotary wing, which meant routing first through Freetown or somewhere else along the coast. In fairness, the Liberian government again offered access to its military airport in town, or safe passage from Robertsfield, but U.S. military planners did not to trust Charles Taylor, nor was it clear that the Liberian government could even guaranty its own safety, with rebel forces already in the city and new reports that MODEL was moving rapidly up the coast. In either case, the Regional Security Officer was not in a position to tell the Ambassador that help was on its way. It was not.

"No disrespect," the Ambassador said. "I'm calling it the 'Slow.'"

Ted Collins sat across from him in his office, jotting a few notes.

The Ambassador scratched his neck, not quite ready to move on.

"It's unethical, really," he said, "There's really no other way to put it."

It was unethical, in his view, for embassy security to be withheld to make the point that he should have closed the embassy while the Kearsarge was on station before the second attack, and that now he should cry uncle. He admitted it was nothing he could ever prove of course, but the facts were that the augmented security had been pulled, post had received no reinforcements, and the city was under attack. The mission under his authority was again down to its small Marine Security Guard detachment and the Inter-Con guards while outside the walls the city was under siege.

When he had called his most trusted sources back home, he heard that Secretary Powell and Secretary Rumsfeld were still at loggerheads about what to do about Liberia. There had been heated exchanges in front of the President, he was told. That Liberia made it to the Oval Office was extraordinary; that it inflamed the passions of the Cabinet bizarre. To the Ambassador it almost sounded like displacement from residual tensions over Iraq, where weapons of mass destruction, the *casus belli*, still had not been found, and security over the past several weeks taken a turn for the worse. It was what it was. At this point the questions he had to answer for himself and his mission were what risk was still acceptable and how long could the embassy hold out.

"Sir," Collins said, "We're going to have to focus on embassy sustainability and survivability. Between Hersh's crew and the Marines I'm reasonably confident we can keep the perimeter secure, especially with Greystone open, unless there is a sustained attack on us. But we are monitoring water, food, and cash. We're burning through all three, especially cash with all the overtime the Inter-Con guys are pulling. We can make it a while longer, but sooner or later something will have to give."

The Ambassador nodded soberly. Fuel was rationed to the keep security lights on and the servers cool enough in the chancery, to protect communications systems, but the cisterns had drawn down rapidly. Ordinarily, the embassy contracted with local fuel and water services for regular delivery. The fuel depots were on Bushrod Island and they took potable water from wells on the outskirts of town, but by all accounts the area by the pump station was contested. Drivers took great risk to go for refills.

"Nothing has changed," he said after a time. "If we close the embassy, the international community will have no platform left for a response on the ground. Even if you get the ceasefire back in place, who's going to be here to talk to the government? Who's going to keep the pressure on Charles Taylor, on the rebels, to solve this thing? I'm not talking about the negotiators in Accra, that process will continue. I'm talking about the kids in the bush. The ones with the guns who fight the war."

He paused and looked at the ceiling, searching for words.

"If they don't see we're still engaged, why stop fighting?"

The Ambassador's voice betrayed a husky note of fatigue.

"You know they just might win," he said.

"In Washington?" Ted Collins clarified.

The Ambassador nodded.

"Don't get me wrong," he said, "we have our boosters."

A Rolodex spun in his mind. "Secretary Powell, I think, understands what we're trying to do, Walter Kansteiner is working the issue, and of course Jendayi Frazer, the Africa Director at the National Security Council, supports us. But I would not be honest with you all if I did not say there may come a point—" he spoke with difficulty, perhaps surprised to hear the words escape his mouth "—where I just might have to give in."

"But we're not there yet, sir?"

"No," he said, "we're not."

The embassy cafeteria was full again. Relief organizations headquartered in Europe decided it was time, again, to draw down. Everywhere the Regional Security Officer looked, he found people sleeping in corners, on chairs, by the barstools. The Ambassador hosted evacuees at the residence: Abou Moussa, the top United Nations official in Liberia, had been ordered to leave, and Geoffrey Rudd, the European Union Head of Delegation, who had only just returned from the peace talks, had also been told it was time.

Evacuations were coordinated by just a few embassy officers. This time, at least, the crowd was mostly doctors and other humanitarian workers, many of whom had arrived after the first attack, but were used to coming and going on short notice in difficult spots. Assets were only slightly easier to secure. United Nations staff negotiated safe passage with the Liberian government for a convoy of land cruisers to Robertsfield, where a charter jet would collect the diplomats and fly them to safety. As for those who could not be accommodated on the flight, contract helicopters might take them out again, so long as conditions were permissive. Mortar strikes on embassy property did not meet the criteria. Still, Ted Collins felt that the country team had things reasonably well in hand until, late the third night of the attack, he stopped by the cafeteria and saw a barrel-chested man alone at the bar.

The Regional Security Officer recognized him from around town and knew him to be affiliated with a religious institution, one of the temperance-based ones. The man rose from his stool and walked over to Collins and asked if they were going to be able to make it out. Collins paused. He was honest to a fault. "If we can, sir, we will," he said cautiously. "I promise you that. Right now, I don't know."

The man nodded and closed his eyes and drew a deep breath. Then he walked with purposeful gait into the main part of cafeteria and sat down at a table stacked with dinner plates and crumpled napkins. He set a blue nylon laptop carrying case on the table. He had lost everything he owned, he said, save his passport. He picked up a half-full glass of water, looked at it, and poured it slowly onto the floor. Then he set it back down on the table. He lifted the flap of the carrying case and pulled out a bottle of Johnnie Walker. He unscrewed the cap with due care and filled the glass to the brim. Then he screwed the cap back on, rose and took down the entire glass.

"I knew I'd need this," he said.

It scared the shit out of Collins.

Before he called it quits for the night and tried to grab a couple of hours sleep between the incessant calls with Diplomatic Security, Collins briefly checked the news. The stories were either endless loops about the murder of someone named Lacy Peterson or pixilated videophone images of "embeds" broadcast from nameless, featureless towns in Iraq. Nobody back home knew was going on in Liberia, or what they were trying to accomplish. Then, suddenly, on the crawl, he caught something about President Bush calling for Charles Taylor to step down. He jumped to his computer.

It had occurred around lunchtime in Washington. The stuttering link brought a video of a Hilton conference room where a well-heeled crowd at a "U.S.-Africa Business Summit" murmured in anticipation of the arrival of the President of the United States. Less than a week before, the White House announced that President Bush would shortly tour five African nations. Naturally, Liberia did not make the cut. The President's speech, Collins learned, was billed an outline of his vision for U.S.-African relations.

The President entered the spotlight to a wave of applause. Africa did not feature regularly on the stump, so he warmed up slowly. The United States was "fully engaged," he said, "in a broad, concerted effort to help Africans find peace, to fight disease, to build prosperity, and to improve their own lives." He praised African leaders who understood the "power of economic liberty and the necessity for global commerce," but added that "the promise of free markets means little when millions are illiterate and hungry, or dying from a preventable disease." Laudable words, with a catch. "It is Africans," he said, "who will overcome these problems." To skeptics, this was taken as code that meant: the United States had no plans and does not care enough to help out.

But then: "In Liberia," the President said, "the United States strongly supports the cease-fire signed earlier this month. President Taylor needs to step down—" he paused just long enough to ensure he'd been heard, "—so that his country can be spared further bloodshed." The audience applauded vigorously.

Collins peered at the screen, stunned to watch the Commander in Chief call out Charles Taylor by name. It was the first direct sign that the decision to keep the embassy open, to report in real time the urgency of the ground situation and assist Americans in trouble, had been affirmed at the highest levels. Strong words did not appear randomly in a presidential speech. Officials throughout the chain spent time corralling information from the embassy, from the observers at the peace talks, from other sources, and internal debates had taken place, and drafts written and rewritten, to produce a statement that was as calibrated to advance a specific policy objective as it is dramatic. It was the breathtaking power of the pulpit. In one sentence, Collins realized, the President made the work of the embassy relevant. Liberia, of all places, was now newsworthy.

The prevailing notion of diplomats is that they are cynics, and the image comes to mind of a swank reception and a man, most certainly a man, dressed in a suit, drink in hand, waxing pessimistic on the state of the world with other men in suits as they watch with following eyes the feathered women strut by in their shimmering evening gowns. The word evokes for most the sense of a class of people who could tell you quite assuredly that things are broken and cannot be mended, and, for a nation that prides itself on getting things done, to be a diplomat is, in a sense, un-American. Diplomacy, as a corollary, is most commonly viewed as gab, artifice, empty talk, and so to make it palatable for constituents in the United States some sort of active, muscular verbiage is often appended and you end up with "Dollar Diplomacy" and "Gunboat Diplomacy." The Ambassador always found it strange that his profession was seen in such negative light. As a Cold War officer for the first half of his career, he knew the critical role diplomats played in the balance of powers and he also knew that to achieve anything you had to be an optimist.

You had to believe in a better tomorrow.

He admitted to himself that he had slipped of late, that the second attack made him question if there was a way forward, and given the threat to the lives of those under his command he also knew it would be irresponsible to charge blindly ahead. A guard and gardener lay dead, along with scores of others, and bodies were piled at his doorstep. But with the news that the Charles Taylor had been called out by the President, a president known to back up his words, he finally had a signal that Washington was getting with the program, that the policy would not just be on paper.

"We made the 'in' box," he told the Regional Security Officer, aware that, in tone, he had pulled a one-eighty from the last time they spoke. "Liberia has friends in Washington and we have compelling story. I'm sure some folks are pretty upset to see Liberia jump in the queue, but now it's up to us to leverage the support and make progress on our foreign policy goals. We might be able to accomplish something after all." Collins found himself smiling at his boss allowing a smile. Then it was back to business.

They had to consider how the President's words would be received. Other countries would react differently if the President of the United States demanded that their leader step down. Retorts, recriminations, and mass protests would almost certainly follow. Rocks might be hurled at the gates, flags burned, and effigies knocked around like piñatas. Or there could be an outright attack on the chancery. But this was Liberia. The street was with America and so too, in spirit, were many officials in the government.

"They want," the Ambassador said, "to be on America's team."

The job of a diplomat is to get along with people so that you can most effectively promote your country's interests. Diplomats always risked the perception that, in building ties, they forgot for whom they worked. It was called "clientitis." Ambassador John Blaney could never have been accused of being soft on Charles Taylor but, at the same time, it would have been wrong to say that he and his senior staff did not have good ties with the Taylor administration. Lines of communication on both sides stayed open and many of the diplomats and officials on both sides got along quite well personally. It was in their perceptions of the roots and realities of the crisis that they disagreed.

The Ambassador called his contacts in the Liberian Cabinet and was relieved to hear that their policy to engage had not changed. Minister of State Jonathan Taylor, Charles Taylor's nephew and an ordained minister, listened respectfully as the Ambassador glossed the statement from the U.S. president, noting that for Liberia to be on the agenda should be seen an opportunity. They had Washington's attention. Minister of State Taylor thought well enough of John Blaney to admit to an internal conflict in the Liberian government. "It is because of the role of the United States," he explained. "If your president makes a definitive statement like that, you have very little wiggle room. We know our government has to do something. It's a statement by the most powerful man in the most powerful nation on earth. But we also consider America our closest ally."

Most of the Liberian senior advisors said they believed that they could not afford to, nor did they wish to, further alienate the United States. Loyal as they were to their president, they had to look to Liberia's future. The government's credibility with the public, everyone agreed, rested in part on how it managed relations with the United States. Hardliners wanted to make America the enemy, but, with the war going badly, the advisors decided they could not lose the street any more than they had. They scrambled for a way out.

"President Taylor," Jonathan Taylor said, "was troubled by the statement. Maybe it took him by surprise. I can hear him thinking, 'But why would the man say this? I am the legitimate president, I'm under attack, and then he tells me to leave my country.' President Taylor was thinking, 'What is it that I've done.'" Maritime Commissioner Benoni Urey had a slightly different take. He said he was irritated that the message had not passed through private diplomatic channels, delivered by the Ambassador or the State Department. The admonition was all too public. "But President Bush acted on misinformation," he concluded. "He got bad advice, so it's not his fault."

The Ambassador was told that President Taylor rallied his team, as he always did. National Security Advisor J.T. Richardson said that, when they gathered at White Flower, the mood was somber and no one knew what to expect. But Taylor walked in, looked around, and simply told them, "George Bush says I must leave. Guys, calm down. Remember, I already said 'I will leave *if...*'" He instructed them to prepare a response and said the thinking should be, "I challenge you, George Bush, to provide security to the Liberian people should I leave. What semblance of security they have is because I'm here."

It was not much of a semblance at all, but Richardson feared it could get worse. The government controlled less and less territory and nobody anywhere in the country was doing much governing. Things were paralyzed. There was no economy anymore, no opportunity. Entire cities and towns were cut off from the world. "The rebels would be worse," the National Security Advisor insisted. "We have to make sure the people of Liberia are not overrun if President Taylor leaves. Like it or not, a lot of these people are fighting not for John T. Richardson, and not for the government."

Richardson paused, for emphasis.

"They fight for Charles Taylor."

The next day, in Washington, the Harry S. Truman building, in the fourth floor offices of the Office of West African Affairs, Liberia Desk Officer Andrew Silski pulled a single sheet off the fax machine. "The Government of Liberia," the release read, "welcomes the interest that the United States President George Bush has taken in the Liberian conflict and urges the United States government to remain proactive in the peace process. The Government is encouraged that the United States is supportive of the International Contact Group for Liberia, ECOWAS, the African Union and the United Nations to bring a successful conclusion to the peace talks in Ghana..." The question of resignation was finessed. "The Liberian Government reiterates President Taylor's declaration made in Accra, Ghana on June 4 that he will not be part of any transition government."

16

THE DISPLACED

The day after President Bush spoke, Jenkins learned the rebels had abruptly quit Monrovia again. As if a fever broke, the skies went silent and grey. Rebel negotiators in Accra claimed their forces withdrew to Bomi Hills to give Charles Taylor a last chance to step down. It was not clear that either side had gained much tactical advantage, as Liberian government forces more or less held the line, which is to say that the rebels never reached downtown proper, but the "fish-in-a-barrel" strategy failed entirely, if only to judge from reports of a wild caravan of cars, listing with loot, that the rebels had driven back to Bomi Hills.

When he ventured into town, Jenkins found a city worse for the wear. Faces in the crowds bore a sedimentary sadness, layers of trauma compacted in their features. Shanties were everywhere now, flimsy shelters of canvas, cardboard, and flattened hubcaps. Duala and Red Light were foul-smelling tracts of turf covered with splintered plywood. Here and there blackened chicken wire was etched into the ashes of recent fires. The stench of uncollected refuse and excreta rose from pools of standing water in pits in the road or along the curbs, where the drains backed up. North of Bushrod, the old camps for the internally displaced stood empty, fields trampled and fallow, littered with the bamboo stakes and scraps of canvas of abandoned shelters.

Nearer to the embassy, Greystone hosted a permanent population of people with nowhere else to go. Jenkins walked up the narrow lane, waved to the guards, and entered the compound. What he saw weighed on him, heavily. Greystone had long been known as a safe haven, and in the fiercest fighting in the nineties people had gone there and the danger passed them by. Back then the fighters had mortars too, but nothing ever hit the compound. People came to believe over time that rockets could not explode there, because it was an American installation, that rockets would somehow be deflected away. So when the rebels attacked this time, Jenkins heard again and again from local people: "If you come to fight your war, we'll just go to Greystone. After you fight your war, we will go back home." But this time the compound had been hit.

Vagabond mats were spread on the grass and sand among the giant buttresses of the fig and rubber trees, and whole families sheltered there beneath the shaggy, dripping canopy. By day they bartered for tins of grain or trekked to the swamps on the outskirts of town to scavenge for potato greens or net eels from the rice fields, while small children squatted like pigeons and pecked at spilled maize at the curb. By night, when the guards shut the gates, they huddled around charcoal fires, eyes red with the dark smoke, as the walkways echoed with the strains of *Danfo Driver* from a radio here or there, played over and over on warped cassettes until the batteries ran down. There were no medical services. Cholera broke out and women who could not make it to hospital gave birth in the dirt and leaves.

Everything reeked of damp, dirty linens.

For Jenkins, it was a hall of mirrors. Everywhere he looked he saw reflections of himself. He had lived it: a life interrupted, deferred, maybe derailed. To be a refugee or an internally displaced person, especially in the first days of flight, was to cast aside, at least for a time, the customs that defined everything you knew about the world and replace them with fear, uncertainty and new, shifting rules. Over time you adjusted, you adapted, because that's how you got on. But it was not the life you had known, or planned, or expected.

At a different time, Jenkins knew, the people at Greystone were lawyers and teachers and businessmen, or tradesmen or farmers, or students finishing their studies. At a different time, they would have risen, dressed the children for school, prepared breakfast, then headed to the office or the market or the field. Their days would have been filled with whatever amusements and pursuits were common to their town, or village, or culture, and on Sundays they would have donned their finest hats and dress and shoes and sung their hearts out at church, then taken dinner together with family and friends on vast tables covered with hand-knit doily. In the evenings they would have watched the English Premier League on wooden benches at the corner bar, or chatted with friends, kicked the generator a few times, and argued and made love on hand-washed sheets. At a different time.

Or maybe in a different place. The misery was not new, Jenkins thought sadly. It had all happened before in Liberia. It had all happened to him. It was as if it were 1990 all over again: the lawless, violent streets, the people hiding from the rain in the hollows of trees under cardboard and plastic bivouacs. He was overwhelmed by a sense of impotence almost as degrading as when he himself had been forced to flee. Militia were in the streets hunting down Mandingo just as, thirteen years before, on then-President Doe's orders, the republican troops hunted Gio and Mano people.

Back then the violence was rationalized as retaliation for the slaughter of ethnic Krahn in the countryside, but it really did not matter who cast the first stone. Jenkins was of Mano descent and dropped out of high school when it became clear that he would be killed for his ethnicity. He had hesitated at first, because he was so close to his degree and because he was unwilling to believe things had gotten that bad. It was not the reality he had grown up with. He changed his mind when, on his way home from school one day, he spotted a childhood friend in military fatigues toting an automatic rifle. His friend was ethnic Krahn and had joined the Armed Forces of Liberia loyal to President Doe, and Jenkins was torn about whether to greet him, since they had not seen each other for a nearly a year, or to pass unnoticed. He opted for the safer course.

That was his last day at school in Liberia.

17

WE LOVE YOU GEORGE BUSH

Callously, President Taylor took a victory spin through the city. Fergy was downtown, drinking tea with his friend Jimmy Eid, a local businessman who dealt scratch cards for the mobile phones. The men and women that turned out for the motorcade were not the usual rent-a-crowd. They seemed to be blocking the street and the motorcade nosed its way through tentatively. Jostling, shouts, then the chant: "We want peace, no more war!"

Protesters rushed the street and four or five men lay down like misplaced highway divides on the hot, sticky pavement. The lead driver balked and stalled out as crowds encircled the chain of black and white cars. Fists in the air, ignoring the rifles and belts of grenades in the pick-ups, they chanted and slapped the hoods and windows. Engines idled heavily. From the rear, security jumped down. Shots and screams filled the air, but nobody was hit. The crowds recoiled as the men and women in at the front of the convoy rolled out of the way and everyone broke for the alleys. Still they chanted.

"We want peace, no more war!"

Fergy called back to the embassy.

"Taylor's done," he said.

Charles Taylor wasn't finished, but he was chastened. President Bush's sound bite was ubiquitous. He repeated, "President Taylor needs to step down!" On AFN, pundits took the blunt words as a shot across the bow, which led them to speculate as to what the President might do if Taylor did not quit, and more specifically whether he was prepared to give the Liberian president Saddam Hussein treatment. From everything the Ambassador could see, a decapitation strike wasn't on the agenda, but pressure to take some sort of action swiftly mounted from other quarters. Key voices abroad urged the United States to re-engage in Liberia and send peacekeepers. United Nations Secretary General Kofi Annan called publicly for the United Nations Security Council to authorize the United States to lead a humanitarian intervention. Many of those who so recently accused America of a rush to war in Iraq lambasted it for dragging its feet on Liberia. They overlooked, the Ambassador noted to his team, that the United States had not sent peacekeeping troops to Africa since its star-crossed mission to Somalia, ten years past, not when Liberia needed them in the mid-nineties, not even to stop the genocide in Rwanda.

Astonishingly, U.S. peacekeepers became a possibility.

The Ambassador watched agape as CNN White House Correspondent John King reported that President Bush was "prepared" to send between one hundred and five thousand peacekeepers to Liberia, but that the deployment would be limited to four months at most. Yet divisions within the Cabinet percolated in the press. King said that Secretary Powell argued for a United States "commitment" to Liberia, while the Associated Press reported that Defense Secretary Rumsfeld opposed sending troops because U.S. forces were already stretched thin in other parts of the world. "Rumsfeld," Associated Press noted, "also doubts there is a compelling United States interest in Liberia's affairs..."

The Ambassador had no idea how things would shake out.

At the start of the Independence Day holiday weekend, Press Secretary Ari Fleisher stepped to the podium in the White House briefing room to field questions about President Bush's upcoming trip to Africa. He wore a grey suit and stood as usual with his back to the White House seal and the royal blue valances. Liberia cropped up immediately.

"Are troops a serious option?" Fleischer was asked.

And—"Will the West Africans get an answer that they want?"

ECOWAS just pledged to send five thousand peacekeepers.

Only, they wanted America to support the operation with troops too.

Fleischer nodded slightly. "The United States," he said, "is working with regional governments to support the negotiations and to map out a secure transition to elections, which have been called for in Liberia. The President is determined to help the people of Liberia to find a path to peace. The exact steps that could be taken are still under review."

"So you aren't ruling out that U.S. troops might go to Liberia?"

"I'm not ruling it out."

Night in Monrovia. Over the handset Ted Collins heard Post One. "Be advised," the Marine said with an edge in his voice, "a large crowd is headed toward the embassy." The mobile network crashed and he could not reach anyone. The first thought was that Charles Taylor had reconsidered his measured response to President Bush and turned loose a mob. Maybe he finally decided to remind everyone of the consequences of taking on an African warlord on his own turf. Collins left his office and walked down the hall to Post One, where he found the Marine on station and Gunnery Sergeant Aldridge.

Noise rattled the lobby windows. More Marines appeared at the armory in their battle dress uniforms. Silent and stern they passed out weapons and ammunition belts. On the monitors, hundreds upon hundreds of shadowy figures slipped through the lamplight like swallows fill the skies before nightfall. No one could tell what was happening. The Regional Security Officer pushed open the Chancery doors. Outside the air was stifling. A strange and heavy sound, a chant, filled the trees and lapped at his cheeks like a stiff wind. He caught the mixed smells of sweat and liquor and perfume. By the gate, crowds swayed like sea grass through the bars. Drums beat in the distance.

At first the words were indistinct.

They came together unexpectedly.

"Hey George Bush, we love you!"

The thunder of clapping and chanting. It was a block party, not a mob. Revelers packed the street, dancing where the bodies of their countrymen lay only two days before. They stomped the pavement in a fevered, rhythmic dance, almost as if they intend to drive the spirits of the departed deep into the earth.

"We love you-o George Bush, that's a fact!"

"O George Bush, we love you-o George Bush, that's a fact!"

Jenkins Vangehn, also outside, finally got through to the Political Officer on the mobile. Radio Veritas had picked up the White House briefing. For most Liberians, radio was the only tether to the rest of the world. For once, they heard something hopeful. Fleisher's hedge played to their believing ears like a promise of better days. After weeks in cramped, stifling flats, behind locked doors, or beneath damp cardboard and water-logged thatch, celebrations were in order. "They're jubilating!" Jenkins shouted.

"Why—I don't get you—what for?"

"American Marines coming here—"

"But we didn't promise anything—"

"Everybody say, 'Chop time finish!'"

Jenkins was lost to booming chants.

"No more looting, we want peace!"

"No more looting, we want peace!"

The radio crackled, "Stand down!"

People spilled out of Greystone to get in on the fun. The crowd swelled and absorbed them. Now the rhythms came so strong they seemed to rustle the trees, shake the last, full mangos from their branches. The sound spread across the city like the wings of a great bird taking flight, as though in every dark and candlelit bar, in every alley or stairwell, Liberians stamped away in passionate unison. Ted Collins shook his head in wonder, keyed his handset and told the Marines to stand down, then lingered a few moments in the warm glow of the lights that illuminated the flagpole.

"We love you-o George Bush, that's a fact!"

"O George Bush, we love you-o George Bush, that's a fact!"

Their hope in America knew no bounds.

The jubilating went deep into the night.

PART FOUR

THE HAST

The HAST team mobbed

18

THE PRESS

A journalist once said the Africa beat was always a challenge: "You cover so many countries that you basically learn to write a story that starts 'the mood of country X is...' while you're passing through customs." Country X was now Liberia and the foreign press streamed through customs nearly simultaneous with the departure of the United Nations charter flight that evacuated the last of the non-American diplomats. At the moment Monrovia had only one serviceable guest house with somewhat reliable generators, so inbound reporters were met at the airport by a small scrum of fixers, local stringers, and taxi drivers who charged increasingly steep fares to clear the oil cans and rags from the trunks, toss in the ruck sacks, and drive the thirty-odd forlorn miles to the capital, where they dropped them at the Mamba Point Hotel, which did not disappoint.

"The Mamba Point," said Karl Vick, "is the hotel you think you're going to stay in when you go to Africa as a foreign correspondent. I personally spent four years on the continent before finding it. It's not just the veranda overlooking the surf and the local hovels, and the swaying coconut palms, and the rusting ceiling fans overhead, and the baby goats in the courtyard where the washer-women gossip. It's that there really is an arms dealer and a government minister at the bar, and some slimy little creep who identifies himself as the 'First Lady's Official Photographer,' and asks, 'Is there anything you need? Uppers? Downers? Women?'" Vick was on assignment for *The Washington Post* and, like so many others who had just arrived, was still somewhat mystified to find himself in Liberia, let alone to discover that a hotel there could be overbooked.

It was not the first time. The Mamba Point Hotel had the distinction to be the only international hotel not looted during the factional fighting in the nineties, when you could not move more than a few blocks without encountering a checkpoint where someone would be wearing body parts. The sightline to the southeastern gate of the embassy compound, fifty yards off, played a role, and militia would hold their weapons above their heads and wave white rags whenever they passed under the scopes of the Marines, who, as now, took positions on the roofs of the chancery and outbuildings. In local lore Adolphus Dolo, *nom de guerre* General Peanut Butter, also kept an eye on the hotel, as it was a favored watering hole for his patrons and others who could pay.

At the start of the second attack, there was not much business to be had, which is why Fergy often found himself alone at a table when he stopped for a beer. Months had passed since anyone felt the urge to hit the play button on the "world famous" singing bass mounted on the wall of the lounge. During the second attack, *New York Times* West Africa Bureau Chief Somini Sengupta was one of the first to arrive. She had flown into Liberia for a few hours in May for an aborted meeting between Charles Taylor and The United Nations High Commissioner for Refugees, aborted when the Liberian president failed to show, but this time the plane landed during the second attack. Hardly any cars wanted to venture into town and, when she finally found a beat up cab that would make the drive for fifty dollars, the ride in was sketchy, foreboding. It was raining hard and at the first checkpoint there was an accident, a sports utility vehicle had slammed into a small, private bus. A body lay in the street. The soldiers at the checkpoint were on edge. They did not know what was happening in town.

The Liberia story, she said, was important for an American newspaper. This was America's patch in a weird sort of way. She came to cover it because she sensed it was an important moment for the region. She had just come from the conflict in Cote d'Ivoire, where everyone talked about the "Liberianization" of the war, but her sense was that Cote d'Ivoire and Guinea had their hands deep in the mess and that Liberia's story was not so much a civil war as a regional, internecine cycle of betrayal and revenge. For several years the pattern had been dry season attack, wet season retreat. Something seemed different this time and it just had to be recorded. She did not know what to expect.

Thirty-six hours later, it was hard to find a table on the veranda. The bar and restaurant hopped with the clink of beer bottles, the tap of keyboards, and the static of cell phone chatter. Everyone came: beat reporters of course, but also network correspondents, television crews, and freelancers looking to make a name and catch on somewhere. Many had flown in from Iraq, where they spent the past several months lurching around in the back of Humvees but, when the story tired, jumped at the chance to go somewhere wet and green. As staff dropped green vinyl tarps from the eaves, to keep out the gusting rain, and nailed clear plastic bags filled with water to the posts, to chase off the flies, the reporters bartered for cars and drivers and access to Charles Taylor and his camp. The graveled lot between the hotel and the Mezze House was a jigsaw of cars and pick-ups with "TV" or "PRESS" duct-taped across the doors and windshields.

Fergy could not figure out what all the fuss is about. Liberia had been a forgotten conflict for years. Wire services he expected to be there, and big papers with regional bureaus did not surprise, but when major television news divisions staffed up the story it was clear that something else was afoot. Only one thing he knew could draw that kind of attention: the deployment of U.S. troops. Which made sense, except that, when he checked the message traffic, he had no indication that anyone had ordered anything. A FAST platoon was nowhere in sight, let alone a peacekeeping mission. In the Washington press, in fact, anonymous sources talked about "preconditions" for any U.S. deployment, with Charles Taylor's prior departure at the top of the list. So why had the press come?

The Ambassador summoned his security team.

"Ever heard of a 'HAST'?" he asked.

Ted Collins and Fergy looked at one another.

"Well," he said, "they want to send us one."

He handed out copies of a press release.

The Pentagon, it stated, was assembling a survey team to depart for Monrovia to "assess" Liberia's humanitarian needs. "The composition of this Humanitarian Assistance Team (HAST) will include subject-matter experts to be able to best advise the theater commander about requirements for a potential humanitarian assistance mission. There has been no decision on what additional United States Forces, if any, will deploy to Liberia. The mission of this team is to clarify the humanitarian situation in Monrovia for United States decision makers." It did not exactly sound like the cavalry.

The Ambassador folded his arms in a huff.

"No one needs to come to Monrovia to tell *me* there's a humanitarian disaster here. We've got thousands of people and no toilets at Greystone! The well is contaminated and we have no way to feed them. We've got people sheltering under the stands at the national football stadium. What is it they don't get?"

"It's a mess, sir," Collins agreed.

"Look," the Ambassador said, "Two things. One, if we have to take on extra folks, then I want my team too. We need to make sure Ed Birgells gets back. He is critical to our assistance efforts here and the military can't do it all. Second, I guess this is part of a whole process. I don't know what the end game is, but we need to be as helpful as possible. Whoever these experts are, they will probably have their own agenda, but we should call European Command and see how best we can assist. I don't want them running around the country on their own."

"Roger that," said Fergy.

The Ambassador took off his glasses and rubbed his eyes.

"The key to this HAST will be their instructions."

"You mean if they've already been told what to write."

"For the record," he said, "I never recommended American troops. I think that the United Nations is the way to go. But I don't like what I'm hearing. I think Washington wants it to be ECOWAS. That's fine, of course, but ECOWAS should not have to do this alone. They will be sucked into the war like before. We will have to help them out, if that is the decision. ECOWAS can lead, but we need to support. If the HAST is here to set up a false choice of U.S. troops or cut bait altogether, that won't work for us."

The United States invested for years in West Africa's security architecture through the Economic Community of West African States, advising, training, and equipping African troops for precisely a Liberia-type mission. West African countries had a self-interest in ending the conflict in the heart of the region and, in theory, their troops could deploy faster than, say, United Nations peacekeepers, which required Security Council authorization and long lead times to line up budgets and troop contributions. At the same time, they would be reminded at every turn of their last intervention in Liberia, which many Liberians just viewed as another faction, plagued by allegations of brutality and corruption. The ECOMOG peacekeeping operation, they said, stood for Every Conceivable Moving Object Gone. And it was the ECOMOG exit strategy that gave Liberians the election that brought Charles Taylor to power. The rebels, the Ambassador guessed, would reject the deployment of ECOWAS peacekeepers if they thought Taylor would use the peacekeepers as a buffer to set himself up for an indefinite "transition."

"We can't let history repeat itself here," he said.

Post One reached the Ambassador at the residence. He took the call at one end of the long, empty dining room table as he ate leftover snapper alone. Outside the sea was grey and dark and the light melted into severe line of the horizon. It was Colin Powell.

"Mr. Ambassador," the Secretary said.

"Good evening, Mr. Secretary."

The Ambassador felt a slight hitch in his own voice. He had been at the game along enough so that he was not overly impressed by title, and had been sworn in by the man, but as a former career Foreign Service Officer he still felt a small thrill to receive a call from the Secretary of State. Ordinarily a Secretary's call sheet and schedule were meticulously planned by staffers, with times agreed upon and talking points prepared days in advance by principals and officers who spent untold hours volleying emails and attachments back and forth until the language was just so. Of course sometimes Colin Powell, still very much an Army man, just picked up the phone. But with the Department's global representational responsibilities, and crisis always astir somewhere in the world, it was rare that an ambassador at a small post in Africa would ever hear from officials placed higher on the organizational chart than the Assistant Secretary for African Affairs, let alone the Secretary. It meant that Liberia was on his mind. Of course, the Ambassador thought with a wry smile, it also meant the news out of Monrovia was disturbing enough to warrant the call.

"We know it's been rough out there," the Secretary said.

"It's okay," he said, then laughed, "for the moment."

The Secretary chuckled in acknowledgement.

"John, look," he said, cutting to the point, "The White House is getting serious about a stabilization force for Liberia. The current thinking back here is an international security force spearheaded by ECOWAS. We might bring a couple of the West African battalions over from Sierra Leone to start, then deploy a larger ECOWAS contingent after we've got them trained and equipped. How does that sound to you?"

"First of all this is great news," the Ambassador said. "Even if we get a peace accord in Accra, it's the only way to end the war. My own view is that after ECOWAS comes in we should transition to a full United Nations 'blue hat' peacekeeping operation. Given the history here, it's going to take the broadest possible international effort to stamp out the war. ECOWAS does not have those kind of resources. Regardless, we never got the JVT, so we need peacekeepers here as soon as possible to separate the warring parties."

"So ECOWAS, then the United Nations as a follow-on force."

"Yes sir, Mr. Secretary."

"That's how I see it too."

The call ended and the Ambassador rose and walked to the sliding glass doors. The balcony was a long, wide, and elegant, a few floors above a lawn, a rocky beach, and the seawall beyond, perfect for sundowners or lamp-lit soirees. Outside the air was thick, salty, filled with sound of the surf. Not for the first time the Ambassador experienced a brief sadness at the thought that Robin could not be there to take in the view, that she would never be there, nor his daughters, that it would be for him alone.

His thoughts returned to the call. They had come a long way in three weeks. There was no talk this time of closing the embassy and instead Washington was engaged at the highest levels on finding solutions. It was more than he could have expected and it meant that peacekeepers, for the first time, were a real possibility. Steps in the right direction were being taken, plans drafted, budgets crafted. He had long ago recognized that diplomacy was a complex, collaborative discipline, like filmmaking, where myriad people worked at various levels and you could not expect to control the entire process, only shape it, and prod it along with well-timed interventions. As the president's point man on the ground, his job was to make sure the right people had the right information at the right time, and of course he had to make the right call, and win support for it, when it was his moment.

One thing troubled him. The Secretary never mentioned the upcoming military-led humanitarian assessment. Granted it was a Defense Department initiative, so not under the Secretary's authority or control, but with the pressure so recent to close the post and pull everyone out, it was a curious decision to say the least to insert an assessment team into the mix. It would be more bodies to look out for if the violence flared again and nobody had briefed him on any exfiltration plans, if it came to it.

So what was the game?

19

THE NIGERIAN OFFER

Independence day was a well-choreographed event at embassies around the world, entailing months of staff-wide "countdown" meetings and the solicitation of sponsors, days with caterers selecting the hors d'oeuvres, hours of rehearsal, countless edits of the speeches, and painstaking review of a guest list that included hundreds of local officials, businesspeople, and expatriates. In light of the circumstances, however, the Ambassador decided that a modest ceremony, with a simple memorial for the guard and gardener they had lost, would be more appropriate. The staff set out rows of metal folding chairs in the cafeteria, poured orange soda and wine into plastic cups, and set them out on a folding table, then called around to the few expatriate Americans they could still reach.

Forty or so guests, staff included, filled the seats. The Ambassador walked in quickly, flanked by four Marines from the Detachment. A cassette tape was inserted into an old deck with portable speakers, set atop the cash register, and everyone stood for the worn, scratchy recording of the national anthem. The Marines presented the colors. The Ambassador gave a short speech that spoke to the courage and the resilience of the Liberian people, the tragedy of the losses, and the hope for a better future. He read slowly the names of the departed and called for a long moment of silence, and prayers for their families. When it was all over, people clapped tepidly, made small talk by the drinks table for ten minutes or so, swished their lukewarm wine around, and left.

Nobody was in the mood for a party.

Robertsfield, or Roberts International Airport more formally, was a long gray strip of tarmac in a stretch of coastal grasslands and palms bounded to one side by a slow, winding river, on the opposite banks of which stood the pale, orderly rows of rubber trees of the old Firestone plantation. If you had flown into Robertsfield to take a post at the U.S. embassy at any point in the months leading up to the rebel attacks on the capital, the first person you would have met as you descended the rolling staircase to the bright, warm tarmac at Robertsfield would have been Conneh, a tall, affable expediter, head shaved and shining, dressed in a colorful embroidered shirt, looking back at you through rose-tinted aviators, waiting to extend you a damp handshake, grab your passport and customs forms, and lead you to an immigration booth that looked like a confessional with the top knocked off. You would have almost certainly flown in from Europe after a short layover in Ghana, and before you had your bearings you would have been led through a dim, crowded baggage claim, where ads for local hotels were hand-painted on the beige walls, your suitcases and backpacks would have been tossed in the trunk, and you would have found yourself in the backseat of a white four-wheel drive Chevrolet Suburban headed to town as green lowlands drifted by. Just about the time your head would clear, Conneh would swing round, straining against the seatbelt, point to a small collection of zinc-roofed huts along the roadside and say, in his deep, earthy baritone, "Smell No Taste." Then he would laugh from the belly.

Back in the day, when engineers from the United States had come to survey the site that would become Robertsfield, they pitched tents in a sandy patch a mile or so from the Firestone plantation and hired day laborers to begin to clear the land. In the evenings, the engineers grilled marinated meats and vegetables over open fires. Smoke drifted over the low dunes to the palm groves where the local help would pause as they hunched over plates of rice and potato greens, all they could afford, inhale the rich, sweet scents, and try to imagine dinner spreads over at the American camp. After the airfield was completed, a few of the workers stayed in the area, built modest homesteads, and called the place "Smell No Taste," after the memory of the meals they knew they had missed.

Smell No Taste was little different than any other Liberian village in that children ran around in the dust and kicked footballs of wadded plastic and yarn, tawny dogs lay in the hot shade flicking their ears, and women carried well water in plastic buckets on their heads, and yet the short distance to

Robertsfield meant that those who lived there could see every plane take off and land, and they knew the regular flights by sound, so that whenever a new plane turned up they would call their friends at the airport and find out what was going on. Mid-afternoon July 5, 2003, they heard the wash from the engines of a white jet with green markings, which appeared against the blinding blue skies, passed low over the clustered homes of Smell No Taste and landed at the airport. The usual calls confirmed that this was something out of the ordinary and those with the energy and inclination took to the road on foot to catch a glimpse of the visit of Nigerian President Olesegun Obasanjo, who, they learned, had arrived for a tête-à-tête with President Taylor.

Robertsfield was not an ideal site for a summit, but it was understandable that Obasanjo did not want to drive into town. The terminal stood off to one side, a forlorn frame of black concrete, the rest of the structure burnt to the ground long ago and never rebuilt. A long, squat, rectangular building served in its stead, functional enough with a departure lounge with no view to the runway. Wedged between it and the old terminal stood the VIP lounge, a small cream-colored outbuilding with sliding glass doors, recessed lighting, and white leather furniture. The red carpets smelled of the must that carpets hold in the tropics when the cooling units have been turned off for some time.

President Obasanjo stepped out of his jet to the songs of a few thousand well-wishers clapped and danced from a safe distance as he was ushered with his bodyguards as quickly as possible across the tarmac and into the VIP lounge. Journalists were staked by the entrance, having been tipped to the event, and mingled with the small crowd, waiting in the feathery shadows of the pepper trees with their recorders and notepads, lured the thirty-five miles to the airport by the possibility of a new angle to the Liberia story.

Two hours passed. When the presidents finally appeared, they walked over to a small lectern where they stood side by side, both dressed in white, President Taylor in a short-sleeved safari shirt with matching pants and President Obasanjo in a traditional robe and zebra-striped pillbox hat. They smiled benignly at the assemblage and clutch of press. "We are here as brothers," President Obasanjo said, "as neighbors, as those who feel that what is happening in Liberia could happen anywhere in Africa, and that Liberia needs a lifeline to solve its problems." Charles Taylor nodded at his side.

"I thank my big brother for coming," President Taylor said. "He has extended an invitation and we have accepted an invitation... We believe that the participation of the United States right now is crucial. We embrace it. We invite the United States to come full force and assist in the process to bring peace back to Liberia."

It was a perplexing statement and could have been mistaken to mean that Obasanjo had come to whisk Taylor into exile at that moment, but it was not to be. The peacekeeping force proposed, President Obasanjo intoned, should deploy in a very, very short time. Only after that would the question of the safe haven be relevant. The two presidents smiled and shook hands, then President Obasanjo and his retinue made their way back to their jet. Taylor waited until wheels up, then hopped in his black Mercedes, and drove off, the crowd cheering an appropriate time before wandering off as the journalists found their drivers, ducked into their rented cars, and headed back to the darkening city.

At the embassy, Ambassador Blaney received the brief from Jenkins with cautious optimism. Taylor's exile was now a precondition for peacekeepers and Obasanjo showed pragmatism and political courage in extending an offer. He would take flak in Nigeria for sheltering a warlord who had been responsible for Nigerian deaths during the previous ECOMOG deployment, and from other quarters, especially in the United States, for not remanding Taylor immediately to the Special Court. Exile was not imprisonment, and Taylor would presumably still be able to influence events on the ground in Liberia. Still, it was incremental progress and the outlines of a workable peace were taking shape. Of course, the Ambassador considered, it all might be a charade, a way for Charles Taylor to bide his time until he could achieve decisive victory on the battlefield.

Taylor, he reminded everyone, was no coward.

20

THE HAST

U.S. presidential trips are always headline news in part because presidents travel with press in tow, but those reporters not fortunate enough to be on Air Force One or a charter flight, those who are not based out of New York or Washington, generally pre-stage at various stops along the route and provide local color or B-roll footage that can be spliced into the coverage where appropriate. It was unusual that so many reporters who otherwise would have been in Senegal, the first country on the President's itinerary, converged on the hedgerows on a sun-splashed embassy compound hundreds of miles down the coast, in a country the President would not visit, to film the deployment of a military team whose purpose and composition nobody could describe with precision. They were certain only that the events were intertwined. President Bush, after demanding that Charles Taylor step down, could not tour Africa for the better part of a week without doing something to resolve the crisis in the one country on the continent most associated with the United States, and maybe this military team was a first step. So the press camped out in Monrovia and waited for President Bush to declare that he would order U.S. combat troops to Liberia to enforce a peace and maybe even topple the Papay.

The embassy walkways were marked with the yellow pastels of flowers fallen from the temple trees and the air was rich with the scent of rotting almond husks. The Ambassador, Ted Collins, and Fergy stood on the service road behind the cafeteria, by the swath of green above the helipad, looking at the concertina wire scribbled across the top of the seawall and the sharp line the horizon beyond, dividing the white-grey sea from a white-blue sky.

The windsock rippled in a soft breeze coming off the water. The Ambassador allowed a slight frown as he listened for the sound of the helicopters. He was concerned that the HAST was a diversion, a way for someone to put off a decision on troops until after the president left the continent, then, once the Liberia story played out, turn the whole thing off. Diplomacy, he knew, was often as much about outmaneuvering agendas back home as it was about carrying the day abroad, so he told his staff that, even if the HAST were a charade, they would support the exercise to the fullest, though he was concerned it would raise false hopes on the Liberian street. Behind him, the jaunty fence of photographers and television crews took light readings and panned for the best shot. Electric cables plugged into portable generators covered the pavement like party string and CNN set up for a live telecast with a satellite dish strapped into a flatbed parked to the side.

Landing lights blinked faintly in the glancing sun. Tandem blue and white Mi-8s appeared over the sea, wavering in the heat like the first dabs of watercolor on wet paper. As they drew near, the wind picked up and brushed salt and sand against the faces of the onlookers. The first helicopter came in low, dropped over the seawall, and bobbed lightly down to the grey square of tarmac. Marines from the long-awaited FAST platoon, sent as force protection for the HAST, jumped out and moved quickly into their crouches, then raised gloved fists and signaled the all clear. It was quick, efficient, and not particularly dramatic. Navy Captain Roger Coldiron clambered off.

Coldiron was dressed in green fatigues, shirt rolled up at the elbows. Deep shadows under his eyes and a yellow hue to his olive skin suggested far too many hours slumped in nylon jump seats trying to block out the grinding din of the C-130 that carried them from Europe to Africa, followed by a long, cramped helicopter flight from Sierra Leone. A coffee, a smoke, and some shut-eye were in order. Collins ambled down to the helipad, greeted him over the pulse of the rotors, and escorted him to the Ambassador. Together they started back up the hill, leaving behind others on the team, mostly reservists a few years removed from basic training, to labor stiffly with their kits. The Ambassador paused at the bank of cameras to let the press have a moment, which the Captain, to judge from his glassy-eyed expression, had not expected. Fluffy microphones at the end of black booms hovered at their chins and print reporters crouched in front of the pack and thrust up hand-held digital voice recorders. Shouting started at once, like in the movies.

"What's your mission?"

"How long will you stay?"

"What will you recommend?"

Narrowing his eyes like someone who thought he might have been pranked, the Captain first glanced over at his press attaché, who nodded and smiled with unhelpful enthusiasm, then scratched the back of his neck and responded as anyone inexperienced with the press might: he started to talk. The journalists leaned in to catch his words, but all he managed to stammer was "Look, it's been a long ride and we're here to see what we can do." At the next barrage, the Ambassador stepped in and mercifully cut it short with a few choice phrases culled from Washington-issued press guidance. A gentle nudge steered the Captain away, which sent the reporters digging for their mobiles to call their other contacts at the embassy, most of whom stood just a few feet away, and yell at them.

"That's it?!"

One of the women who cleaned the office had thoughtfully set on the coffee table a glass vase with delicate brown and white tiger-striped orchids clipped from the Marine house garden, and the Ambassador allowed a smile as he moved the vase to his desk to clear the table for his concessionaire's map. It was reason enough to do everything in his power to ensure that the embassy in his care would stay open and that the dedicated Liberians who staffed it would have a place to work. Map out again, the Ambassador rehashed for the Captain the basic geography of the conflict and offered some simple facts and figures on humanitarian crisis. For his part, Coldiron relayed that the parameters of his report were not particularly well-defined, but he expected to be in country a week or two. The Ambassador asked about the HAST security detail and was informed that it was in fact half of the FAST platoon he had requested, but they were under explicit instructions to protect the HAST, not the embassy. Irked though he was at the gamesmanship in the chain of command, the Ambassador decided to let it go. The HAST, after all, worked out of the embassy, so to secure one was to secure the other, if it ever came to that. He was grateful for the extra shooters. It helped that Ted Collins told him that the FAST platoon leader, Captain Greg Kuni, was as fine a young officer as he had encountered and that he "got it."

Half an hour into the brief, the Ambassador saw Coldiron's head start to droop and remembered he had to wrap up quickly because he had promised an interview to Brendt Sadler, CNN's Chief Middle East Correspondent, who had inexplicably been dispatched to Liberia. By the time he made it back down to the cafeteria the other journalists had cleared out. The CNN crew fixed a small microphone to his lapel, handed him an earpiece, and positioned him with his back to the sea. Sadler spoke to camera with a few remarks then threw it over to the studio in Atlanta. The Ambassador realized too late he was on live. Disconcerted, he stood on the breezy lawn, flushed from the heat, as the voice of Bill Hemmer, "American Morning" anchor, bubbled in his ear. The CNN crew did not provide a monitor so he stared earnestly at the dark eye of the camera and blinked at the slight delay in the feed. Hemmer got right to it.

"Is there a need, Mr. Ambassador, for U.S. troops at the moment right now, perhaps immediately, to make sure that aid gets to the people who need it?"

John Blaney smiled self-consciously.

"Well," he said, "that's a decision that the President of the United States will make. Our mission here right now is just to provide the support and the access for this team to take a look strictly at the humanitarian situation. They'll be going to hospitals; they'll be going to IDP camps. They'll be meeting with non-governmental organizations and other experts in the humanitarian area here in Liberia."

"What have you recommended—"

Wind tufted the Ambassador's hair unkindly.

"—to the White House and the President?"

Normally before a senior official spoke with media he or she held a "murder board," where staff asked tough questions and corrected missteps before the cameras rolled, but the Ambassador did not have the staff or the time and there had been no murder board and now, from the leading nature of the question, CNN wanted him to say to a domestic U.S. audience that President Bush should send troops to Liberia. "Well," he said cautiously, "we've made some recommendations. But I'm not in the habit of trying to box in or preempt my President's decisions. He'll be making his own conclusions on what to do in terms of United States troops or an international stabilization force."

Warming to the moment, he paused ever so slightly.

"Let me just say," the Ambassador said, taking a chance, "that I think that the President has put a lot of impetus behind a change in leadership, which is needed in Liberia, and also to underscore the importance of the ceasefire and emphasize the need to do something about a very serious humanitarian situation." He added that the overdue Joint Verification Team was needed urgently to cement the ceasefire.

In Atlanta, Hemmer listened politely. Perhaps he realized he was not going to break any new ground when he heard mention of a "JVT," a detail far too technical for an audience dropping in on Liberia for the first time and on which he likely had not been briefed, but as a professional, he tossed a last obligatory curveball. His tone was casual, friendly. "And finally, sir," he said, "in your estimation right now, if U.S. troops came to Liberia, could they, indeed, keep the peace there, or is this a situation that may continue to unravel as American troops put their lives on the line in Western Africa?"

The question elicited a wry smile.

"Well," the Ambassador said, "I think the capability—I think American troops are capable of just about anything, but the decision is up to the President. I think there is a need for greater stability and I think I'll let it go there."

Out came the earpiece and off came the microphone.

The next day, President Bush landed in Africa. At the Presidential Palace in Dakar, Senegal, he attended a gathering of democratically-elected West African leaders, including Ghanaian President John Kufuor, who held the ECOWAS rotating chair, and afterward took questions from the press. Dressed in a dark blue suit and cornflower blue tie, he was prepared to discuss democratic progress in Africa and his program to address HIV/AIDs, tuberculosis, and malaria, the raison d'être for the trip. The reporters had another issue in mind.

"Can we ask you about Liberia, sir?"

"We had a good discussion about Liberia."

"Have you made a decision?"

"The President of Ghana is the leader of ECOWAS. I told him we'd participate with ECOWAS. We're now in the process to determine the extent of our participation. And I really appreciate the President's leadership on this issue. Charles Taylor must leave. The United Nations is going to be involved. The United States will work with ECOWAS. The leaders of ECOWAS were at the table, all of whom are concerned about Liberia, as are we, and are concerned about a peaceful Western Africa."

"Does that mean you'll send troops?"

"We're in the process," President Bush reiterated, "of determining what is necessary to maintain the ceasefire and to allow for a peaceful transfer of power. We're working very closely with ECOWAS. The President of ECOWAS is with us today, the President of Ghana. He and I had a good discussion. I assured him we'll participate in the process. And we're now in the process of determining what that means."

"Do you have to wait until Mr. Taylor is gone?"

"We're in the process of determining what that means."

Fergy convinced European Commission Aid Coordinator David Parker to come over to the embassy to brief to the HAST. As an aide worker with six years already in Liberia, the tousle-haired Briton was skeptical of the whole exercise. USAID had teams that could steer cash to relief groups to hire local staff, set up distribution networks, or leverage existing ones, and move food and medicines quickly to those in need, but Parker had never heard of a unit of military reservists flying in to assess how bad things were. For all he knew, they were there for intelligence purposes. Fergy argued that this was important, that the HAST could pave the way for peacekeepers, and that they needed to hear from the real experts. He also said he would kick in a six-pack of beer. Parker relented and early the next morning endured the indignity of waiting at the gate while the local guards called Post One, then the Regional Security Officers, then Fergy, before letting him through, even though before the crisis he had been a regular at the cafeteria and the Marine happy hours.

The bar was converted into a briefing room. Stools were pushed into a corner to make room for flip charts and briefers stood in front of the Heineken signs and spoke loudly enough over the low hum of the liquor coolers. Haggard but somewhat rested from a night on the carpeted floor of a vacated bungalow, the more than thirty combined engineers and shooters slumped into plastic chairs or against the walls and sipped lukewarm instant coffee. Major Phil Spangler stood in the back by the dartboard tried to figure it all out. EUCOM message traffic a few days before stated that a civil-military expert was needed for a Liberia mission, but Naval Forces Europe, NAVEUR, would lead the effort. A colleague had been tapped, but had already been down with the ESAT for the attempted NEO and had to cancel plans with his fiancée, but after he reworked their reservations things went haywire again, so Spangler volunteered in his stead. Spangler had not heard much about the NEO other than the Ambassador did not want it, so it wasn't done.

Why and how the HAST was assembled was somewhat of a mystery to the HAST members themselves. The team had never worked together before, but orders were cut, holidays curtailed, and arrangements made for weapons to be drawn, and suddenly they found themselves in Mildenhall, England, at a desolate air terminal, waiting for a C-130 to Rota, where they would link up with their FAST security elements then head to Africa. Spangler was the only one, it seemed, with any experience with humanitarian needs assessments. When the room settled, Parker pointed to a map. Cross-hatched areas reflected rebel-held lands and nearly all of the map was cross-hatched, a reminder that, increasingly, the capital was the last spot under government control, although everywhere "control" was a loose term. Between the rebels and the militia, relief agencies could not operate safely.

"Security," David Parker said, "is the key."

"I don't know the first thing about Liberia," Coldiron confessed.

Parker's eyes narrowed. As the European Commission Aid Coordinator, he had briefed dignitaries and heads of international agencies for years. But he was as unfamiliar with the U.S. military as they were with the standard relief pitch and jargon. On the fly, he went big picture. "We have a humanitarian crisis here," he said. "The civilians are caught in the middle of a nasty civil war. Several hundred thousand are homeless. No safe drinking water, little food, and with the rains upon us, cholera, dysentery, and the rest of it."

The Captain grimaced into his mug.

"If someone," Parker said forcefully, "if *anyone* can establish security on the ground in Liberia, the relief agencies can do their jobs and some others might come in. But, without security, we can't provide food, shelter, or medicine. This has been Liberia's story for many months, even before the latest attacks. It's that simple."

"Moooo" issued from near the doorway that led to the cafeteria.

Everyone turned, confused, as Fergy ducked out to take the call.

Fergy could not hear clearly. It was an Admiral of some sort, who kept saying he was aboard Air Force One. Fergy wasn't one for protocol, but it was highly unusual for any officer of high rank, let alone an Admiral on the President's plane, to track down a Senior Master Sergeant in Liberia. The Admiral told Fergy he was the President's aide. He said he wanted Fergy to know that Air Force One was waiting for the HAST report and expected a draft to be emailed to the plane within forty-eight hours. Then he yelled as if talking through turbulence. "The FAST Marines aren't there for you!"

"Yessir."

"Their job is to protect the HAST, not embassy security. Do you copy?"

"Yessir. Copy sir."

Fergy clicked off, cussed, and shouldered his way back into the briefing room. He bent over Captain Coldiron and gave him a quick readout. The Captain turned awkwardly in his chair and stared at the embassy's Operations Coordinator.

"Why'd he call you?"

"I got no idea. Sir."

"I don't get it."

"Everyone calls me these days."

The Captain held up a hand. "The plan," he announced, "has changed." Parker stood with marker poised at a flip chart. "Gentlemen," the Captain said, "we have two days." Mugs clattered roughly on the countertops. Chairs raked against the deck floors. As if class bell had rung, the HAST members hustled toward the exit, though nobody knew where they were headed. Parker shook his head, rolled up his maps and charts, and flashed Fergy a look of annoyance.

"I got up early for this," he said.

As soon as the gates opened, the Ambassador knew they were in trouble. He sat with Captain Coldiron in the second car in an embassy convoy Fergy organized to take the assessment team to clinics and camps around town and even through the tinted, blast resistant panes of the armored Chief of Mission Land Cruiser he could feel a chorus of engines fire up, flushing egrets from the trees and grasses, as a dozen or more taxis, jalopies, and pick-ups played bumper cars in front of the embassy. Refugee camps and field clinics are no strangers to visits from dignitaries and celebrities whose photo-ops can help raise funds and awareness, but "assessments" are most often low-key affairs, a few men and women from aid organizations with sun hats, water bottles, and fanny packs who walk the grounds with local colleagues and ask questions about baby weights and pit latrines. A safari derby of thirty odd cars carrying an ambassador, military engineers in battle dress uniforms, a fully armed security detail, and a press corps that had run short of laundry options after a week in country was a sight as astonishing as it was unexpected, not just for camps and clinics but for the entire populace of a war-torn capital.

Word whipped like dust devils through the streets and alleys and every-where men, women, and children jumped up ran to the curb. As the convoy rumbled through the city center, crowds three or four deep lined both sides of the street the length of the route and waved and danced and twirled rags in the air and chanted. Captain Coldiron stared at the sea of white tee shirts and paisley wraps and turned to the Ambassador and asked innocently what was the occasion. "You!" Blaney returned with a short laugh that belied his private reservations. He toured IDP camps when he first arrived and had been mobbed each time. He knew the crowds could get unruly and dangerous even if the intentions were good. Coldiron flashed him a skeptical look and self-consciously waved back at the ten thousand smiles sliding across the glass.

At New Kru Town, crowds swirled around the cars like a revivalist con-gregation. Sweat and dust bright on their faces, clothes blanched from the elements, women waved palm fronds and banana leaves as drums beat wildly and ululations floated above the general hubbub. Children's fingers blossomed against the windows and left behind a mist of tiny prints. The convoy nosed through the narrow blocks of the slums until the bodies were so thick in front it could go no further. Then came the thunderous serenade:

"We want peace, no more war!"

"We want peace, no more war!"

"We want peace, no more war!"

The Ambassador and the Captain cracked the doors and alit. Hot, moist air fogged their shades. It smelled of dust, sweat, dried grass, burning garbage, and diesel fumes. Children surged after them, buffeting them against the high, white washed wall that separated Redemption clinic from the street as if they were caught in a wind tunnel. Faces rushed up and fell back, hands grabbed at their arms, slapped their backs. If the street held a thousand people, there were three thousand, five thousand. A low black doorway appeared on the left and the Ambassador and Captain ducked in behind Assistant Regional Security Officer Brad Lynn and a couple of shooters. Inside, several attendants in white throws with red MSF logos greeted them and led them to a small courtyard shaded by a few pepper trees in which stood a small hand pump that had been spared during the attacks. Deafening chants vaulted the walls and crashed into the courtyard.

"We want peace, no more war!"

"We want peace, no more war!"

"We want peace, no more war!"

Guided by staff into the clinic, which had reopened to patients a few days before, the Ambassador and the Captain passed through the narrow grey corridors shot through with the smells of iodine and bedpans. Coldiron bent to talk for a few moments to a frail man on a diarrhea bed, a possible cholera case, then straightened up and glanced around, lines of distress chalked across in his features. Behind him, several members of his team trailed like lost sheep and seemed to forget to take pictures.

The *New York Times* correspondent was not impressed. Somini Sengupta stood in a wedge of shade and watched as the feverish chants rained down the bewildered military engineers. "What the hell kind of assessment is this?" she said. "It's madness. You can't hear a damn thing! What can they possibly learn this way?" She closed her pad without any notes made her way back to her car.

Over the handsets, Fergy was shouting.

"Move out! We got to move out!"

HAST members and reporters hustled into the street. Crowds hurtled toward them, swept them across a narrow causeway over a dry streambed cluttered with brown reeds and trash, and pushed them roughly in an open lot of dried, packed clay that served as the produce market every couple days. Amid the froth of faces and dancing bodies the arc of white embassy Suburbans appeared, bumper to bumper, Fergy up on the rail of CD 58 waving his arms madly and shouting.

"Where's the Ambassador?!"

He swept the crowds with field glasses, looking for his principal, looking for guns. As an Operations Coordinator, charged with logistics, he was appalled at how awry things had gone but there was no time for self-critique: he knew the only fix was to get the team out of there as soon as possible, drive north of the city, let the mania die down bit. Across the tumult of bouncing heads and scarves, at the far end of the lot, he noticed a dilapidated two-story cinderblock schoolhouse that sagged on its foundation like a weary hobo. Palm fronds flapped at the doors, which suddenly sprung open. Through the churn he caught a glimpse of the Ambassador's head, thin hair matted against his forehead. A narrow canal opened and he hustled toward the cars with Captain Coldiron in tow. Fergy slapped the roof hard, spun his hand, and the rest of drivers hit the gas.

North of the Saint Paul there was little to suggest that rebel fighters had twice taken that route in the space of a month, little hint of any war, in fact, save the absence of car and foot traffic along a major artery into the capital. Here and there Fergy spotted a woman walking slowly toward town with small bundles of tired potato greens on her head, bound no doubt for Duala market, but that was it. The land was wide and empty and off to the side the grasses grew long among standing pools of rainwater.

The caravan eventually reached Iron Gate, which was neither iron nor a gate, but rather a small, concrete tollhouse on the highway divide that most closely resembled a public toilet. As the last permanent police checkpoint before Kle Junction, it earned a reputation over the years as a point of no return, beyond which lay the unimaginable terrors of the bush. It was lightly manned. To the right a row of plywood and branch shacks had been erected along the footpath between the tarmac and the napier grass. Ten or fifteen militia loitered in the shade, smoking joints and chewing leaves. Nobody lifted their weapons but a young man with a wisp of a beard sauntered up to Fifty-eight.

Fergy cracked the door to speak with him.

Photographers raced past the Ambassador's window, cameras slapping roughly at their sides. They turned their lenses on one wiry teenager who stood rigid against the green, arms tense but automatic weapon pointed down, a scarlet bandana on his head glaring like an open wound. He scowled but never flinched. Some of the militia on the benches were children, ten to twelve years old, and more than a few wore women's wigs, the hair pieces tilted sloppily on their heads like mannequins taken out to the trash. One boy had donned swim goggles, now nearly opaque with dust.

Fergy knew the kid at his door and knew he didn't have much authority other his assault rifle and mobile phone, but he was saying they could not pass. Wisps of marijuana smoke curled past. Fergy wiped the sweat from his brow. Behind them, the unruly column of cars huffed and labored in the heat like winded buffalo.

"Your Defense Minister says it's okay," Fergy said.

The kid stared at him impassively.

"Okay," said Fergy. He dialed his mobile. It was a quick chat and when he finished he snapped the phone shut and stuffed it in his vest pocket. "You sorry, stupid-ass motherfucker," he said to no one in particular. Then,

"Sonnofabitch." Over his shoulder, he spied CNN's chief Africa correspondent and cameraman, recording. The correspondent grinned and Fergy just shook his head.

"Did they deny you access?"

"Hell yes they denied us access. We got to go back."

The Ambassador and Captain Coldiron watched the exchange up ahead, muted by the dusty glass and armor. It was a setback, the Ambassador knew, and a cautionary note that the Liberian government was not a true partner, that the militia could turn on a dime, and that peacekeeping in Liberia could be messy even if the street were with you. This was still Charles Taylor's city. In Somalia, less than a decade ago, the simple job of protecting food deliveries during a famine had drawn American troops into lethal firefights. Many in Washington said that Liberia would be no different.

Fergy swung the convoy around.

They moved fast and reached Bushrod altogether too soon. The streets were still jammed at New Kru Town and thousands of buoyant bodies pressed in on the cars, delighted with the unexpected return. Horns blasted to no avail, and the convoy slowed as the crowds bobbed alongside in their flip-flops.

"Hey George Bush, we love you!"

There was a muffled pop and the Ambassador felt a jolt, as though the car had struck something. The driver hit the brakes and Brad Lynn called up to Fergy, who jumped out of the lead car, pushed his way back through the delirious tapestry of faces, and found a pair of small feet beneath the chassis. A child had caught himself on the front wheel and was dragged under. Men swarmed the car pointing, shouting. Photographers rode up in taxis on the shoulder and angled for shots. The Ambassador dabbed his forehead with a pocket handkerchief. It was hard to tell what had happened, whether the child was still alive or how badly hurt. He had seen crowds turn like flames and pummel and burn cars for less, but in the frenzy were none of the telltale signs of anger, no fists or rocks, only the joyful, strident chants. But the international press was out there too and he imagined a lede that the HAST had run over a child. Anyone back in Washington who opposed troops for Liberia would seize on that as more evidence of the unnecessary risks and complications of humanitarian interventions. The rest of the story would be lost.

Shouting and pushing, local men locked arms and cleared space for Doc Lish to shoulder through. He knelt down and carefully extracted the child, cradled him in his arms, then jogged to the next Suburban and slapped at the window. As soon as the door opened he laid the child in the lap of the Political Officer. The boy was all of six years old and wore a tattered tee shirt and shorts. A long, deep gash ran across his belly like rope burn, terribly raw but not bleeding. The Political Officer cupped the small head in his hand and elevated him slightly. The boy's hair was coarse, filled with sand, and with bloodshot eyes he looked up at the stranger holding him and wailed in fear and pain.

The convoy could not move. The crowds cheered and bounced like they were on pogo sticks. On foot now, Fergy pushed his way to the front of the lead car. Elbows bowed out, he cleared a path like a tracker beating a path through the jungle while overeager young men emerged from the crowd to help the cause, kicking and beating away men, women, and children with the backside of their hands. In the mania, nobody seemed to care. Palm fronds flared, people sprayed bottles water into the air, and everyone danced.

At Bong Mines bridge, the column stopped again.

Suddenly, a burst of automatic weapons fire.

Panic. Everyone broke for the mounds and gullies along the road. Men and women ducked reflexively and stumbled over one another, bent as they ran as if the ground had tilted against them. Fergy ducked behind an open door, but when the gunfire stop he poked his head up and found himself staring at a wide swath of empty road with a dozen armed men clad in black uniforms advancing on the convoy, the elite Anti-Terrorist Unit. Behind him, he heard a dozen doors swing open and the Marines jump out and lock on targets. Fergy turned his back on Taylor's men and waved wildly.

"They're just firing in the air!" he yelled.

FAST platoon leader Kuni looked straight past him, intensely focused on the ATU, who had stopped abruptly at the sight of the Marines and the guns. Eyes narrowed. Sweat beaded on foreheads. Fingers tensed. In the second car, the Ambassador leaned forward and tapped Brad Lynn on the shoulder. "Tell our guys go climb back in," he said. Outside, Fergy kept yelling, "They cleared the road for us!"

The ATU helpfully lowered their guns.

"Get back in the cars!" Fergy shouted at the Marines. Doors slammed, tires screeched, and the air filled with exhaust. Fergy drew his gun for the first time and slapped at each car as it went by like a pit crew director. The convoy roared past the ATU and the madding crowds cowering in the ditches. Broken pavement punished the shocks and they reached the south end of Bushrod before anyone remembered Fergy.

"Birdie, Birdie, you still with us?"

Fergy's voice snapped like a whip.

"Fuck you all; I found my own ride!"

Back in the chancery, the Ambassador looked a little flushed. "Um," he said, "I think I'll sit out the next round." Captain Coldiron tapped his foot absently as he looked over some old black and white prints of a visit to Liberia by Franklin Delano Roosevelt, back in the forties, that hung on the wall in the reception area. Roosevelt was smiling in the bright sun and talking to Winston Tubman, who held office for more than thirty years altogether and even declared himself president for life. Coldiron did not know what to make of the crowds and it seemed to him, almost, that they were prepared to sacrifice a child if it would bring peacekeepers. "Things are bad here," he said, "anyone can see that."

Ed Birgells, all knees and elbows folded into a seat cushion across from the Ambassador, shook his head in disbelief. The USAID Country Director, who had only just been evacuated a week or so before on orders from Washington, was still coming to grips with the fact that he was back in Liberia. He had never wanted to leave in the first place, but, once it happened, he looked forward to some family time. His feet had been on U.S. soil for all of two days when he received a call from the State Department, who told him they needed in Liberia anon. He bristled. The next day he took his daughters to see the fireworks at the National Mall and the day after that he was on a Delta flight to Brussels, with connecting flights to Abidjan and Monrovia.

On the ride in from the airport it had struck him how quiet the city seemed, tranquil even, compared to the chaos of the second attack. The Ambassador called him to the front office before he even unpacked and told him to assist a Navy Captain who had been put in charge of some sort of assistance program. His head had been in a complete fog as he sat in the back of the white sports utility vehicles and watched the overeager crowds slap at the hoods and cheer. He really had no idea why the military was getting into the relief business and he looked forward to getting back to his small office in the corner room on the second floor of the Consular outbuilding and having a few minutes to take stock.

The medical unit called. The Ambassador learned, much to his relief, that the injured child would be all right. He had run too close to the wheels and the gash, though painful, was manageable. A HAST medic and Doc Lish patched him up and the next day Becky, the local nurse, would take him back to New Kru Town and reunite him with his family. It did not make the headlines: between the militia at Iron Gate, the Anti-Terrorist Unit standoff and the wild crowds there was more than enough to cover.

Captain Coldiron was irritated though. "The reporters asked me," he said, "isn't all the adoration exhilarating? I don't think it's particularly exhilarating. These people aren't celebrating because of me or my team. They're expressing hope, not joy. They think we represent an end to their troubles. The children's faces all looked so optimistic."

"I'm worried," he said, "they don't have reason to be."

Defense Minister Chea said Iron Gate was all a misunderstanding. "People on the street think this is it," Chea laughed, "that the Americans are on the ground. That's what they've always looked forward to. If you talk to any ordinary Liberian, they feel now there's hope, hope that all of the warring factions will be placed in one cage and locked up and the keys thrown in the deepest part of the Atlantic." The HAST was turned back at Iron Gate for one reason. "Sovereignty, of course," Chea said. "We're happy to have you on board. But somebody should see that we're still a government. It's an official visit and there was supposed to be a courtesy call. I waited for the team to come by my offices."

Sovereignty is inarguably a basic principle of international relations, the core authority of a nation state. Nobody anywhere wants foreign military teams racing around their country without oversight, even teams on ostensibly humanitarian missions. But not every government has lost control of eighty percent of its territory and relied on a mix of children, drug addicts, and a praetorian guard to defend the capital. The whole episode was, from the Ambassador's perspective, gamesmanship. As he saw it, President Taylor knew full well the hope Liberians placed in America and appeared to believe that if he could flip the narrative, erase the sins of the past, and be seen as the man who brought in the peacekeepers, maybe, just maybe, he could cut a deal to save himself.

Only, the United States did not want anything to do with him.

21

THE REPORT

President Bush was midway through his Africa trip. For forty-eight hours the major U.S. networks juxtaposed his trip with images of the Liberian crowds, but then the HAST left the streets to write their report, the narrative moved on, and Liberia vanished from the news, lost in the digital drift. In the cafeteria, Captain Coldiron was out of time.

It was not much of an assessment, but the HAST had seen enough. They had seen the displaced squatting under the stands at the football stadium, cooking in the stairwells of the Masonic temple, huddled in the arcades of elementary schools, and building cardboard and garbage shelters against the buttresses of towering figs at Greystone. They smelled the stink of the clinics and hospitals, bleach in short supply, and witnessed the dying. They had tasted the bitter greens and weak tea that families survived on and listened earnestly as aid workers explained the need for security. The tidal rush of the crowds still rang in their ears. They had seen the child soldiers at the roadside.

Now they had a few hours to make sense of it all. On the red and white checkered tablecloth they set up a single laptop and spread out fact sheets and charts they collected along the way. When they flipped through their notepads, they discovered the ink bled in the heat and damp. It grew dark. Overhead, the lamps fluttered with the pulse of the generators. Major Phillip Spangler scratched his cheek in concern.

Major Spangler was a Senior Civil Affairs Plans Officer for Special Operations Command Europe, based in Stuttgart. He had a high forehead, thin, sand-colored hair and spoke in earnest, measured tones. His towering frame offset the erudite look of his small, wire-rimmed glasses. Before the

Liberia gig he had reconstructed police offices in Iraq. He said, like a man apart, "The HAST just visited camps, hospitals, and ports. We have to produce an interim report for Air Force One but we don't have a template. We don't know how to present our findings, whatever they are. You need a depth of facts, detail. You need to be able to say, as a fact, there are thirty thousand displaced people at the national stadium and that they consume fifteen liters of water per day. Then you can match capabilities with needs." But they did not have those kinds of facts.

Nobody knew what to write, he shrugged.

Mug in hand, Captain Coldiron squinted at the laptop. Different team members stabbed at drafting and editing. The cursor blinked heavily on the grey screen as words appeared and disappeared. Beside the keyboard, coffee stains spread intricate patterns, like imprints on a mud cloth. From time to time, the Captain packed his cigarettes in his palm, patted his pocket for his matches, and headed for the door. Outside in the lamplight he listened to the sounds of the surf and strange birdcalls and the rustle of the almond leaves. He was ornery. They had two pages of rudimentary analysis and the pressure was real. In his view the request from the military chain of command was more of a demand, that someone had come to the conclusion that intervention wouldn't help, that things weren't that bad, that someone else should help Liberia, not the United States.

Coldiron had come to Liberia with the intent of producing an honest assessment and that was what he was determined to produce. He had received very brief and succinct orders and he only knew to do what he thought was right, and that's what every member of his team did. What they clearly did not do, he knew, was give the answer that the chain of command wanted. But he had made O-6 and already done better in his career than he had ever hoped, so he was willing to let the chips fall where they may. He was equally sure that for a long time he would be quite unpopular in some political circles.

The night of July 10, Secretary Powell briefed reporters in Pretoria and Ambassador Blaney found the full transcript posted online. From a Holiday Inn, Powell said that United Nations Secretary General Annan would meet President Bush upon the President's return from Africa. Liberia would likely be discussed and, he added, "Our assessment team in Monrovia has about finished its work and I expect that we'll be getting a full report from them on the humanitarian situation. And this weekend, in Accra, Ghana, a United States team will be meeting with ECOWAS military leaders to assess what will be required to move the ECOWAS troops into Monrovia and to support them, and as part of that assessment, what role the United States might play or ECOWAS thinks we should play."

Liberia looked to receive African peacekeepers again.

"The preference," he noted, "is to lead with ECOWAS, with the United States playing a role of support. I expect over the next several days as we finish the assessment in Monrovia and get the report, and hear from the military assessment team working with ECOWAS... the President will be in a position to make a decision."

Would he have HAST report before the Annan meeting?

"I'm reasonably sure of that," the Secretary replied.

After five countries in five days, President Bush left Africa. Ambassador Blaney caught the CNN International broadcast of the final photo opportunity. At the presidential villa in Abuja, in the shadow of Aso Rock, the granite mountain that loomed over the Nigerian capital, President Bush stood beside Nigerian President Obasanjo, resplendent in dark spectacles and a rose and grey African gown. After a few words of praise for the respective roles of Nigeria and the United States in the emerging world order, the two leaders fielded questions. President Bush was greeted with a familiar topic.

"What about Liberia? Will America send troops?"

"The President and I," President Bush said, nodding to his solemn host, "just talked about Liberia, and we are—our assessment teams are still in place. We need to know exactly what is necessary to achieve our objectives."

His tone was direct and comfortable.

"The first objective, of course," he said, "is for Mr. Taylor to leave the country, which he said he is going to do. And I want to thank President Obasanjo for his leadership on that issue. It's been a tough issue, but he's led. And the world is grateful for that."

He spoke with well-briefed precision.

"Secondly," he continued, "we've got a commitment to the cease-fire. And therefore, we need to know exactly what it means to keep the ceasefire in place. Thirdly, we've got a commitment to relieve human suffering and we need to know what that has required. And so we're still in the process of assessing."

President Bush paused ever so slightly.

"And I told the President we would be active."

"See a decision next week, sir?"

A press officer moved to wrap it up.

"I'm not sure when yet, Randy."

At the Mamba Point Hotel, the news did not go over well. With the HAST sequestered, the reporters assumed details of the findings would emerge in a day or two. Instead, the Pentagon went silent. President Bush flew away from Africa with no decision on U.S. peacekeepers and it dawned on the press corps that the HAST story was finished and maybe Liberia was finished as a lede. The HAST findings, whatever they were, would not be released. The news cycle tumbled on and big media's interest vanished.

Brendt Sadler returned to the Middle East.

Ambassador Blaney accepted where they were in the story arc. He was determined not to let the embassy be viewed as too far ahead of the policy, so he had to play the long game. He had to convince Washington that the humanitarian crisis was so bad that it demanded an international response of some sort (easy), but not so bad that it was hopeless and that any intervention would be a waste of time, resources and, possibly, American lives (difficult). Especially in Africa, especially after Somalia. If he got the balance wrong, and in public, those who wanted to quit Liberia would probably get their way. Washington would not be shamed into action. But there was a process to reach decisions and if the HAST and embassy reporting returned enough detail so comfort could be reached that a military and humanitarian response was doable, that, despite the chaos on the ground, the U.S. could play a positive role, then that was where they needed to be. The good news was that, from all he could tell, they had started to make progress.

The HAST had another benefit: it helped post return to growth mode. With a full military team and force protection on deck, the State Department allowed a modest rise in the headcount. The Defense Intelligence Agency sent a new Defense Attaché, Colonel Sue Anne Sandusky, to fill the gap and let Fergy return to his actual duties. Mike Mezaros, a Washington-based civil servant who had been to Liberia several times before, and may have been the only one to raise his hand this time, flew in to help with consular affairs. Mezaros was popular with the local staff because he took lunch in the local staff canteen, pitching in for potato greens and rice slathered in palm oil and laughing it up with the motor pool drivers and office staff with his attempts at Liberian English.

Extra bodies had plusses and minuses of course. Embassy staffing was lean for the crisis and it was not easy to accommodate the needs of dozens of troops and other experts, even though you needed all hands to get to more normalized engagement, if the Liberian peace process ever took hold. The Regional Security Officer still could not believe the cafeteria found a way to feed everyone. Maybe, he grinned when he thought about it, they had been way overstocked before things went haywire. Fergy, with all his great ties around town, had been critical to their logistics effort even though it had nothing to do with his job description. Throughout the crisis the embassy kept topping off on water, fuel, and food stocks, but it was always touch and go.

None of this was of much interest to the thirty-odd reporters who extended their stays at the Mamba Point only to find themselves once again left with Charles Taylor, a tenuous ceasefire, and quiet days in a cesspool of a city. The nights grew long. Late, after filing deadlines were met, they repaired to Kamal's and sagged into the creaky rattan chairs to shoot the breeze over beer and mezzes. Scuffed fingernails picked damp labels from the bottles. Oil-stained tissues piled up on the tables alongside half-eaten baskets of pita and dishes of olive pits. Beneath the slow fans, in the dim glow of the lamps, cheeks and brows shone like wax in the heat. Somini Sengupta lifted her beer to her lips.

Dark eyes flickered in the shadows cast by the short brim of a canvas sun hat that covered her close-cropped black hair. She possessed the razor sharp intellect and the caustic wit you might expect from a *New York Times* reporter, and she was not afraid to tell anyone she was disappointed in her own government. As a taxpayer.

"We paid for the HAST assessment," she said, "to come to Liberia for a few days and assess the obvious, which is that there's a gigantic humanitarian crisis staring you in the face. You don't have to be a rocket scientist to figure that out. There are people shitting on the beach, there are people pouring out of these balconies, there are children everywhere."

She shrugged at the darkness.

"So what's the point of that?"

A couple weeks later, the *Los Angeles Times* broke the story. By then, the HAST was long forgotten and the story received little attention. In the article, the reporters stated that the HAST did, in fact, complete an analysis and deliver it to Air Force One while the President was in Africa. "The team," they wrote, "urged that the United States immediately deploy a 2,300-strong Marine Expeditionary Unit to stabilize the country and protect civilians." Citing officials on the President's trip, the reporters wrote that "on Air Force One, the initial draft of the team's report made the rounds of State Department and National Security Council officials, including national security advisor Condoleezza Rice... The report was also distributed to top officials in the Army's European Command, which oversaw the team, and the Joint Chiefs of Staff." According to their sources, a second report was filed a week later. The second report had "a stronger humanitarian focus and less specific language over whether the United States should provide the emergency force or merely support a West African-led one." They left the reader to conclude it was watered down.

But the first report, they asserted, never reached the President.

22

A TENSE CEASEFIRE

L iberia had dogs that did not bark. Basenjis, as they were called, supposedly had a noble lineage as Pharaoh's hunters, but in the clearings on the roadside they looked like nothing more than tawny, flop-eared curs passed out in the hot shade. Colonel Sue Ann Sandusky said she did not know much about basenjis, but she had her own theory that all the dogs in West Africa were bred from a single mother. To build her case, she counted dogs with white-tipped tails. Admittedly, there were many.

"Twenty-six, Ma'am," said Fergy, at the wheel.

They were on their way to Gbarnga, a ruined town a hundred and twenty miles east of Monrovia, about a four-hour drive on a dry day. As a rebel, Charles Taylor had based there for a time and still kept a farm in the area. The word was that the rebels overran the farm a couple weeks back but it had been recaptured. If the rebels ever did seize Gbarnga, they could attack Monrovia from two directions. But they did not see any rebels. They did not see anyone at all. An eerie, abandoned land floated past. In the bright, steaming light, vegetation was piled along the road like compost, burying the past. Rubber plantations were overgrown. The grey, scarred trees staggered beneath shawls of vines and moss. Weeds blanketed the fields like fresh thatch. Here and there, concrete pads and crumbled walls told of a lost home. Mustard plants and grasses reclaimed the yards from the dust.

The Colonel said, "This is how I remember it."

The Colonel had flown in from Abidjan the day after the HAST showed up, but spent the first forty-eight hours in country wrapped in a wool blanket on the leather couch in her office, laid low by malaria. She was reprising a role she had in the late nineties. At that time, Charles Taylor had just been elected and the national disarmament campaign was underway that, in theory, would pave the way for reconciliation. The soldiers practiced for the big day in the shade of the mango trees, with broomsticks for rifles. The campaign didn't work. Everyone wrapped their good weapons in plastic and buried them, then turned in rusted, useless pieces for a bag or two of rice.

The war resumed soon afterward.

Sandusky once vowed she would never serve in a country at peace and she was on track. She had a thin, taut face and wore drooping aviator frames that lent her a doleful look, but she was most easily recognized for her shock of white hair that poked out from beneath her weather beaten Army Ranger cap and cut a jagged line at her nape, the same hue as the lamb's fleeces they used to sell on bamboo racks by the roadside before the war got too hot. To the Liberian street she was known far and wide as "that white-haired lady," or, to the more theatrically inclined, "Silver Bullet."

A basenji loped across the road. "Look," she exclaimed, "twenty-seven!" She jotted something in a green, coaster-sized pad. Colonel Sandusky's notes, which she turned into lengthy reports, were legendary for their detail. Throughout the day she recorded everything in sequence, salient facts and observations from the road, or the name and contact for anyone she met. Even, it seemed, her running count of the basenjis. As she hunched over to write, her thin shoulders did not fill out her fatigues and her patches bent on her arms like creased baseball cards under a car seat.

"I didn't see the white tip," Fergy said.

"That can't be—are you sure?"

"Yes Ma'am."

The Colonel shook her head.

"Well you may have missed it!"

"Ah, okay," Fergy rolled his eyes.

The purpose of the trip was to let Ed Birgells and Captain Coldiron assess what was left of USAID-funded assistance projects and to check on the security situation upcountry. It was always different, Fergy knew, outside the capital. At a makeshift clinic at Salala, they looked in on a nine-year-old boy who lay limp in a cot at the back of the tent, behind the older patients, staring at the patterns of shadow and mold on the sagging canvas. Thick gauze covered the length of his arms and the bandages were damp and discolored and reeked of sepsis. He breathed in short, shallow rasps and, when you looked closer, his eyes appeared to be covered with a white film, like a fish that had been left in the bottom of a boat too long. The nurse said the boy's name was David and that he had lost his family at Gbarnga.

The militia had captured the child with some others and carried them to Gbartala. The kids got hungry and went to the forest to look for food, but the militia accused them of trying to run away. David was tied to a pipe and left overnight. The cord was too tight. When the militia saw the gangrene they cut him loose and let him wander off. He walked through the bush for two days to reach Salala. As the embassy officers stood there, a fly landed on the boy's face and picked at the crust from his eyes. The nurse brushed it away and it settled on a rack of empty pill jars. The boy's mouth twitched, but his eyes were vacant. Even if he lived, he would not have use of his arms, all for the misfortune of being in the wrong place at the wrong time.

Conditions at the clinic had deteriorated since the last time an embassy team visited, three weeks before the first attack. The shelves were bare, the cots were mostly empty, and anyone who could be moved had been, carried closer to town. Two huge IDP camps just to the north of Salala had emptied, leaving behind a ghostly grid of sticks and trenches. Further on, outside Gbarnga, they found the charred ruins of the Phebe hospital, which USAID had poured tens of thousands of dollars into over the past several years as the only viable surgical hospital in the area. Everything was blackened, lost, burnt in some attack or counterattack. This was empty land now, fighting land, where the militia did what they wanted and what they wanted was never good.

The last time anyone Fergy knew had been up that way, David Parker drove some journalists upcountry in the short window between the first and second attacks. Parker told him that they had come upon a checkpoint somewhere along the way where the militia kids lolled around a picnic table, upon which lay a human head. A BBC cameraman leapt out to catch the image, but one of the boys, startled into some small sense of propriety, jumped up and knocked the head into a ditch in a puff of dust.

It was like he knew it was wrong, but not exactly why.

They arrived in Gbarnga as the light mellowed, to a crescendo of cicadas. The effects of war are often worst away from the action. Even in its glory days Gbarnga looked to have been a one-horse hitching post, and the horse,

Fergy thought, was long gone. It was a place, among many, that would have no chance to join the rest of the world so long as the war raged. Most of the block buildings along the main drag had been crippled with rocket propelled grenades. The scent of ash and charred wood hung in the air. The small convoy crested a low hill that led to a market clearing. Liberian General Francis Dolo stepped out of the lead car. Defense Minister Chea insisted they travel upcountry with a government escort. Dolo was from the Armed Forces of Liberia, Liberia's constitutional army that Taylor defeated then sidelined in favor of the militia and the paramilitary. Many of the old AFL soldiers served under Doe, or even Tolbert, but still put on the uniform in the hopes of collecting worthless pensions and to reminisce about the days when America trained them.

A few, like Dolo, still held a bit of respect in the capital.

Colonel Sandusky stepped out and joined General Dolo and Captain Coldiron in a huddle with local staff from the Phebe clinic. Fergy sauntered off for a smoke. It was a bit strange for him to return to his regular Operations Coordinator job, to a strictly support role. For five or six weeks he was in every meeting with the Ambassador and the Regional Security Officer, being asked his opinion, asked for input, and then suddenly the Defense Attaché did all those things. He was okay with it though. With the HAST and the FAST and all the other requests from European Command and the Defense Intelligence Agency, he had his hands full as it was. And he liked her, though best he could tell, she was going to drive him crazy trying to keep her from getting herself killed.

Nearby, a few young men and women loitered on the dusty periphery of a barren lot strewn with bottle caps and cigarette wrappers and bits of plastic. Hardly any stalls were open. The women spread their meager offerings on gunny cloth on wooden benches. Pinch-sized clusters of peppers. Lean, gnarled yams rusty with dirt. Soft and stinking papayas. A few cloudy jars of palm oil and a string of small, blue and white detergent packages. The presence of U.S. military drew little interest. Sullen gazes followed their movements. The men might have been militia, the women perhaps camp followers, who trailed the fighters through the bush as cooks and lovers and slaves. Or they could all just be survivors who refused to flee: tired, bitter, and stubborn.

Corn roasted over a charcoal stove, the sweet, charred scent filling the air. Dressed in a soiled white tee and Capris the color of sunflowers, a woman squatted by the stove on a low stool with her arms draped over her knees. She chatted with another woman in a local patois as she swished away the smoke. From the corner of his eye, Fergy caught a bearded man glaring from the recesses of a timber shack. He wore a red mesh football jersey, jeans, and high-tops. A bike messenger bag was slung over his shoulders.

The corn seller frowned.

Colonel Sandusky's voice cut through the heavy air.

"Load up—time to move."

They had stopped five minutes at most. Overhead, cumulus rolled in and the low sun intensified in the narrow band between the forest and the clouds. Heavy doors slammed shut and the white cars wheeled out of the lot in a billow of dust. The convoy headed back to the cracked strip of tarmac that pointed toward Monrovia. The Colonel poked her finger at the window. Strange shadows flickered along the stucco walls. In among the ruins, a shirtless boy in sagging blue jeans carried a rifle with a rusty bayonet. Behind him, another, and another. Grim-faced, they trotted toward the road with inscrutable intent. The convoy was more than three hours from the embassy.

"Not good," the Colonel muttered.

It was clear that chain of command ran directly to White Flower and General Dolo did not have much authority in Gbarnga. If the course of the war was hard to predict from Monrovia, it was murkier still deep in the bush. It was hard to see how the Liberian peace talks in Ghana, or all the discussions in foreign capitals of international peacekeepers, had any connection to this reality. Far from their Papay, left to their own devices, the militia would shoot anyone or anything if the mood struck them, maybe even a convoy of Americans. Fergy hit the gas. The other drivers followed suit and the swell of the engines wiped out the sound of the bush. The militia boys shrank in the mirrors and disappeared. Storm light cut through the clouds and the town behind briefly glowed like the treasure of forgotten kings. A light rain began to fall. The jungle closed in.

They were safe again in the darkening land.

Elsewhere in the bush, Colonel Sandusky heard, the rebels already grew restive. It was mid-July and, in the week since LURD left Bushrod Island the second time the Accra peace talks had gone nowhere, the U.S. military assessment yielded nothing and Charles Taylor was still in power. It mattered little to

LURD that ECOWAS heads of state had met and the Secretariat was lining
up budgets and troop contributions, or that U.S. military advisors deployed
and assets were being pre-staged throughout West Africa, all of which indicated
peacekeepers were likely headed to Liberia. The Colonel guessed that all the
rebels knew, as they trekked through the coastal marshes to the south or idled
on moldering porches in Bomi Hills, watching drafts of rain over the ridges,
was that Charles Taylor still held court at White Flower and played for time.
Peacekeepers, to their mind, would serve only to reinforce the status quo. On
July 11, the LURD Secretariat issued a chilling press release, which hit the
local press a day later, or the same day President Bush left Africa:

> A Nation is built on three key factors: the constitution, the mechanics
> of its operation, and the respect it inspires. Taylor has misused and
> dehumanized the dignity of Liberia. He must therefore leave now and
> give chance to LURD to restore the downtrodden dignity of Liberians
> and Liberia in the comity [sic.] of Nations. The leadership of LURD
> considers the deployment of ECOMOG while Taylor lingers on as
> preposterous and unacceptable. If there is no war, there is less of a pos-
> sibility for an attack. LURD ascribes to a credible stabilization force
> that will operate from a position of neutrality and to usher Liberia a
> stake of sustained peace.
>
> Taylor's government is widely considered to be on its last legs.
> Therefore, it will be totally unacceptable for any troop deployment
> in Liberia, before Taylor's departure. This will enhance his ability
> to remain in power and to further tarry. TAYLOR MUST LEAVE
> NOW, before any deployment. While we hope for the best we are
> braced for the worst; therefore any troop deployed before the depar-
> ture of Taylor must be prepared for a firefight. NOTE: Any troop
> deployment before the departure of Taylor shall be viewed as a means
> to prop-up Taylors dying regime and to further prolong the crisis.
>
> LURD's initial commitment and pledge to restore durable and
> sustained peace to Liberia remains undaunted.

That night, the Defense Attaché, the Regional Security Officer and the
Political Officer huddled in the fluttering light of the Ambassador's office.
The Ambassador tapped his faded map of Liberia, spread out on the coffee
table. Tracing the thread of ink that ran the forty-two miles from Monrovia

to Bomi Hills and the empty green space beyond, he muttered concern that the fighters in the bush might not be on the same page as their negotiators at the peace talks. "We still don't have a Joint Verification Team," he said, "so anything could spark another attack and there's nobody to throw a flag."

Colonel Sandusky scribbled intently in her notepad.

"This statement by the rebels is not helpful," the Ambassador said. "They talk about attacking peacekeepers, which is exactly what can't happen if Liberia is to have a chance. If this turns ugly, everyone might just walk away. Now I understand from our delegation at the peace talks that the rebel negotiators are already walking this back a little, but they are not my concern. I am worried about the commanders in the bush, the ones with the weapons. I am worried there could be a disconnect with their leaders."

Resistance movements often have voices speaking at cross-purposes, especially at the start, and LURD in its brief existence had at least a half-dozen people on record with widely-divergent views on their aims and objectives. Sekou Damate Conneh, most recently a used car salesman, emerged earlier in the year as LURD's nominal leader, but how he orchestrated the fighters and political operatives was entirely inscrutable to outsiders. That he appeared to derive at least some of his influence from his wife Aisha, a soothsayer who had the ear of Guinean President Lansana Conte, did not clarify anything.

"We need," Sandusky said, "to contact the rebel field commanders."

"Yes," the Ambassador agreed, "that's long been a blind spot for us."

The Ambassador frowned, rose, and walked to the window. Through the louvers the fig trees were ghostly in the security lights, and the liana hung from their branches like pythons. "Our near-term diplomatic goal is clear now," he said, turning to his team.

His eyes sparkled through his sea glass lenses.

"We have to ensure the vanguard force is seen as neutral."

23

THE PRAYER RALLY

When there is rain, and heat, and nobody to beat back the green, nature takes over, but Jenkins still found himself surprised at how quickly it happened. Along every stretch of pavement, along the old sidewalks, weeds shot through. Fences were shaggy with overlapping layers of vines and broadleaf, and grasses grew so tall they bent under their own weight sagged over walls and culverts. At Waterside, at Red Light, at all the old markets, trash piled high in the streets, islands of filth with mud rivers flowing around them. And amid this riot of muck and weed, the displaced tried to scratch out a living.

Jenkins recorded what the families had: a few clothes, a plastic mat, some plastic buckets. Maybe an extra pair of flip-flops. They draped gunny cloth from the arcades and window lights to block the sun and the rain and cooked rice or collards, handouts from the relief organizations, over tin cans with hot coals. Children hustled all day to win a few extra coins to buy bouillon to flavor the rice, or fistfuls of macaroni. Nobody could afford an entire box, so dry noodles were meted out in small portions and sold off in plastic bags. Proper vendors were scarce, Jenkins noticed, for want of business. Even the wholesalers at the "buy your own thing" market could not find many takers. The concept of the market was simple enough: after your property got looted, you could buy back what had been stolen from middlemen or even the looters themselves, at a premium of course. But the usual buyers, the Lebanese and the Indians, had mostly fled, and nobody else could afford that imported crèche or those high thread-count sheets.

Jenkins took advantage of the calm in Monrovia to send his mother, brothers, and sisters to Guinea. One brother stayed behind to look after the house, but for the first time in months he had some small peace of mind that the family would be all right no matter what happened to him. The last few walkabouts he had done through town, militia accosted him and accused him of spying for the United States. Sooner or later they would grab him. He moved in with the Political Officer for a time, and relied on his mobile phone and a stack of scratch cards to work his contacts. People treated him as though he had more authority than he did. They told him to tell the Marines to come rescue Liberia. All he could do was pass along his views and hope that the country team would make the case to Washington that something should be done to help. He had faith in the Ambassador, but he had seen so much death and destruction that it was hard to be optimistic. The ceasefire held for the moment, but the peace talks made little discernible progress.

Where, he wondered, was the urgency?

Jenkins learned that Charles Taylor decided to hold a prayer rally at the national stadium, but he dared not go. Hardly anyone turned out for the event, save Somini Sengupta, a few other foreign correspondents and the captive audience of more than ten thousand displaced people who now lived under the bleachers. The stadium was a massive concrete facility built on the outskirts of town by the Chinese government, as a gift to the Liberian people, and included an all-weather track and world-class football pitch, when the groundskeepers had a chance to keep it up. It had the advantage in this iteration of the war to be, so far, well out of range of the mortars tossed into the air at the front lines.

The prayer rally coincided with a massive distribution of food and "non-food items," in the parlance. The International Committee of the Red Cross, or ICRC, which ran the event with Liberian charities, had prepped for two days. At the Delegation warehouse on Bushrod Island, Kim, an ICRC Logistician from Denmark, hired sixty-five daily workers to pack everything. His nine trucks made nine runs each to the stadium. It was load, go, load, go, load, go. On the all-weather track, people lined up in the sprinting lanes in the light rain and waited patiently for three sets of supplies from the back of the trucks. First a roll of sleeping mats, *lappas* and soap, then a blue plastic bucket filled with salt, beans, and cooking oil. Last, fourteen days' rations of maize in gunnysacks. Kim said that, when he walked through the dark corridors of the stadium, he saw that the people were grateful, eating the maize, because they did not have anything else. "Of course," he laughed, "they also carried the maize into town for sale. But we're helping many, many people."

The rain cleared and the heat came. It was a sweltering day. Taylor lured the press out to the stadium with the promise of an important announcement. Somini and the other journalists milled in the infield with a handful of Taylor loyalists and bodyguards for the better part of an hour or two. A smattering of displaced people stood in the bleachers with confused looks on their faces. Everyone else waited patiently in line for their buckets. At the midfield seats, microphones sprouted from an enormous black lectern beneath a sagging canvas canopy. Several rows of chairs were arrayed on the dais. A gospel choir and the Armed Forces of Liberia band were on hand to play the standards.

The stadium shuddered with the rumble of a small motorcade, punctuated by the staccato drone of a motorbike. Charles Taylor emerged from a black sedan. His bodyguards halted the distributions. The gospel choir broke into "It's a Miracle God," a song, Somini noticed, about the possibility of miracles. As the soulful voices swelled in the scorching air, two men circled the track on a motorbike, brandishing rifles. On the dais, President Taylor appeared with Vice President Moses Blah, Taylor's wife, two former United States Congressmen from the Bible Belt, who somehow had flown into Liberia for the occasion, and a diminutive Houston-based Indian preacher introduced as "Dr. K.A. Paul."

Taylor smiled and waved to the barren stands. Liberia's President dressed in blinding whites. "My decision to step down," he said wearily, "is based on the fact that the greatest gift I can give you now are two things. The gift of life and the gift of peace. My life is no more important than your lives." Applause like light rain. Hand raised in feigned protest, Taylor's voice clouded over. "If I were to leave this country before the peacekeeping troops arrive in this city," he said, "I see disaster. I see trouble. I see murder, mayhem. I see rape. I see total destruction."

The journalists were disappointed. This was nothing new. Except for Dr. K.A. Paul. The happy little man in the Nehru suit seized the microphone and smiled benignly through a bushy black mustache. He placed a hand on Taylor's forehead. "President Tyler has made mistakes," he intoned. "I have made mistakes. We have all made mistakes!"

"Where did this guy come from?" Somini wondered.

"And why does he keep calling Taylor 'Tyler?'"

Dr. Paul exclaimed, "My friend, Charles Tyler!"

Days later, at the Mamba Point Hotel, Declan Walsh reflected on the event over a beer. Declan was a lanky, mop-haired Irish journalist who flew in at the tail end of the HAST mania to report for *The Irish Times* and *The Independent*. From afar Liberia had seemed to him like a West African hell *par excellence* and he had the impression that it was one of the most dangerous and volatile places in Africa, run by a rogue President who didn't give a damn about what anybody thought. He read reports about conflict diamonds, illicit timber trade, mercenaries, and other nefarious characters, shady deals at the port and people getting bumped off. Before he came over from Nairobi, his base, he called the BBC's Paul Welsh and asked him wasn't Liberia in the midst of the great dramatic story about the final days of Charles Taylor. "You know," he said, "an evil dictator holed up in his palace, about to be toppled, overrun by rebels?"

"Well," Welsh replied, "we're running out of stories. It doesn't look as if Taylor is about to fold. There's been some sort of stalemate."

It did look that way, despite all the diplomatic activity in capitals.

"Once American involvement came in, though," Declan said, "the British papers were really keen on the story. But when I stepped off the plane, I thought Liberia looked like a lot of these places, kind of rundown and slightly humdrum. Normal, in a sense. It was obviously very poor. But it wasn't, well, your imagination can run away from you, and you can think things are going to be sinister and dark all the time, whereas of course they're just confused and messed up." But the prayer rally left an impression.

"Well," Declan said, glancing at his notes, "it was a bizarre spectacle." Dr. Paul announced an "international day of fasting for peace" would be held in Liberia in ten days' time. He was astounded. "Here was K.A. Paul saying that Taylor was a misunderstood man, that Taylor had personally pledged to him that he would leave the country. He talked about how he, K.A. Paul, was personally friends with all these great world figures like President Bush, and how he had sold his jumbo jet to give money to the poor. Then he appeals to these people to fast—all these people who were already starving, refugees who were bombed out of their houses, living under the fucking stands of the city stadium." Declan rubbed his temples like he had a headache.

"The whole thing was hallucinogenic."

The rebels, it seemed, were not amused. That evening, word reached Monrovia of new clashes at Kle Junction. Around town people had taken to calling the first two rebel attacks "World War I" and "World War II." Now, as rumors of a third assault darted through the narrow streets and the dark, dank, overcrowded slums, the gallows humor resurfaced.

"World War III coming-o," they said.

PART FIVE

THE THIRD ATTACK

Liberian Support Operation

24

THE THIRD ATTACK

T he *Far Side* calendar on Fergy's desk said it was July 19, 2003 when he got the first call that the LURD rebels had attacked Monrovia for the third time in two months, three and a half weeks after their second attack, less than a fortnight after the HAST arrived and five days after President Bush and Kofi Annan had what they called a "meeting of the minds" on Liberia. It was the blink of an eye, really, for Washington, for West African military planners and for the Liberian peace negotiators in Ghana. In nearly any war, when the shooting starts, a great deal of energy is expended on finger-pointing, as though there is some moral edge to be gained as the offended party. The rebels argued that their attack was provoked, which the government denied with equal vigor. With no Joint Verification Team in place there were no neutral observers to assign fault, not that it mattered anyway. In Monrovia there was a sense throughout the city that this was the final battle for the capital and likely for Liberia itself. Maybe nobody wanted it, Fergy thought, but nobody could stop it either.

Gunnery Sergeant Aldridge mobilized the Marine Security Guard detachment and once again Scramlin, Muniz, Weeks, Adams, Stovall, and Brown found themselves gathered at the armory while outside, gunfire and mortar blasts pulsed in the overcast sky like the din of some distant freeway. The reports Fergy had were not good. The rebels' ragtag columns smashed through Taylor's feeble defenses at Kle Junction, at Iron Gate, at the Saint Paul River. LURD clearly had cashed in their chips and brought down the bulk of their forces from Bomi Hills, perhaps as many as a thousand fighters, and had deputized hundreds more en route. They also may have linked with elements that had been fighting up in Gbarnga, so that their numbers swelled to the thousands. By noon of the first full day of the assault, they reached the north end of Bushrod Island, six and a half miles from Mamba Point.

Then something odd happened. A wave of cheers surged through the streets. Dances broke out, foot stomping jigs, and children sprinted gleefully down the slopes toward Bushrod Island waving bandanas, tee shirts, any old scrap of cloth they could get their hands on. The *New York Times* reporter called Fergy from Via Town, the southern end of Bushrod, en route to the Free Port. Buffeted by hoots hollers on all sides, Somini pressed her sun cap to her head tried to find out if what everyone around her was saying was true, that West African peacekeepers had landed to save the day.

"Everyone thinks they've docked at the port," she shouted.

Fergy had not heard anything. The "Free Port" of Monrovia was so-called because cargo in transit could be stored duty-free at the facility pending re-export to other countries in West Africa, a feature which had helped Liberia become a regional leader in entrepot trade in the three or four decades before the war. During the ECOMOG mission in the nineties, the Free Port served as command headquarters for West African peacekeepers, and it was in a shabby office building with confetti marble flooring that Samuel Doe had been caught and brutalized. Given that it was still the spot that nearly all food and fuel entered the country and it had a defensible perimeter and space enough for armored cars and heavy weapons, it was not unreasonable for Liberians to believe that the new wave of peacekeepers would stage there. Only it was not true.

Media reports back in the United States stated that U.S. military advisors had only just started to work with ECOWAS to plan a humanitarian intervention of some sort, but nothing indicated they were anywhere close to deployment. There was the thought that, if anyone had landed, it might somehow be the Joint Verification Team, but Fergy quickly confirmed the JVT was still stranded in converted shipping containers at the airport in Sierra Leone. It was probably just a rumor, he told Somini.

It played out as a cruel joke. Delirious crowds who rushed to the Free Port to greet phantom platoons of West Africans ran unwittingly toward the advancing front, like a flock of sparrows at the edge of a violent storm. At the embassy gates it was no different, as men, women, and children galloped along with rosy smiles, whooping and cheering. It was heartbreakingly beautiful, Fergy thought, all the headscarves and tee shirts glittering like stained-glass across the road, shimmying banana leaves held aloft.

"We want peace, no more war! We want peace, no more war!"

Boom. Boom. Boom. Mortars, clustered, hit everywhere. At the Free Port, Liberian Defense Minister Chea stood with a handful of troops under the green and white arches, beside the white concrete wall blackened with mold upon which were mounted the cheery words "Freeport of Monrovia Welcomes You." Two pistols buckled across his chest, Chea waved his arms wildly. "You've got to get off the street," he shouted at the crowds. "There's an active war just a few miles away. No reason for you to be here. We know you want to see the peacekeepers, but if and when that happens, the government will inform you." It was a noble gesture, if futile. It was not until they heard the blasts that people were convinced, then they rocked and swayed like sleepwalkers startled back to the waking world. Rage and shock tinted the crowds, then panic.

Everywhere militia emerged from the alleys, dressed for battle. The boys wore pastel wigs, women's clothes, and white face, "to confuse the bullets," they said, and they were angry and sullen and high on whatever. They complained to Somini that they had not been paid, that they lacked ammunition, that they did not want to fight anymore. They were upset, but they knew they had no choice but to fight. Special Operations Division police appeared and scattered the crowds with shotgun bursts. The black-clad units whipped anyone they catch with sticks and bicycle tubes and even the militia boys scurried for cover, stumbling over women and children who clustered like ruffled birds in the ditches.

Finally the streets cleared.

The day before the attack, Colonel Sandusky and Fergy had driven well north of the city, north of Iron Gate, to Combat Camp, to investigate rumors of clashes at Kle Junction. Combat Camp was a village of sorts that the government used to give the militia a break when they were fighting up at Kle, but, at least from the roadside, it looked more like a country bus stage, a few wooden benches on a dirt rise along the road and some concrete structures with no roofs standing empty amid the long grass. Nobody was there, nothing was going on, so they turned the car around and drove back to town, the land silent beyond the hum of the engine. When they reached Monrovia, they heard that Defense Minister Chea had just been quoted on the wires that the rebels were eight miles from the capital, and advancing. In their brief to the Ambassador, they could not explain the contradiction. It seemed impossible to Fergy that an attack was underway because they had heard nothing, but he had been wrong before.

The next morning General Yeaten led a group of reporters out to Iron Gate to hold a press conference, and the Colonel and Fergy tagged along in Fifty-eight. Yeaten was driving, Fergy noticed, a Toyota that had been commandeered from one of the international relief agencies. At Iron Gate, the Liberian flag officer told the reporters that the frontlines had advanced and were now south of Kle Junction. The rebels might be in Sasstown by then, he said, a quarter mile from Combat Camp. "We are observing the cease-fire," Yeaten assured everyone, "but the rebels are not observing the cease-fire. We are defending and they are carrying on shelling toward Monrovia."

Fergy stepped away from the cluster and listened. He still could not hear the sounds of war and he turned to a CNN reporter nearby who confirmed that, indeed, there was nothing to hear. Colonel Sandusky strode past him toward Fifty-eight, lost in her own thoughts, as though she were ready to drive off without him. "Where the fuck is she going?" he muttered to himself. "I've got the keys." They had to move anyway. Roland Duo, who held some convoluted title but was basically a top commander for the militia, had not been happy to see the Defense Attaché at the press gaggle, let alone Fergy, whom he had seen snooping around in the past. He pulled General Dolo aside, who was out there as well, and said "Get your guests out of here."

The Colonel and Fergy headed back Monrovia, taking the long route via Somalia Road, but no sooner had they reached the city than Fergy's phone rang. The rebels, he was told, had taken the Saint Paul River Bridge. "You got to be kidding," said Fergy and they reversed course again. This time they only got as far as the Bong Mines Bridge, halfway along Bushrod Island. Yeaten and Duo were there together again, only Yeaten had changed into civilian clothes, which was, Fergy noted, against the laws of armed combat.

Parked off to the side, on the dusty shoulder a hundred yards from the old overpass, it was hard to avoid that hollow sense that creeps in when you find an abandoned industrial lot. To the right stood several white-washed concrete buildings, windows, and doors sealed with security gates, walls stained red by bleeds from the corrugated tin roofs that had rusted to the color of Spanish tile. To the left rose an earthen embankment, sandy, spotted with weeds, that marked the edge of the port area, beside which stood a row of telephone poles, wires slung low and tangled uselessly, while beyond could be seen piles of gravel and ore that had never been shipped and petroleum silos.

Colonel Sandusky walked over to Yeaten and Duo.

She wanted, she said, to go a little further up, to take the Jamaica Road turnoff. "No, no, no" they said, "you can't go." Around them the street filled with militia, which meant one thing. Militia fight, Fergy knew, and government forces stayed behind. When you were surrounded by militia, you knew you were at the front line. They had the big guns with them, the 20 and 50 calibers, and one, bagged up, that might have been a Gatling gun. The Colonel got back in the car and Fergy backed up a few yards and pulled off to one side to see what would happen next. There was an uneasy calm in the air, like the moment in a dark room before a match is struck. Then they heard the shooting, and mortars.

"I think we should go," suggested the Colonel.

"Nah," said Fergy. "Let's watch the reaction."

Every now and then bullets zipped by.

Then gunfire erupted all around them.

They saw Yeaten and Duo jump in their cars and pull away.

"Okay," said Fergy, "it's time to go." As he turned onto the road there was a big boom behind them and the car lunged forward. A few blocks later they ran across Yeaten again. Fergy started to ask if they should stop again, to see if the defenses would rally, but the Colonel cut him off before the words were out of his mouth.

"No," she said, "we've seen enough."

As the fight engulfed Bushrod Island, Jenkins watched helplessly as still more crowds appeared at Greystone desperate for shelter from the lawless city, pressing in to claim the last sandy patches beneath the almond and breadfruit trees. In the first two attacks, Bushrod Island absorbed much of the surfeit of displaced when the Montserrado camps to the north disbanded, but its own residents for the most part stayed put. With World War III underway, the exodus now came from the island itself, as war-weary families finally quit their homes and fled to the cape. All morning old and new homeless streamed across the bridges, heads bowed piteously to the black crest of Snapper Hill and Mamba Point. Those who stayed behind were now caught between the war and the waters, a hostage population, their lives once more dependent on the whims of feral, hopped up children.

Once again bobbing buckets and bundles filled the streets as fretful crowds eddied and whirled outside the embassy gates. The displaced had reached Mamba Point on luck, courage, and calloused feet, but if a shanty under a tree counted as a reward, it bent the mind to think what anything worse might look like. Relief agencies drew on repurposed money from USAID's Office of Foreign Disaster Assistance to deliver rudimentary services to those camped at Greystone and elsewhere. Food and water were distributed, latrines dug, a triage clinic and cholera ward erected. Tarpaulin was found for some of the shanties. It was not enough, Jenkins realized sadly. At each new surge of displaced people, things fell apart. Rations were gobbled up. Tarpaulin, bamboo, and plywood stocks vanished. Vapors of excrement and ammonia polluted the air. People in rags massed on the black stones between the warehouses and the trees and, hands locked behind their heads, looked up in anguish as the heavens darkened with new rain. Jenkins returned to his quiet office shaken.

The voices of his countrymen echoed in his mind.

"Tell George Bush to send help!" they begged.

Or, "Don't suffer your Liberian brothers!"

On the roof of the chancery, Corporal Anthony Adams did not feel like much of a hero. You could have told him, as the Ambassador had, that without the Marine detachment the embassy would have closed, that diplomacy would have had no platform, that Liberia would probably have been finished, but it was small comfort as he looked over the fear and frustration below. The Marines did what they were asked with what they had was how he put it to himself, but not for the first time in his life was he acutely aware of how much events were out of his hands.

Adams had been raised in Georgia, the son of two Army parents, so the call to service ran in his veins, but he lost his sister to a car crash a decade ago and his mother six years later to breast cancer. At the first chance he had to control something in his life, he enlisted in the Marines. After Parris Island boot camp he worked his way through Aberdeen Proving Grounds and Camp Lejeune before receiving orders to attend Marine Security Guard training at Quantico. Monrovia was Adams' first embassy, but, unlike most of the other Marines at post, he knew something of the place from an old instructor who had served there. Still, it had been surreal how quickly the city had unraveled. He had arrived five months before, in March, less than three months before the first attack on the capital, and it seemed like yesterday that the detachment had been down at the beach volleyball court, filling sandbags and hauling them up to the roof to build the bunkers just in case… He was all of twenty-three years old.

Mortars impacted, palpably close. Throughout the morning, government-held areas to the north of the city had been rocked with explosions. As the rebels fought their way down Bushrod Island, Monrovia proper and Mamba Point swung into range. Syncopated blasts, felt but unseen, filled the air with shock waves and strange smells. In the ringing silence that followed, your ears filled with a yellow, molten pulse. A few blocks from the U.S. embassy, smoke scribbled into the sky. In the street, more anger.

"This should never happen!" men yelled.

"America could have stopped this attack!"

Corporal Adams silently held his post.

In the executive suite, the Ambassador took a call from Assistant Secretary Kansteiner. Kansteiner did not beat around the bush.

"John," he said, "Everyone in Washington is following this."

"Okay," said the Ambassador, unsure where he was headed.

"I'm told the President is going to make a decision soon."

"On what?" the Ambassador said, just to be clear.

"On whether you need to close the embassy."

Another call came through. This time it was Secretary Powell. He did not mention anything about closing the embassy and the Ambassador did not ask. He wanted a quick brief on the situation and, after the Ambassador provided it, he said he had one question.

"Is this another Iraq?" he asked.

"No sir," the Ambassador replied. "It isn't." He ran through his points. Americans were not the targets of the attacks. The United States was generally respected in Liberia. It was critical for the embassy to stay open to help stave off the disintegration of the country. The embassy took necessary precautions to protect its people. When he was done, there was a pause as if the Secretary sensed he had something to add and waited.

"I can't guaranty, Mr. Secretary," he said, "that there won't be U.S. casualties."

"Understood," the Secretary said.

The Ambassador called his Beltway sources. Liberia was hot, they told him, and not in a good way. Secretary Powell and Secretary Rumsfeld were again arguing openly and in almost personal terms in front of the President, who wasn't happy. Secretary Rumsfeld hewed to his line that there were no strategic interests at stake and Liberia was a distraction from the main effort in Iraq. Secretary Powell retorted with equal force that the United States had the capabilities to help and that it must support its West African partners. It was by far the most combative of any debates anyone had seen within the administration. The President, he was told, was sick of the infighting and at one point just threw his hands in the air.

He was, they also said, leaning toward doing right by Liberia.

The Ambassador called his team together. They crafted a brief statement to be passed to the foreign press at the Mamba Point Hotel. Bluntly the Ambassador called for the LURD to honor the terms of the June 17 ceasefire, respect human rights, and negotiate a political settlement in Accra. They still had no way to reach the LURD field commanders directly, so the one paragraph release was the only means to get across the embassy's views. They could only hope the rebels monitored the airwaves, listened carefully, and came to their senses. If not, there was no telling how many people would be killed.

"Moooo." Conversation stopped. Fergy shrugged, reached into his chest pocket, and pulled out his phone, which he deftly flipped open and cupped to his ear while moving to a corner. The Ambassador and his security team waited patiently as the Operations Coordinator conversed in low tones. When he came back to the table he told them that a photographer had been shot.

"An American?" the Ambassador asked.

"European. They want us to get him."

"Where is he?"

"Hard to hear. Bong Mines Bridge."

"We just came from there, sir," said Colonel Sandusky. "It's the front lines."

The Regional Security Officer grimly shook his head.

"They need to take him to JFK, they're the only ones who can do surgery."

"That's what I told them," said Fergy.

The Ambassador flushed. The embassy did not run an ambulance service and could not mount impromptu personnel recovery operations through the war-torn streets for everyone who had chosen to be in country despite fair warning. It could also put more lives in jeopardy to do so. He knew the casualty report could very well be the first of many and though he had no power to prevent members of the Fourth Estate from making their way to the front, he wished that in taking personal risks they could better see that they could put the broader effort to save Liberia in jeopardy. Dead reporters did not help the case that the crisis was manageable, and through two attacks the red lines had not changed. The U.S. government writ large still had zero tolerance for official American deaths in Africa and if the Ambassador lost any of his American staff they would still shut the embassy faster than he could say "NEO." Game over.

Ten minutes on, another moo.

"No shit," said Fergy, headed for the door.

"What's up?" Ted Collins asked.

"They dumped the guy at our gate."

Downstairs, outside, the light was warm and yellow and the shadows had started to stretch across the grounds. At the turnstiles, a man was on the ground. He wore a white shirt, yellow belt, and khakis, and the front of his shirt, at the belly, was bright with blood. Marines shouted for a gurney. Nobody could find one. There was a commotion and suddenly a large Marine appeared, bent down and in one startling motion slung the injured man over his shoulder. Fergy was stunned at the Marine's effortless strength, but there was no time to lose, so he waved and started to walk toward the medical unit. The Marine fell in behind him, the bloody man tacked to his shoulder awkwardly like a beetle pinned against the felt.

Captain Coldirion arrived with a HAST medic and together with a couple other Marines and *New York Times* photographer Mike Kamber, who had brought his injured colleague to the gates, the party hustled the five hundred paces past the flagpole at the front of the chancery, down through the shaded palm groves of the Marine house garden, past the empty palava hut and through the motorpool parking lot until they arrived at a five-story white and teal block of condominiums, in which, on the first floor, the medical unit was found. In a small, white room the Marine slid his charge heavily onto the examination table as the paper slipped and crackled, then stood back, chest heaving, and removed his helmet. Doc Lish and several FAST medics scrambled with drips and scalpels and, when they ripped away the man's shirt, they found a mess.

"He's got to get to JFK," Doc said.

"Got it," said Fergy.

"We can only stabilize him."

Fergy stepped out and called David Parker, who knew the team at JFK. In the parking lot Kamber paced like a caged animal. Nearby, Stephan Faris, a freelancer, stood by in silence. They had been with the photographer when he got winged and Kamber's white shirt and blue cargo pants had blood on them. Somehow they had flagged down a pick-up and convinced them to drive to the embassy, their colleague bleeding out as they climbed the bluffs in the rattling back pen. Fergy told him there was nothing else they could do at this point and at that Kamber stopped abruptly, as though struck, and headed toward the gates. "I gotta get back out there," he said, "I've still got work to do."

The afternoon light gave way to a gauzy, grey evening. The International Committee of the Red Cross surgical team at JFK hospital agreed to take the patient, but they did not have an ambulance to spare. "You have to bring him over," Fergy was told. He went with Doc Lish to the Regional Security Officer, who grabbed his deputy and together they repaired to Collins' office to stare at the wall, which was covered with a satellite image of the city streets. JFK was on the far side of town, in the Sinkor neighborhood, some distance from the front, so long as the rebels had not infiltrated from multiple directions. There would be militia checkpoints, it would be dangerous, but the alternative was to let a man die in the medical unit. As a Regional Security Officer, Ted Collins was paid for his judgment and he took a common sense approach wherever possible. He was not the type to wrestle with decisions, but this was an instance where both options could have bad outcomes. Still, when he joined Diplomatic Security he told himself he would try to do the right thing, always. The right thing here was to get the man to surgery.

They rolled out in a three-car convoy. Fergy led with Fifty-eight, FAST platoon leader Captain Kuni riding shotgun. Assistant Regional Security Officer Brad Lynn drove the health unit's armored Suburban, which served as the ambulance. Seats had been stripped out of the back so the gurney could slide in. FAST Marines and several HAST members stuffed themselves into the last car, a security follow. The streets were broken and deserted, as empty as Fergy had ever seen them. Mortars struck from time to time, white puffs on the sides of buildings followed by a small shower of debris. Gunfire was general and even a mile and a half from the front militia were everywhere, shooting in the vague direction of the ridgeline and sometimes shooting at each other in fear and confusion.

Now and again the convoy passed men and women who had been caught away from home or shelter and tried to make their way back. They crouched low at the corners, paused to gauge the direction of the last shots, then launched themselves into the streets, bent low, and sprinted with comical gaits, almost like marionettes with strings tangled. Fergy kept his foot on the gas pedal, blowing through makeshift checkpoints of string and branches before bewildered foot soldiers had time enough to think to shoot at the sparkling white cars. They drove fast and tight, so tight the bumpers scraped from time to time. On the far side of the Executive Mansion, Fergy keyed his radio.

"Anyone know where JFK is?"

Doc Lish, in the ambulance, laughed as if it were a joke, but Fergy had never been there before. The hospital was the largest facility that side of town, a four story concrete block, shoebox-shaped, at the end of a paved drive and sweeping lawn. They had blown past the gates and had to circle back. Once at JFK, Fergy and Brad Lynn stayed in the cars while members of the HAST team carried the patient into the hospital, Doc Lish at his side the whole time. The transfer of the patient went smoothly enough, but when Doc got back to the car he shook his head. The patient's blood pressure had dropped off the charts and they nearly lost him. He was still a long way from safe. The cars regrouped, everyone loaded up, and they swung back out into the wide, silent streets of Sinkor.

The return trip did not go as planned, not that Fergy had much of an opportunity to plan. In the brief time they had been at JFK, Anti-Terrorist Units had set up a barricade near an abandoned, bullet ridden building owned by the Libyans, a stone's throw from the Executive Mansion. Raised fists and rifles halted the embassy convoy. The soldiers sported full kits, with Kalashnikovs and rocket propelled grenades at least two heavy weapons in flat beds. They trained their sights on the embassy cars and Captain Kuni tensed, jaw grinding, veins popping. "What's the plan?" he asked.

There are not too many options when you are stuck at a checkpoint with rifles trained on you. "Anyone fires," Fergy said, "we go right through the barricade. But don't worry, these guys won't do anything. They just have their orders. They stopped us because no one gets by when the President is at the

Executive Mansion." An officer approached and told them that, indeed, the President was at the Executive Mansion giving a speech and they had been told to seal the route. He suggested they take the bypass back, but neither Lynn nor Fergy knew the route well enough. Fergy keyed the radio again.

"Alamo, Alamo," he said.

"This is Alamo," Colonel Sandusky replied.

Why the fuck did she choose that call sign, Fergy thought.

"They stopped us. We need you to contact Chea."

Tense minutes drifted by. Fergy leaned back in the wide, comfortable seat and closed his eyes. Between the logistics for the HAST, supporting the Colonel, briefing the Ambassador, and answering interminable requests for information that came down through message traffic, he was getting two to three hours sleep max. Ten minutes stalled at a checkpoint with weapons aimed at him seemed as opportune a moment as any to grab some shuteye. Captain Kuni, next to him, looked ready to explode.

Colonel Sandusky finally reached the Liberian Defense Minister, who eventually turned up and waived the convoy through. If President Taylor ever turned against the United States, Fergy realized as he watched the soldiers lower their weapons and glare at the convoy as it sped away, the embassy could be in a world of hurt.

Liberia was still very much Charles Taylor's court.

25

THE ALAMO MEETING

The Ambassador had just ended a conversation with General Wald, who had just phoned him for the sixth or seventh time and by now had given up trying to convince him to leave, but wanted to discuss the fluid security situation, when Assistant Secretary Walter Kansteiner called back. Kansteiner told the Ambassador that Secretary Powell had spoken to the President and they discussed Liberia and what to do about the embassy. The President made a decision, which was to trust his guy in the field.

"He left it up to you," the Assistant Secretary said.

"Thank you, Walter," the Ambassador replied.

Relief was not what John Blaney felt when he hung up, but fatigue. There was no other way to describe it: a wave of conflicting emotions washed over him. It was, he reflected, easily the most complex emotional moment of his life. He did not consider himself a particularly devout person, but he felt an urge to shout "Thank God." He was that glad for the support, that it was now his call and his alone. At the same time, he felt as never before the burden of command. The mission had already lost local staff. The lives of the rest of his people, the peace process itself, and the lives of so many more Liberians could be saved, or lost, based what he decided. That was not even to mention the very real and lasting regional interests at stake for the country he represented.

It was physical: he could feel the pressure in his chest.

The conference room smelled of warm battle dress uniforms that could use a wash. The Ambassador had called an all hands meeting for American staff and when he walked in and everyone rose, per the protocol, he noticed it was more crowded than it had been in a while, maybe in years, with Captain Coldiron, Major Spangler, and FAST Captain Kuni there alongside his permanent staff. It was encouraging, in a way, as the Ambassador did not have immediate concerns that they could defend the chancery, but it also meant more bodies to account for at a moment that he had hoped would never arrive.

There was no way to sugarcoat it and it was not his style to do so. They were less than a mile from the front lines of a war fought by teenagers and children, whose lack of skill and military training made the fight no less lethal for anyone nearby. Taylor's forces had retreated from Bushrod Island and, though they rained hellfire down on the southern tip of the island from the Ducor Hotel and other positions along the ridge, it was hard to trust that they could hold the Mesurado bridges any better than they had held any other bridges. The rebels were bent on storming the Executive Mansion.

"Well," he said, "it's kind of like the Alamo around here."

Ted Collins bailed him out with a short laugh.

"In all seriousness folks," he said, "we're in the path of the war. We've taken some fire on the compound—" he said, glancing at Captain Kuni, who nodded, "but all indication are that they were stray shots, nothing directed at us. But the point is we can only protect ourselves so much. You need to be under cover unless you have reason to be out, and, if you are out, you need to be wearing a helmet and vest." It was an important message, but it was details, a way to build to the more urgent point he had to get across.

"Sir," Collins said, "if I may?"

The Ambassador acceded.

"Listen everyone," Collins said, "It's about all sustainability and surviv-ability here on the compound now. We have a lot of bodies and we don't have an easy way to replenish our water, fuel, cash, and food stocks on compound. We get our potable water from a well across town, out by Red Light. The truck is still running, but at any time it could be turned back. We are checking the burn rates, but the point is everyone will need to think about conserving. We have time, so we're not at the point where we have to start drinking the swimming pool, but we don't know how long this will last."

The Ambassador put both hands flat on the table, the smooth wood cool against his palms as he collected himself. "Look," he said, "what Ted is saying is right. We don't know how this is going to play out and we really don't know much about the rebels, the fighters themselves, so we don't know their intentions.

Our best analysis though is that we still have a role to play here, that neither side wants the United States to abandon Liberia entirely. It would be easy for us to walk out right now, leave this to the West Africans and the Liberians themselves, but then you could be looking at a repeat of ECOMOG and no end to this war. The embassy is the platform, the only platform left, that the international community can use to make a West African deployment successful. We're that connective tissue that can help ensure they are seen as neutral."

He paused to let his words sink in.

"My decision, for now, is to keep the flag flying," he said in a sober tone. "But I want each of you to know the risk we are taking here, and the dangers, and that none of you has to stay. I commend you all for your courage and your patriotism, but honestly, if this is not what you signed up for, if you think we should not be here now, or if you think that this is not what our country needs to be doing, or even not what you need to be doing, then you have my full support to leave. I don't want anyone to think that I am ordering you to stay. On the contrary, you are more than free to go and we'll get you out."

No one said a word.

The Ambassador rose and pushed the chair back awkwardly. He reached over and tapped the Defense Attaché lightly on the shoulder. "I want you all to think it over," he said to the group, "and let the Colonel know. We can probably still get helicopters in from Sierra Leone. She'll get the roster started." As the officers by the door arched their backs against wall to make way for the Ambassador, a young Marine reached out and touched the Ambassador's elbow. "Sir," he said tentatively, "are you going?" The Ambassador shook his head, "No," he replied, "no, I'll be here." Alone, he walked back to his office down the long corridor lined with plaques, while everyone else dispersed behind him.

Knuckles rapped at the door. Colonel Sandusky came to him and plopped down in a chair with her clipboard. The Ambassador locked his screen, walked over to his divan, and sat down. She had removed her cap and her white hair was matted down like she had been walking at pace in the heat. She knotted her brow and dipped her head ever so slightly, and the Ambassador thought he heard a quiver of emotion in her voice. She told him that she had spoken to everyone and nobody wanted to go.

"They all want to see this through to the end," she said.

The Ambassador felt a lump in his throat.

26

BROKEN GLASSES

Even with Washington's unwavering focus on Iraq, the rebels' third attack on Monrovia drew attention like a pooch that had spoiled the carpet. At the National Security Council, at the State Department, at the Pentagon, phones pulsed incessantly, monitors flashed with streaming news and tabletops disappeared under a precipitate of situation reports and talking points. The Operations Center called the Ambassador almost hourly for updates. In the administration and in Congress, those who wanted to support Liberia and those who wanted to cut losses plied the phone lines to drum up support for a robust response, maybe even a peacekeeping operation, or to urge the plug be pulled.

The Defense Department prepped for both outcomes. Within twenty-four hours of the attack, Secretary Rumsfeld finally ordered the rest of the FAST down from Rota to protect the embassy, once again "at the request of the United States Ambassador," as though it suddenly occurred to John Blaney that extra security might be warranted. More ships were headed to Liberia too. The USS Iwo Jima Amphibious Readiness Group, an "ARG," and its "embarked 26th Marine Expeditionary Unit, Special Operations Capable," were directed to sail from the Red Sea to the Mediterranean as a "precautionary measure." The ARG's three ships, the flagship plus the USS Carter Hall and the USS Nashville, carried 2,500 sailors, with 2,000 additional Marines in the MEU. But the ARG was a fortnight out from Liberia and did not yet have a mission, neither evacuation nor support.

"We'll put them in place in case they're needed," was the public line.

By midday Sunday, the second day of the attack, the battle centered on Monrovia's port. The rebels had not made any more progress. Everything was dark with rain and Ted Collins found himself in a narrow alley of television equipment in the bar, at the back of the cafeteria, on a stool beside Jennifer Eccleston, a radiant Fox News correspondent. Eccleston was a smart reporter who spent the previous day in an oversized helmet and chinstrap talking her way through checkpoints. She also had the striking blond hair and Ivory-girl features that Fox News fans tuned in for and it was disconcerting to see her in the dim light of the bar, amid a thicket of cables, sound equipment, cameras, and flak jackets. The contrast was so great she almost did not seem real, more like a cardboard cut-out you saw at movie premieres. Or maybe, to be fair to her, it was the other way around. She was splendidly real and the wartime bar had been digitally added to a blue screen.

She was there, all the television crews are here, at the embassy's suggestion. As Monrovia collapsed in on itself, more evacuations were inevitable and the Ambassador authorized an announcement that gave any U.S. passport holder the option to come to the embassy immediately for safe haven, so long as they could get there without greater risk than sheltering in place. It was an unorthodox move, since evacuation assets had not yet been lined up and the embassy was no more a hotel than before, but the Ambassador agreed with his staff that it was better for Americans be on the compound and ready to jump aboard helicopters, if they could be arranged, than to be caught in the streets and overrun. So Mike Meszaros and the other staff made the offer to anyone they could track down.

This is who they reached: Sister B at the Catholic girls school, several relief workers, a handful of Liberian-Americans who returned to protect property or business interests, and the host of journalists at the Mamba Point Hotel. Since the French helped in the first attack, reciprocity was in order, and the offer was extended to third-country nationals affiliated with the international press or relief organizations. The embassy also agreed to shelter an eight-person United Nations country team that returned after the HAST arrived, apparently under the misimpression that the war had ended.

This was who accepted: the United Nations team, a couple Liberian-Americans, and most of the international television crews. Not Sister B, who took a gander at the flag pole, saw the stars and stripes flying, and hunkered down with her students; not the relief workers, who assured the embassy that they would reconsider if soldiers knocked at their doors; and most certainly not the print journalists. Somini Sengupta told Fergy they did not think the Mamba Point Hotel was at risk of ground assault. She reasoned that when it was "safe" they would get out and report. When it was not safe, they would stay indoors. An Associated Press reporter pointed out matter-of-factly that it was all relative, that, when she covered the civil war in the Congo, she had spent three weeks in a bunker as artillery pounded Kinshasa. Lulls never lasted more than an hour or two, yet she still found ways to file her stories. Her point was that Liberia was dangerous and unpredictable, but nobody used heavy artillery and the shrapnel could not pierce concrete roofs.

There were still plenty of ways to get killed.

The difference for the television reporters was that they carried satellite dishes and thousands of dollars' worth of equipment. A National Geographic team turned up with fifteen hard shell cases and it occurred to Collins, maybe unkindly, that there should be laws against jumping into a war zone with anything more than you can carry on your back. So given the choice between a few extra nights at a hotel with no fencing and the embassy, the television crews chose the embassy, at least for the moment. Within a few hours, Assistant Regional Security Officer Brad Lynn was at his wits end dealing with reporters who wanted to come and go through the locked, secure perimeter.

Two-way traffic wasn't part of the deal.

Out on a small deck at the top of a wooden staircase that led to the back entrance of the bar and cafeteria, the CNN correspondent was lit up by a strobe to compensate for the dark skies at his back. He dutifully wore his black flak jacket and blue helmet and spoke to camera with a deep, booming voice. Behind him, the almond trees were black and dripping. He was on live.

"We can tell you," he intoned, "we are still very much inside the compound of the U.S. embassy, the heavily fortified compound. And, even as early as this morning, the embassy compound was taking in stray bullets, whizzing past and landing in trees like the ones behind me. In fact, an embassy staffer, a local Liberian working for the U.S. embassy, a guard at the gate, sustained injuries from gunfire. Mortar shells landed barely twenty meters from the embassy gate. So it was very intense fighting up until a few hours ago, Sean."

This, the Regional Security Officer realized, was the advantage of hosting journalists. They told the story of the embassy. For a few brief moments, on a few different networks, Liberia popped into living rooms back in the United

States and viewers heard about an embassy that had not quit. Liberia was not just be some horrible place with terrified people or anything else confusing and remote and easily forgettable.

It was a place with an American presence.

On the dawn of the third day of fighting, the second tranche of the FAST team, led by Captain Robert Lynch, flew in on Pavehawk helicopters that had now forward deployed to Sierra Leone. The Pavehawks came in fast and low in the light rain, flying tandem over the water. They dropped off twenty-one Marines and promised an additional twenty, plus supplies. On their backhaul, they evacuated a couple families and carried away the entire HAST team save Captain Coldiron, a medic or two, and Major Spangler, who still had Civil Affairs work to do. To Fergy, after the madness of the first several days of the HAST runs, and the pressure of the report, it was a strange, quiet departure.

The press did not bother to report it.

Jenkins Vangehn stayed in his office much of the day, monitoring the radio. Whether the rebels or the government had the upper hand was impossible to tell, but it was clear that civilians were being killed at every turn and nobody took any responsibility for any of it. During a brief lull in the mortar wash, Jenkins was able to get through by mobile to Bushrod Island. Two of his contacts told him they had seen firsthand one of the LURD mortar tubes. "Mortar Papay" was an old Armed Forces of Liberia soldier, trained under Samuel Doe, who now cast his lot with the rebels. He and a second set up a small grey tube on a curb in Via Town and played to bystanders either brave enough to creep out of their homes or angry enough with Charles Taylor that they did not care that they were behind the lines. It was all good fun. He gestured toward the distant ridge of Cape Mesurado, toward Mamba Point, and said, "Let's greet them 'Good Morning.'" He asked how many 'Good Mornings' he should send and the crowd laughed along and counted up from one. At four or five or six, Mortar Papay held up his hand and shouted.

"Add a zero. Let's send them fifty Good Mornings."

Children poked through the crowd too. Again Mortar Papay waved at the ridgeline across the river and spoke in his rapid-fire patois. "Your ma there? No! Your pa there? No! Then give them more mortars." He reached into a black duffle bag, lifted out an olive green, tear-drop shaped bomb, stripped away the clear plastic wrap, and dropped it gently into the tube. There was a hollow poof, a blur at the tip like something had flown out, and the tube would fall over. Then, seconds later, a distant bang. Tendrils of smoke sprouted on the horizon. The children clapped happily with no idea that all those shells were raining down on children just like themselves in Mamba Point.

Later it was: "Let's send them fifty Good Afternoons."

Magnus Wolf-Murray was in the Merlin offices a block away from Greystone when the shell hit, very loud, very close, close enough to have struck his building and sent lethal shards of glass and metal through the room. He and the local staff quickly moved to a dim, interior corridor and huddled there, in the dark, listening to the radio handset. On the other end, at the clinic, someone had left the microphone on. Inhuman screaming. Total noise and panic. Magnus keyed in, asked what they needed, but there was no response. Moments later, Doctor Clement, their Sudanese chief medical officer, burst into the office, grabbed extra intravenous drip bags, gauze, and extra surgical supplies and ran back out. Shells were still hitting in the area, heavy impacts. Magnus was not a doctor and hesitated a moment, then said "sod it" and ran after him to support however he could.

As he reached the gates of Greystone, people rushed past with wheelbarrows full of bodies and parts of bodies and dumped them on the curb in front of the embassy. It was women and children mostly, just shattered bodies, and in one bucket, a dead man with an entire arm torn off, another man decapitated. The Merlin clinic at Greystone was built of bamboo poles and tarpaulin and stood on a rough pad of dirt a hundred yards from the entrance. At the explosions the local staff had run, but Doctor Clement tracked them down and ordered them back to work. As Magnus arrived, men and women crowded the waiting room benches, stepping over the inert bodies of children to find space. A thirteen-year old girl had bled out in one of the passageways and nearby lay a man whose skull was cracked open and somehow his whole brain had been sucked out, so there was just sort of an empty shell there and white, lifeless eyes.

You saw things, Magnus thought, you did not normally see.

He made himself useful by hauling the dead out of the tent to clear space for the wounded and dying. Doctor Clement made the best of it, but there were cases that had to go to JFK. It was Magnus' call whether to send an ambulance across town. They had an arrangement with Mercy, a local relief organization, which had the ambulance that Merlin funded to be on call. There was no telling what conditions were like through town, if you would be killed and the van taken, but Magnus took the decision quickly: the need was greater than the risk. An Emergency Room nurse named Jennifer, a volunteer from the United States, said she would accompany with the driver, but as Magnus waited with her at the clinic a call came that the car had been swarmed by a crowd in front of the embassy.

Eighteen or nineteen bodies now lay in front of the embassy, some fresh from the blast at Greystone, while others had been dead longer, their soft, rotting flesh leaking cloudy fluid into the beveled edge of the road. The soft breeze lapped up the smells. A crowd of maybe two hundred young men, heedless of the mortars, milled around the bodies. They were angry now, shouting recriminations at their own dark reflections in the smoked glass of the embassy guard booth. When the ambulance that Magnus had called in arrived, fists beat on the windows and hood, rocking the car on its axels. Reluctantly, the driver backed up. The men returned their attention to the embassy.

"We're going to die for nothing!" they shouted.

"America abandoned us!" others spit in anger.

On the periphery men stooped for rocks, which flew from their hands, nicking the walls with small, sharp flint marks and clattering against the gates with the sound of coins in a tumble dryer. Magnus hustled out from Greystone and pushed his way through the crowd toward the stalled ambulance. The men shouted that they would not let the car collect the bodies from the curb, that the Americans had to look hard and see what they had done. Anger flashed as they mistook him for an American, but enough recognized him as a relief worker that he broke through to the center. He grabbed a couple of the obvious ringleaders and pulled them to one side. "Let the ambulance through!" he shouted. "We need to get the living to the hospital if we want them to stay living!"

They let the ambulance pass.

The men soon dispersed, tired and hopeless. The bodies lay there, untended, like trash in an alley behind a diner until Merlin, or the International Committee of the Red Cross, or "Rescue Mother," an heroic Liberian woman with her own ambulance, came and took them away. Only the Muslim Fula people were buried quickly. Across the street, eight or nine boys in sandals and trousers broke up the earth with shovels and picks in the bald broken-glass lot next to the embassy's Public Affairs offices.

Jenkins heard what was happening and slipped out to watch. Granite and packed clay made for tough digging. The boys could not reach six feet. They wrapped the dead in bed sheets. Bronze bracelets were placed on the hands or ankles, so the bodies could be identified for reburial if the chance ever came. Koranic verses were read, silent prayers said. Afterward, Jenkins walked back to his office, sat down at his desk, and wept. It could have been him or his family, he thought, to have been buried in such a manner.

Television cameras panned over the pile of bodies. In the United States, nightly news programs ran the quick, incomprehensible images in loops alongside thirty-second reports that a place called Liberia, somewhere in Africa, was in trouble. Closer in, J.T. Richardson was disgusted with the whole affair. The Liberian National Security Advisor said he heard the screams from his small flat near the embassy, where he stayed when he was not with Charles Taylor at the Executive Mansion or at White Flower. "It was the norm," he said later, "that anybody who was hit by a mortar, you put them in a cart and wheel them past the Mamba Point Hotel for the press, to make sure they get the picture."

He did not care if his view was unpopular.

"I saw it," he said. "The family walks from downtown behind the dead and the moment the cameras appear, they go through this emotional thing. In fact, a crier runs in front and shouts 'they're bringing bodies, they're bringing bodies' so everyone has a chance to grab their cameras, their movie gear, and run down to the junction. It's all on cue. Even a lot of the crying in front of the embassy is on cue."

But how could grief be an act? Why?

"I guess," Richardson said, "they feel press coverage is the only way anyone will appreciate their plight. You know what it would mean if one relative in America sees you on CNN wailing for a cousin? That's a lot of Western Union control numbers." Richardson gnashed his teeth as he thought about it. "The international press," he said, "doesn't want to know the story. They want to see how many people are dying. They want to see how brutal it can get. To show how primitive we Liberians are. We're portrayed as a bunch of barbarians, who eat each other's hearts and kill each other. We're portrayed as people with no intellect, as fools, savages. The press doesn't want to look at the conflict in any kind of intellectual sense—" He waved his hand dismissively.

"—it's all just blood and gore."

27

NEAR MISSES

Throughout the morning, as every morning, mortars pounded the city. Relief workers and print journalists were forced off the streets and once again their headquarters decided to pare down staff, and the population of potential evacuees swelled. As the fighting intensified, the embassy knew it was time to get them off station. Helicopters were on the way and Fergy was called on again to help move everyone out of the cafeteria, which had a flimsy tin roof, down to the administrative building, a hard structure made of reinforced concrete and barred windows. The sprint across the undulating lawn would leave them exposed to stray rounds and shrapnel, but there was no choice. Fergy and Mike Meszaros shepherded the evacuees into a rough line. Then they broke for it.

Soft mist hung in the air, rich with the scents of the grass and the sea. Handset damp and slick in his palm, Fergy fumbled it as he ran and cussed as he had to stoop to grab it off the grass. A split second meant life or death and in war and the guy who hesitated or stumbled was usually the one who bought it. In the distance, the fight popped and thumped on Bushrod Island. The motley line of reporters in ill-fitting Kevlar vests and helmets, and some relief workers in faded tee shirts and fanny packs, slip-slid behind him down the wet, slick paths. Cameramen huffed under their tripods and equipment cases.

Once inside the administrative offices, everyone squatted obediently against the bare white wall on the gray, gritty carpet, their chests rising slightly from the short dash and the thick air of the windowless corridor. Generators rumbled and droned, eclipsing the sounds of the fight so that they found themselves in something of a vacuum. Patience did not last. The relief workers, mostly Europeans, were miffed they could not smoke inside. The television crews chattered among themselves and began to ask questions.

Within a short time, everyone agitated to leave the hallway.

The call finally came. Pavehawks were less than ten minutes out. The Regional Security Officer and the FAST platoon leader strode down the hill to drop smoke in the little swale by the tennis courts, to shield the landing zone. The first explosion hit staff housing just above the commissary. Wooden shingles ballooned up, then collapsed. Black smoke billowed from the rupture. Joe Ellingson, the Facilities Maintenance Officer, lived on the top floor, and, Collins knew instantly, the flat had been shredded with shrapnel. If he were home at the time, he would be dead. He was not.

Screams of abject terror pierced the air from the men and women crouched in the tenements nearby. The next several rounds hit the ocean, pillars of water shooting, rising like the bones of an old temple as the tides receded. Ted Collins looked at Captain Kuni: they were bracketed. No sooner did they start in one direction than a mortar struck. Collins felt ridiculous, like a laboratory rat. They stopped and started and stopped again. They had nowhere to run. Collins pulled the pin on the smoke, the canister got hot in his hand, and he dropped it on the pavement, where it rolled and spun and hissed and spit out a white cloud. They made a mad dash for a shed at the back of the cafeteria.

The blasts were so close they could easily be heard through the block walls of the administrative building. Everyone in the corridor knew that they must have hit the compound. Reporters clamored to open the doors and have a look. Fergy and Mike Meszaros had to keep everyone at bay and also refused to confirm the hit, in case the embassy had been targeted. You never confirm a hit. Voices rasped at Fergy's hip and he realized too late he forgot to turn down the volume on his handset. "Commissary took a round," someone said over open channels. The reporters all heard it.

"Are you being targeted?" they shouted.

Fergy had no idea. Probably not, given what was known about the dynamics of the conflict. The embassy still had no contact with the rebel field commanders on Bushrod Island and Charles Taylor's crowd could blow with the wind. Yet the sheer number of strikes in the vicinity of the compound, and the timing, especially as helicopters hovered off shore and evacuees waited on deck, had to give pause. It looked like too much of a coincidence. Colonel Sandusky's voice skipped across the radio.

"The helicopters are still going to try to land."

Sticks were cobbled together again and doors pushed open. Everyone sprinted back uphill to the cafeteria. Bullets winged past, striking the palm trees and the seawall. In back of the cafeteria, beneath the wooden deck, stood a cramped shed cluttered with discarded refrigerators and washer-dryers. It offered only the idea of protection. Captain Coldiron, Colonel Sandusky, and several Marines gathered there as they radioed the Pavehawks. Ted Collins and Captain Kuni ran up, breathing hard. The mortar barrage intensified. Captain Coldiron, Collins thought, seemed cool as a cucumber. He wore his helmet tilted slightly back to show his forehead and bangs and a cigarette clung to his lip so that he looked like an image from one of those old black and white stills of the Second World War. He had a large black radio in one hand and a mug of coffee in the other and seemed totally unfazed by the chaos around him.

Tandem helicopters appeared on the horizon. The Pavehawk crew radioed in. They were told to hold off. Colonel Sandusky brushed aside her white bangs. Concussive blasts shattered across the beachfront. Like hummingbirds the distant aircraft skimmed the grey waves and circled back one last time. They could not hover offshore indefinitely. Fuel would be an issue. It was three hours back to Freetown. Collins desperately wanted them to land, to clear the decks of the evacuees. Five minutes was all they needed. Smoke from the canister he released drifted across the lawn like a fast-moving fog, sliding over landing zone. More mortars. Captain Coldiron and Colonel Sandusky exchanged glances. Coldiron made the call, and they stood side by side in silence, as they watched the Pavehawks tilt against the cobalt sky and dart off. They would not come back for at least twenty-four hours, because there was not enough daylight for the full round trip to Freetown.

If Pavehawks had no way in, Collins knew the embassy staff had no way out. When you started to work the equation down the line, you ended up with all sorts of wrong answers. For Fergy, standing nearby, it was a different kind of stress. He had to turn and face a passel of wet, irritated journalists and aid workers, and tell them that all the running had been for naught, that they had to go back to the grey corridor for a while then in all likelihood camp out on the cafeteria floor another couple nights.

"I'm sorry," he said, "we can't get you out today."

"Then at least," they shot back, "you have to let us smoke!"

"The fuck," said Fergy under his breath.

Darkness came with the low clouds and rains. Everywhere you could hear the sound of water running, off the roofs, off the folds of the leaves, along the curbs and gutters, in the dark chambers of the storm drains. Smells of weeds and fallen fruits, pulped and slick under foot, hung in the air. The embassy was under lockdown, but even for the fighters in the streets there was nothing to do but retreat to the eaves and wait.

Even the mortars stopped. Fergy found himself back at the cafeteria with the press, grabbing a quick mug of coffee. The CNN reporter cornered him. Breathlessly he said he had secured an interview with Liberian Defense Minister Chea, but he and the crew needed an escort downtown and he wanted Fergy to help. Fergy shrugged and put in calls to the Defense Attaché and the Regional Security Office, figuring he would be turned down. To his surprise, he was told he could go.

Downtown was left to the ghosts. Bodies lay everywhere, on the curbs, on the gravel and dirt in the traffic islands, or slumped against walls, a sheen of the rainwater like enamel on their flesh. It did not have the look of executions, but of people who had been struck with stray rounds and dropped in place. Living people were nowhere to be seen, save the gaps between the buildings where Fergy could make out the slender figures and the ember-like tips of the cigarettes and blunts in the shadows.

The Minister was not around when they arrived at the Ministry, nor were there any uniformed soldiers, only a couple hundred militia who were none too happy at the sight of the white embassy sports utility vehicle pulling up in the rain, which forced them to be alert. The CNN reporter phoned the Defense Minister, who said he had just given an interview by phone to the studio in Atlanta. The reporter pushed back and the Minister reconsidered, so the CNN crew set up at entrance and recorded bits for the B-roll.

Daniel Chea showed up in fatigues with a pick-up full of fighters. Fergy stood off to the side as the interview went down, keeping an eye on the militia who milled about with incurious expressions. Then he heard his name called. "Hey Fergy, you scared?" the Defense Minister shouted over to him. "Why you hiding behind your car? Come over here and shake my hand." Fergy looked at him and smirked.

"Man, you're a marked man. I don't want to stand next to you."

They both laughed as Fergy walked up to him.

"You're scared," Chea said, "you're wearing a bulletproof vest."

Fergy slapped the Minister's belly.

"You got yours on too."

"Yep," laughed Chea. Then the Defense Minister turned to face the militia and started to clap and stomp his black boots. Throaty voices followed his lead, whooping and hollering, and the chant grew louder and stronger until, at the peak, Chea punched the air with his fists, ducked into his pick-up, and drove off. The boys kept chanting until the car was out of view, then everyone stopped, turned away, and fired up spliffs. Several wandered up to Fergy and asked him if he had any cash, so he knew it was time to go.

On the drive back, on Broad Street, Fergy spotted a dead man on the sidewalk. The man had a full beard that seemed to tremble as they rolled past. It was flies. They picked the lower part of face apart down to the mandible, and Fergy caught the briefest glimpse of bone as the swarm rose at the rumble of the car then settled again. Moments later, a sharp hiss cut through the air, like someone tore a sheet of fabric. Fifty yards away, a concrete wall exploded, leaving a hole and crooked orange fingers of rebar. It was unmistakably a rocket-propelled grenade, and, just as unmistakably, it had been aimed at them. No other cars were on the street and no other people. It was Fergy's third close call of the war, and he tensed up badly, well aware he had pushed his luck.

Fifty-eight high-tailed it back to the embassy.

The shelling of the American embassy made news back home. In Crawford, Texas, at the dry, dusty ranch where the hot winds carried the smells of sage-brush and cow dung and where the leader of the free world spent his vacations, and sometimes hosted distinguished guests, President Bush fielded a question during a joint press conference with Italian Prime Minister Silvio Berlusconi. The event took place in a spacious, under-lit garage, or warehouse, and the reporters were roped off about fifteen feet from the two rostrums. "We're concerned about our people in Liberia," President Bush said, speaking in front of a flag stand, blue curtains, and an oblong seal that said "The Western White House."

"We'll continue," he said, "to monitor the situation very closely. We're working with the United Nations to affect policy necessary to get the cease-fire back in place. We're working with ECOWAS to determine when they will be prepared to move in peacekeeper troops that I have said we'll be willing to help move in to Liberia."

Elsewhere, in Washington, at the Noon Briefing, Deputy State Department Spokesperson Phil Reeker called out the rebels amid detailed remarks that mentioned, among other things, that the Secretary was closely following the situation. He demurred on whether the specific strikes on the embassy compound had been launched by LURD, but he made it clear that they were under intense scrutiny. "You know," he said, "mortar fire comes from a long distance away, but certainly we have seen this reckless and indiscriminate shelling that has been carried out by the LURD group, that is the Liberians United for Reconciliation and Democracy, and we think that has got to stop. There is a ceasefire that needs to be upheld and all of the parties in Liberia have responsibilities to see that that happens in the interest of the future of Liberia as well as the immediate safety of the Liberian people in Monrovia and those that are there to help them."

In Monrovia, the Executive Mansion wasn't exactly sympathetic. National Security Advisor J.T. Richardson said he did not think the attack on the embassy changed anything. "Washington still wanted Taylor to leave," he said. "If I had any doubts before, it was clear you guys supported the rebels. You know them very well and so you let them put on their show." That the embassy had been struck with mortars did not change his opinion. "Okay," he shrugged, "so the embassy was in the path. Okay, so it was hit with mortars. But you know how many glasses my houseboy breaks?"

He laughed cynically.

"I don't pay him," he said, "to break those glasses."

The Regional Security Officer warned the Ambassador not to walk down to his residence but if he had to, for any reason, to vary his times and routes. Certain exposed stretches could not be avoided. The Ambassador snuck in the trip more in the past few weeks than he had before, because it was really his only chance to get some fresh air and stretch his legs. At first he was not sure, but over time it was clear that the face of the wall by the tennis courts was peppered with bullet holes and he took the gradual accumulation of gashes and notches as a sort of a macabre calendar as the fighting dragged on.

It brought to mind a few bars from long ago basic training.

They made him a second lieutenant
They gave him two bars of gold
They made him a forward observer

He lived to be three seconds old

Pfft pfft. There was a hiss and a bang bang as a couple rounds struck chest-high a whitewashed retaining wall a foot or two in front of him. He ducked involuntarily, too late, and glanced around. Several high-rise tenements looked into the embassy grounds, but the shot could have come from anywhere, even the Ducor Hotel high up on Snapper Hill. For about a week the Chief of Mission Residence took rounds from different directions and the Marines stationed on the roof showed him the windows, cracks webbed around the small, clean holes. Captain Kuni told him that his men spotted a rifleman on a nearby balcony one day, cracked off a few rounds, and the guy never showed again. Except here was the Ambassador twenty yards from the nearest carport, the whiff of gunpowder in his nostrils, sweating, limping as fast as he could on a steel ankle to get to cover. So someone still had a sightline and was still bold enough to shoot.

He made it. It took a few minutes for the adrenaline to settle.

The Regional Security Officer was not happy when he called.

"Sir," he said, "let's make sure we're driving you next time."

28

ENDURANCE

Ted Collins now personally drove across the compound in the armored car to collect the Ambassador. He had to park along the side, by the beach, because they had not resolved the sniper problem. One morning, just as he stepped out, mortars shattered across the rocks by the seawall. As he scrambled for shelter, he spotted an Inter-Con guard on the catwalk, at his post, pressed flat to the ground in the push-up pose. He called to him to find cover, but the man shouted back "My post, sir, my post, I can't leave it."

Collins jogged gingerly down the rocky slope and grabbed the guard by the arm. He pointed to a concrete alcove at the back of the Chief of Mission Residence that could offer partial cover. "There, there," he shouted, "you can cover your post from there." Only then did the guard relent. They scrambled up the hill. Moments later a mortar struck the rocks within ten yards of the spot they just left. The guard saluted as he hunched under the little overhang and kept his eyes fixed on the perimeter wall.

As Collins walked made his way around the corner to the front door, he could not shake the guard from his mind. These guys, he thought, risked their lives every day. They knew that if they failed, the country failed. The bravery, the dedication, amazed him. In a crisis, you lived at the edge of your emotions. The Regional Security Officer was overcome. Sometimes you had to laugh, the things that happened were so absurd, and sometimes you just wanted to breakdown and cry.

The Ambassador watched through the kitchen window as the mortars hit the water. They dropped silently in the waves, erupting in huge plumes of white spray. He was on the phone with the Operations Center when the shells hit the front yard and he stumbled into the cabinet, then, back pressed to the wood, slid down to the floor and landed on his butt. "We heard that," said the alarmed officer on the other end of the line. The Ambassador tried to control the tremors in his voice: he did not want a report sent to principals that the embassy was trouble. The house shook again. China skittered across the shelves but Peter George and Saturday Gedeh, the residence staff, skated across the tiled floor and saved it with impossible ballet poses. They hurried into a safe room at the center of the house, where the Ambassador fell into a chair, and turned up the volume on his handset and listened. Marines counted the strikes. In the dining room, a couple bullets pierced the windows and spun on the parquet like dying bees. It was a terrible feeling to hold there with your local staff, in your rumpled suit, in the grey light, waiting for the next explosion and wondering if anyone else had been killed on your watch.

He was relieved when he heard Collins knock on the door.

The day brought heavy downpours. Firefights were woven into the rap of the rain sluicing down from the sky and battering the zinc roofs. The Ambassador raised the blinds in his office and looked out through the security grates and rubber trees at the relentless grey that erased the horizon, and knew that nothing could save the day. It was already half over and the government told the press that the body count in town already reached more than six hundred. His thoughts turned to his wife. Monrovia was four hours ahead of Washington and he knew she had already been at the office for a while. Since she too worked at the Department, the alerts from the Liberia task force would no doubt have hit her screen the moment she logged in.

He did not want Robin to worry any more than she already did, so he made it a practice not to talk through every up and down and she did not ask. They talked on the phone most every day, but they tried to keep it light: stories about the kids or Nixie the dog, or mundane things like bills and taxes. It helped him more than her, he guessed. There were times when he just needed to let her know that he was alright, or just let her know that he was thinking of her, which was another way of saying he did not want to feel so far away from the woman he loved. He typed out a quick email.

FROM: John Blaney

SENT: Tuesday, July 22, 2003 1:22 PM

TO: Robin Suppe-Blaney

SUBJ: Hello!

Just a quick note to let you know that I am okay and that I luv you.

me

The response came five minutes later.

FROM: Robin Suppe-Blaney

SENT: Tuesday, July 22, 2003 1:27 PM

TO: John Blaney

SUBJ: Re: Hello!

I LOVE YOU TOO! (Yes, I know that's shouting)

Robin

The lights in the office were off and he sat there a long time in the half-light, the lenses of his glasses blue with the luster of the reflection of the monitors. Rain tapped against the window in intricate patterns, like henna designs. A few hundred yards away in an overgrown compound, people were dying of cholera, dying of stray rounds. He had seen to it that money was released to the relief agencies, ensured they had access to the property, made the case for more resources, but nothing he could do at that moment could change the immediate reality. No one person could save Liberia. He had already done his part to try to head off the crisis. He had pushed Charles Taylor as hard as he could to negotiate with the rebels at a time when the government had the stronger hand, and now that the rebels were at Taylor's throat there was still no plan for a transition and it was awful.

He thought of his family and friends and colleagues and he knew that there would be no reproach from any quarter if he simply lowered the flag. He knew everyone on his staff had someone who was worried about them; he knew that in some respects it might be easier for some of the local staff and the guards to release them from their commitments and tell them to go look to their families and leave the embassy behind. He thought of how his own sister had to gloss the truth for their elderly mother even though she herself was worried sick. But then he thought about how he had responded when she wanted to know why he stayed. There had been no hesitation. His sister was an artist and he explained to her, you paint so beautifully, and this is what I do, diplomacy is to me what art is to you, and I need to stay here and do this.

The Ambassador knew that war was not a static condition: it was marked by extreme unpredictability, which is why it was sometimes described as a force that essentializes life. Under the stress of the mission, he had to remind himself that in daily life, in life without war, anything could happen at any time to anyone. But he also knew that people were not wired to live in a state of existential terror, so you get adept at pushing the thought of mortality from your mind. War forced you to confront it.

At the same time, because men make war, the act also reflected, however perversely, men's collective tendencies. Even in violence, he realized, men sought the routine, the familiar, which was why, in a drawn out conflict, there were bound to be long stretches that reverted to some sort of common rhythm, like the beats in a drum circle. Surprise might be the greatest tactical advantage, but once the fight was on, and the enemy engaged, both sides tended to wordlessly agree on times to attack and times to fallback, refit, and regroup, until the next surprise. Four days into the third attack, the Ambassador sensed that the Liberian war had fallen into such a rhythm.

In the street Jenkins told him that Liberians asked: "Who cook it and not done?" The meaning, roughly, was that the rebels controlled Bushrod Island but somehow could not take the city. Militia held strong at the Gabriel Tucker and the Old Bridge to Waterside. Somalia Drive, the eastern flank of Bushrod Island, was hotly contested, as rebels crossed and re-crossed Stockton Creek and met stiff resistance with every surge. But nor could Taylor's loyalists mount a sustained counterattack.

So it went, back and forth. Mortars at dawn, so regular Mike Mezaros tabbed them the "LURD alarm clock," followed by the mad cackle of automatic weapons and the wasp-like hiss of stray rounds. As the morning wore on, the Ambassador noticed, the mortars tapered off, the shooting came and went and thick clouds blotted out the sun. In the afternoon, hard rain palpitated on the roofs and swelled the pools in the cratered pavement. At dusk, the skies cleared briefly, as if to draw a last breath, before a crescendo of explosions chased the light away. Nighttime brought more rain and merciful silence, save the hoots and hollers of looters downtown, which the Ambassador could hear from his bedroom, or an occasional, bone-chilling scream that could only have meant a violent death.

Not unexpectedly, American network interest did not last. After the strike on the embassy, the reporters could squeeze only so much mileage from the set shots of themselves on the balcony with their backs to the sea. U.S. helicopters finally returned with the rest of the FAST and were able to evacuate a diminished pool of relief workers. After the near miss during the mortar attack a few days before, it was as anticlimactic as the HAST departure. The evacuees were tired and ready to go and everyone just hauled their bags down to the landing pad like tourists at the end of a long beach holiday looking forward to their own showers, beds, and pressed shirts. They boarded the helicopters without incident and flew off to Freetown. The embassy organized a separate convoy to Robertsfield for the network television reporters, who had arranged a charter flight, but most of the wire services decided to take their chances and simply went back to the hotel. The Ambassador did not like the thought of reporters still out in the streets but he, like his staff, was relieved to have the decks clear for the time being.

At the embassy, the Marines saw action. One FAST Marine was grazed by a bullet across the cheek and another struck in the helmet. The round circumnavigated the Kevlar shell and dropped out on the bridge of his nose. The Marine was amped when he passed around the helmet. Small black tears in the cloth cover looked like the mark of a kill shot.

In town, the body count steadily climbed. The great tragedy of the Liberian war, of nearly any war, was that non-combatants paid the steepest price. Each morning, when the fighting spiked, a locust cloud of brass and steel arced across the skies and dropped on the people, piercing the trees and roofs and tents. In Los Angeles, the gangs sometimes told the story that there were some bullets that just drifted through the air for as long as it took until they found someone to kill. In Liberia, it never took long. The shortwave radio in Jenkins' office broadcast each new horror: seven shredded by a mortar blast at Newport Junior High; four dead and fifty-five cut up by a shell at the Great Refuge Temple on Front Street; thirty to forty people winged by bullets every day at Greystone.

Magnus Wolf-Murray hired a hundred day laborers and sent them to the beach to fill old rice bags with sand then build a "wall of life" along the Greystone walkways so that people could take cover at the worst moments, but the neck-high pile of swollen white gunnysacks could only do so much. In the military, the term "sniper" denoted a person with a highly specialized skill set, so nobody at the embassy wanted to make the case that snipers targeted Greystone. Hersh Hernandez and his Inter-Con team did not get hung up on the technicalities. They knew that not all of the rounds were strays: too many people had been hit. It was said that militia took pot shots at the compound from the haunted window lights of the Ducor Hotel, maybe to remind the people that the Americans could not protect them, maybe just for the thrill of watching someone die. Kaetu Smith went to the far corner of the compound, close to Benson Street, and climbed the rusted ladder of the water tower. At the pad at the base of the tower he lay flat and pulled out his binoculars. On the ridge of Snapper Hill he spotted a man with a rifle in the saddle of a tree. He wore a local military uniform. The Inter-Con guard watched helplessly as the man peered through the scope of the rifle at Greystone and pulled the trigger. That's what he was doing. Every time the shots passed, Kaetu heard the sound.

"It's a different kind of scream," Hersh said, "when someone gets hit."

29

RECONSTRUCTION

Nearly any forward deployed unit in a war will at times find itself unable to advance without decisions and support from command. You can only go so far on your own. The Ambassador knew that, for the moment, his mission could do little more than protect itself. Others, elsewhere, would have to advance the peace process.

In the U.S. federal government, in general, policy and resources flowed from a scrum of meetings and paperwork known to those inside the Beltway as the "interagency process," which was basically the way different parts of the government tried to find common ground and collaborate. To most the words were synonymous with "bureaucracy" or "quagmire," though to anyone not familiar with the way the federal government operated it would more aptly have been described by one word, spoken in derision: "Washington."

In a crisis, the Ambassador knew, the process tended to be more focused, driven by the White House through the National Security Council, or by the State Department or the Defense Department, but that often meant that even more people were added to the mix. Where only a few people worked the Liberia account a few months before the siege, now hundreds, if not thousands, had something to say about it. Their activity was replicated in other capitals and international institutions the world over and the bureaucratic machinery ground on until collectively, somehow, a rough consensus emerged about how to help Liberia and who would pay for it.

The first concrete evidence that high-level diplomacy would pay off came on a rainy Friday in late July, when word reached Monrovia that the Economic Community of West African States announced it would send 3,250 peacekeepers to Liberia. The name for the operation would be the ECOWAS Mission in Liberia, or "ECOMIL." Nigeria agreed to contribute the lead battalions, 1,300 troops in all, and the first battalion was to slide over from Freetown, where it deployed under United Nations authorities. A second battalion would be sent sometime afterward. It was welcome news, but it caught the Ambassador's eye that the timetable was unclear. Nigerian President Obasanjo also caveated that the peacekeepers could not deploy without a "complete cessation of hostilities." In Monrovia, it was hard to fathom how that condition could be met.

Still, the Ambassador had more signs that help was on the way. In Washington, the White House announced that President Bush directed Defense Secretary Rumsfeld to position "appropriate military capabilities" off the Liberian coast to support the deployment of the ECOMIL peacekeepers. The United States' military role, it was underscored, would be "limited in time and scope," giving way to United Nations peacekeepers in the not-to-distant future. The State Department separately granted Pacific Architects and Engineers, a logistics contractor, ten million dollars to provide the West African troops with transport, equipment, and communications as needed.

The prospect of U.S. engagement kept Liberia current and questions popped up at the oddest moments, the Ambassador noticed. The same day Nigeria announced its troop contributions, President Bush held a joint press conference with the Palestinian Prime Minister at the Rose Garden. The two leaders stood behind a single lectern with the presidential seal and two microphones and each read prepared remarks on the Middle East peace process. When the President opened the lawn to questions, Liberia came up first. The President answered with his hands for added emphasis. "We're deeply concerned," he said, "that the condition of the Liberian people is getting worse, and worse and worse. Aid can't get to the people. We're worried about the outbreak of disease. And so our commitment is to enable ECOWAS to go in. And the Pentagon will make it clear over time what that means."

He glanced down a moment, but clearly knew his points.

"Secondly, it's very important for Charles Taylor to leave the country. Third, in order to expedite aid and help, in order to make the conditions such that NGOs can do what they want to do, which is to help people from suffering, a cease-fire must be in place. And finally, we're working very closely with the United Nations. They will be responsible for developing a political solution and they will be responsible for relieving the U.S. troops in short order. And so we're working all of these pieces right now… But today I did order for our military, in limited numbers, to head into the area to help prepare ECOWAS's arrival, to relieve human suffering."

Shortly afterward, Colonel Sandusky and Fergy briefed the Ambassador that the President's order triggered a cascade of plans and actions. The U.S. European Command directed the Southern European Task Force, SETAF, to stand up a "Joint Task Force" for Liberia with the express objectives to help ECOMIL deploy and to prevent a humanitarian catastrophe by creating a secure environment for relief organizations to do their work. "JTF" was a term for a force that drew assets from more than one branch of the military for a specific, limited mission. Joint task forces did not stand up too often, but, when they did, requests for forces were issued to the different parts of the armed services who controlled the required assets. The Defense Secretary cut the orders. For Joint Task Force Liberia, all four branches pitched in. The Navy and the Marines provided the bulk of forces and equipment via the three ships of the Iwo Jima Amphibious Readiness Group and the embarked 26th Marine Expeditionary Unit. But the 3rd Air Force's 398th Air Expeditionary Unit, U.S. Army Europe's 21st Theater Support Command, and Army Special Forces also supported. In short, Joint Task Force Liberia was certainly not on the scale of Multinational Forces Iraq, but nor was it a small operation.

Major General Thomas Turner headed the operation out of SETAF headquarters in Vicenza, Italy, but task force elements were to be deployed to Ghana, Sierra Leone, Senegal, and Nigeria and other West African countries. As the first order of business, SETAF dispatched a small liaison team to Ghana to, as it was reported in the press, "interface with the ECOWAS political and military leadership and to conduct a handover from Special Operations Command Europe, who had initial responsibility for a potential noncombatant evacuation operation in Liberia." According to the Army, the liaison team provided the JTF commander with situational awareness about the West African plans for deployment and mission execution. Logistics were also part of the process, involving close coordination with ECOWAS, the United Nations, and Pacific Architects & Engineers. Separately, Major General Turner created a "forward coordination element," to work with Ambassador Blaney and the country team in Liberia. The Forward Coordination Element brought together SETAF command staff, Marines and operations, logistics and communications personnel.

They would be SETAF's "eyes on" in Liberia.

As he monitored the uptick in international diplomatic and military efforts to save Liberia, the Ambassador took stock. Smart guys played chess while everyone else played checkers went the old trope. The chess pieces had finally aligned and coordination between the United States, Nigeria, Ghana, the United Nations, and ECOWAS moved at nearly unmatched pace, especially considering how many entities were involved, of such size and complexity, with so many overlapping authorities. He knew it had taken far longer to field peacekeepers in Bosnia, or Sudan, or nearly everywhere else. So yeah, John Blaney thought, finally he could see some progress. It did not mean peace was at hand and that he was ready to stop drinking the Buitenverwachting Christine.

In Liberia, in real time, the chess game did not matter. The way the Ambassador saw it, the fighters still played checkers. If you were at the wrong end of a bayonet, or in the path of the shrapnel or brass rounds, you were stacked with the other chips and taken off the board. The Ambassador stifled his frustration. He wanted badly to stop the killing and he was acutely aware of the limitations of his authority. Tactical patience could not save lives today, but he had no choice but to wait. Blood would run. He had to keep his focus on the lives that could be saved in the future. The embassy had to stay open to provide an in country diplomatic platform for the peacekeepers. But he did not know, realistically, how much longer he could hold out. Every day was worse.

Despite the moves from ECOWAS and the United Nations, the news from the peace talks in Accra was not encouraging. The Liberian sides would meet, talk, then walk away. In the abstract the issues were complex and important, things that took time to sort: who would succeed as president, when new elections could be held, who would be eligible to run for office. Absent a war, it was understandable they could not be resolved quickly. But there was a war and every delay, every bit of posturing, cost lives.

The Ambassador reviewed his choice to stay or go daily, even hourly at times. The embassy lost another guard, capped in the back of the skull at Greystone. The Ambassador took the report like he had been struck across the cheek with the back of a hand. It was a visceral reaction. He saw men faint before, long ago, when he was in the military, and there was something deeply unsettling about the sight of an adult dropping wordlessly to the ground. He could picture the guard at his post, black cap low on his brow, then, suddenly, falling to the pavement and that awful delay until the pool of blood appeared.

There were moments now when there was no one to call, no questions to be answered or reports to be received, and he just leaned back in his chair and stared at the cheap, round, butt-ugly black and white federal wall clocks, and thought that if they could just make it another day, or hold out another couple of hours, things might start to improve. On the phone with the Operations Center or in front of his staff he stayed calm, upbeat even, but, left alone, his apprehensions returned. They were one very bad moment away from mission failure. He tried to take the long view, but patience was not his strong suit. The embassy, he knew, had to move forward and advance an agenda, not just endure, if they were somehow to emerge from all this.

The embassy was under lock-down. The Regional Security Officer would only let a few people pass into the streets, for discrete missions. Fergy made it out from time to time, but even he was under restrictions, able only every now and then to head down to the Mamba Point Hotel or find his way to the flat of his friend Ziad Sankari, the Lebanese Consul who was as overworked as he was trying to meet the needs of the hundreds of Lebanese expatriates trying to hold on through the war.

The USAID Country Director was often called to the executive suite, mostly as a sounding board but sometimes, Ed Birgells suspected, because the Ambassador simply wanted the company. One day, when the mortars hit so hard he could not find the time to walk the fifteen yards back to his office, and he loitered in the hallway between Post One and the Regional Security Office transfixed by all the men in uniform calling this person or that, pointing to maps and grids plastered across tables, and otherwise looking busy, even though, at the moment, there was not a damn thing they could do about the bursts of shrapnel that kept them as penned in as he was, Birgells was told that the Ambassador had asked him to come upstairs as soon as possible.

"Whaddya need, sir," he bellowed as he walked in unannounced. Birgells did not care much for protocol and certainly did not suffer fools, but he was also old-school in his respect for hierarchy so he rarely addressed the Ambassador without sticking a inserting a "sir" somewhere into the sentence.

It also helped that he liked the guy and respected what he was trying to do. The Ambassador, for his part, knew that Birgells did not fit the model of people from his agency, who generally disliked bluster but were far more defensive about their work, and he thought Birgells was the perfect match for his team. The man knew how to get things done that squared with mission objectives. As soon as Birgells showed up he logged off, walked around his desk, and took up his usual seat on the divan.

"How did the call go?" he asked.

The day before the Ambassador asked Birgells to sit in on an interagency conference call with Washington, the purpose of which was to determine how much funding Uncle Sam would steer toward Liberia and what would be done with it. The call had been total chaos. No one could agree on anything. Everyone talked over each other and as soon as someone said something, others would immediately start shouting down the person.

The Ambassador shook his head but not in surprise.

"We need a post-conflict strategy for Liberia," he said.

"Yessir," said Birgells. He liked it. It was a gutsy call given the intensity of the fight and the gridlock at the peace talks, and given that the international response, though shaping up, was still hypothetical. He shifted his weight, pulled a notepad from his pocket, looked around, and swiped a pencil from the desk. Then he jotted some notes.

"If we get peacekeepers," the Ambassador said, "they cannot operate in a vacuum. We are going to need a robust disarmament, demobilization, rehabilitation, and reintegration package for the ex-fighters. Something that takes them off the battlefield for good and gives them a stake in, let's call it, the 'New Liberia.' If we don't give these tens of thousands of child fighters some sort of alternative to war, they will be right back at it. We also need a strategy for getting the country back on its feet economically. And I want Treasury advisors in here too, because they can't keep running this place on suitcases of cash."

Birgells wrote so fast the lead broke.

"They screwed up DDRR here last time and it came back to bite them. I want a serious education component here. The fighters need to be able to go to school, to try to help them become productive citizens again. There's a whole generation of kids here who know only war and refugee camps. Now we might see all sorts of calls for a truth and reconciliation commission and the like and that is for Liberians themselves to work out. But there is no economy here. We need to help them create jobs, keep the kids busy until the idea of picking up a gun starts to become a less normal response to everything. I'm thinking of work programs like the old Civilian Conservation Corps, where kids learn some discipline and teamwork while also rebuilding the national infrastructure."

Birgells peered at the Ambassador over his reading glasses.

"Write up the strategy and we can cable it in through State."

"Yessir," Birgells said. "How much should we be budgeting?"

Ambassador Blaney paused and thought awhile, running numbers.

"How about a hundred million dollars," he said, still mulling it.

Birgells nodded again. It was a nice round number. The Ambassador thought about it some more and openly wondered about the disparity between what was being spent in Iraq and the money pegged, annually, for all of Africa. The Iraq money was not in the budget and the administration was prepping an eighty-seven billion dollar supplemental request to Congress to fund the war effort. In that context, a hundred million dollars to help fix Liberia, if peace ever came, would be a drop in the bucket.

"Let's go for two hundred million," the Ambassador said, slapping his knee.

"Two hundred million it is," Birgells said.

He stood up and left the office to go plan.

30

NO MONKEY, NO DOG

ews that West African peacekeepers had been identified and committed and would be supported by the United States military did not produce any happy crowds at the gates. Throughout Monrovia, everyone just tried to stay alive. The hail of gunfire continued apace. Canvas cots sagged with the sick and injured lined the halls of the hospital. Doctors and nurses labored in overheated operating theaters, without fans, cutting brass and shrapnel from flesh and bone. They worked as quickly as they could, round the clock, but still more came. It got so bad they made a clear plastic bin the size of a city trashcan and tossed the bullets in. It was half full after only a few days.

Downtown was still deserted. Gaunt, vagrant militia boys wandered from hollow to hollow. Red was the color of the season, as ochre tresses and scarlet bandanas were all the rage among the killers. Militia battlewagons careered through the alleys, nothing more than tin can sedans with the doors stripped or overfull pickups, battered and painted with crude tiger stripes. A few trucks had sandbags and heavy machineguns mounted badly on the roof, and Jenkins saw one drive past the embassy gates with a human skull for a hood ornament. The atmosphere was, as *Irish Times* and *Independent* reporter Declan Walsh put it, like of one of those cheap arcade games where you drive around in a crappy car, at high speeds, and bad guys popped out of deserted alleys and side streets.

Foreign correspondents were undeterred. They made daily pilgrimages to the front to report the latest outrage. At Waterside, where the Old Bridge crossed to Bushrod Island, they picked their way through the filth and rubbish and caught up with the militia, the teenagers and children who defended the city from teenagers and children across the waters. The first time Declan made it down there he copped to his own fears. Automatic weapons could be heard throughout the empty market. In abandoned shops and stalls, he came across young fighters loitering in the shadows. Most were weirdly relaxed. They smoked marijuana and fiddled with their guns. From time to time, as if on impulse, they dashed into the street, onto the bridge, and danced a jig to mock someone on the far side. They sprayed their weapons until the clips were spent and ran back to shelter.

That, Declan realized, was why people were dying on Bushrod Island, and in Greystone, and outside the Mamba Point Hotel. The fighters held their machine guns at their hips, or sideways over their heads. The burst of rounds flew into the neighborhoods, lashing the innocent, as unavoidable as sand in a squall. It was as much a farce as a war. Agence France-Presse's Emmanuel Goujon said when he saw the child fighters at play he realized he had no power. As a journalist, he said, his only role was to address some concerns, to witness, to share what he saw. He filmed the scrawny boys sprinting to the bridge, shooting and dancing, shooting and dancing. But as he filmed, his attention was on his craft and his own survival. He was aware of every movement. Only later, he said, when he looked at his footage, did he realize what he had captured. It was totally irrational. He could not make sense of it.

The rains were relentless but the city went thirsty. Monrovia relied on a network of private wells for potable water and most were now inaccessible or contaminated with shit and poisons and parts of bodies. In better times, the White Plains pump station to the northeast, by the Saint Paul River, channeled water to a gantry on Bushrod Island. Tankers carried the water to homes and businesses throughout the city while a water main supplied the island. Soon after the start of the third attack, White Plains flooded and the pumps shorted out. The mainline ran dry. Deep Well One, a European Union-administered bore hole several miles to the southeast of downtown, was now the only source of water for wide-scale distribution. Unfortunately, someone had to drive the tankers through town, fill them, return safely, and distribute the water. Even if they could get through the checkpoints, the shelling too often prevented them from moving out.

The job of marshaling the effort often fell to the European Commission's David Parker, his deputy Jean Chahine, their friend Bob Khoureiy, and their local drivers. Bob, a Lebanese expatriate, found himself involved with the relief effort simply because they needed a hand. Sallow and taciturn, with furtive eyes, Bob managed the family business, a print shop that printed all of the city newspapers on an old German press, and was usually good for a few hands of poker on his off-nights. The business was shuttered for now, so he answered when his friends called and asked for his help.

"It makes the time pass," he said, sort of joking.

They hauled water to every major concentration of displaced people, wherever Merlin or the International Committee of the Red Cross or anyone else had set up water bladders. They had all lived in Liberia long enough to believe they knew enough faces around town, even among the militia, that they could talk their way out of any jam. Familiarity did not shield them from stray rounds, or shrapnel, or the fickle moods of the children at the checkpoints. In the street outside Greystone, they hooked a hose from the tanker to the nozzle of an old pipe, set up during another crisis, and waited for the cisterns to fill, crouching behind the tires of the rig as the bullets smacked the pavement, leaving small, lethal chalk marks. They had no other protection. "People need water," Jean Cahine said. "They come to you. What else can you do?" He knew water tankers made for big targets, but he shrugged it off. "You have to be brave sometimes," he said. "Either brave or crazy, but you have to do it."

At the embassy, strict conservation measures were implemented. The Ambassador bathed in the water from his de-humidifier. It worked well enough, he convinced himself, as he squatted in the tub and scooped soft water from the plastic tray with a coffee mug. Except the water was soft and it was difficult to rinse away all the soap. When he finished, he just dumped the rest of the tray over his head. Outside the gates, a daily trail of women and children from the Masonic Temple and Greystone paraded down the hill to carry plastic pails and yellow jerry cans to a small natural spring that bubbled from the ground in a vacant lot between the Mamba Point Hotel and the south gate of the embassy, on a rocky slope strewn with rubbish and overgrown with weeds and stunted banana trees. They risked the hail of gunfire to fill the containers and haul the water back to their shelters to drink and cook and wash. Some people brought soap with them for a quick bath. Privacy was not an option, so men and women just stripped and scrubbed down in front of one another. They called it "Adam and Eve," after the first garden, where there was no shame.

Jenkins had lived the hunger before. He took small comfort knowing that his mother and siblings were safe, but as he watched small kids slip out of Greystone at dawn to try to hustle for food he was drawn back again to the night, thirteen years before, that his aunty and uncle pressed some cash into his hand and asked him to try to reach Kakata, where they heard the markets were open, and bring back supplies. They had been holed up in the house in Gardnersville for weeks on end and, though they had the money, the streets were too dangerous to buy food. Ribs started to show.

Jenkins hid the cash in the waist of his jeans. He had lost fifty pounds already and it was hard to tell he was carrying anything at all. In the streets bodies lay everywhere and the bandana pressed to his nose could not keep him from inhaling the stench. He found a pickup headed north, paid for the ride, and managed the first day to make it about fifteen miles, to Fendell, to the campus of the University of Liberia Science College. Checkpoints had been set up every mile or two, it seemed, and the rebels who manned them demanded to be called "freedom fighters." Anyone who hesitated was deemed an "enemy of the revolution" and detained. At Fendell, a hundred thousand displaced persons were massed at the campus. People were being taken away and shot. It was like hell.

At Kakata, the market serviced fighters, smugglers, and camp followers. Jenkins bought cassava, plantains, sugar cane, avocados, and some greens and fruits, enough to fill a gunny sack that he tossed over his broad shoulders like a peddler. He caught another pickup headed back to the capital, paid the tithe, and made it home the same day. The wife of a rebel commander owned the truck and they were waved through the checkpoints with little trouble. When he arrived at the house, the door was cracked opened and he entered to find clothes strewn everywhere. His aunt, uncle, and cousins were gone. They had to be dead. It was the lowest moment of his life: eighteen years old and alone in the city that had taken those he loved. He kicked aside his sack of food, fell to his knees, and wept. He did not know what to do. He knew only he had to find a way out.

In a place where rifle and machete rule, the easy thing to do is embrace a binary world of wolves and sheep, and join a pack. Sometimes there is no choice: you are taken. For youth there is always the allure of power and of being part of something larger than yourself. It is the tinder of rebellion and terrorism. The first kill must be the hardest: after that it is just work. The surprise is not that so many do such evil, but that so many do not. For Jenkins, it never entered his mind to pick up a weapon.

Thirteen years on, the capital again under siege, Jenkins ran across a boy the spitting image of himself. Francis Gallo used to come out for football and kick around with the men. His mother told him to go to Greystone, to build a thing to live there. He argued that the situation there was not preferable, that anything could drop there, but she had told him no, the Americans had a deflector in that place, so you can go there, and nothing will happen. So he left his family and went to Greystone.

Inside, he heard a sound in the trees. Then it blasted. He ran under a concrete roof. A second mortar landed. He decided to run, away from the compound, out of Greystone, but a friend called him: "Come back! They're still launching. You can't go." Just as he was about to run again, the thing landed, and he saw a woman with a baby. The thing tore the woman's stomach. The baby never died. The baby was crying, and the mother died. And he saw another girl, with her head split. He didn't believe it; it was like a dream to him when he saw it. When the shells stopped, he ran from Greystone, and his mother saw him, and cried, "O, it was in Greystone."

"I told you Greystone was not safe," he said.

She said it was true, what he was saying. So they went to the Wellington flats, a tenement down the street. Inside, people were suffering from the heat. Some people were dying from cholera. Some were sitting there crying from bullets, because they couldn't go to the clinic. There were twenty or twenty-five people to a room. Every time there was a launch, people would leave the rooms and crowd into the stairwells. They would sit out the fighting there, and then go out for rice. Francis' mother gave him money. Sometimes the launching started again while he was out.

Then there would be running here and there, here and there.

At night, sometimes, the Anti-Terrorist Units tried to recruit him, but they didn't get him. He and his friends sat by the road, and the soldiers came by in a car and jumped down and chased them. One night, they caught him, and started carrying him off, but one of the soldiers recognized him, and said "I know this guy. He is not a fighter. All he does is play soccer and go to school."

So through God he escaped.

Just as Jenkins once escaped.

The World Food Program food stocks were warehoused at the Free Port. This was the rice, maize, and bulgar wheat that the relief agencies relied on to feed the hundreds of thousands of displaced people. With port inaccessible beyond the front, they had nothing to distribute. Malnourishment rates spiked and people started to starve. Far from the city, in the direction of the airport, miles beyond the range of the mortars, markets were open and the staples of potato greens and cassava were readily available to anyone who could afford them. But the banks were closed, out of cash, and the money transfer offices shut, so the usual remittances from abroad stopped as soon as prices jumped.

Fergy had predicted it. After the first attack, he negotiated a fair price with the traders and stockpiled rice for the local staff, which the embassy now sold to them at cost. At eighteen dollars per bag, it was a fifth of the going rate on the street. Distributions took place twice a week in a covered arcade at the consular outbuilding. Staff hauled the sacks back to their offices and tried to figure out how to take them home without getting robbed. Word got out that the embassy had rice and on distribution days crowds massed at the gates to wait for family members or to see if they could catch sight of someone they knew. When the guards peeled back the razor wire, supplicants pressed forward. In among the crowds, militia boys eyed every transaction. If they spied someone carrying something, they stalked him or her up the street and pried it away at gunpoint. Satan, a local commander, beat people with a stick and threatened to storm the embassy.

Jenkins parceled out his allotment in sandwich bags to his one brother who had stayed behind to keep an eye on the family house. From Gardnersville, the boy was forced to walk "around the world" to reach the embassy, a circuitous route to avoid the firefights at Bushrod Island that took him many miles through Red Light, ELWA, Congo Town, and Sinkor. They disguised the rice as much as possible, strapping the bags to his waist, as Jenkins himself once hid cash on his trip to Kakata. He wore loose clothing with deep pockets, so no one would suspect him.

Not everyone had a brother in the embassy. Families grew faint with hunger and the bellies of the small children bloated. Rumors made the rounds that on Bushrod Island the rebels broke into the World Food Program warehouses and meted out rice to the locals. Men and women from government-held areas began to make their way to Bushrod via Stockton Creek, risking their lives in the treacherous and disorienting mangrove swamps. "Scratch Water

Crossing" was what they called the trek, Jenkins was told, because the channels were polluted and the abrasive grasses and mangroves left hideous rashes on those who survived. Many lost their way and drowned. For fifty Liberty some people put their fate in the hands of wild-haired men with machetes who claimed they knew the way through and how to avoid the militia and the rebel scouts. But when they reached the Free Port, the rebels grabbed them anyway.

"Any monkey?" the rebels called out.

If you were with Taylor, you were "monkey."

"No monkey!" the people shouted.

The rebels stared at them to make sure.

"Any dog?" the rebels called out again.

"No dog!"

If anyone hesitated, he was pulled aside.

"Anybody know this guy here?" the rebels said.

If no one spoke up, they led the man away.

31

THE PRESS CONFERENCE

Bracing rain battered the city. The Atlantic tossed against the shoals. Lightning played hop-scotch along the dark horizon. Bursting rain-drops left a low halo of mist over the grass and pavement. The embassy grounds sank beneath torrents of water so deep you had to set out blocks and planks just to walk anywhere. Everywhere you could hear the sound of water moving through the land and at times it seemed as if the entire city rested on a porous matt of dirt, sand, and clay and was about ready to slip off the bedrock, into the sea, to be crushed by the undertow or dragged out with the riptides.

It was Liberia's national day, but there would be no celebrations this year, so it seemed to the Ambassador as good a day as any to hold a press conference. The fighters on both sides of the Mesurado had yet to rouse themselves from their wet shacks and venture into the rain to shoot at each other. Hardly any shells fell on Mamba Point. At the embassy, in the consular waiting room, overhead fluorescents cast the white shine of supermarket aisles across the tidy rows of plastic bucket seats. Local staff shuffled in with an easel, flip chart, and wooden podium, which they set down with a rough, hollow thud. A short time afterward, the room filled with the squeak of rubber boots and the rustle of slickers as a passel of reporters arrived. Writers plopped unceremoniously into the front row and conversed with one another or jotted notes on rain-softened pads. Behind them, television crews erected tripods and fiddled with the lenses. Everything smelled of wet cotton, like gym clothes that had been left in a locker too long.

In red magic marker on the flip chart someone had sketched a crude map of greater Monrovia, including the Cape, the Mesurado River, Bushrod Island, the Saint Paul River, and, farther north, along the road to Kle Junction, the Po River. It was July 27, eight days into World War III, the siege of Monrovia, and it was a Sunday, though by now the date and days of the week seemed irrelevant as the hash marks of life.

Twenty-four hours earlier, the Ambassador huddled with his staff in his office. "Our problem," he has said, "is the front lines of this war run right through heart of the city. That's an impossible situation for peacekeepers. You can't keep the peace, if we get one, with fighters on both sides stacked on top of each other like this. Even if you get a ceasefire, one yahoo can end it. And both sides can take pot shots at the peacekeepers." Which happened the last time ECOWAS sent peacekeepers, Colonel Sandusky balefully pointed out. "Right," the Ambassador said, "The West Africans can easily be drawn into this conflict just by defending themselves. We have to find some way to separate the rebels from Taylor's forces. And the humanitarian agencies need access to the port."

"Just ask them to pull back," the Political Officer said.

The Ambassador cocked his head and looked at him.

"You can do it, as the United States Ambassador."

The Ambassador, seated on his customary divan, folded his hands. Charles Taylor would probably agree to a local ceasefire, he speculated aloud, but it couldn't be unilateral. They still had no contact with the rebel commanders on Bushrod Island. He made the point that the commanders had to buy into any ceasefire or it would fall apart, no matter what their political masters said. Not that they said anything productive. For the better part of a week, he had been told, Washington tried to pressure the rebels through its team in Ghana and its embassies in neighboring Guinea and Sierra Leone, where rebel leaders cropped up now and again, but to no avail. Despite public protestations to the contrary, rebel leaders appeared to be indifferent to the situation in Monrovia. Just a few days before, during some of the heaviest shelling, one of their negotiators granted a television interview. The man sat by the hibiscus bushes and the blue tile pool at a four star hotel in Ghana, sipping cocktails. Over his shoulder, a voluptuous brunette woman in a tight black bikini spread out her beach towel and dipped her painted toenails in the sparkling water, seemingly unaware of the cameras a few yards away. On a split screen, while the rebel jawed and smiled, the editors looped images of Liberians mourning their dead.

"You could call them out publicly," the Political Officer said.

Enough international reporters were still in Monrovia. If a press conference were convened, the Ambassador could use it to put pressure on both sides. His voice would carry extra weight because of the unique status of his office in Liberia. Judicious words now could send a powerful message to the rebel field commanders and serve as the opening salvo to get diplomacy back on track on the ground, in Monrovia.

The Ambassador mulled it over, lost in thought.

This, he confessed, was very high-risk stuff. If he went forward with it, he would place part of America's reputation on the line by saying what had to happen, without any prior communication with the rebel commanders. It would be different than anything he'd ever tried before. This wouldn't be the same as talking to military generals about a ceasefire. He wasn't talking to General anybody, because he couldn't.

He considered not doing it. "Look," he said, when he had a moment to reflect, "it wasn't what I had learned. This was not what I had done for years. My whole career had dealt with private diplomatic contacts. You prepared the groundwork, you made prior contact. If I did this in public, the LURD might come back and say 'Hell no.' That could ruin the embassy's credibility as a mediator." But he went ahead with it.

"Frankly," he reasoned, "we have no other choice right now."

Within minutes he was on the horn with the Liberian Defense Minister. "What if LURD pulls back to the Saint Paul River Bridge?" he asked. "What do you think? Would Taylor accept that?" Defense Minister Chea pointed out that the Saint Paul River, the northern boundary of Bushrod Island, was part of Monrovia. It was within mortar range for large swaths of the city. He said that the June 17 ceasefire agreement, admittedly now just a fiction, but still the operative document for the start of political transition, stated that the rebels should pull back to Tubmanburg, Bomi Hills, the base from which they launched their offensive. Or at least Kle Junction, thirty-six miles from the capital.

The Ambassador told him he doubted the rebels would agree to that. Surveying his map of Liberia, he suggested the Po River, a thread of water strangled by bamboo groves well north of Bushrod Island, but closer than Kle Junction. There was nothing at the Po save a small bridge, but it was an obvious natural boundary. "I think President Taylor would agree to the Po," Chea said. Afterward, the Ambassador turned to his team.

"I don't care how, but we need a way to reach the rebels."

The Ambassador arrived in the company of an embassy staffer holding a paisley umbrella. Cheeks rosy with the oxygen-rich air, he disappeared behind the podium with his statement, then looked around with a thin smile at the bedraggled reporters as though he was pleased with the change of scenery. Washington had given him the green light to hold the conference and he spoke confidently, backed by the full authority of his title and the United States seal. He delivered the message in his usual no-nonsense style.

First he laid the groundwork for his proposal by underscoring U.S. support for West African peacekeepers and by alluding to the impending arrival of U.S. warships off the coast. He cited President Taylor's own statement that he would leave. Then he cut to the chase. "I now ask," he said, "both LURD and the Government of Liberia to cease fire and to use the Po River as the new demarcation line between their forces."

The cameras whirred, the reporters scratched out their notes.

"This new demarcation line," the Ambassador said, "will leave Kle Junction, an important supply route, entirely in the hands of the LURD and will require LURD to make only a partial withdrawal from its recent gains. The Government of Liberia has said that its forces will not pursue LURD as they withdraw to the other side of the Po River." He motioned to the flip chart, indicating the boundaries of his proposed local ceasefire. Resolve stiffened the timbre of his voice. "The LURD," he said, "needs to accept this proposal to show that they have regard for the people of Liberia, that they are not indifferent to the great human suffering that is taking place here."

With that, the embassy was front and center for the diplomacy.

Within a few hours, the rain let up and the fighting resumed. The Ambassador's press conference did not grab any headlines, but the story flooded the wires. The press generally reserved judgment, but no sooner had a few shells fallen than Reuters announced "Liberian Rebels Reject U.S. Calls to Withdraw," while an Agence-France Presse banner proclaimed "Liberian rebels step up attack on capital, turn down U.S. offer."

Read closely, though, most of the articles included a crucial statement by LURD Chairman Sekou Conneh. In pronounced contrast to the LURD's July 11 press release that threatened to attack *any* peacekeepers, Sekou Conneh told the press by telephone that "We agree to fall back, but we want peacekeepers to come. We don't want to hand the port over to Charles Taylor." It was a start. The rebels accepted in principal that they would not control the capital after Taylor left, if he left.

The Ambassador was confident he had positioned the embassy to broker the safe deployment of West African peacekeepers, and any United States troops that might support them. He set forth in public the parameters of what needed to happen on the ground: the rebels had to leave Bushrod Island, head to the Po, and humanitarian aid would resume fully. But international peacekeepers would have to fill in behind the withdrawing rebel forces. If Taylor's men rushed into the vacuum, all bets were off. Unfortunately, peacekeeping forces were still not ready. From New York to Vicenza to Accra, ECOWAS, the United Nations and the U.S. military were negotiating budgets, logistics, and troop contributions.

Discussion shifted to possible implementation.

Reports trickled in to the Ambassador and his team that small steps had been taken toward a new ceasefire. U.S. African Affairs Deputy Assistant Secretary, Ambassador Pamela Bridgewater, on assignment in West Africa, hammered home the Po River proposal in meetings with rebel negotiators. Two days later, on Tuesday, July 29, rebel negotiator Kabineh Janneh suddenly announced in Ghana that LURD rebels would initiate a unilateral ceasefire. "The information about the ceasefire was delivered to our forces at six o'clock," he told the press with some assurance. "We will pull our forces from the front line and we will remain at Monrovia's port pending the arrival of peacekeepers."

Only, it was not quite so clear.

"I gave the order today to my troops to cease fire in Monrovia for humanitarian reasons," LURD Chairman Sekou Conneh confirmed, with a caveat. "Our unilateral ceasefire will be effective only when Taylor will stop attacking us. He is still trying to cross the bridges by force," Conneh said. So the fight continued. For Ambassador Blaney, the critical question was whether the rebel negotiators were on the same page as their commanders in the field. For his part, Sekou Conneh said that he knew the Ambassador wanted peace and didn't want casualties, and he understood the diplomat's role and the need to handle it at the combatant level. But, he insisted, based on past experience, LURD had every reason to doubt Charles Taylor. He told his men to maintain their positions.

"If Taylor does not cooperate," he ordered, "continue to advance."

32

MODEL

I t had become practice for the people in the embassy whose job it was to know what was happening in Liberia, people like the Regional Security Officer or the Political Officer, to stop by the Defense Attaché's Office late in the evening and compare notes with Colonel Sandusky. She could most often be found behind a parapet of papers on her desk, bent like a bent nail over her keyboard, her thin features grim and drawn as she rapped out reports with the fervor of a concert pianist. To the extent she slept, she bunked on her office sofa, a hard black vinyl piece upon which a wool blanket was scrunched at one end like a bird's nest. Nearby, on the floor next to the glass-top coffee table covered with glossy military magazines and gun catalogues, could be found a cardboard box of meals-ready-to-eat with its flaps roughly sawed open by a Leatherman.

Colonel Sandusky spent much of her day liaising with the ECOMIL team and in contact with Liberian commanders to ensure she had the latest reports from the front for her briefings with the Ambassador. In gaps between the firefights she often had Fergy drive her down to the Ministry of Defense where the disinterested guards stepped aside and let her tramp up a concrete stairwell lit with rain light to find the Defense Minister, who was often in combat fatigues, often on his mobile phone, talking to the press or barking orders at someone, pacing around his office. Chea had a husky voice made huskier still by sleepless nights moving through the city to buck up the troops or hand out provisions, and it did not help that he had four or five phones and took every call. So the Colonel was a bit concerned when, one day, one entire day, she could not reach him at all.

The Colonel heard the sound of a knock at her door, which was open, muttered something at her screen, hit the "print" key, swiveled in her chair and handed the Political Officer a few sheets of paper. She said, "Try this." A few minutes passed as he read her latest report. Her level of detail, coupled with analysis, was breathtaking. He pitied the staff at SETAF or wherever that would have to break it into bullet points when they passed it up the chain. He handed the pages back to her with a nod and she scanned the text with pursed lips, as though dissatisfied. She looked ready to break out a red pen.

"The Ambassador and I haven't been able to reach Daniel Chea," the Political Officer said. Colonel Sandusky ran her hand through her white hair. It was hard to tell whether she were more bothered that, as a Defense Attaché, she could not reach the senior military official in the country for however long, or simply that the man had disappeared while the city was under siege. Restlessly she picked up her Thuraya, scrolled to Chea's number, and waited. As if on cue, she got through. She held her free hand over her opposite ear as if she could not hear him clearly.

They talked briefly. "He said he's in Buchanan," she said when the call ended. The Political Officer looked at her quizzically. Cataracts in the road would be treacherous now, after weeks of rain, meaning the eighty-six mile drive southeast from Monrovia to Liberia's second largest town would take at least four hours. Daniel Chea was not a foot soldier like Benjamin Yeaten or Roland Duo, so did not necessarily have to be at the front lines at all time, but most of Charles Taylor's Cabinet at one time or another strapped pistols to their hips and circulated with the militia, and it was obviously an inopportune moment to step away from the city. Colonel Sandusky frowned.

"He said he's visiting his mother."

Quality time with family was important, on that they agreed, but the real story was that the MODEL rebels were on the move in the southeast, and Buchanan, Liberia's second largest city, was about to fall. The house of the mother of the Liberian Defense Minister was in the path of the advance and Chea had taken steps to protect his family, but he was, he admitted, pessimistic that the government could hold the city much longer. Militia and government troops lacked the resources or desire to hold fast. They knew also that the defense of Monrovia was the main effort.

After he had been briefed, the Ambassador was disappointed but not surprised. Every time diplomacy made incremental progress, it seemed, setbacks were dealt. For two months, the LURD rebels grabbed the headlines, now MODEL wanted attention too. He had tried to head it off a few days before. He had taken a call from a MODEL leader in Philadelphia, of all places, and the man ranted that MODEL might be "forced" to attack Taylor's defenses in the southeast. The Ambassador urged the husky voice on the other end of the line to negotiate at the peace talks and not exacerbate the crisis. He knew that Buchanan would probably be attacked no matter what he said, but he also knew if he stayed silent it might be taken as an invitation. So he tried to convince the man to hold off. For his efforts, he was treated to an invective-laced tirade against Charles Taylor, a litany of the many wrong-doings. From that the Ambassador guessed that MODEL did not want LURD to hold all the cards at the peace talks.

No less alarming, he reflected, was the thought that it was possible to run a West African insurgency from Philadelphia. Apparently all it took was tortured rhetoric, a few wire transfers, and a web site or two. Twenty-five bucks and a couple Kalashnikovs could start a war. At least Mike Mezaros saw the humor. He said when he first came to Liberia on temporary duty, back in the nineties, he befriended several members of one of the factions. Years later, safely back in Washington, he received a call from one of them who announced happily that he had bought a condominium in Mike's neighborhood. "It's kind of fun to get to know everybody over here," Meszaros said, "but *jeeze*, it's another thing to have a real live warlord living down the block from you!"

The problem, the Ambassador reminded his security team, was that if Buchanan fell, nothing more than fifty miles of very bad road lay between the rebels and Robertsfield. Tactically, they all knew if the rebels seized the airport they would cut off the most obvious exit route for Charles Taylor, even if he really did vacate his office. If their goal was to put his head on a pike, the march north would be the logical next move. That, in turn, would complicate the peace process. It was hard to envision landing heavy, slow C-130s with rebel rifles and rocket-propelled grenades trained on the airstrip. If MODEL controlled Robertsfield, peacekeepers might not be able to deploy.

The last Tuesday in July the Ambassador received word that MODEL took Buchanan after no more than a day or two of skirmishes. Later that day it was reported that Gbarnga fell too, to the LURD rebels, which meant the half of greater Monrovia and a wedge of beach southeast of the city was about all the territory the government could be said to control. Across town, the war effort soured, Charles Taylor held court with the press. In an interview with *Newsweek*, he dispensed his patented equivocations. He said, "I'm going to step down, hopefully… We'll begin the process of my transition, to wherever I'm supposed to go, *if* I'm supposed to go. Do I leave office as a free man or with the indictment over me? These are political decisions that have to be taken."

Nigerian President Obasanjo's offer of safe haven still stood, as far as the Ambassador could tell, but everyone knew it did not resolve the Liberian president's troubles with the Special Court for Sierra Leone. Charles Taylor's confidants still insisted he would rather die fighting than face trial for atrocities that occurred in a war in another country. They did not think he would leave Liberia without an amnesty deal, and he seemed to confirm as much. President Taylor told *Newsweek*, "Once I'm stripped away from my supporters I'm standing in left field alone. Somebody thinks I'm going to go out there where I'm exposed to the elements. That's not going to happen. Now is the time to sit down and get involved in some hard negotiations."

Advisors considered Taylor's defiant streak a source of strength. Maritime Commissioner Benoni Urey said, "Even in the face of the greatest danger, Taylor impresses to you that all is well, like nothing bothers him. And he always gives you hope. Like, 'Don't worry, man, it will be alright.'" But, Urey conceded, "If you get too carried away with believing in Taylor, it becomes dangerous to your own security. Because the man has guts. Nothing really moves him. I say, 'My man, nothing really moves you?' And Taylor replies, 'Man was made to die.'" Still, the new parlor game in town was to guess the end. Rumors of all sorts of nefarious schemes reached the embassy team. Taylor would take to the bush to fight on, some said. Or get cash and weapons from Libya and other old patrons and counterattack to devastating effect. Or take the Nigerian offer, or accept some other secret handshake, and jet off to freedom and comfortable retirement. None of the theories were entirely implausible, but each reflected a growing sense that change was in the air.

Negotiators at the peace talks, the Ambassador learned, had started to talk as if Taylor's days in Liberia were numbered, one way or the other. It still did not generate much momentum. Draft peace agreements circulated, but the sticking point was who would take over when Taylor stepped down, or was forced from power. It was not a minor detail. Who got to run the country was, in fact, the point of the entire war. The government argued that any peace agreement should follow constitutional strictures, which meant the vice president should be sworn in should the president resign. Negotiators proposed to keep a rump administration in place until credible national elections could be organized, which everyone knew might take years. To the rebels, it smacked of a way to allow Taylor to pull the strings from afar. Vice President Blah was not known as a vocal leader and they believed that Taylor would direct him from exile. Both rebel factions rejected the proposal out of hand. If Moses Blah became president, they let it be known, the war would not end.

Even with Liberia's political transition up in the air, military planning for the peacekeeping operation proceeded apace. The Joint Task Force Forward Coordination Element slipped into embassy Monrovia with a seven-man team led by Lieutenant Colonel John Del Colliano, Executive Officer of the 26th Marine Expeditionary Unit. The MEU had most recently seen action in Iraq, but Del Colliano, a twenty year veteran, had been just about everywhere else too, even Somalia. He had been there in the early nineties when the Marines escorted the food convoys with gun ships to try to protect them from marauding clans until they became targets themselves. He was with the teams that extracted the last U.S. forces soon after the Blackhawks went down. It had been chaos.

If he had any scars, they did not show. In fact, it would have been hard to sketch a better Marine right down to the shaved head, severe brow, and granite stare. He strode bolt upright along the walls to look over the embassy perimeter defenses, never flinching as stray rounds cracked overhead. As for what he saw in the streets, militia slinking back from the front with soiled bandages, sunken chests and jaundiced eyes, or bodies covered in mango leaves carted past in wheelbarrows, he spoke with professional detachment. "You could," he said, "just look around and know that this was a troubled place."

The Ambassador viewed the arrival of the Forward Coordination Element as an important step forward and directed his staff to lend whatever support it could to the team, scaring up cars, cots, and computers. Del Colliano set up in the Regional Security Officer's shop and space was cleared in the political section for Major Mike Shinners, a young Army officer tasked with relaying reports from the field back to the ships of the Amphibious Readiness Group and SETAF headquarters in Vicenza. The team had not been on the ground more than an hour or two when they found themselves in the executive suites receiving a briefing from the Ambassador.

Del Colliano and Shinners listened attentively, their trained poker faces unable to suppress mild surprise as the Ambassador outlined his proposal to the LURD rebels to withdraw from Bushrod Island. SETAF had planned for two contingencies: support ECOMIL and evacuate the embassy. Having focused primarily on the evacuation, Shinners admitted he had expected the Ambassador to say, "Okay, you finally got here, now please evacuate us." In the wake of the Ambassador's briefing, he realized that the embassy would take it as a failure of diplomacy to close down. Or, as Del Colliano deadpanned, "It seemed the evacuation piece was not something the Ambassador was willing to do."

The Ambassador was pleased they understood his game plan. Simply put, President Bush had made a decision to help Liberia, and the Ambassador viewed it as the embassy's job to implement that policy. The Ambassador knew that he still faced malicious compliance from certain quarters: narrow interpretations of the decision. He fretted openly that the mandate to support ECOMIL might be diluted, so that the willing and capable sailors and soldiers who showed up at the embassy might be handcuffed. At the same time, he was proud to have highly trained professionals on deck and was impressed with their adaptability and flexibility. "Every wave of military support," he told his team, "begins the same way: 'Let's prepare evacuation plans!' But then I talk to them, explain what we're trying to accomplish, and they realize that evacuating the embassy is a dead-ender. Then they know they need to get on with the real mission. And they do."

They were still a long way from anything like success, but stepping back from the Washington infighting, the sequence of military moves in the offing was the best response possible for this kind of crisis, even though it had been ad hoc. If you were to plan U.S. participation in an international humanitarian intervention in the abstract, the Ambassador supposed, you would have wanted a team to conduct civilian evacuations, a team to secure the embassy, and a team to help prepare and secure aid delivery. You would have wanted a joint task force to marshal assets and, for maximum international credibility, you would have leveraged regional players for both troops (ECOMIL) and diplomacy (ECOWAS), before giving way to the economies of scale and sustainability of a robust United Nations operation. He wasn't happy about how it had gone down, not at all, but it really did not matter what contortions that they had gone through to get to this point.

The resources teed up were about as good as it got.

33

THE FORCE COMMANDER'S

RECCE

The press provided a breakthrough. The Political Officer was on the phone with a foreign correspondent a couple days after the Ambassador's press conference, trying to convince her that the diplomacy was lurching forward even if the effects were not yet readily apparent in the streets. She said she was not sure the rebels saw it the way the embassy did. He asked with whom she had been speaking and she said she had come across the numbers for a couple of the LURD field commanders on Bushrod Island. Apparently they were now on the Lonestar network, having grabbed their share of phones and scratch cards during the attack. "Oh," he said casually, "We've been in touch with them too, but I haven't been able to get through today. What numbers you have?"

No need to admit the embassy was still in the dark.

Suspicion passed through her tone like a fleeting shadow. "I can give you a contact," she said, "but I would ask…" She let her voice trail off. It was a war where the reporters were all staying together at the same hotel and often piled into the same taxi, talked through security together, helped each other out, but they were still each looking for their ledes and scoops, and contacts mattered. "Don't worry," the Political Officer replied, "We won't pass it around to the rest of the press corps." He scribbled the digits on the back of an envelope. As soon as the call ended, he punched in the number. Long rings went unanswered but, on the second attempt, a husky voice jumped through the receiver.

"Who's there?"

The Political Officer identified himself.

"Hello Mr. Political Officer. Pleased to meet you."

"I'm looking for the LURD."

"This is Alhaji Sekou Fofana."

"Yes, are you with the rebels?"

Fofana answered cautiously.

"I'm Deputy Secretary General for Civil Administration, L-U-R-D."

"Mr. Fofana, our Ambassador is trying to reach you guys."

"Well," Fofana said, as if pleased, "we're happy to talk to him."

More pieces fell into place. On the last day of July, in Accra, Ghana, an Extraordinary Summit of ECOWAS Heads of State and Government convened. The guest list provided a powerful statement of West Africa's commitment to ending the Liberian crisis. In attendance were the presidents of Ghana, Nigeria, and Togo, joined by ECOWAS Executive Secretary Chambas, International Contact Group for Liberia Co-Chair Akufo-Addo, Nigerian General Abubakar, who was the official mediator of the Liberian peace talks, and U.S. Assistant Secretary of State for African Affairs Kansteiner. ECOWAS decided to dispatch promptly to Monrovia a delegation of the Foreign Ministers of Ghana, Nigeria, Togo, along with Executive Secretary Chambas, to arrange for President Taylor to hand over power and depart Liberia. Noting that Taylor said he welcomed international peacekeepers and that LURD pledged publicly to hand the Free Port over to peacekeepers, ECOWAS called for the establishment of transitional national government in Liberia once ECOMIL peacekeepers deployed and Charles Taylor departed. They left it to the Liberian negotiators at the peace talks to sort out the details of the transitional government and appoint an interim head of state.

Evidence that ECOWAS had made good on its pledge of peacekeepers appeared in the Monrovia at the end of the week in the person of Nigerian Brigadier General Festus Okonkwo, the ECOMIL Force Commander, who flew into Robertsfield with a ten-person reconnaissance team. "For weeks," the Ambassador said, "the question has been: are we going to hold the bridge, or have we gone a bridge too far? If you look at it like a military man," and he liked to remind that he was once a military man, "this is the first genuine sign of relief. We no longer have to hold the bridge alone."

Robert Azemard, the Ambassador's driver, had not had much to do over the past several months. He detailed the car regularly, dutifully logged the short trips from the Chancery to the Residence and kept the gas and oil topped off, but much of the time he napped on a chair in the carport or, when mortars or bullets or rain kept him under cover, he stood by patiently in a small waiting room or sometimes joked with the Marines at the command post they had set up in the house. So he was surprised as anyone when, during a sustained mortar attack, he took a call from the Ambassador, who told him to have the car ready. Five minutes later the Ambassador, in an excitable state, showed up with the Assistant Regional Security Officer, and together they hopped into the armored car and had Robert drive them thirty-five miles southeast to Robertsfield.

On his return, a couple hours later, the rosy-cheeked Ambassador grinned like a schoolboy who just played hooky as he recounted how he had hurried out onto the dark runway and caught up with the Nigerian general amid a crowd of photographers, confused airport officials and well-wishers. Smartly dressed in a black beret and forest green fatigues, the General towered over the Ambassador. "I was so happy to see him," the Ambassador confessed, "I thought about hugging him." Photographic records reflected dazed smiles and a handshake in the white light of the flashes.

At news of ECOMIL, Lebanese traders in Liberia began to bet heavily that the peacekeeping operation would move forward. It was high risk, high reward. The Royal Hotel in Sinkor, somewhat removed from the front, reopened its doors just in time for the Force Commander's "recce." What it lacked in ocean view it made up for in ambiance, with arched doorways, arabesque lamps, and a well-stocked bar. The entrepreneurial gambit paid off. The ECOMIL team overnighted there and not a few journalists checked in.

The next morning the ECOMIL team met with Liberian military staff, toured JFK Hospital, and stopped by the Ghanaian embassy, only to find the gates locked, doors bolted, and windows shuttered. They had no contact with the rebels. It was like any other formal military exchange, they thought, until they passed through downtown. By the time they made it to the U.S. embassy for a meeting with the Ambassador, the West African officers looked, for the most part, unsettled by what they had seen.

Heat seemed to follow them into the chancery. Damp in their berets, heavy olive green fatigues, and black boots, they marveled at how empty and ruined the capital looked. The Chief of Staff, Ghanaian Colonel Theophilus Tawiah, confided that his first thoughts were that ECOMIL would not be able to keep to the timelines they had set for themselves. They talked about deploying on Friday, August 15, more than a fortnight away, but it occurred to him they might be asked to come sooner. It was clearly an urgent crisis. He was not sure whether either Taylor's forces or the rebels would accept that. He was not even sure who controlled Monrovia. When ECOMIL came with troops, he worried aloud, it could be to fight for the city.

General Okonkwo settled comfortably into a leather chair beside the Ambassador and folded his hands in his lap. Fifty-two years old, with flat, untroubled features, dark, distant eyes, and a quiet voice, Okonkwo proved a reassuring figure. Before he was tapped for the assignment, he had been Principal Staff Officer for the Nigerian Armed Forces Command and Staff College, in Jaji, Nigeria. It was not a combat role, but he had been in the Nigerian military for thirty years and this is not his first time in Liberia. In the mid-nineties, he had been the Ground Task Force Commander for ECOMOG. Back then, he recalled, he witnessed terrible things. They often awoke to severed heads on pikes outside their camp. From what he had seen so far, this iteration of the Liberian war was "not as terrible as before." This time, he felt, ECOWAS was also better prepared.

With ECOMOG, back in the day, he recalled there had been scant planning. West African troops were dispatched on a moment's notice, without proper equipment or training or logistical support. Reconnaissance had not been conducted. Now, General Okonkwo smiled, ECOWAS had different capabilities. Three days ago, the day of the Ambassador's press conference, ECOMIL had held a planning session in Accra, Ghana, where they met with the U.S. Ambassador to Ghana, U.S. Major General Thomas Turner, and a number of other officers from Joint Task Force Liberia and the United Nations. General Okonkwo understood from that session that the United States would help ECOMIL secure the Free Port, when the time came. Now, with his recce in progress, the Force Commander could see firsthand the challenges he faced, identify barracks for troops, and smooth the way with the Liberian government for the ECOMIL deployment. He would have to land his first battalion at Roberts International Airport, which was still squarely within territory still held by Taylor's forces, unless MODEL attacked.

Colonel Tawiah recounted the ECOMIL planning session with a good-natured laugh. The Colonel had soft features and a lovely smile and he tended to wrinkle his nose when amused. He wrinkled his nose and said that he had just met Okonkwo for the first time a half hour before the planning session. When everyone else showed up, they heard that the Force Commander should present his plan for the ECOMIL operation. "We had no idea," he confessed, "what was really happening in Liberia. But everyone asked that we go and present a plan." Luckily, he said, some United Nations staff officers had worked on something. ECOMIL modified and adopted it, briefed with a director of intelligence, and hashed out a concept of operations.

Their main objective, they told their U.S. counterparts, would be to secure the Free Port of Monrovia for humanitarian aid and hold their ground until United Nations peacekeepers could come to relieve them. The key would be to have enough troops in place to secure Robertsfield and central Monrovia, a thirty-five mile strip of territory, before moving to the port. They decided they would deploy one Nigerian battalion from the United Nations Mission in Sierra Leone as soon as possible, since they had been told the United Nations could release the battalion. A second Nigerian battalion trained in Nigeria by the United States would follow soon after. Subsequently, other West African nations would contribute troops, once identified by a team, supported by the United States, that traveled from country to country to assess capacity and capabilities.

After General Okonkwo presented the plan, General Turner had asked where the United States could assist. The ECOMIL staff learned the United States would lend officers to help with logistics, operations, administration, and planning. The Nigeria general officer was pleased. West African teaching, he said with a wry smile, was quite different from the American system. "Americans go into details on everything," he laughed, "but we don't, because the equipment is usually unavailable to meet such planning. But we added what we felt we needed and our plan was accepted."

A Force Commander's reconnaissance was also suggested. West African capitals expressed serious reservations about sending an ECOMIL recce into Liberia without any sort of ceasefire in place. But, General Okonkwo heard through his own channels, Nigeria's leaders were worried about the rising death toll in Monrovia. Nigerian President Obasanjo was not prepared to wait any longer. If they delayed ECOMIL, Okonkwo heard, the situation might deteriorate further and, in the end, ECOWAS might decide not to send the ground troops after all. His recce was green-lighted.

In his office, the Ambassador spread his trusty concessionaires map on the coffee table and placed pencils and stone paperweights off to the side to indicate the Saint Paul River, the Po River, Kle Junction, and Bomi Hills. Index fingers pressed white against the soft paper and hardwood beneath, he demonstrated the proximity of the front lines to the embassy and showed how the city was split.

"LURD," he said, "controls Bushrod Island, including the port. Someone has to convince them to leave, to put some degree of separation between themselves and Taylor's forces. It will be very hard right now for ECOMIL to interpose itself between the two sides. They are right on top of each other. I've asked the rebels to pull back as far as the Po River. If they do, your forces will have to deploy in the vacuum they leave behind, as a buffer, or Taylor's militia will just walk in and claim victory." Studious expressions on the African faces indicated the Ambassador had their attention. Measured in tone, he laid out the stakes without preempting any military decisions. "The country's food and fuel stocks are at the port." he said. "We're basically out of food on this side of the river and thousands of people are starting to starve. Bushrod Island is the key to everything."

It was important, the Ambassador stressed, for the peacekeepers to contact the rebel commanders directly, in addition to the government, not just rely on the statements of rebel political leaders in Guinea and Ghana. "You must be seen as neutral," he said, "and you can use our embassy as a diplomatic shield for contacts on both sides." General Okonkwo nodded slowly. "Diplomatic shield" resonated with him.

"Does the embassy have a way to reach the rebels?" he asked.

"Why yes," the Ambassador said, "I've spoken to Cobra myself."

General Okonkwo folded his arms as if impressed. His phone rang in his breast pocket. Holding a hand up in apology, he took the call. The ECOWAS Extraordinary Summit in Ghana had just concluded. His recce was recalled. ECOMIL troops, he learned, had been instructed to deploy on Monday, August 4, in four days' time, more than two weeks earlier than expected. With a burst of boots and chairs scuffing the carpet, the recce team stood en masse and readied to leave. The Ambassador jumped to General Okonkwo's side to escort him to the door. On the way out, he urged Okonkwo to leave at least one member behind in Monrovia to show continuity and General Okonkwo, who said he had the same thought, selected Colonel Tawiah. The Colonel readily accepted, though he confessed that he was still not convinced that the ECOMIL mission would be peaceful. But, he said later, "I realized, as we listened to Ambassador Blaney, that it might be possible to use diplomacy to achieve a lot of things."

That evening, at the Royal Hotel, General Okonkwo and his staff were deep into the lounge chairs when Colonel Sandusky appeared in the doorway, walked up to him, and handed him several phone numbers written on white scraps of paper torn from the pages of a common stationary pad. When General Okonkwo called the first one, he reached someone called Kamara, and Kamara said, "Okay, any time you are here, you should see us." The General said he was a bit relieved that he was able to talk to the rebels, so that it did not look like he thought that they were not important, or as if there were problems. It was good news for ECOMIL and for the embassy, too: both the government and the rebels were willing to meet with the peacekeepers. "Under ECOMOG," the General recollected with a grimace, "we weren't even allowed to enter Liberia."

In the wake of the Force Commander's recce, mortar attacks in the capital gradually abated. Heavy fighting continued at Stockton Creek, the eastern boundary of Bushrod Island, as LURD gained some ground along Somalia Drive. But downtown, for the first time in several weeks, nobody was shredded with exploding shells. Perhaps it was only coincidence, but, Jenkins heard, Mortar Papay had been killed.

Contacts told him that Mortar Papay had been executed by a rebel commander because he had killed too many civilians and was giving LURD a bad name. LURD Deputy Secretary General for Civil Administration Sekou Fofana confirmed the death later, saying that Mortar Papay had been "fired" by another rebel. "Yeah, man," Fofana said, gruffly, "Mortar Papay hit the guy with a wheelbarrow, and the guy happened to be armed, and he fired him. Mortar Papay died instantly. That's the story." Apparently the "firing" itself violated LURD "Standard Operating Procedures." When news of the incident reached General Cobra, he gathered the other rebel commanders on Bushrod Island. "Everyone agreed," Fofana said pointedly, "that, in order to avoid future 'confusions,' whereby people fire one another for one person's business, they needed to carry out what the Standard Operating Procedure said."

It was unclear whether the Standard Operating Procedure was a written document that the fighters carried into battle, or just a set of precepts that they all memorized. But apparently rules were rules. "That is," Fofana said, "if you kill willfully, be it soldier or civilian, without genuine reason, without trial, you will be killed. You fire somebody, we fire you. So this fellow who killed Mortar Papay was automatically executed. That quieted down the whole thing immediately. It was finished. And nothing bounced back."

As Monrovia settled into an uneasy stalemate, the Ambassador heard that high-level diplomacy made more progress. The United Nations Security Council passed a resolution, introduced by the U.S. mission in New York, that authorized the United Nations to deploy a peacekeeping operation to Liberia in the near future. The United Nations would take over from "the Multinational Force," which was ECOMIL and any United States support. It was exactly the mission the Ambassador had advocated and meant that Liberia had a clear path forward. "The Multinational Force," United Nations Ambassador John Negroponte told the press, "is a crucial short-term bridge to our goal of placing United Nations peacekeepers on the ground in Liberia as soon as possible... The Multinational Force can now deploy, confident of the support of the Council and the knowledge that planning for a follow-on United Nations peacekeeping force is underway."

He also explained the ECOMIL mission succinctly.

"Peacekeepers on the ground will secure the environment for the delivery of humanitarian assistance. Their presence will support the implementation of the June 17 ceasefire agreement... [and] safeguard security in the wake of Charles Taylor's departure from the Liberian presidency." Negroponte then reminded everyone of a key proviso. "I cannot emphasize how crucial it is for Charles Taylor to leave now."

That same day, the ECOWAS foreign ministers and Executive Secretary Chambas flew into Monrovia to meet with President Taylor, only to learn that the Head of State was not available. It is easy to disappear in Africa, but still surprising if you are the man of the moment. By one account, the delegation was told that Taylor was in Buchanan to rally his men. By another, they were told that Taylor was at White Flower, but delayed the audience because the ECOWAS team had not followed protocol. Most troublingly, there was the story that reached Karl Vick of *The Washington Post* that placed President Taylor on a plane in Ouagadougou, Burkina Faso, grounded by torrential rains, waiting to return from a secret trip to Libya to buy weapons in violation of United Nations sanctions.

"We will wait," Chambas told the press. Sure enough, the Liberian president resurfaced the next day. As the only ECOMIL representative in country, Colonel Tawiah accompanied the West African dignitaries to the Executive Mansion. Inside, he said, the talk was frank. They pointed out that President Taylor himself had insisted that if peacekeepers landed he would be ready to go. Well, they said, the peacekeepers had come, so he should go. Colonel Tawiah stood by quietly. It seemed President Taylor wanted some guarantees. First, he wanted the Foreign Ministers to intervene with the Special Court for Sierra Leone indictment. They replied that they had done all they could, but it didn't appear as if the United States and the United Kingdom were prepared to support such a move.

"Well," Taylor said, "if I have to go, I want to leave in dignity."

In Liberia, Tawiah noticed, even on the most vital decisions a tendency to focus on process could crop up. The Ministers' timeframe for Taylor's departure—immediately—was too short. Both Houses of the Liberian Legislature, President Taylor explained, had to go through the process of awarding the presidency to his vice president. He glossed the fact that nearly all members of the legislature were in exile. He said he wanted a big ceremony, because he would make a big sacrifice. He requested that a number of his fellow heads of state be on hand. And he wanted to leave Liberia a free man, free to return any day.

No guarantees were given. When the two-hour session disbanded, Taylor met with the press and announced that he would step down from office in nine days, on Monday, August 11. It was not exactly the ECOWAS timetable, but it was not too far off either. Reporters asked whether he would leave the country on the same day too and go into exile.

"I'm not," he replied coyly, "going to tell you right now."

Successful policy, really success in anything, demands that analysis and assumptions are constantly revisited in light of changed circumstances. The Ambassador long assumed President Taylor would not leave other than in a blaze of glory. Now he started to have some confidence that maybe Taylor really would just step down. He had spoken with members of Taylor's inner circle, who insisted it was a done deal.

Minister of State Jonathan Taylor said his uncle, the president, asked him to lay the groundwork for exile. Liberia was isolated as any country in the throes of a violent conflict, but it was still part of the fabric of West Africa and there were means to close the distances. Nigerian Foreign Minister Adeniji escorted Minister of State Taylor to Nigeria in a Falcon jet. They landed late at night and Jonathan Taylor was ferried in a black sedan to the villa of President Obasanjo. The Nigerian president was at a banquet.

Minister of State Taylor waited in a spacious living room the Nigerian Foreign Minister and the Governor of Calabar. When President Obasanjo turned up, near midnight, they spoke about the details of who might accompany Taylor into exile, what sort of security would be provided and so on. As discussions wound down, President Obasanjo pulled the Minister aside to deliver a message to his uncle. "Tell him," Minister Taylor heard, "we will try to do the best we can. I will not come to Liberia myself, but I will send my aircraft."

Minister Taylor nodded, but the Nigerian president had more.

"Tell my brother," he said, "that he must not change his mind."

PART SIX

FRONTLINE DIPLOMACY

"Reverie" (World Press Photo of the Year)

34

THE CROSSING

On Monday, August 4, exactly two months since the start of the Liberian peace talks and the public announcement by the Special Court for Sierra Leone of the indictment of Charles Taylor, Colonel Sandusky and Fergy stood on the tarmac and watched the first West African peacekeepers touched down at Robertsfield. After all they had been through, Fergy could hardly believe the day had arrived. Colonel Sandusky, as usual, had her mobile phone wedged between her cheek and shoulder as she talked to contacts and simultaneously scribbled notes in her green field pad. In all, just over 200 troops landed the first day, with nearly 600 more, plus several armored personnel carriers, due by the end of the week. President Taylor and the Liberian government kept their word and ECOMIL deployed without incident. A happy crowd of several hundred Liberians rushed the tarmac and foisted General Okonkwo onto their shoulders and danced and sang.

In Monrovia, at least in the government-held areas, the news was greeted widely with relief, even, it seemed, by Taylor's loyalists. To read the press, General Okonkwo and the 776 men of the first Nigerian battalion would have no trouble whatsoever securing the airport, the capital, and the thirty-five miles in between, let alone Bushrod Island and the Free Port. It would be, consensus said, an easy mission. To those charged with carrying out and supporting the mission, men and women like General Okonkwo and Colonel Sandusky, history strongly suggested otherwise. Local fighters had a poor track record of respecting the authority of international interventions, and if it were not enough to recall that peacekeeper blood had been spilled in Liberia in the recent past, you needed only to look next door to Sierra Leone, where just a few years earlier the very rebels said to be backed by Charles Taylor took more than 500 United Nations peacekeepers hostage. From a military planning standpoint, the risks to the West African force could hardly have been greater.

Nigerian troops had deployed amid two mercurial rebel armies and equally unpredictable government forces, with no local ceasefire in place. The single battalion had no heavy weapons, little in the way of transport, no headquarters, no barracks, and no fortified positions, yet they were expected to control thousands, maybe tens of thousands, of intoxicated and ill-disciplined fighters staggering around with Kalashnikovs, mortar tubes, and rocket-propelled grenades. Objectively, it was mad.

In Washington, these all represented sound reasons to not put more U.S. boots on the ground, though in Liberia itself people wondered why the Americans would let the West Africans do it all on their own. The United States, foreign correspondents were quick to point out, was missing a chance to play hero. Ambassador Blaney acknowledged the point and admitted he would have loved to see joint U.S.-ECOMIL patrols, but, he underscored, whenever the subject arose, he had never argued for U.S. troops. The policy was to support the West Africans to solve what was, at heart, a West African crisis and, as he saw it, to say that ECOWAS or ECOMIL could not handle it did not give due credit to their intensive, high-level diplomatic efforts or their military capabilities. Of course the peacekeeping troops lacked some logistical capacity, but that was precisely why the United States helped with planning and equipment, and three U.S. warships were en route.

At Greystone, strings of rain drifted from the low clouds and beaded on the cheeks and yellow slickers of the guards. Near the front gate, the black and yellow steel arm of the barrier gave way to the wet drive beneath the dark, somnolent canopy. When Ted Collins first arrived at post, the previous Ambassador let chickens run wild on the compound. He received them as gifts whenever he visited community projects and the chickens roosted on the barrier. When cars drove in, the arm lifted, and the fowl just slid down, crashing into one another in a billow of feathers and squawks. Collins always laughed when he recalled it. "At that point," he said, "I just knew something was wrong with this place."

The chickens were long gone. Acrid odors assaulted the nostrils, smoke, sweat, piss, and the rotten pulp of small fruits that fell from the trees and were stamped like dog shit into the rocks and flagstones. When Jenkins wandered over to check on things, he marveled that in just a few short weeks Greystone had become a barter town. Looted items were the currency. Children leaked into the alleys and returned with shower slippers or cloth, sold what they could and took the "small money" to their parents to buy bouillon cubes. Canteens opened along the main drive, places like Ma Fatu's and Jay Bon's, shanties with a few plastic seats and wooden stools that served "all throughout," until one in the morning, for anyone who could pony up a few Liberty. They ladled out thin pepper soup and "Cook Bowl," which meant anything cooked, a bit of rice with cassava leaves, potato greens, and bitter ball, the tart yellow eggplants grown in the bush.

Meat was scarce. Some resorted to "issue." "We don't call it dog," said Kaetu Smith, Inter-Con's Senior Local Guard Force Commander. "In Liberia, normally, when you eat dog, people tend to look at you so. Instead you say, 'O, I got the issue here-o.' So as soon as you say that, those that are eating dog will know straight that's dog you're selling." For the worst off, there was "bullet bounce," protein biscuits from the relief agencies that were so tough to break it was said even bullets would bounce off them. "When you eat them," Kaetu said, "you have to drink plenty water so the bullet keeps bouncing in your stomach." Many, Jenkins noticed, still could not afford anything. Along the walls of sandbags, pale and hungry faces sat listlessly on the curbs. They waited for food distributions while their children squatted in the mud and puddles, bellies poking from their grey shirts, snot crusted around their noses and vacant eyes. It was not the dramatic famine from desert climes that you sometimes saw on television, skeletal people collapsed in the dust under the thorn trees beside the desiccated corpses of their cattle. Instead, it was a slow rot and decay, like the rust and molds that softened the tin and cardboards of the bivouacs.

At night men got drunk and fought. Kaetu Smith tamped down the rowdiness. Sinewy and coiled tight as a grip-hoist cable, he had a steely gaze, sharp, angular features and, when he doffed his cap, a diamond-shaped patch of grey that suggested somehow that he had passed through dark times. The "Mayor of Greystone" was his informal title and he was both feared and respected by everyone for knocking heads to keep order. "Anytime day or night," he said, "they can call me to the gate or somewhere else to solve problems. Basically I correct people, put them outside the gates if they're stubborn or don't want to let the others rest. I enforce the rules. Especially 'no guns.'"

Jenkins was surprised to learn that militia often came by Greystone to rest or visit family. At the gates, they tried to intimidate the Inter-Con guards and sometimes threatened to kill them. Kaetu worked out a compromise. Weapons were stashed in a plastic bin when they entered, then retrieved when they left. Somehow it worked. "Now even LURD fighters come to Greystone," Kaetu noted with a shrug. "Some of them have family here too. You know, in our war sometimes we have brothers fighting against each other. Late at night, when they get tired, maybe they pay something small and come across the bridges. Sometimes they even bring rice."

That fighters could cross the front so easily told Jenkins there was fatigue on both sides. Front lines softened in places and the Liberian war seemed to turn into an elaborate kabuki drama, or else a theater of the absurd, albeit still lethal, with teenagers on the banks of the river still dancing and shooting until their puppet masters told them enough was enough. It was hard to know what either side was trying to accomplish and the rebels were inscrutable as ever. Jenkins was frustrated. It made no sense to him that people were still being killed, that, even with the lull, bodies were washing up on the shores. Like everyone he knew, he sensed the end was near, but nobody knew how to finish it.

The day the first ECOMIL peacekeepers landed at Robertsfield, Richard Butler, a freelance British photographer, called the U.S. embassy to say he had crossed the front lines. In a chipper voice he explained that he had negotiated with the militia and with the rebels on both sides of the Mesurado, then walked across the Old Bridge from Waterside to Bushrod Island. Everyone was perfectly civil to him, he said.

LURD Deputy Secretary General for Civil Administration Sekou Fofana corroborated the story. Embassy officers were now in contact with Fofana, but calling a rebel was tricky business. There was no manual for it. Neutral tone and language seemed the best course, especially in absence of any deep grasp of either cultural or linguistic context. Fofana was more personable than could be expected for someone who managed a siege of his own capital in the company of men who called themselves Cobra, Dragon Master, and Iron Jacket. It also helped that the rebels seemed to have a positive view of the United States and always took embassy calls. "Well," Fofana said, "I met the British man physically and we talked. Afterward, I put him in my car with the intention of escorting him back to the bridge. We went as far as the edge of the Old Bridge and the man said, 'Put me down, don't risk your life.' He told me that if by accident he was killed on Bushrod Island it would be blamed on LURD. So what was on my mind was that the man was more comfortable with us than with Charles Taylor's soldiers."

"So he walked back across the front lines?"

"Yes, I myself saw him walk back. Nobody fired."

In most conflicts, the reporters said, both sides are covered. In Liberia, only James Brabazon and Tim Hetherington, two British journalists, had traveled with the rebels in the past few months, and then only during the second attack. Very few others had ever spent time with them, although maybe a year before the siege Emmanuel Goujon of Agence-France Presse met them in the bush and got to know a few of their leaders. A tall, lean Frenchman with sallow skin the color of nicotine, dark eyes and a thick, black goatee, he chain smoked as each evening he rapped away at his laptop on the verandah of the Mamba Point Hotel. He was stuck on the government side of the Mesurado with the rest of the press, frustrated, to be sure, but resigned to the circumstances.

"Normally," he said, "when you cover civil wars like this, it is understood that one person can't cover both sides." It was a question of logistics and of basic security. If you reported from one side, he shrugged, the other side branded you as an enemy collaborator. He himself had run into trouble in the Congo. After he reported from rebel-held territories, he learned that he wouldn't be permitted to reenter Kinshasa. "They threatened to cut my hands, to cut my balls, or to shoot me," he said.

"I had many choices, but all of them were a kind of suffering."

In that context, Richard Butler's gambit created a stir at the Mamba Point and the Royal Hotel. Now all the journalists wanted to cross the front lines and interview the rebels. They had plotted it for days anyway. Many had never been to Bushrod Island, which, close as it was, seemed like a foreign country. With peacekeepers at the airport, they sensed change in the air. Firefights still peppered the days, civilians were still being killed, but the press found out that during lulls or after dark fighters from both sides had started to congregate in the middle of the bridges and smoke weed together.

Reporters called the U.S. embassy for an assessment, but the Ambassador told his team to reply in the only responsible way, which was to recommend that crossing the front lines should not be tried. The war was not over. There was no capacity to extract anyone. With so many militiamen around, in varied states of sleep deprivation and intoxication, it was easy to imagine an ill-timed rocket-propelled grenade sparking a pitched battle, with peacekeepers, relief workers and journalists caught in the middle. Plus, at any moment either side might make a new push. The embassy's counsel was taken under advisement and promptly ignored. A day after Butler's adventure, the Political Officer received a panicked call from a photographer at the river's edge: "Somini is trying to cross. She's with a couple others. It's insane. They negotiated with a couple stoned guys. They're shooting above their heads, they're almost shooting right at them." Nothing could be done.

It was not the first time the *New York Times* reporter had tried to cross. She had heard that the rebels had set up some kind of field hospital at the brewery on the north end of Bushrod Island and she wanted to report on it. So she went down to the beach, to the fishermen sitting by their wooden boats, to see if they would ferry her across the water. The fisherman stared at her. The hundred dollars she offered didn't move them. They said, "Are you out of your mind? We don't cross the river, because if we're seen coming back, Taylor's men will kill us." Undeterred, she called several LURD generals and won their approval. They were very friendly. "Yes," they said, "come on over."

She had better luck the second time. At Waterside, in the company of a *Financial Times* correspondent and several photographers, she walked over to some militia and asked if they would hold fire as she and her friends crossed the Old Bridge. "Yeah," they said, "it's almost a ceasefire now, it's all cool." One of the photographers wrapped a white tee shirt around a stick and waved it. Somini smiled. It was impressive, she thought, that at least one of them had the good sense to have a spare tee shirt in a camera bag.

War is remembered by the damage to things that have been built, but it leaves other marks on the land. Brass casings covered the Old Bridge, deep as a shag carpet. Ankles turned as the spent rounds wriggled underfoot with the empty sounds of small, broken bells. They could not take one step without rolling on them. Gunfire rattled somewhere nearby. It was a good thing, she told herself, that they were crossing the Old Bridge. It seemed as if the shots were coming from the Gabriel Tucker Bridge, further upstream.

The far side was completely deserted. "Hello," Somini yelled, "hello, are you there? We're journalists!" A man with shades appeared in an alley and motioned them forward. They could still hear gunshots and ducked behind a cement wall. Somini had no true point of contact. Someone who called himself "Dragon Master" had given her permission, but that was it. By phone he just said, "Come anytime." It wasn't much of a plan. At the time, she reasoned, somebody had to cross at some point. Bullets zipped past as the crouched by the wall. When she peeked into the street, she spotted corpses a few paces away. It was the closest she had ever been to dead bodies. An overpowering stench filled her nostrils. She could not look too closely, but one might have had its legs hacked off. She and her cohort made their way to the man in shades. Then it felt like a Mad Max tour of rebel land. They were led through the alleys by a bunch of drugged-out rebel gunmen, endless alleys, going back and forth, back and forth, through and through, with no idea where they were headed. She just said, "Take me to your leader, I've spoken to him on the phone."

A short time later, Declan Walsh made it down to Waterside, arriving about a half-hour after Massimo Alberizzi from *Corriere Della Sera,* an excitable Italian journalist, crossed the Old Bridge. Declan had been delayed scouring the Mamba Point Hotel for a flak jacket. He finally borrowed one from Reuters, who had a spare after a cameraman left. He felt guilty about taking someone else's protection, but they owed him a favor anyway, he reasoned, because they were in the room next to him and ran their fucking generator every day, right outside his window. At Waterside, the stalls were deserted. Garbage was piled in the streets like mounds of storm debris. The fighters were very agitated. One well-built young guy wore just a ragged tee shirt and sneakers. He raced around like a crazy man, pumping his rifle and shouting. It was, Declan thought, psychotic. The kid had a mad look in his eyes, drug-induced, where the pupils go small. A mad sparkle.

Fighters tried to bum cigarettes. Relationships between strangers in war are often transactional: Declan couldn't tell if the smiles were an act. They could turn on him in an instant, he guessed, and if they did no one could rein them in. He ran into Commander Cairo Poo Poo, a young man dressed in a black velvet jumpsuit. He asked about the name. "Cairo," Cairo Poo Poo said, "as in the city." And Poo Poo... Well, here the guy went into a fast rap and Declan couldn't write it all down, it went too fast, but the bottom line was, "You can smell me, but you can't dodge me." He told Cairo Poo Poo he would like cross the bridge to the rebel side. And he did not want to get shot on the way. Cairo Poo Poo assured him it would be okay, so Declan made his way to the rails. It was kind of like a bungee jump, once you took the first step, you just had to keep going.

He wore jeans and Bata boots and carried nothing more than a pocket-sized Canon and his black Kartasi notebook, the small notepad he brought with him from Nairobi. He was almost out of pens, which were oddly hard to come by, but he had one last ballpoint. Unfortunately, he had forgotten his glasses. The far side of the river was a blur. Out of nowhere, two local Médecins Sans Frontières staffers adopted him, waving an enormous white MSF flag. They told him they had been shuttling back and forth for hours and would escort him across. Banner raised high in the hot, heavy air, they made their way to Bushrod Island, where they were met by a grinning fighter, pants down by his knees, penis dangling. Several kids in wigs drove past in wrecked cars painted with crude tiger-stripes, screaming up and down, pulling hand-brake turns in the middle of the road.

The detritus of war was everywhere. Off to one side, Declan saw dead bodies. They had been stripped and, as far as he could tell, executed. Not knowing what to do and having no clear plan, he walked forward with the MSF volunteers. At first, no one took any notice. They wandered in the midst of a hellish chaos and Declan thought it was like they had a little bubble around them. People would run towards them and maybe gesture, or say something, but nobody asked where their papers were, or where they were going, or what they were doing. He asked after Massimo and MSF directed him to a hardware store, on the left-hand side of the road. Indian men stood on the balcony and when they saw him coming the gate creaked open and he found himself mounting a concrete stairwell.

Upstairs, he found the Italian journalist. A wounded Indian lay in a dark room. The man had taken a stray round. MSF guys were on the phone, trying to figure out how to carry him back across the bridge. The Indians showed Declan around the house. Their bathroom had been shelled and in its place was a gaping hole the size of a car and a pile of rubble. The toilet was intact, Declan noticed, but the shower destroyed. Bullet holes polka-dotted the living room, light glowing through. The house faced the front lines, so anything that came over from the government side of the river hit it broadside. The Indians hid deep in the flat. These guys, he thought, were nuts. They stayed on Bushrod to protect their businesses and locked themselves up for weeks on end, living in really close quarters, eating tinned food and cornflakes, while all hell broke loose around them.

Somini and the others met up with Sekou Fofana. The rebel administrator seemed eager to show them that people in the area were happy and loved the LURD. It was interesting, she admitted, that a lot of people came out into the streets and chanted things like "LURD, we like you! LURD, we like you!" They clapped too. But she guessed she would never know how much of that was orchestrated. In a rebellion, the smart play is to avoid picking sides until you know who will win. Fofana honked his horn and basked in the applause. "Are we harassing these people?" he asked rhetorically. Finally they met General Cobra, the top commander. He was very weird, Somini observed. He wore a beret and he was missing some lower teeth. He didn't speak English well, at least not coherently, though with that it seemed a full complement of teeth could not have helped. None of this stopped her from reporting. "What happens if Taylor doesn't leave?" she asked.

"I will move him," Cobra replied. "I will attack him militarily."

Other rebels were introduced. All the officials, Somini noted, had fancy titles. So-and-so was the Assistant Commissioner for Recordkeeping. Someone else was in charge of protocol. Another did military training. But Sekou Fofana answered all the questions. "Dragon Master" introduced himself as Dragon Master, but later said he was also known as "K1" and as "Sekou Kamara." When she had spoken with him on the phone, she imagined him to be some big cheese, but in the flesh he was a young, personable guy.

He seemed like a guy you could talk to, she reflected.

Declan hoped to get to rebel headquarters to announce his presence and get a sense of what was going on. He and Massimo grabbed a lift with a Toyota pickup overfull with LURD fighters, their weapons hanging over the side. The rebels were pretty nice about it. They were civil. They even kicked out one or two others to make room. But it was close quarters and nobody had washed in a while. The pickup dropped them at Club Beer instead. Just as everyone had heard, the brewery had been converted into a field clinic. Declan was appalled. A dirty wooden bench in the loading bay served as an operating table. Local nurses and medics, who had no medicines, worked with crude, non-sterilized instruments. He watched as they basically chopped open some guy on the table. The man had a wound in the bicep and they cut into him. No dignity, no hygiene.

The medics even admitted they weren't doctors. They were just local people who didn't really know how to perform surgery. They tried their best to help. The man on the table just screamed in agony. Blood flew everywhere. Declan made his way to the back of the building, where a ward had been set up in the canteen. The rebels had stashed two men there who had such severe gangrene they couldn't be left with others. One told Declan he was rebel who had been imprisoned by his comrades. To be a rebel and be branded a traitor by rebels must be a most bitter turn. They bound him, chucked him in a confined space and left him for a week, and the wounds from the ties went septic. White bandages covered his arms, but they were completely soaked through. Declan winced when he looked. The better part of the arms just rotted away. You could smell the diseased flesh. Beside him, another man had been shot in the leg and gone untreated for too long. Gangrene had spread through his body. These poor men, Declan thought. Imprisoned in their bodies, obviously on the verge of death, and no one could do anything.

Declan and Massimo made their way back to the river and met up with Somini and the others. By now, they noticed, CNN and others had crossed the bridges in cars, but they were still on foot, so they waved their tee shirts again and walked back across as a group. Marijuana was the smell of change. At the center of the bridge, rebels and militia stood together in the fading light, smoking and chatting amiably. It was pleasant, in a way, but it was getting fraught and tense on the streets. Looters were out already. The reporters were all anxious to get back.

Plus, they were really screwed for filing deadlines.

Back at the Mamba Point Hotel, Somini sat down at her laptop. She had noticed that Bushrod Island had plenty of food, especially rice and chickens. Duala market was thriving again. Spaghetti, canned meats, and toothpaste were readily available. It was abundantly clear to the reporters that the Free Port had been looted. "Divided by a series of bridges," she wrote, "the rebel- and government-held halves of this capital compose a bleak landscape of haves and have nots... One side, controlled by the besieged Liberian President, Charles Taylor, has little food or fuel, but a sufficient supply of drugs and doctors, thanks to international aid agencies. The other side, held by [LURD rebels], has no drugs or doctors but plenty of food and fuel, with the [port] of Monrovia under rebel control."

And that was her lede.

That evening, the Ambassador slid his mouse across a grey pad and waited for the monitor to flicker to life. A banner headline popped up: "Bush Orders Six to Ten Troops to Liberia." Reading further, he found the White House announced publicly that President Bush had authorized a small contingent of United States troops to Liberia, possibly as many as twenty, to assist ECOMIL. It was the Forward Coordination Element. "Six to ten" did not an army make, but now, officially, there were U.S. "boots on the ground."

The Ambassador and his security team met in his office. The light was dim as candlelight and the air-conditioners grumbled like junkyard dogs. From his divan, elbow propped on the armrest leaving one shoulder awkwardly higher than the other, the Ambassador squinted at Colonel Sandusky across the coffee table as she briefed him that journalists and a few aid workers had passed between the warring parties and made it to Bushrod Island. He listened intently then said, as though pitching an idea, "The strategic reasons to stabilize Liberia haven't gone away and the humanitarian crisis is worse. But everyone has to remember that, if and when Charles Taylor leaves, we have a way forward so long as everything comes together sequentially." In the best of circumstances, "peace in Liberia" was far off. In any war there are no shortcuts. It did not help the Ambassador to know that throughout his career he had been uncannily accurate in predicting likely outcomes, starting with the collapse of the Soviet Union.

"First," he said, polishing his glasses with a handkerchief, "ECOMIL had to move out from Robertsfield and into Monrovia. Then they have to push onto Bushrod Island and secure the Free Port to open a route for food aid. At the same time, the Liberian peace talks in Ghana have to produce an agreement, so that the ECOMIL peacekeeping deployment, with all its risks, does not happen in a vacuum. Next, United Nations peacekeepers have to replace ECOMIL and deploy throughout the country, which means the rebels have to cede control of the territory they now hold so that Liberia will not be 'balkanized.' Then everyone would have to disarm. All sides need to be disarmed, demobilized, rehabilitated, and reintegrated into society. And the economy needs to be kick-started."

He took a stab at a joke.

"So our jobs are safe for a while."

Colonel Sandusky could not manage a smile. The Colonel rarely smiled these days, though she otherwise had a dry wit locked behind her hangdog frown. She was frustrated, everyone was, that U.S. "support" for ECOWAS was still undefined. She knew that the three warships of the Iwo Jima Amphibious Readiness Group were on their way, but their orders had not been clarified. The Ambassador was rightly concerned that their mission would be to sit offshore and monitor the situation, rather than actually help. He called it "Operation Float." If that were the case, and the Liberian fighters figured it out, there would be no reason to stop the war. The key, the Ambassador emphasized, was for everyone to understand in no uncertain terms that the United States had ECOMIL's back.

The Colonel sat aside her green notepad and leaned forward. She removed her cap and her white hair instantly became the brightest point in the room, reflecting the dull luster of the lamps. "I'm concerned," she said, "about ECOMIL moving their troops from the airport into town without some sort of ceasefire in place. One accident and this whole thing could blow up. Charles Taylor also could see this lull as a chance to regroup and launch a new attack. The same goes for the rebels."

"I agree," the Ambassador nodded. "I think we need ECOMIL to talk to Cobra face to face, to remind him, as the top LURD commander, of the pledge by LURD political leaders to leave Bushrod. General Okonkwo would have to be willing. That's the only way to make this happen. We have to go to them. I don't think they'll come here."

"You mean you want to go to Bushrod Island?"

He grinned, his eyes lit with a bit of mischief.

"Whatd'ya think? Can we get away with it?"

"You mean cross the front lines?"

"The press did it."

Ted Collins grimaced. As Regional Security Officer, it would be a hell of a call to let his Chief of Mission cross active front lines. If anything happened, there really was no fall back. The number one rule for a Regional Security Officer was to not lose the principal. Here was his boss telling him he wanted to travel through a nest of Kalashnikovs and rocket-propelled grenades to hold talks. Still, the Ambassador understood the dynamics in Liberia as well as anyone could, and he knew the stakes. "Sir I think we can pull it off," he said quietly, nodding his assent. "If both sides agree." The Ambassador grinned, then caught himself again, as if he remembered others were still in the room.

"It will be risky of course," he said, "and no guarantees."

Diplomacy meant risk. This, the Ambassador thought, was maybe what his whole career led up to, the essence of why he had joined the Foreign Service: the chance to make a difference, the chance to end a war. The window, he knew, could slam shut on a moment's notice and he simply could not let that happen. He was grateful to Collins in that moment for not undercutting him. Casting about the room, his eyes rested on the print of Mandela. "If we go across the Mesurado," he said, "and something goes wrong, a misfire, an accident, or anything at all, the consequences will be awful for the diplomatic process. If General Okonkwo or I are harmed, all of this could end."

He rubbed his brow. Earlier in the day, LURD Chairman Sekou Conneh issued a statement from Rome, of all places, where Sant'Egidio, a powerful Catholic organization, brought him to urge him to pursue the path of peace. Conneh publicly reaffirmed LURD's plan to turn the Free Port over to ECOMIL but, he added, "We don't trust Charles Taylor and we are sure he is not going to step down. It will take some force." It was not clear what force he meant, or how his remarks would be interpreted by Cobra and his men on Bushrod Island. Ambiguity as such from rebel political leaders could lead to a new bloodbath. The LURD Chairman, after all, was not in Liberia to clarify his intent.

"I'll go," the Ambassador said. "It has to be done. We have to build confidence that ECOMIL is neutral and get the rebels to turn over the Free Port. The only way to do that is to cross the front lines and tell them in person that we're serious."

The Ambassador glanced at the city map on the coffee table, and he noted the short distance across the two bridges that linked Bushrod Island to the rest of the city. A few weeks ago it had been a ten-minute drive to the port in light traffic. Now the simple logistics of the trip were hard to fathom. The Colonel, ever the pragmatist, leaned back and flipped open her pad again. "We have to coordinate with the government," she said.

"Let's make it happen," the Ambassador said decisively.

35

AMBASSADOR, PEACEKEEPER, REBEL

othing in the dishwater hue of the skies or the off and on spit of rain suggested that anything good could come of the day. A quartet of white sports utility vehicles and a golden armored Chevrolet rolled cautiously in a tight convoy through the grey veil along the ridge of Mamba Point. A large star spangled banner hung in heavy folds from the thick black antenna of the lead vehicle. At the Masonic temple, the men and women in the atria rose wearily from three legged stools and overturned buckets and stared at the passing cars. If the Americans were on the move, it meant something was afoot, but the weeks of siege blunted their curiosity and they made no effort to wave or move to the street. Children who once chased after the cars now peered mistrustfully through slim gaps in the green tarps draped over the windows. It was still too dangerous to be outside.

In the city center, the convoy picked up a police escort, a couple black sedans and pick-ups. Several press vans pulled out of the alleys and followed at a careful distance. No other cars were on the road and within a matter of minutes the group reached the footings of the quarter mile span of the Gabriel Tucker Bridge. CD-58 was the lead car, Fergy at the wheel. In the jump seat, Nokia glued to her ear, brim of her olive green hat so low it pressed down on the wire frames of her glasses, Colonel Sandusky volleyed calls between the government, the rebels, and the embassy cars. Variables shifted from moment to moment. Huffing engines idled near a battered police bunker. Child soldiers in tattered clothes and high-tops lolled around in small clusters, eyes nearly as vacant as the men they killed.

A thumbs up told Fergy the Colonel finally got what she needed.

The convoy crawled at the pace of parade floats along the long, subtle rise toward the center of the bridge. In his car the Ambassador blanched at the number of scars and hash marks of gunfire on the concrete rails. Spent shell casings carpeted the length of the drive as if someone dumped box after box of ammunition. Brass and copper popped and rolled and jingled under the tires. Militia, full of piss and vinegar, chanting war chants, jogged on foot in front of the convoy. They could easily be mistaken for an attacking force, it occurred to the Ambassador, and he waved his hands through the tinted glass to urge to them to turn around. They would be lucky if the rebels did not open fire the moment they came into view. No one took him seriously. Liberia, he thought, could never have a lasting ceasefire with warring parties that close to each other. Certainly, he thought, not with that many child soldiers on either side of the river. It was totally impractical.

Mild vibrations against his chest let him know he had a call and he reached into his suit pocket and pulled out his phone. He did not recognize the number. It was not the best moment for a call, but he felt a strange compulsion answer. European Command was on the line, as best he could tell. The voice was scrambled. A man said he had to relay a message to the Ambassador from the Supreme Allied Commander, General James Jones. The line cleared a bit. The massage was that General Jones had ordered the Ambassador not to cross the bridge. "You all could be taken hostage or killed outright," the man added by way of explanation. The Ambassador coughed to buy himself a moment then, with due courtesies, reminded the caller that he worked for the President, not the General, and in any event it was too late as they were already committed.

Next to him, General Okonkwo smiled generously. "I hope you know what you are doing, Mr. Ambassador, or things will get very sticky for us," he said. "I hope I do too," the Ambassador said, and they both laughed, at least in part to ease the nerves. Clicks and slaps from the jump seat told him that Brad Lynn had a fully loaded semi-automatic rifle at the ready. He could see the knuckles of Robert, the driver, white and yellow across the steering wheel. It was comforting, in a way, to know that everyone understood the stakes.

Defense Minister Chea escorted the convoy to the midway point before

Colonel Sandusky jumped out of her car, much to the alarm of her Operations Coordinator, and waved vigorously that it was time for the government forces to turn around. The Minister finally yielded and fell back, taking the young fighters with him. Watching it all unfold, Fergy marveled at the lack of uniformed military on the government side. It was all militia, kids decked out with their fright wigs and tee shirts and colored flip-flops. Wigs, kids, wigs, kids. If a city was defended only by children, it was defenseless.

An uncommon breeze scuffed the surface of the river and the restless currents appeared as black and grey stripes brushed with whitecaps. Colonel Sandusky reached Dragon Master on the phone. Fergy advised her that once they hit the far side of the river, the banks of Bushrod Island, they needed to make positive identification immediately or he would turn the car around. The Colonel nodded and peered through the murky streaks of rain on the windshield and spoke into her phone.

"I don't see you, Dragon Master, I don't see you."

It took a leap of faith to rely on the word of a rebel, even for an appointment, as a rebel was, after all, someone who had violently rejected the entire social order. They started a gentle descent toward the southern tip of the island. Fergy applied the brakes to no avail. A conveyer belt of brass shell casings carried them forward and the car started to fishtail and skid off the road. He realized he had no way to turn around. At the last moment, he regained control. Hundreds of fighters, most of them children, came into view.

One car back, Brad Lynn turned around in his seat.

"Sir, I think we're outnumbered," he deadpanned.

As they hit Bushrod Island, Fergy did a double take. The entire press corps was staged there, standing in rebel-held territory amid the rubble, barbed wire, and the splintered wood of the checkpoints. Cameras rolled. The journalists towered above the child soldiers like schoolteachers. There was no sign of any rebel command and control. As far as Fergy could tell, the child soldiers on Bushrod were indistinguishable from the child soldiers back across the river. Some of them shouted and ululated.

The whole thing, he thought, was fucking stupid.

Via Town, the southernmost neighborhood on the island, bore the brunt of the crossfire throughout the siege. The business district was unrecognizable. All the buildings were shot up. Like a construction site after the wrecking ball, the pavement was cluttered with barbed wire, splintered planks, and blasted chunks of concrete, the rust-colored ribs of rebar jutting skyward like bones in the strata after a massive slide. Blackened apartments, gutted by fire, had melted on their foundations into charcoal pools. Sheet metal billboards once bright with crudely painted advertisements were now so punctured with bullet holes they look like enormous cheese graters turned on their sides. A mangled lime green bus tilted in a ditch on the shoulder of the road, its frame so shredded with gunshots it assumed the lace-like aspect of a bug-eaten leaf.

Fighters in blanched yellow and brown tee shirts glared at them. The rebel assault rifles looked new, newer than anything Charles Taylor's militia had, the wooden butts dark and shiny as polished chestnut. Rebel graffiti was scrawled everywhere in black spray paint on walls and steel curtains: "No Monkey." Peering through the windshield in a trailing car, Lieutenant Colonel Del Colliano thought he had never seen a place shot up like that. That said something. Even Baghdad, roughed up as it was, seemed to him to have fared better by comparison, save places hit with JDAMS. He had confidence in the Ambassador and his ability to assess the situation and if John Blaney would put himself out there, unarmed, then the Marines would be there with him.

But he gained a whole new respect for the diplomatic process.

You could not pay a guy enough to go through the frontlines like that.

"Look," Colonel Sandusky pointed, "Dragon Master." A lithe young man still growing into his frame appeared off to the right and waved at them as he talked to the Colonel on his mobile phone. Dragon Master had the smooth skin of someone who could not yet grow a beard and he wore aviator shades and a bandana. He carried an assault rifle, with a pistol strapped to his side, and, as CD 58 approached, he motioned Fergy to follow his pickup, a looted four-wheel drive with hand-painted camouflage. Fergy fell in behind him, followed by the other embassy cars, then the battlewagons, and a scramble of press. They drove north, away from the front along the wide central boulevard, hydroplaning through curbside pools the color of chocolate milk.

He had no idea where they were headed.

The Ambassador gazed out at the people in the alleys and side streets, gawking at the convoy packed with uniformed military and, at the rear, the largely unwashed Fourth Estate. To his mind, the residents of Bushrod Island looked astonished. For all he knew, they might have thought the U.S. ambassador had been captured. Along the road they passed the rag-doll shapes of men and women who had clearly been executed, stripped naked, their hands knotted behind their backs with electric cable. The bodies were bloated, the flesh in places yellow-purple and orange and flaking off, and parts of the faces seemed to have spilled into the gutters. In other places, white skulls and ribs were strewn about in the mud, as though fresh graves had been unearthed.

General Okonkwo, seated next to the Ambassador, was disgusted. Bodies were everywhere and nobody cared. It was something, he thought, that was discouraging for everybody. The rebels looked at those bodies every day and just passed. There were even bodies in the water. You saw the swollen bodies, the way the people were living near them, and nobody cared. The rebels, he grimaced, just sat around and ate their food and it didn't even bother them. Some of the fighters wore whiteface or dresses or strange outfits of wigs and chiffon and spikes and chains, but he had seen it all during his previous deployment and was not bothered by the outlandish dress. He simply could not shake the thought of the unburied dead. His head swayed slowly in disapproval. "If human beings can leave bodies that way and eat around them," he said, "then anything could happen. You have to be careful. These are not correct people."

The past intrudes on the thoughts at the oddest times and, as the Ambassador mulled how best to approach Cobra, he found himself thinking about spacing. His step-grandfather, Keye Luke, had been famous in the old Hollywood studio system as a "go to" actor for Chinese character parts. In the seventies he took a role as blind Master Po and often invited the young John Blaney to the set. It was a surreal place: a set for Camelot hung by ropes in the dark rafters, just above the range of the cameras. He helped Luke put on white contact lens with pinholes and a couple of times his step-grandfather had him stand in for David Carradine, the star, as he practiced his lines. "Grasshopper, take the stones from my hand," and that sort of thing. He was known as "One Take Luke" for his perfect recall, so it was not for memorization but rather to practice the distance and spacing between the characters, because he could not see. It did not help that the studio blew dry ice across the set to make it spooky, or that Carradine's large dog Buffalo ran wild on the set and knocked Luke off balance time and again. How close, the Ambassador wondered, is too close, when you are talking to a rebel commander, and how far was too far.

The convoy stopped at the gates of the Free Port. A man awaited them under the archway. His mouth was drawn in a taut, tense scowl, clamped tight in anger, as if to let you know he was someone you wouldn't want to cross. He wore a red beret with a gold-leaf insignia, aviator sunglasses, and a thick, black beard that added necessary heft to his sunken cheeks. A billowing camouflaged jacket, white tee shirt visible at the collar, added to the impression that he had killed men, or ordered them killed. Four or five young men at his side, rifles drawn, looked willing to do whatever he ordered, and it was then that the Ambassador knew that before them stood the LURD Acting Chief of Defense Staff, Aliya Seyah Sheriff, also known as General Cobra, the architect of the siege.

Cobra had words with Dragon Master, almost yelling.

It was all, the Ambassador admitted, a little chaotic.

Dozens of fighters lurked in the lots visible through the arches and in the shanties across the street. The rebels did not lack for grenade launchers. The Ambassador took a deep breath and stepped out of the car, General Okonkwo right behind him. "Hello," he said, hand extended, "I'm Ambassador John Blaney. I'm glad to meet you." Cobra returned a limp, clammy handshake. He didn't look too well, the Ambassador thought.

The Ambassador said that they had come to speak with the rebels and hear their views, just as they said they would. He quickly introduced General Okonkwo. His respect for his Nigerian counterpart grew by the second. The General placed himself completely at risk. It was not lost on anyone that Nigerian troops had been killed when they last tried to land at the port, nor did anyone forget that a similar meeting thirteen years ago ended in the murder of the Liberian president. The place had some sordid history. Of course General Okonkwo and his men were armed and they had U.S. Marines with them, but it would have made little difference. If the rebels attacked there would be no good outcome.

ECOMIL Chief of Staff Colonel Tawiah was a bit more confident that it would not come to that. He didn't expect the rebels to pull any tricks with the Ambassador present, because this was Liberia, where most everyone liked the United States. It would have been very different if the peacekeepers had gone in alone. So, he thought, the Ambassador's contribution was very, very crucial, because he went in personally, flying the big American flag, which the Liberians respected. But nobody really could be sure...

The press corps caught up and clambered forward, forcing the principals into an ever-constricting circle so that the Ambassador was almost shoulder to shoulder with the rebel leader. He did not like the spacing at all. Jostled from the left and the right, the noise of the skies and the street clouding their ears, it would be impossible to convey the tone and tenor of his message, let alone the message itself, standing there at the gate.

"Can we go somewhere else to talk?" he asked.

Cobra grunted. Then they were back in the convoy, hurtling along the wide, empty central artery of Bushrod. Burnt and shot up cars lined the route. Here and there at long-abandoned pump-stations, gas was for sale in plastic bags hung like intravenous drips from hand-made metal coatracks on the islands where the pumps once stood. War is most often associated with entropy, with disorder and destruction, but in some ways it preserves. On the left-hand side a tall earthen embankment ran on for a mile or so, over the grassy ridge of which could be seen the white petroleum depots and the grey, conical hills of pelletized iron-ore that never made it onto the last ships before the miners went bust.

As they neared the Bong Mines Bridge, midway up the island, the rebels veered into the walled compound with a split-level office building and enough space for a fair number of the cars to park out front. "Cape Maritime Agency" read a sign out front. A gallery of children, most of them toting guns, gawked at the cars from a strip of grass by a cinderblock wall. One child was shorter than his rifle, which he dragged by the muzzle like kids might pull a red wagon. Scabs of dry mud covered his cheeks and he wore frayed high-tops and an oversized tee shirt that hung below his knees. Passive, unblinking eyes took in the arrival of the Americans as if they were watching television on mute, entranced by the shifting images but impervious to the heaving engines, shouts, banging doors, and the sounds of gunfire that could be heard on and off beyond the walls. There was the urge to reach out to the children and take away their guns, but no sooner did the Ambassador and General Okonkwo step out from the cars than they were ushered by older fighters into a dark entrance hall of semi-opaque glass, tiled like a public restroom, and up a musty, dog-legged staircase.

Fergy found himself with Robert, the Ambassador's driver, and the cars. What the fuck, he thought, as he looked at all the children with guns looking at him. Holy shit. Moses Blah once said that children made good soldiers because they were easy to control, but to wage war successfully took sustained effort and if the mind of a child could be defined by one characteristic it would be a tendency toward distraction. Two of the kids set their Kalashnikovs casually against a chain-link fence and started to play tag. They were no more than nine or ten years old. They played for a time, shrieking and squealing, oblivious to everything around them. When they tired, they picked up their rifles and walked away. My God, Fergy thought. These are really just kids. Nearby, another child hugged an assault rifle tight to his chest with one arm and in his free hand he held a plastic whiffle ball gun.

It was not clear he knew the difference.

Inside, the Ambassador and General Okonkwo followed the rebels up a dog-leg staircase to a corner office on the second floor. The office appeared seldom used. Dark, sweating, wood-paneled walls were bare save a water-stained map of Denmark in a simple frame. The upholstery was sandy and abrasive to the touch, staples peeking through like dormitory furniture. The Ambassador and General Okonkwo squeezed their way through a crush of reporters and photographers to find General Cobra already seated behind a wooden desk, bare save an elephant carved from rosewood, a porcelain figurine of a bucking bronco, and an abacus. The Ambassador reintroduced himself, Cobra made a few tough remarks about how Charles Taylor had to leave the country. Cameras filmed, flashes bounced off the ceiling, then rebel bodyguards muscled the reporters out.

Rusted hinges and brittle plywood squeaked as the door slammed shut. Backlit by rain light filtering through a single, grated window, Dragon Master and a gaggle of other field commanders stood behind General Cobra. Even with the reporters gone, the dank, stuffy room left little space for the strapping Nigerian soldiers, the Marines, and all the rebels. The Ambassador and General Okonkwo were ushered to simple wooden chairs. When everyone settled, the rebels circulated cans of stale Pringles. Coca-Cola was also offered. Colonel Tawiah smiled. It meant the rebels looted the port. Most of the team did not eat the chips, but the gesture, he thought, showed a lot of good will.

In negotiation of any type it is critical to know with whom you're dealing. As the Ambassador sat on the hard, small seat in and looked across at Cobra, it occurred to him that he knew next to nothing about any of the rebels. In the State Department, staffers provided "paper" to senior officials before they met someone important. "Paper" generally meant talking points and biographical information. The Ambassador generally eschewed paper, because he knew his brief and did not like make-work. In this case, biographies would have been helpful, but, even if there had ever been anything in the files on the likes of Cobra, it would have been burned long ago. Cobra and the men who stood behind him were, until that very moment, marginal in Liberian history. They were Mandingo, they were Muslim, they came from the border areas, and, as a class of people, they had been left out of Liberian governance from the start.

Nobody knew their names and that was the point.

General Cobra had fought Charles Taylor before as a member of one of the old factions that dominated the conflict in the nineties. He had also long ago served in the Armed Forces of Liberia, which meant he may have had American training along the way. At no time before was he considered a senior leader, the type that made it into history books, but whatever his past, fighters under his command held half the capital and at least half the countryside. He dictated the fate of the city and maybe the country.

An uncomfortable silence ensued, which the Ambassador mercifully ended by reintroducing himself and General Okonkwo a third time. Discussion, such as it was, centered on the Ambassador's proposal that the rebels withdraw from Bushrod Island to the Po River. The Ambassador stressed that now that ECOMIL had come to Liberia, Cobra and his men could turn the Free Port over to them, confident that Charles Taylor would not claim it after the rebels left town. The rebel commander looked irritated but said nothing. The Ambassador added that the LURD Chairman had signed a ceasefire agreement, and he noted that he understood that the rebels wanted peace.

It all seemed too much for Cobra.

"You negotiate with me," he yelled, slamming his fist on the table and knocking the figurines to the floor. "Only me. I don't take orders from Sekou Conneh. I command the army. I am going to take Monrovia and Taylor-men will pay in blood for what they have done. In blood. We have the tactics, we have the men, and nobody can come and save them. We will control the city and I will make the decisions."

Cobra turned to General Okonkwo.

"I already know this man," he sneered.

It was meant as an insult. General Okonkwo rose up from his seat to full height approached the desk. General Cobra circled round and the two men stood chest-to-chest, trash talking in mutually unintelligible dialects. It was clear that they had met in Okonkwo's previous deployment in Liberia and equally clear the memories were not fond. The Nigerian Force Commander towered over the smaller, thinner rebel, but he was easily outgunned. Sweat slid down foreheads and temples, eyes narrowed, and throughout the room fingers crept onto triggers. Seconds ticked away.

The Ambassador jumped up and separated the two men with his hands. "Look," he said to Cobra and his men, his voice dry and one note from breaking, "I'm here to represent the American people to the people of Liberia. Not just one side, you know. I'm here for everyone. So that means I'm your Ambassador too." General Okonkwo finally stepped back. He was not going to let the rebel commander disrespect him, but anyway, he thought, he had already done what he had come to do. ECOMIL made its intentions known to the rebels, right on the first day. The objective was to open up the port, and move LURD back to the Po River. That was what was mentioned to them. And they never said no.

But, he took note, General Cobra kept his options open.

Sekou Fofana took hold of the discussions. He made it clear that rebels would follow the decisions of their political leadership, but that they would need to consult again even though the Ambassador had assured them that Sekou Conneh would support opening the port for humanitarian assistance. It cooled things down. Colonel Tawiah, at the back of the room, heard the rebels talk tough. He also heard them ease up a bit. They had not, he heard them say, come to occupy Bushrod Island. They marched on Monrovia to get Charles Taylor out. But when the Ambassador suggested that they leave, they said no, they were soldiers, they could not take any decision like that. They needed to hear from their political leaders. Still, from Colonel Tawiah's perspective, it was good that the Ambassador raised the topic, even though it was the first meeting. It set the thinking positively about the real intentions of ECOMIL, of the United States embassy, of everybody.

As for the rebels, Sekou Fofana was the most articulate. Colonel Tawiah noticed that Fofana could talk and convince, or try to convince. Cobra had very few things to say, but he was somebody who could easily get angry and act funny. You could be talking nicely and in a moment he could change. Fofana insisted on behalf of Cobra and the others that the militia quit Monrovia if the rebels gave up the port. The Ambassador and General Okonkwo did not like the idea of any preconditions, but pledged to raise the matter with the Liberian government. Finally General Okonkwo allowed a laugh. "I would be more than happy if the militia were removed from the city too." Cobra nodded.

"Well," Cobra said afterward, "I was impressed. I decided then that we would work with General Okonkwo, as an African brother, in order for peace to come. As we saw it, the ECOMIL were administrators. They had come to Liberia to do a peaceful job. LURD were fighting for the Liberian people and ECOMIL was going to save them." He said he would again receive the West Africans on Bushrod Island, so that they could see for themselves the rebels' intentions. "As for Ambassador Blaney," Cobra said, "he seemed to have some technical know-how about how to bring peace. He was to be commended for the tireless work he did for the Liberian people. But, at that first meeting, we didn't have full trust in him, or ECOMIL." The Ambassador should have brought some Coca-Cola, he added. "LURD had Coca-Cola, but we thought the Ambassador had more."

The meeting ended cordially enough. The rebels agreed to a follow-up in a few days' time, which, for Colonel Tawiah, was a significant outcome. If you fixed another time for somebody, he said, it meant that you were ready to hear more. Outside, in the parking lot, Ambassador Blaney and General Okonkwo found themselves encircled by a throng of reporters, wet tape recorders and microphones thrust at their faces. The Ambassador spoke first and kept his remarks brief. He called the meeting productive. "I'm here," he said, speaking carefully, as if still gathering his thoughts, "to try to talk peace and make sure the ceasefire that the parties have signed is respected."

"I think it is a good way forward," General Okonkwo added.

Even Cobra managed a few words. In a throaty voice hard to hear above the idling engines of the convoy, he said, "President Taylor has to resign and leave Liberia and we will leave the port to the international peacekeepers. He has to leave the country totally." To hear them tell it, the rebels on the whole were satisfied. Afterward General Cobra called LURD Chairman Sekou Conneh by satellite phone and briefed him in detail. "Frankly," Sekou Conneh said, "we were surprised the ambassador went to Bushrod Island. Even I was surprised. I saw it on television. General Cobra and the United States Ambassador were talking and communicating."

"The visit," he said, "gave our fighters a lot of confidence. It had showed them that the Ambassador could handle the situation. They saw that he could merge the city and that the LURD fighters could stay in the country without problems. If the Ambassador could drive from Taylor's side, visit them and go back, that was a major sign of peace." Still, the LURD Chairman fretted that something might happen to the Ambassador or General Okonkwo if they crossed the front again. He said it was dangerous to come and go through Charles Taylor's fighters. He did not trust Taylor at all and did not want the rebels to be blamed for any incident. In his view, the Ambassador had taken a huge risk. That nothing happened, Sekou Conneh took as a sign that Taylor and his forces were tired. "He didn't do anything," he said, "but if he had been angry, well, Charles Taylor's men killed peacekeepers in Liberia before. They killed Nigerians before."

"And" he added, "Taylor is sly in organizing things."

The call from Secretary Powell came after the Ambassador was already back safely in the office. The Secretary noted that the Ambassador had not run the traps with Washington before crossing into no-man's land. The Ambassador conceded the point, but the Secretary let it go and listened intently to his brief. After a few minutes, the Ambassador thought he heard a smile through the phone, and the Secretary gave him what was, in all likelihood, one of the mildest rebukes in diplomatic history.

"It was great, John," he said, "but I sure wouldn't try that again."

36

A PIECE OF PAPER

The evening he returned from the front lines, the Ambassador debriefed with his security team and reviewed the headlines from Liberia. Everyone looked a shade paler than usual. Nobody had a full night's sleep in more than two months and it was hard to imagine any rest coming soon. Thin as she was, the Defense Attaché at times seemed to disappear into the shadowy folds of her fatigues. Across from her, the Ambassador sank back in his seat, the collar of his cotton button-down bunched up around his neck like a soft tortoise shell. After the Regional Security Officer provided the latest updates on embassy security, talk turned to the press coverage of the trip to Bushrod. On balance, it was favorable, although the media pointed out that the peacekeepers were still moored at the airport, far from the capital, waiting for their full battalion and armored personnel carriers. Monrovia was still very split, and a food crisis spiked in government-held areas.

Skirmishes were reported to the east of Bushrod, along Somalia Drive.

"Our meeting with Cobra was just an icebreaker, really," the Ambassador said, scratching his sparse goatee and betraying a hint of pique. "Some of these reporters seem disappointed that we didn't conclude peace in Liberia right then and there. I mean, my gosh, we've been meeting on the Middle East since I was an entry-level officer in the Foreign Service and I'm supposed to do everything in Liberia in one shot?"

It was, he added, as if the carefully choreographed meeting meant that Monrovia had been reunified and that anyone could pass freely through the front lines. They could not. If you pulled the same stunt with the right coordination, you might likely be, as Lieutenant Colonel Del Colliano liked to put it, "not very far from never seeing home again." When ordinary Liberians tried, either to find food, or family, or to make their way home, they were shot by one side or the other and their bodies tossed in the river.

At least, the Ambassador noted, international efforts to stabilize Liberia were for the moment on track. The confluence of objectives, resources, and attention by Washington, ECOWAS, and the United Nations, unfathomable just a few months ago, meant that Liberia's last, best chance for peace was at hand. They were by no means in the clear and they still relied on the work of dignitaries, diplomats, military brass, and civil society activists at the peace talks to identify a new path for Liberia. He reminded everyone that the rebels could, without rhyme or reason, rethink their public pledge to cede Bushrod Island, or MODEL could attack the airport, or Taylor could counterattack, or Taylor could refuse to step down and leave Liberia. "The latest information we have," an aide to Nigerian President Obasanjo was quoted as saying, "is that Mr. Taylor appears to be, at the present time, unwilling to take us up on our offer [of asylum]. It appears he is imposing fresh conditions. That matter will obviously have to be looked into." Taylor's spokesman once again confirmed that the Liberian president still wanted to be shielded from prosecution by the Special Court for Sierra Leone before he left Liberia, "if" he left.

The Ambassador shifted in his seat, straightened, and brushed out the wrinkles in his shirt. Voice firmed as the thoughts coalesced in his mind, he said that from his meeting on Bushrod Island he took away the notion that the rebel commanders listened, to some extent, to their paymasters at the peace talks. But they needed to be incorporated into the peace process somehow, to avoid misunderstandings. "What we need," he concluded, "is something that the political leadership can sign off on and that the field commanders can also sign off on." He broke out a notepad.

"In my experience," he mused, "people in Liberia are very procedural. In fact, even with the country completely shattered, even with child soldiers on both sides of the river, everyone from Charles Taylor to the rebels talks about the need to respect the Liberian constitution." General Cobra, he said, was a world apart from those discussions but if he did not feel vested in the process, any agreement hashed out in Ghana would be impossible to implement on the ground in Monrovia.

The Ambassador's eyes sparkled.

"We need," he said, with a quick sweep of his fist, "a local agreement, maybe a written local ceasefire that has color of law. Something that would ensure that the rebel commanders stick to their political leaders' pledge to turn the Free Port over to ECOMIL and withdraw from Bushrod Island. It would also force LURD leadership at the peace talks, or wherever they are, to stick to the bargain."

"You mean a piece of paper?" Collins said.

The Ambassador bobbed his head. Others jumped in and for a few minutes they discussed whether to include ECOMIL and the Liberian government. In the end, they decided that adding more parties might create unnecessary complications. "It should be very straightforward," the Ambassador said. "It's just meant to allow LURD to make a gesture and come out of it positively. Because at my press conference, I challenged the rebels that if they cared about the Liberian people, they had to show it. This can be LURD's chance to start to look responsible, not just like a bunch of rebels that are killing people indiscriminately." He turned to his Political Officer.

"You're a lawyer, you draft it."

Twenty-four hours later, the Ambassador handed a draft "Unilateral Cease-fire and Disengagement Declaration" to General Okonkwo. It stated that the rebels would turn over the Free Port to ECOMIL and withdraw from Bushrod Island, as far as the Po River, just as the Ambassador called for in his press conference, in order to permit humanitarian aid to reach the people of Liberia. The declaration was to be signed by LURD Chairman Sekou Conneh and Cobra, as the top battlefield commander, and witnessed by ECOMIL and the United States. No true legal obligations would be created, but it would sanctify, in writing, the rebels' intentions to cooperate with the peacekeepers.

General Okonkwo was on board immediately. To his mind, anything that could help hold the warring parties to their promises would be useful. His objective was to win broad acceptance for ECOMIL as neutral peacekeepers. Based on his own experiences, a written pledge was important. So long as everything was only spoken, he noted, there was nothing to back up any action by the peacekeepers. If, on the last day, the rebels said they would not move, there was nothing that would give ECOMIL the justification to move them by force. But with a paper, a written declaration, he said he felt it would be far easier to say "Okay, you agreed, you signed this paper, so you have to move."

President Taylor's advisors were less sanguine. Sovereignty was their concern, as ever. "It is not fair," the Defense Minister chafed. "The government isn't part of it and it is happening on Liberian territory." In the end, Taylor waived his concerns through his intermediaries. "You're trying to hold the LURD to something written," Chea conceded, "because what's written and signed can't be easily denied. If that's your objective, so be it. We support anything that will remove the rebels from Bushrod Island."

All that was left was to deliver it.

37

THE PRESENCE PATROLS

International peacekeeping operations in general abide by three mutually reinforcing principles: impartiality; consent of the parties; and the non-use of force except in self-defense. The difficulty in deploying armed men and women into someone else's war is that culture, language, and history influence the first two principles, which makes the use of force in self-defense more likely. The history of West African peacekeeping interventions in Liberia suggested that a cautious, methodical approach might be the best way to avoid confrontation with the locals, especially since there was no peace agreement between the warring parties, and the "consent" they had given to the mission was contained in a month-old ceasefire agreement that all three sides had violated.

From a tactical perspective, the last thing that a general officer wanted was an undermanned team spread out across an immense territory in a series of positions that could not be defended, resupplied, or easily exfiltrated if someone started shooting. Yet that was exactly the situation General Festus Okonkwo found himself in five days into the ECOMIL deployment. The Ambassador knew these risks. Everything he experienced over his career also taught him that the chance to make peace could be lost as quickly as it emerged, that the low embers of a dying fight could so easily be stoked into flame. It did not matter how tired of war people were or how low was the morale of the fighters. Liberia had already lost so many chances over the years that it was now or never.

The Ambassador encouraged General Okonkwo to conduct "presence patrols" in Monrovia even as he waited for his full complement of troops. It was a simple concept: once or twice a day, drive the thirty-five miles from

Robertsfield to Monrovia, swing through the capital, show the people that ECOMIL had landed, and signal to the warring parties that it was time to start thinking that the fight was over. Like any commander worthy of his rank, the Force Commander had serious reservations, especially with MODEL in Buchanan, just eighty-six miles to the southeast. He was also decisive.

Less than twenty-four hours after General Okonkwo held his face-to-face with the rebels, he rolled the dice. Two or three diesel powered armored personnel carriers and a few rented pickups rumbled past Smell No Taste on a quiet, sunny morning and disappeared down the pencil-grey thread of pavement that pointed to the capital. As soon as smoke from the engines wafted through the huts and fruit stands on the outskirts of town, calls were made and people ran to the road. Crowds of tens of thousands sang and chanted the welcome. From the shadows of the walls of the embassy, Jenkins watched the slow procession mount the hill at Mamba Point. It seemed as if everyone in the city found a bleached white tee shirt or headscarf that they somehow secreted away through the rains and the fighting for precisely that moment. The street transformed into a luminous, undulating salt flat, the brilliant noon light flashing across the happy, sweat-stained faces and upturned palms. Frenzied handkerchiefs pin-wheeled above the hopping, bouncing heads.

Ululations floated through the air.

"We want peace, no more war."

Packed uncomfortably in the back of their pickups, like metro passengers at rush hour that tried to shoulder in before the doors slammed shut, the Nigerian troops were a haphazard collection of arms, legs, and bayonets. Netting on their helmets was stuffed with leaves and grass, as extra camouflage, but there was nothing to hide from. Adulation, if unexpected, has a curious effect on the psyche: it causes embarrassment. Frozen smiles were plastered across the Nigerian faces as they took in the kelp-like bed of Liberian hands and fingers that swayed around them, trying to touch them and hand them children. Somini Sengupta did not know what to make of it all as the patrols passed the hotel. The *New York Times* reporter had covered the HAST, and the attendant madness, but she had also seen Liberian hope turn to anguish when peacekeepers did not deploy in time to stop the third attack. She saw the embassy pelted with rocks and men and women wail over the bodies of their kin piled on the curb. After the horrors at Greystone, she was not alone among the press in thinking that a certain anti-Americanism would kick in.

"But," she admitted, "it never really did."

As much as differences of faith can be a cause of conflict, it is just as true that faith is what sustains so many through the ravages of war. In Liberia there was no shortage of it. Still, as an outsider, Somini could not easily reconcile what she had seen people endure with the spectacle of the crowds pouring into the streets to celebrate the coming of the West African peacekeepers. They knew that Monrovia was still split between government forces and the rebels, and that other rebels held Buchanan and that President Taylor was still in power. Yet there they were, happy. "Based on what?" she said. She doffed her sun cap to reveal a close-cropped tuft of lush, dark hair. "I just don't get it. As a human being, I fail to understand what the optimism is based on, on how you can just keep turning out and smiling and waving your hankies in a genuine, believing way."

General Okonkwo did not question it. He was pleased the presence patrols were a success and nobody got shot. "People were jubilating," he smiled. "They were happy we were there. The first time we came, as ECOMOG, we were received with bullets. That's all past. This situation is different. At least there's some hope."

Elsewhere in the city there was a different sort of frenzy. President Taylor submitted a letter of resignation to the Liberian Congress that stated that he would step down in a formal ceremony in four days, on Monday, August 11, at 11:59 a.m. At that moment he would transfer the "mantle of authority" to Vice President Moses Blah. Until then, he held power. Questions arose among Liberians whether Congress could accept the letter, since most legislators had fled and the Congress had been defunct, for all intents and purposes, for months now. Apparently, enough were around for a quorum.

The radical idea that Charles Taylor might actually leave had a strange effect on the lawmakers: they decided to loot the capitol. It was not a bad choice, as far as what might be taken. The capitol was a domed building across the street from the Executive Mansion with a grand, airy atrium, red carpets on operatic staircases, and glass chandeliers designed, no doubt, to impress upon guests the splendor of the body politic. In the space of a few hours, they ran out with all the fixtures. They dismantled the halls piece by piece, unbolting the chairs, lifting the doors off the hinges, and prying up squares of carpets with X-Acto blades. Even the commodes were ripped out. It helped that there was no water.

It was not much of a vote for the future.

38

THE ARMS SHIPMENT

A stocky man in khaki shirt-sleeves and black pants stood resolutely with his back to the seawall, waving at Ted Collins. Stratus clouds over the Atlantic were suffused with pink and laid across the sky like white socks accidentally washed with a new red beach towel. The coconut palms dipped and swayed in the breeze. The Regional Security Officer could see the smile as he approached. "We hope for peace to come!" the guard shouted.

He smiled. Collins had seen the man hold his post during a mortar attack, knew what he had put on the line for the sake of the embassy. It was not just the guards, of course. The entire local staff, from men like Jenkins in the political section, to the cafeteria workers, the maintenance, administrative and public affairs staffs, and the motorpool drivers, who drove the convoys, had risked everything to keep the embassy open. Many had been stranded on compound for days on end, unable to reach their homes, sleeping under their desks. Others had seen their families torn apart or their houses destroyed. Conneh the expediter had been trapped near the front and spent five days flat on his belly, unable to raise his head more than a foot or two because of the intensity of the firefights in his neighborhood. He subsisted on spoonfuls of broth.

"We're still trying," Collins said.

In Liberia, handshakes ended with a twist of the palms and a finger snap. The guard reached out and they snapped fingers. As Collins walked away, it occurred to him that if the guard had a say, if any of the embassy staff had a say, the war would have ended long ago. The root of Liberia's problem, of course, was that they did not. The guards, the staff, and most everybody else in the country had been disenfranchised for too long, hundreds of thousands of people menaced by gangs with Kalashnikovs and bayonets.

It was the nature of failed states and rogue regimes. The fate of the vast majority of people was out of their hands. As a Regional Security Officer, whose job it was to look at the crime and violence and darker aspects of the countries to which he was posted, he knew also that it took work to keep a failed state failed. Given the chance, most people simply wanted to provide for their family, worship as they pleased and, the words were true, pursue happiness. Liberia had suffered untold traumas, yet, whenever it was safe, Liberians flocked to the markets, to the beach, to school, to their churches and mosques, just like anybody else anywhere else. It took effort to create and sustain a level of violence and depravity that could thwart the tide of those aspirations.

More than African interests were at play, unfortunately. Liberia had no munitions factories, yet somehow militia and rebels had Kalashnikovs and mounted guns made and supplied by someone who was most certainly not Liberian. As the fighters battled from town to town and village to village, someone most certainly not Liberian profited, paid in gold and diamonds plundered from the country's creeks and riverbanks. Collins knew the value chain: someone manufactured weapons or their components, someone paid for them, someone shipped them by air, or sea, or land, someone received them, someone distributed them, and Liberians killed with them. Over and over.

Peace was near, but the profiteers were not done.

The arms trade snaked back into Liberia like the mambas that the guards killed from time to time on the black rocks by the shore. After the first presence patrols, General Okonkwo and his command staff went back to the Royal Hotel, took their dinner at the round tables beneath the patterned lamps, and chatted awhile in the palava huts out back. Defense Minister Chea showed up to deliver a simple message: President Taylor wanted to see them urgently. He said he would confirm the appointment, but he never did, so the general and his men stopped waiting and repaired to their rooms.

At one o'clock in the morning, General Okonkwo called Colonel Tawiah to his room and told him there was trouble. He said that the troops at the airport reported that an unidentified aircraft landed and wanted to offload several pallets of cargo. A small plane that flies into a country at war under cover of darkness can be assumed to be up to no good. The Force Commander told the troops to monitor the activity closely. He immediately rang the ECOWAS

Deputy Defense Secretary, in Ghana, and relayed the story. "Hold the plane," he was instructed, "and find out the contents of the cargo."

General Okonkwo gave the order. The peacekeepers were already suspicious, because Liberian defense forces turned up, and they were in a foul mood because the Liberians pledged to provide them lodging, but had not done so, so they were forced to bunk in a musty hangar at the far end of the airstrip. It was dark, and late, and wet, and when they pried open the container they discovered weapons and ammunition. Over the protests of the Liberians, they impounded the container and waited for guidance.

At daybreak, General Okonkwo and Colonel Tawiah set out for the airport. No sooner had they hit the road then the general's mobile rang. President Taylor wanted to see them, so they detoured to White Flower, where the guards hastily admitted them. Inside, President Taylor acknowledged that his government sought to import weapons. By way of explanation, he argued that Liberia was a sovereign nation and had a right to defend itself in a time of war. ECOMIL, he said, had seized the arms. General Okonkwo, he said, should head to the airport and see what he could do about it.

As he listened, Colonel Tawiah realized that President Taylor actually thought they could be convinced to ignore the shipment. When the Liberian president saw that General Okonkwo would not release it, his face fell and he seemed perturbed. "The issue," General Okonkwo told him politely, "is no longer with you. It is now an ECOWAS issue. You can get in contact with the ECOWAS Chairman to resolve it."

At Robertsfield, General Okonkwo and Colonel Tawiah found Defense Minister Chea and General Yeaten. Nigerian troops milled about the impounded weapons. A small white aircraft was hobbled on the runway. Apparently it tried to leave without asking, which angered the peacekeepers. They shot out the tires. After some back and forth, General Okonkwo agreed to let it go. From his perspective, ECOMIL had no business with the plane. His problem was the cargo. The Defense Minister tried to rationalize the shipment. Dismissing the United Nations arms embargo, he said the war wasn't over. The government did not trust the rebels on Bushrod Island and was concerned the rebels in Buchanan would get "adventurous." It had been made clear to them at the Liberian peace talks in Ghana that ECOMIL was not going to grow to full strength overnight. The peacekeeping forces on the ground would not be enough to cover attacks by both LURD and MODEL. The Liberian government, the Defense Minister said, was just being practical.

Chea told General Okonkwo that, personally, he didn't want war. He pointed out that his signature was on the much-abused June 17 ceasefire. But the Liberian government didn't have too many choices left. Soon after the ceasefire was signed, the rebels attacked twice, then MODEL struck the rear flank. Government forces had been pushed into a tight spot. To his mind, ECOMIL had one simple mandate: to separate the warring parties. "So," he reasoned, "if the Liberian government could get a hold of something to keep the lines intact, to stop 'these guys' from more attacks, that should be okay. ECOMIL was outnumbered and needed some help."

The peacekeepers, he said, should not mind.

General Okonkwo and Colonel Tawiah both told him, "We mind, because the same bullets could be used against us." There is a common tendency to fall back on arguments of principle when you realize that things have moved beyond your control, so even as Defense Minister Chea conceded the point, he still wanted to know whether they agreed that every sovereign government had the right to self-defense. The peacekeepers were less interested in the philosophical points than the crate of guns on the tarmac.

"ECOMIL," General Okonkwo replied, "will take care of it."

The attempt to smuggle arms just four days before the date the Liberian president pledged to vacate his office was a clear signal that Charles Taylor had plenty of fight left. ECOMIL's intervention was a serious setback to the government's war effort, but also showed the neutrality of the West African force. Ambassador Blaney called General Cobra directly to brief him. As usual, Cobra wasn't much of a conversationalist. Eyebrows rippled from time to time as the Ambassador tried to make sense of the mangled grammar that filtered through the receiver, and, when he hung up, he jutted out his lower lip and exhaled. Cobra, he thought, sounded satisfied with ECOMIL's actions, but had also taken particular interest in the fate of the jet and asked him about it several times. When he repeated that it had been released, Cobra sounded somehow pleased.

Then it occurred to him: the jet supplied both sides.

39

THE DELIVERY

General Cobra was not one for pleasantries. He stared across his desk at Colonel Sandusky, Colonel Tawiah, and the Political Officer. The tchotchkes and abacus from two days ago were gone and in their stead were a wind-up green dinosaur and rubber figurine that was half-man, half-hammerhead shark. Colonel Sandusky placed two sheets of paper on the desk and with two fingers slid them gently to Cobra. The rebel kept his eyes fixed on his guests and did not move. This was, the Colonel explained, a written "Unilateral Cease-fire and Disengagement Declaration" that simply affirmed what LURD already agreed, that they would withdraw from Bushrod Island, as far as the Po River, and turn over the Free Port over to ECOMIL. A copy would be couriered to Chairman Sekou Damate Conneh, the Political Officer added, but everyone would be most happy if General Cobra were to sign it as well, since he commanded the fighters.

Cobra stayed quiet. One of his men picked up the pages and made like he could read them. Everyone sweated. The rebels, Colonel Tawiah observed, looked like they had not slept much in many nights. Cobra tilted his head back with an upside down smile and sniffed, maybe in agreement. Colonel Sandusky eased back in her chair and glanced at Colonel Tawiah, who nodded in evident satisfaction. The draft declaration, he observed later, clearly gave Cobra and his staff a bit of importance. To his mind, the rebels would feel a little bit constrained by the gravity of a paper agreement. It was progress.

"Sir," Colonel Sandusky said after an appropriate pause, "if possible, we would like to get over to the Free Port, just to see what the conditions are as we prepare for the handover." They knew they were pushing the rebels a bit. It had not been as easy to arrange the visit and there had been a series of miscommunications. It was late afternoon already, another gloomy day with the light fading fast, but since the Free Port was the objective it should be seen by someone before game day. Cobra sniffed again and this time it seemed slightly more definitive in assent.

Colonel Sandusky glanced at the Political Officer. He leaned forward. He impressed on Cobra the need to protect any American citizens that might be in rebel-held territory and to put the embassy in contact with any of whom they might be aware. "There is a little girl," he said, "she is at a church. We have been in touch with Sekou Fofana, who told us that you guys would let us take her back with us for evacuation." Finally, Cobra nodded.

He hissed through a set of yellowed, broken teeth.

"We know of her," he said, "we will take you there."

The embassy was not set up for search and rescue. It had neither the personnel nor the technical expertise and, as with other services, largely relied on host country resources for personnel recovery. But under John Blaney's direction they were going to do the right thing if the chance arose. The embassy had gotten word that an American child, a six year-old girl, was trapped behind the rebel lines. The mother, a Liberian who emigrated to the United States, called the State Department to see if there was any way the girl could be carried out and flown home. It was not uncommon for children of recent émigrés to be returned to the nation of their heritage to be raised by grandparents or extended family, at least until school age, as their parents worked to save and pay the bills. It was less common for them to be trapped in an old wooden church in a shantytown under fire and patrolled by armed children not much older than they were. Nothing could be promised. There was money to be made from hostages, so even raising the topic was a risk.

But the embassy staff saw a chance and took it.

A mad derby of sedans, sports utility vehicles, and battlewagons wheeled out of the Cape Maritime Agency compound and thundered across Bushrod Island. Five minutes later, give or take, they pulled off the road at a modest, whitewashed church with a tin roof and powder blue eaves. Above the cross, the clouds had broken a bit to reveal a deepening blue sky. A small crowd greeted them at the steps, grandparents, pastor, and congregation decked in calico prints and herringbone jackets. In a row of austere wooden pews the Political Officer found the girl, a thin child with angelic features, dressed in her Sunday best, a chiffon and white sateen dress, with her hair tied up with beads. Her grandmother was also in white, with a white headdress and neon green sandals.

They spoke for a few minutes in soft voices and the Political Officer explained that the girl's mother asked that the embassy evacuate her to the United States. The grandparents already knew that not everyone could go, but the family chose her nineteen-year-old sister as an escort. The faces around them were wrought with grief and tension. They wanted the child carried to safety, but they had also raised her, brought her up in the church community. It was hard to let go. She looked at her grandparents, soft brown eyes wide in fear and confusion. Her sister, slim and pretty, soothed her as best she could. A quarter-mile away the corpses of executed men were sprawled on the sidewalk, unburied, and in that world it seemed a miracle this family, that any family, had been spared. Houses of worship had not always been respected. Charles Taylor, it was said, lost his father years before in a massacre at a church on the other side of the river.

They moved to the altar, where the family and the pastor gathered in a circle. Hands clasped in the fading light, they prayed for the girls' safety and for the war to end. Voices broke and lips trembled, then the grandparents knelt to embrace the child one last time. They walked to the door. At the steps, the press surged forward. They closed ranks around family, cameras flashing red lights, microphones jabbing, voices loud as paparazzi, veins in their faces popping as they pelted a six-year old with absurd questions. Caught off-guard, the Political Officer froze. Beyond the crush the convoy idled along the street, as gunmen in knee-high athletic socks and construction boots prowled restlessly.

The small hand squeezed tighter and the Political Officer snapped to it. He broke through the gaggle with the child and her sister in tow. The reporters sprinted ahead, crouched down every few steps, snapped their pictures, then popped up and barreled on. The child was overwhelmed. The Political Officer broke for the nearest car, a Jeep. The door opened and the child, eyes glazed with tears, was bundled in with her sister. Microphones and cameras lunged forward for one final take. The manic, booming voice of a CNN correspondent ripped through the cacophony.

"Little girl! Little girl! How do you feel?!"

40

THE NEGOTIATION

O f all the ways people imagined President Charles Taylor's term might end, to the extent they even dared imagine it, a resignation and peaceful transfer of power to the vice president, in the witness of several African heads of state, was certainly one of the least likely. "Charles Taylor" to many was synonymous with mayhem. He was also the Papay to his followers. He had set the terms for Liberia for more than a decade. That he would go gently into the night was unthinkable. Everyone was on guard, Declan Walsh said, that he would pull something special, somehow. What it would be, no one knew. "But," Declan said, at least in the press, "we had all built up this idea of Charles Taylor as this great escape artist and cunning master of illusion. He was the man who escaped from jail in Massachusetts, eluded the best efforts of the international community to corner him for years, committed terrible deeds, and manipulated his country's politics for his own Machiavellian ends. So there was this idea that he would find some way out of this, even at the end, even when it looked like he has fewer and fewer options." It was hard to find any Liberians who disagreed.

Still, Fergy learned, plans for a ceremony proceeded. The Centennial Pavilion, a stately convention hall in the style of mission architecture that sat on the bluffs above the river, was selected as the venue. It was the traditional site of presidential inaugurations. In every drama there are stagehands and, while most anyone vested in Liberia was preoccupied with the big questions like the fate of Charles Taylor, someone had to worry about bunting. Crews were dispatched to scour the plaster off the pavilion until the shots started to fly and the protocol officers realized it might be best to opt for a place a bit

further removed from the frontlines, or at least out of sight range of the rebels.
The Executive Mansion was the default.

The embassy was again overcrowded, the Ambassador noticed. Lights at the
landing zone flashed constantly as helicopters from the three battleships somewhere off the coast came and went. Men and women in uniform shimmied
past each other in the narrow halls with charts and briefs, and the lunch line
at the cafeteria grew. Ben and Jerry's ice cream appeared in the commissary
iceboxes and sold out in a matter of hours, which might have been faster had it
been advertised. Names and dates started to fill the executive calendar, which
the Ambassador still kept himself, as members of civil society made their way
to the embassy and as he ramped up military consultations.

It was encouraging, the Ambassador thought, but he had to remind
everyone that they were still in the middle of a war. There was no peace agreement. The city and country were still divided. People still died every day in
nasty ways. "It's imperative," he told everyone he met, "that neither LURD
nor MODEL tries to take advantage of this situation. After Taylor leaves, if
he leaves, many of his fighters will feel abandoned and anything could happen.
ECOMIL will be the only defense for the capital and their base is at the airport
thirty-five miles away." Neither rebel movement had agreed to a transitional
arrangement that would allow Moses Blah to hold the presidency and there
was a very real possibility, the Ambassador cautioned, of a coup against Blah.

General Okonkwo sat comfortably in the Ambassador's office, sipping instant
coffee the Ambassador prepared. "What we need to do," the Ambassador said,
"is meet with Cobra and his gang on Bushrod Island as soon as possible after
Taylor leaves, to finalize the hand-over of the Free Port and the whole island
to you guys. The longer the rebels hold onto it, the more they will think of it
as their own, where they control the access and call the shots. We can't have
'LURD land' and 'MODEL land.' We can only have Liberia."

The Force Commander agreed. The "balkanization" of Liberia happened
before. When Charles Taylor himself had been a rebel and controlled most
of the countryside, but not the capital, he called it "Greater Liberia." The
two current rebel factions between them held sway over eighty percent of the
country, so that even if ECOMIL fulfilled its mandate and secured Monrovia
for humanitarian relief, broader peace was by no means guaranteed. The hope

was that a quick, decisive move by ECOMIL to secure Bushrod and the Free Port after Taylor's departure would show all sides it was time to put down the guns and go home. General Cobra would have to play ball for that to happen.

The Ambassador turned to Lieutenant Colonel Del Colliano.

"It would be good," he said, "if the Iwo Jima Amphibious Readiness Group could come pop into view as soon as Charles Taylor departs, so that no one gets any funny ideas. Fly some sorties. I think it will have a calming effect on the whole situation, just like the Kearsarge did. What do you think? Will that be possible?"

General Okonkwo nodded. His chair was too small and he sat with arms folded and legs crossed, head tilted forward, brow creased slightly. He said that he understood that Joint Task Force Liberia would help ECOMIL secure the Free Port. This was important, he said, because, until his second Nigerian battalion deployed, he did not have the armored cars or the manpower to secure Robertsfield, Monrovia and Bushrod. Even then, it was a lot to ask. Prudence was needed, given everything that could go wrong. It would take little to upset the delicate equilibrium that settled across the front.

"I hope we can make something happen," the Ambassador said.

Left unspoken were his concerns that, from everything he heard from his Beltway sources, the interagency back home was split as ever on Liberia. The Forward Command Element and the FAST notwithstanding, Secretary Rumsfeld and others of like mind fiercely opposed U.S. "boots on the ground," while Secretary Powell and those more in favor of the Liberia mission insisted that there should be robust support for ECOMIL, albeit for a limited time. The President even tried to settle it at a principal's meeting. "Take the port," was what the Ambassador was told that the President said. It made sense. The Free Port was a discrete, defensible area and U.S. troops would only be needed for a month or two until ECOMIL reached full strength. Some dangerous incidents were bound to happen, the Ambassador admitted, but on the whole he was certain the Liberian combatants would respect American professionalism and firepower, which in turn would bolster ECOMIL's credibility and capacity. Yet nothing Colonel Sandusky or Lieutenant Colonel Del Colliano briefed to him indicated that the Amphibious Readiness Group and the embarked 26th Marine Expeditionary Unit were prepared to set up camp by the piers.

"We'll work on the sequencing sir," Del Colliano said.

At White Flower, Charles Taylor's advisors struggled to come to grips with the increasingly real possibility that their boss would step down and leave Liberia. On the night of Sunday, August 10, the eve of the transfer of power, long-time supporters gathered around in the sitting room and stared disconsolately at the ivory white piano and the Versailles-style furnishings. Minister of State Jonathan Taylor admitted he had mixed feelings. At his uncle's request he had personally coordinated the logistics of the departure. "On balance," he said, "if that was what it took for peace, then he had to go. But even in those last moments, there were still people in our policy area that felt that he should not leave. Even President Taylor seemed as if he would hedge. It was a difficult decision and the President said, at one point, that he was just prepared to retire to his farm. He said he would not leave Liberia, but he would just give up politics. He would not bother, he would not interfere."

Taylor had, in fact, publicly floated this idea from time to time.

"The practical side of that was problematic," Jonathan conceded.

Everybody silently pondered what might happen. Maritime Commissioner Benoni Urey said it was one of the saddest times of his life. Then President Taylor strode into the room and commanded, "Gentleman, look alive!" When the president took his seat, he thanked everyone for working in his government and said if he had offended anyone, he was sorry. He followed with a prayer and blessings for everybody. "Life," President Taylor told them, "is a difficult thing. We must learn to accept the good and the bad. I will be going tomorrow, but we must stick together. There's strength in unity and we must not let all we worked for go away. I'm leaving because I've been perceived as the problem. Now the whole world will see I'm not the problem in Liberia."

Urey glanced up and saw many of his colleagues weep. His own brow was creased in dismay. He admitted he conceded defeat. "But," he sighed, unsettled, thinking about how it had come to this, "we should have been more obedient to the Americans, because they were it. We should have realized no nation is an island. The world order had changed. These problems should have been solved long before it all came to this."

He rubbed his cheek wistfully as he recalled the scene.

"In the end," he said, "our weakness was diplomatic."

PART SEVEN

HISTORY ON THE BRIDGE

Ambassador convoy headed to turnover ceremony

41

GOD WILLING, I WILL BE BACK

Monday, August 11, started with rain. At Robertsfield, sports utility vehicles kicked up spumes of water as they pulled parallel to jets that landed through low clouds. Umbrellas opened and men in suits hustled over to the stairs to try to shield visiting dignitaries from the elements. Charles Taylor was on-hand in black shirt-sleeves to personally welcome three fellow presidents: African Union Chairperson Joaquim Chissano of Mozambique, ECOWAS Chairperson John Kufuor of Ghana, and Thabo Mbeki of South Africa. Other dignitaries turned up as well, including Togolese Prime Minister Koffi Sama, ECOWAS Executive Secretary Mohamed Ibn Chambas, and General Abdulsalami Abubakar, the mediator for the Liberian peace talks. Time moved quickly now.

After tough negotiations in Accra, the rebel factions accepted that President Taylor would yield his office to Vice President Blah, who would hold it until the stakeholders at the peace talks agreed upon the structure of a transitional government. Still, U.S. embassy officials spent the morning urging Sekou Fofana to ensure that LURD would not advance after Charles Taylor left. He assured them that they would not. Ophoree Diah, *nom de guerre* "Iron Jacket," one of the top rebel commanders, was less certain. From the Gabriel Tucker Bridge, Iron Jacket said he had orders from General Cobra "to make sure that Taylor will move." If Taylor did not move by four thirty, Iron Jacket himself would break ceasefire and by six o'clock the rebels would take the whole city.

"We are prepared for that," he vowed.

The ceremony was held in the great hall in the Executive Mansion, a room that left the indelible impression that it had been designed in tribute to both French interior design and the Paris discos. Mirrored pillars rose thirty feet to support a ceiling of honeycomb tiles, lit by crystal chandeliers. The walls were white with gilded inset panels, the floors polished marble, and the furnishings wood with fake gold leaf and floral needlepoint.

Invitations to the big event were hard to score, but staff added a dozen rows of plastic deck chairs to accommodate the overflow. The Ambassador made the fatal mistake of arriving on time for the 11:59 a.m. handover. It was already crowded and unbearably hot, because the government did not have enough diesel to run the air-conditioning overnight. As noon approached, President Taylor and the other African dignitaries were nowhere to be seen and the Ambassador wilted in his chair. He had a bottle of water with him, but the event was going to be, he realized too late, an exercise in bladder control. The Acting Chief of Protocol at one point approached and asked him who was the current dean of the diplomatic corps. The Ambassador had no idea. The man paused and thought a moment. "You are," he exclaimed. "You're the last Ambassador left." And then he pointed to an empty seat a couple of chairs over. "There. That's where the dean of the diplomatic corps sits. Move there." He did. It was not really a better seat.

Several hours late, the parade of African leaders arrived. The Armed Forces of Liberia band, seated in a dark balcony above the hall, roused themselves and banged out a few tunes that sank through the thick air and eventually petered out. President Taylor finally appeared, walking in amid a quartet of grim bodyguards in long, stifling leather jackets. The Liberian president looked small and solemn in a white suit with the green sash of his office across his chest. At the dais, he offered a curt greeting to Vice President Blah and then the two of them sat on their "thrones," ornate wooden chairs painted gold with red plush cushions. The ceremony began with an invocation and kind remarks from the other African leaders. Then President Taylor rose to give his final address to the nation.

His tone was sober, a touch weary. There were no notes. He spoke in the measured cadence of a confession, one that has played in the mind many times before given to voice. The audience was quiet, attentive, like nurses at a hospital, aware of what it was to watch a man who knew he was passing into history. There in the hot, dark hall, in the presence of men of high station, before a bank of cameras and microphones that would broadcast his remarks around the globe, Charles Taylor finally commanded a stage that he was long said to desire. He knew his decision as an elected president to step down in the interests of peace was in many ways unprecedented in the region. He had not yielded to a democratic uprising, the "people power" so common in the world, and not, truth to be told, to military pressure from the rebels. He could have fought on. Instead, he bowed to concerted pressure from an amorphous "international community," which was the United States and its allies, and ECOWAS, and the African Union, and the United Nations Security Council.

He wanted the sacrifice acknowledged.

"You must now seize this opportunity to help Liberia," he said. "I want to be the sacrificial lamb. I am the whipping boy. You know, it's so easy to say, 'because of Taylor.' There will be no more Taylor after a few minutes. And now the Liberian people need the good." Taylor's voice filled the hollows and crevices of the great hall. Even on television the usual shifts and coughs were muffled. Women fanned themselves silently with their programs. Endings are times for parables and Taylor turned to an old standard.

"There is a story of three cows," he said in a conversational manner. "There was a red cow, a white cow, and a black cow. They were friendly with Lion. After Lion had eaten up all of the little antelopes around, he decided that he would have a meeting with the cows, to discuss future meals. And so he met them and talked, but he kept the secret. The secret was to wipe out these three cows, but they did not know."

Nods in the audience.

"So," Taylor continued, "he went to the white cow and the red cow and said, 'Listen guys, there is this black cow. I don't like how this fellow looks. So, I'm hungry. Let me just eat him and you guys will be fine.' And the other two cows said, 'Yeah, go ahead and eat him.' He grabbed the black cow, he wiped it out."

From time to time, an air horn sounded.

"Lion got hungry again," he said. "So, he came to the white cow and said, 'You're white, you got no problem. This red cow is trouble. Let me eat this red cow.' The white cow said 'Of course, go ahead and eat the red cow.' He ate the red cow."

By now, everyone guessed the end.

"When Lion got hungry again," Taylor smiled, "he came to the white cow. The white cow said 'O! But you promised that you would not do this.' But he said, 'You should have known that if I had wiped out the red cow and the black cow, you're next!'"

He cast a long glance at the visiting leaders.

"I say to my colleagues, the Chairman of the African Union and the Chairman of ECOWAS, Africa is at the crossroads. In this new one-world government, we must be very careful. Liberia is a soft spot. Decisions are not being made in our capitals. They are being made in foreign capitals. You must be careful. Today is Charles Taylor. The black cow is going. The red cow is waiting out there!"

Uncomfortable laughter and damp-handed applause rippled through the audience. The message resonated for many, the tension between sovereignty, the core of national identity, and the new world order. For a moment, Charles Taylor effectively swept aside the mess that he had created for himself, blood diamonds, child soldiers, and the rest of it, and raised in its place the specter of a sinister one-world government that preyed on the weak and the guileless. Colonel Tawiah, who spoke only for himself, said he understood it well. "It can come true," he said. "The international community, not necessarily just the United States, can jump on anybody, at any time, without any excuse. The precedent has been set, and it can be used well, or it can be misused."

Point made, President Taylor went on to say all the right things. He urged Liberians in the Diaspora to come back to the country and rejoin the political process. He urged the negotiators at the Liberian peace talks in Ghana to conclude a peace agreement. "I want to thank everyone," he said. "I want to thank President Bush, even though we have had some disagreements, and I think I'm entitled to my opinions, just as he is entitled to his. I believe that he's a Christian and I know he has a good heart even though he has been misled with lies and disinformation. I know that God will reveal the truth to him. I have nothing against him. I believe he has made decisions based on the lies that have reached him. But the Republic of Liberia will survive, and I know he means well. I urge him to do everything to help ECOWAS and this country to move forward."

There was a generosity, a softness, and for a few brief moments the world had a glimpse of what might have been, to see what those who believed in Taylor had always seen. The intelligence, the oratory skills, the melody of the words that could cut across class and race and nationality and offer hope through the darkness. It took an act of will to remember that even as he spoke a mile away there were scared, half-clothed boys crouched at water's edge with rifles poised in the expectation that before the day would end they would kill or be killed. Boys that bore arms for a cause that was his name.

As President Taylor basked in the applause, deep emotion crept into his voice, as though he wanted to draw out the moment but was acutely aware that, with every word, each breath, he was closer to the end. Softly he praised the African leaders and ECOMIL, then spent a few long moments to acknowledge the contributions of Nigerian President Obasanjo. Suddenly, there was no one left to thank. Eyes heavy, he looked out across the drooping, sweat-stained faces and spoke for the last time as president. His words seemed to drift and hang in the air like soap bubbles, as though you could watch them for a moment before they burst and vanished forever. "I leave you with these parting words," he said, eyes twinkling. "God willing... I will be back."

A dented bugle sounded a single, sickly note. Vice President Moses Blah rose from his seat. Charles Taylor lifted the presidential sash from his chest and draped it upon Blah. Liberia's new president placed one hand on a Bible and took the oath of office in his soft, throaty voice. Then Charles Taylor stepped from the dais and sat with the other guests. He was no longer the head of state of the Republic of Liberia.

President Moses Blah did not speak long.

"I'm a unifier," he said. "I don't want to fight."

Everyone applauded, the ceremony ended and the band struck up.

Ambassador Blaney watched as the former Liberian president walked with the African presidents down the center aisle and left before the rest of the gallery. The plan, he heard, called for Mr. Taylor, private citizen, to escort the leaders back out to Robertsfield. Then he was supposed to leave Liberia in their company. It struck the Ambassador that this would be the last time he saw the man. He decided not to go to the airport. He felt it was not appropriate. Emotions were running high.

At Robertsfield, Fergy stood among hundreds of Taylor loyalists who milled about on the tarmac at under the watchful eyes of ECOMIL peacekeepers. The former Liberian president was huddled in VIP lounge with the other African leaders. Everything was strangely calm. Fergy guessed that Taylor must have told his fighters he would only be gone a short time, otherwise he could not see how they would have let him go. It would have been, "Wait, I worked for you and you are quitting on me? I'll kill you."

A Boeing 767 stood at the ready. A commotion was heard. Heads turned, necks strained, and a murmur arose. Holy shit, Fergy thought, this is really happening. The large elbows and hands of the bodyguards cleared a path and a diminutive figure appeared, walked quickly to the plane, and jogged up the rolling staircase. On the steps, men in dark suits scanned the clamor below for signs of trouble. It was over in a matter of seconds. At the low, curved arch of the door, Charles Taylor turned briefly and waved a white hanky, a wistful look in his eyes, then ducked into the plane.

Dr. K.A. Paul, Taylor's spiritual advisor, struggled up the stairs after him, only to be turned back. Black hair disheveled, he grinned in sheepish confusion and seemed to stumble on his way back down. Jet engines fired up and ECOMIL cleared the tarmac. Fergy stood back and watched the plane taxi to the end of the runway, make a slow turn, rev its engines, speed down the tarmac, and lift off into the glaring white skies.

Around him, the immensity of the moment overcame people. Grown men and women cried and fell to their knees as though taken ill. Even the broad chest of General Momo Jiba, as fierce a fighter as Taylor ever tutored, heaved with sobs. He pressed his meaty hands to his head like he wanted to squeeze out the anguish. Here and there, anger percolated. "This would never have happened except for the Americans," Fergy heard. "Papay would never have left except for those people."

Holy shit, he thought, now what do we do? We got rid of Taylor. How do we put this country back together? It's not going to be as easy as everyone thinks. Yes, it's a win, but where do we start? Where the fuck do we start? The LURD still controlled half the city. MODEL was down in Buchanan. Fergy was at a loss. You lived through all that shit and you were thinking the whole time if Taylor just left it would be so much easier. Then he goes and now what do we do? Fergy flipped open his Nokia.

"Wheel's up," he said.

Minister of State Lewis Brown had been told several weeks before that President Taylor would go, on one of his trips back from the peace negotiations in Accra. The only question had been where to go, for continuous safety and security, and in the end it was Nigeria. The Minister was still emotional.

Because, he thought, there were thousands and thousands of Liberians who had believed in Charles Taylor, who had given their lives to defend the ideals. Thirteen years before, he remembered, he had been driving along the Buchanan highway, after dark, and he had turned the headlights off, so he would not be detected. Then he heard screaming, and he saw movement in the road, and he took a chance with the headlights. He turned them on, and he saw a hand wave in the gray, dusty light, from the brush. He pulled over. It was an injured fighter. He didn't know him personally, but the guy was one of theirs.

The man had taken a bullet in the gut, and he had tied his wound up with a rice sack. It didn't look good. He drove the guy to the hospital in Buchanan, and they said he needed an operation immediately, so Brown drove him down to the hospital at LAC and woke up the doctor at two-thirty in the morning. The bullet had been in there a long time, and fibers from the rice sack were in the guy's intestines. They tried to help him, they were impressed with his strength, but there was little they could do. The man was suffering, but he didn't complain. Instead, he grabbed Lewis's hand.

"Thank you, Comrade Brown," he said.

Brown had no idea the guy knew him, but they had been at university together.

"You guys," said the man, "were the advocates of change."

He pressed his dog tags into Brown's hand. The man passed a few hours later. He had never forgotten him. It was overpowering, it was like losing a brother. And now Brown walked beside Charles Taylor, and their fighters had been standing around crying, knowing that Papay was leaving them. He needed, he felt, to give some vindication, for all the guys who had given their lives. How do you account, he thought, for the living and the dead? When they had reached the stairs, his wife rang, frantic.

"I see you climbing the plane on CNN. Where are you going?"

Lewis Brown paid his respects and walked back down the stairs.

It was hard, Defense Minister Chea thought, to imagine the day had come. Because of President Taylor's style of leadership, people were not going to imagine the day when he would relinquish and leave. Up to the very point when President Taylor got on that plane, there was a question for most of his supporters of whether he would leave. Even as he walked to the terminal, until he walked up the stairs and waved one last time, the question was: "Did it happen, was it real?" Because that was the kind of person he was.

A man full of life, powerful, a charming person, a very tough orator.

No, Daniel thought, it can't be happening. It's not real, it's a dream. Then he was angry, he was frustrated. Because it didn't have to happen. They had opportunities to turn things around. They were a small nation. They were not poor, but—because they had not done their homework properly—they were poor. They had the natural resources, but they were still very poor. It did not matter. They could not fight the world. They could not be at loggerheads with everybody. Over six years as a government, they should have done everything to keep the people on their side. And unfortunately they had not.

When President Blah first headed for the airport, following Charles Taylor's convoy, he had it in mind to bid farewell to the other African presidents. He did not, he insisted, truly know Mr. Taylor's plans. When he saw Mr. Taylor boarding a plane himself, he was confused. Where, he thought, is Taylor going? And then he saw Taylor's personal bodyguard crying. He had thought that maybe Charles Taylor was going into the plane to say goodbye, but then he was waving, and his people were weeping, and he was gone.

President Blah was worried. Now he was the President, and he was going back to town, and, wow, what was this, he was in a big presidential limousine, and he didn't know any of the personal security people. They were President Taylor's personal security people, and they were taking him back to town again. "Well," he said to his wife, "we have to be strong." At least he had a few of his own guys with him. He had been asked by the head of the security services to change his security detail, to get rid of his old guys so the palace could bring in some new guys, but he had refused. They could all come to work, he said, but he would have his personal guards in there too.

Jenkins had stayed in his office the whole day and listened to the radio. He was tense throughout. He never believed that the man would leave. He thought he was buying time and that, at any moment, Charles Taylor would change the game. Taylor was the dominant political and military figure his entire adult life, and it was inconceivable to him, and so many others, that the man would just get on a plane and fly away. As he listened to the farewell speech, it dawned on him that maybe Taylor really would leave and there would be a chance to end the fighting. He was overcome with relief as he heard that the plane had taken off and Taylor was gone. For the first time in a long time he dared to let himself think that this must be the start of the end of the civil war. He walked outside and heard songs in the street. Young people danced and rejoiced with palm fronds and banana leaves.

It was one of the happiest days of his life.

In Greystone, the people listening to the radio and eating Cool Bowl outside the bamboo and tarpaulin shops were happy. "Let the man go," Kaetu Simth heard them say, "let the man go." Then a rumor circulated through town that something was happening at sea. People left their dark apartments, and their tents and bivouacs, and wandered down to the beach. Small crowds gathered on the rocks, and on the sands at the water's edge.

National Security Advisor J.T. Richardson had not gone to Robertsfield. He had spoken with Taylor by cell phone shortly after the ceremony at the Executive Mansion. "We'll get in touch," J.T. heard, "but protocol here is too difficult."

"No problem," J.T. said.

When he heard the rumor of the arrival of U.S. ships, he went down to the beach instead. Why not? The ships, he noticed, hid over the horizon until Charles Taylor finally left. Now everybody was on the shore cheering—yah, yah, yah—and then nobody was even coming on land. It was all unnecessary, he thought. All those people fighting, they just wanted jobs. In fact, he corrected himself, it had been about an imagery of jobs. The rebels and their backers had been in exile so long, they were still imagining how government ministers used to operate twenty years ago. Now, he said, ministers flew economy class. They got down in New York, he thought, they had to take a cab, because they were scared as hell to call their ambassador because they had not paid him in eighteen months. But the guys fighting against Charles Taylor, they were remembering driving up to the airport in limos. It's not working that way guys! "If I got an upgrade," he muttered, "it's either because I have the miles, or somebody has given me credit."

Still, he said, someone had wanted Charles Taylor to give them jobs. Taylor could have given them jobs, or whatever they wanted. It all could have been avoided, he thought. If the government's courtship of the Americans had come to some sort of fruition, then this could have been avoided. But, he thought, people's minds were set.

And all those people died unnecessarily.

At the beach, people drummed and danced. On the horizon, wavering like a mirage, a trinity of grey, indistinct forms appeared, the spires and towers of the three warships of the Iwo Jima Amphibious Readiness Group. They steamed into view coincident with Charles Taylor's departure. The skies rattled as gunships buzzed the shoreline. The message was unmistakable: the United States military had arrived. The people on the beaches waved and shouted. Jenkins called back to the embassy from the edge of the water. "They think," he said joyfully, "the Americans can see them from their ships."

Maybe they could.

As evening fell, Bushrod Island erupted with gunfire. The first thought was that Cobra and Iron Jacket and the rest were on the move. The Political Officer finally reached Sekou Fofana, but it was difficult to hear his voice over the mobile. The LURD rebels had held Bushrod Island for going on three weeks, but, with Charles Taylor gone, all that lay between them and the Executive Mansion was the river, a few children toting Kalashnikovs and the rebels' written pledge to the Ambassador. The Ambassador wanted to meet them that day but ran out of light. Their intentions were unclear.

"Mister Fofana, Mister Fofana," the Political Officer yelled.

"Wha'you say?"

"Tell me you're not attacking the city!"

"We're not attacking," Fofana barked, "we're celebrating!"

"What's all the noise?"

"Charles Taylor ran away!"

"You're not shooting *at* anyone?"

"No, we're shooting to the air!"

Fofana laughed his husky rebel laugh. "No monkey!" he shouted as gunfire crackled around him, a cacophony like a Chinese dragon dance, with all the red strings of firecrackers setting off at once. Grenade blasts added punctuation. Men and boys hooted and hollered in the background. Reggae music drifted in and out.

"Stray rounds can kill us over here," the officer shouted.

"Okay, okay—but I can't stop the boys. They're happy!"

Over the receiver, bleating, like a goat.

"Mister Fofana?"

"Yes?"

Bleating. Loud.

"Is that a goat?"

Gunfire and bleating.

"Wha'you say?"

"Is that a goat? Do you have a goat with you?"

Laughter and gunfire and bleating.

"Well," Fofana said, "the goat is happy too!"

42

THE AGREEMENT

The day Charles Taylor left Liberia, President Bush was at a Marriott in Aurora, Colorado, to announce the nomination of Mike Leavitt as Administrator of the Environmental Protection Agency. It was not a venue to discuss developments in West Africa, but the President who called for Taylor to step down would not let the event pass unnoticed. "First," he began, "I want to make a comment about some foreign policy. Today's departure of Charles Taylor from Liberia is an important step toward a better future for the Liberian people. The United States will work with the Liberian people and with the international community to achieve a lasting peace after more than a decade of turmoil and suffering."

Then, as he had all along, the President set the broad parameters for the way forward. "The United States," he said, "will help ECOWAS and the humanitarian relief organizations to get aid to those who need it. I appreciate the efforts of many African leaders, most especially Nigerian President Obasanjo, Ghanaian President Kufour, South African President Mbeki, and Mozambique President Chissano. Their continued leadership will be needed in the weeks and months ahead as a new government is formed and the Liberian people seek to chart a future of peace and stability."

With that, he returned to the domestic matter at hand.

Statements from many quarters, most notably from Ghanaian President Kufuor and, separately, LURD Chairman Sekou Conneh, proclaimed that the civil war was over. As ECOWAS Chairman, Kufuor was well aware the staggering obstacles to peace that remained, but he artfully tried to steer the process. Everyone knew it was premature to celebrate. There was no peace agreement. The capitol was still divided. Buchanan was under rebel control. New President Moses Blah controlled certain elements of the national forces, particularly his own kinsmen from Nimba, but it was not clear how many would lay down their lives for his administration. Many of the militia wandered off to the bush, despondent, or stashed their guns under mattresses and melted into the crowds. If the rebels decided to swarm across the bridges, they could bring Monrovia to its knees.

ECOMIL only had a battalion and a half.

More than three weeks since the rebels occupied Bushrod, hunger was acute on the government-held side of the river. Tens of thousands of people fixed their hopes on the rice stocks at the Free Port, behind rebel lines, and waited desperately for the reunification of the city. Despite the comings and goings of journalists and some relief workers across the bridges, Liberians still could not go. Fighters on both sides controlled whatever trade occurred. There were reports of skirmishes near Buchanan. Richard Butler, the freelancer who had first crossed onto Bushrod, made his way down south and reported seeing along the side of the road bodies that had been cleft by machetes from sternum to groin. The MODEL rebels interned several thousand civilians in a church compound. Some people were said to have been executed when they left to find food.

Talk stirred of ethnically-based violence.

The Ambassador, General Okonkwo and Joint Task Force Liberia were on the same page. The priority now was to convince General Cobra and his men to sign the "Unilateral Cease-fire and Disengagement Declaration," then set a specific time for the rebels to cede the Free Port and Bushrod Island to ECOMIL. That would allow the peaceful reunification of the capital and the influx of humanitarian assistance.

It meant one more time through the front lines.

Faxed copies of the declaration bearing the signature of LURD Chairman Sekou Conneh arrived before they set out. Conneh had not taken the decision to sign lightly. He had recently flown to Accra and booked a room at the Golden Tulip. Late one night, the United States Ambassador to Ghana brought him a paper. While she waited, Conneh and his advisors debated amongst themselves. As they understood it, the declaration said LURD would voluntarily pull back from the Free Port, as far as the Po River, to allow unfet-tered relief operations in Monrovia. It was necessary, everyone agreed, because Liberians on the other side of the river were starving.

They had been in contact with General Cobra and others in the field. The United States Ambassador to Liberia, Cobra told them, wanted him to sign the document in Monrovia. Rebels, as a rule, don't like to sign things. Cobra sought advice from rebel leadership, because many of the fighters were not happy with the proposed declaration. They did not want to leave the Bushrod Island or the port, which they had won in battle. LURD Chairman Conneh also expressed concern about ECOMIL, since the previous experience with West African peacekeepers had gone badly. In his view, ECOMOG had added fuel to the fire. "At that time," he said, "the peacekeepers supplied guns and ammunition to the Liberian factions. Maybe not the officials," he added care-fully, "but some connections there." They went along in some senses. The difference this time was interesting, because Americans were involved and the United Nations would come.

That made him comfortable.

"We also do not want," he told the others, "Taylor's men to reclaim the Free Port." ECOMIL was deployed thirty-five miles away, on the far side of Monrovia, at Robertsfield. That was the concern. Many LURD fighters wanted to hold the port indefinitely, until there was a comprehensive peace agreement and a nationwide disarmament campaign. Still, Conneh thought LURD should sign the declaration because they wanted to respect the inter-national community. They were fighting for a change and they had been assured that Charles Taylor would leave. He did. So they had to sign, Conneh admitted, they had to leave the port to ECOMIL. He signed with a Parker pen.

As the joint ECOMIL and embassy convoy crossed the quarter mile span of the Gabriel Tucker Bridge, the front lines were eerily quiet, like an abandoned corral in one of those spaghetti Westerns right before the ambush. Someone had swept up the brass. Plastic bags tumbled across the road in the slight breeze. When they reached the island, fighters were harder to spot, but came out now and then at the sound of the engines. In places small groups of women sang and shouted for peace. At the Cape Maritime Agency, in the corner office, they found General Cobra planted behind his desk exactly as when they last met him, his features taut and rigid as if rendered in wax.

The usual gang of commanders stood behind him. The small room stank like a city loading dock in August, a compost of sheetrock debris and restaurant trash. LURD Deputy Secretary General for Civil Administration Sekou Fofana turned up in a blue pith helmet and matching tartan shirtsleeves. Short and barrel-chested, he had dour, bloodshot eyes, rugged sideburns, and the sunken cheeks of someone who had spent time in the bush subsisting on swamp rice and potato greens. The numbers in the room oddly favored the visitors. In addition to the Ambassador, General Okonkwo, Colonel Sandusky, Colonel Tawiah, and the Political Officer, Major General Thomas Turner, and the Joint Task Force Liberia commander, had flown in to join the mission. Lieutenant Colonel Del Colliano and retired Colonel Michael Smith, on a State Department contract as a plug to ECOMIL, also found spots against the back wall.

Major General Turner was a quiet man with silver grey hair, a clean, small face, and remote blue eyes that seemed to look through you at some fixed at some point on the horizon. He sat on a sofa beside General Okonkwo with his helmet on his knees, his flak jacket tight across his chest, boots together. "I wouldn't miss that joy ride for all the world," he had told the Ambassador when he learned that there would be another trip through the front lines. Before the trip he had let the Ambassador know Washington had placed constraints on what he could do with the firepower at his disposal, such as no combat flights for his aircraft. The Ambassador shook his head and floated the idea of training missions or other activities that could help the pilots log flight time, at which suggestion the general paused, then winked. Now, in the stifling room, after everyone settled, Turner straightened up, narrowed his eyes and just stared at Cobra.

The Ambassador handed Fofana the fax with Sekou Conneh's signature. "Charles Taylor," he said, "is gone. It's time to talk about the port. ECOMIL needs to come in so that we can deliver food to those who need it. Your chairman, Sekou Conneh, signed this 'Unilateral Cease-fire and Disengagement Declaration.' The idea, as we discussed before, is for you to turn over the port to ECOMIL and to leave Bushrod Island."

"I was not there when that was signed," General Cobra said. It was an interesting comment. It crossed everyone's mind that the negotiations could go spectacularly bad if the rebel commander decided that victory belonged to him and his fighters and he broke ranks with his political leadership. But Fofana, as the senior political operative on the ground, grabbed the fax, huddled with the others, and muttered something to Cobra, who replied, as best as anyone could make out, that without Conneh's signature he might not relinquish the port. Several of the men challenged the authenticity of the fax.

Fofana put it all to rest. He declared that they accepted the signature for what it was. Which did not mean the rebels were ready to comply with what was written on the page, he then noted. General Okonkwo spoke up with a touch of impatience. "It's too late," he said, "Your Chairman has signed the papers in good will and you have to accept it, because the papers are already signed. But you can sign too and you should agree too." Cobra visibly bristled and fell into sullen silence. Behind him, his men retied their bandanas and rolled their necks and chattered in guttural exchanges in their local patois.

Sekou Fofana sat on the corner of his chair and tried *sotto voce* to frame the problem. "Liberia is," he admitted, "a difficult country. Something starts and everybody else joins. In the end, people try to tribalize it, every group blaming everyone else. But I am Mandingo and I have an Islamic background. I don't care who may fear about that. I'm not Osama bin Laden and I don't think I would associate myself with Islamic fundamentalism. I would not. But without the involvement of the Americans, without the Americans on the ground, not just on the sea, we're not going to cooperate with anybody."

His point was that the rebels did not trust the Nigerians. Moments later, Cobra mumbled something about ECOMOG. Over his shoulder, one of his men blurted out that if not for the United States, ECOMIL would not have seized Taylor's arms shipment on August 7, Taylor would never have left and they would be in a bloody fight for Bushrod Island right now. General Okonkwo was a man of great economy of speech. He seemed to be able to raise his voice without actually talking louder. With no visible change in his expression, he folded his arms and shot back that United States warships had not arrived at the time the container was seized, so the rebel didn't know what he was talking about. "Something you don't know," he said, "just don't mention it."

Del Colliano was impressed. Here was a guy, he thought, who was going to control the environment. He stood strong and told the rebels, "This is the way we are going to do it and I want it to happen," and words to that effect. The Ambassador drove the process, but General Okonkwo said, "This is the way I am going to implement this peace." Outside, thin rain fell and the room was lit with a soft, silver-grey light. Through the open window you could see a small patch of sky, a tangle of downed telephone wires, and the darkened windows of a local fish packing company in the next compound. There was a gentle flutter and a pair of laughing doves landed lightly on the wires.

Occasionally, gunfire crackled in the distance.

The people in the room sweated and talked. They talked about the past, they talked about Charles Taylor, they talked about times and movements. If you were to walk in at any point, you might have missed that the real topic was the fate of a nation. Men, women, and children would live or die on what they decided. The rebels had no military imperative to move. It was good to have the Free Port. Cobra had been in a faction that held parts of the city for chunks of time not that long ago. He knew how to hit and run. He did not trust the West Africans and he did not know the Americans, he said.

The doves on the wire took wing.

Suddenly a deafening roar shook the walls and windows. The wind-up dinosaur on desk rattled to the edge and fell to the floor. Harrier jets, two hundred feet off the deck, ripped across Bushrod, the shock waves crushing the flimsy roofs and frames like an inverted earthquake. Fofana glanced at the windows and muttered that he was not prepared to die that day, then he spoke out, shaking his head as if he had sniffed smelling salts. He admitted that, having seen Sekou Conneh's signature on the declaration, he knew straight away that the rebels could no longer stay on Bushrod Island. They had to withdraw. "But," he said, "if the embassy doesn't add its name after our signature, it will be difficult, because the United States embassy is very neutral in the whole arrangement."

The Ambassador assured Fofana he would sign as a witness.

Fofana turned to the others. "Look," he said, "the Americans are involved. No one can fight them except God." They huddled again. After a few minutes, Fofana leaned back to the Ambassador and said, hands out in full bargaining position, "Okay, give us time and we will leave the port, we will leave Bushrod Island. We need—" he glanced over at Cobra, "—three days." A scowl was what passed for assent.

Three days was a long time in a war. The longer it took ECOMIL to get control of the city, the more could go wrong. The front was still active east of Bushrod Island, along Somalia Drive, out by the old cement factory, the firefights almost hourly. Executions were still being carried out. Then there were the threats, anonymous, poisonous, against President Blah, against the peacekeepers, and in reprisal against the rebel commanders. This was not to mention whatever was happening in the rest of the country.

"No," Colonel Sandusky said. "Tomorrow."

"We have shorter time frame in mind," the Ambassador smiled.

"Impossible," Fofana blurted out. "We cannot get everything ready."

The rebels, General Okonkwo reflected, seemed jittery. Tempers flared and he wondered if they thought they were being pushed too much. He understood why Colonel Sandusky spoke up, but he waited for the Ambassador to add more. "Mister Ambassador," Fofana argued, "if it can't be seventy-two hours, please let us stay two days. We need time to prepare. We have to get the word out. We don't have the same kind of communication system as the American military." The Ambassador nodded. He looked comfortable in his seat, hands in his lap, as if he actually enjoyed the discussions.

"LURD people," he said to Fofana, "are of course welcome to stay on Bushrod Island after you turn the port over to ECOMIL. Just not as fighters and not with weapons. You should pull back to the Po River, but individuals can return without their arms. As Liberians, they have a right to move freely within their capital."

This approach won a nod from Cobra and others.

"Please," Fofana said in a softer tone. "Two days."

Ambassador Blaney smiled and extended his hand. "I'll tell you what, why don't we split the difference?" Fofana reluctantly agreed. The time for the handover was fixed for noon on Thursday, August 14. Afterward, General Okonkwo said he was pleased that the Ambassador read things like he did. "The compromise on thirty-six hours solved a lot of problems," he said. "That calmed everything. If the embassy had insisted on only one day, maybe there would have been a clash. Because LURD seemed to feel that one day would not give them enough time to remove all that they had to remove." Allowing a smile, the General added, "LURD needed time to take away enough fuel and all of those things that they had looted. It would not be possible to do that overnight. The transport just wasn't there. There were enough trucks only for the senior rebels, not the junior rebels too. So they needed some time."

Ballpoint pens buckled against the grain of the wooden table, leaving shaky lines and small inkblots as General Cobra and Sekou Fofana signed the "Unilateral Cease-fire and Disengagement Declaration" in triplicate. Then General Okonkwo and Ambassador Blaney added their names as witnesses. When it was done, Fofana laughed huskily, "Without that paper you're not going to get the port off of us!"

Tension seeped from the room and they all stood and shook hands. Beaming, the Ambassador patted down an insurrection atop his head. His wide smile was infectious and even Cobra painfully contorted his lips into a crooked grin for a moment or two. The reunification of the city was a day and a half away. In thirty-six hours, ECOMIL would control the city and food aid and other assistance stashed at the Free Port could finally begin to flow to tens of thousands of needy people on both sides of the river.

Downstairs, Fergy took a call and herded the press into a rough crescent. Declan Walsh found his way to the front of the pack. Marines stood by the cars and children with guns stopped what they were doing and looked at the gathering. What was most striking within the scene, Declan later reflected, was seeing Marines at LURD headquarters, seeing the burly, well-armed men next to these skinny kids with battered Kalashnikovs and women's wigs. You had kind of forgotten, he said, what a real army looked like at that point.

The principals came out. General Okonkwo, General Cobra, and Sekou Fofana stood shoulder to shoulder with the Ambassador, who composed himself quickly. He spoke with hands folded politely at his belt. "We had," he said, speaking slowly, deliberatively, "a productive meeting today. We were able to reach general agreement on the modalities for a permissive entry by the elements of the multinational force into Monrovia's port and for LURD field commanders to turn over control of the Monrovia's port and Bushrod Island to the multinational force elements. This is extremely important for the delivery of the humanitarian relief effort."

The rebels, he announced, would withdraw to the Po River. He stepped aside and Sekou Fofana took his turn. General Cobra stood by grimly in a burgundy beret and flashed a thousand yard stare. There was no opportunity to coordinate a press strategy, but Fofana stayed on message. "We're leaving," he said, "and we will not leave anyone behind. We have no reason for holding on to the port."

Lieutenant Colonel Del Colliano marveled at what he had just seen. After his time in Somalia, Iraq, Haiti, and Panama, he thought he knew everything he ever cared to know about failed states. But Liberia started to change his perspective on a lot of things. "General Okonkwo," he said, "even singled me out at one point before the meeting and said to me, *me,* a lowly Lieutenant Colonel, 'You're not just a Lieutenant Colonel of the Marines. You're a Lieutenant Colonel of the United States. You represent the United

States military. And that is significant.'" Del Colliano smiled as he tapped the patches on his arms. "Not a lot of people," he said, "get the opportunity to stand in a small, hot, dangerous room like that and feel the awesome impact of this uniform."

43

THE FREE PORT OF MONROVIA

Negotiations ended, Colonel Sandusky convinced General Cobra to allow them to see the Free Port one more time before the handover. As the convoy veered through the gate, a group of armed women in bandanas, tee shirts, and black jeans stood and laughed under a flamboyant tree off to the left, across a lot from the Customs building. Female combatants were not uncommon in Liberia and one of the fiercest of the rebels gained widespread notoriety with her *nom de guerre*: "Black Diamond."

The port was a mess. Forty-foot Maersk containers were scattered about like block toys. Doors had been torn off with chains and tractors. The steel frames were askew, as if they had been pushed over by heavy machines. Now and again, heads poked out of the dark recesses of the containers to stare at the string of cars. The port area was a mile or two long, fronting seven-hundred and fifty acres of artificial harbor. Fergy rallied the cars into a semi-circle when they reached the wharf. On foot now, it was hard to believe that these facilities were the focus of talks. A few pitched roof warehouses, a few silos for fuel, did not seem enough to hold a nation together.

Rusted, damaged equipment littered the grounds. Forklifts with no wheels were parked in muddy patches. Down by the water, a massive ship lay half-sunk, tilted into the wharf at a forty-five degree angle as if it tipped offloading something. It was the wreck of the *Torm Alexander*. It had been there for years and many people died attempting to swim into the cargo bay and salvage what they could. In the oily steel of the berth, the lifeless, naked body of a small man floated face down, the skin slowly sloughing off. A crusted spot at the base of his skull marked the entry hole.

A long, stone pier jutted into the water. The port needed dredging for sure, but the draw was still deep enough for relief ships to make it in. Medical supplies and food pallets could be brought in through Robertsfield, but not in quantities big enough to feed an entire city. Fuel and food stocks, the big ticket items, had to travel in freighters through the breakwaters and dock at the open berths. A crane was needed.

Fofana escorted General Okonkwo and the Ambassador along the wharf. He ignored the corpse gently rocking with the tide. Between the warehouses, another body was slumped in the shadows against the corrugated tin like a drunk after closing time. Black stains at the belt tip hinted at the stomach wound that finished him.

The Ambassador had seen enough.

The next day, Bushrod Island was chaos. Civilians stormed the streets to loot. The rebels broke into the largest warehouses and, by the hundreds, people snatched dusty sacks off the pallets and left trails of rice like white cobblestones in their wake. CNN broadcast the story. The reporter breathlessly talked over the footage. "Civilians," he said, "literally, like thousands of them, taking whatever they can on their heads and with wheelbarrows, however they can, looting the port area that is to be surrendered to the peacekeepers in less than twenty-four hours. Some of them literally under the eyes of the LURD rebels. The rebels told them to take whatever they could right now, because they're supposed to surrender this port." Nearby, Sekou Fofana lost patience.

"We are totally in control of the situation," Sekou Fofana told the Associated Press as, the reporter noted, fighters in construction boots ran after looters, shooting in the air, and beating them with chains, plywood planks, and anything else they picked up. There would not be much fuel or food left by the time ECOMIL had the chance to restore order, whenever that would be. It was not that different from what had been seen in Baghdad after the regime fell. It was a chance for some small redistribution after so much suffering. They carried off whatever they could. In Baghdad they had the chance to steal everything from computers to antiquities. In Liberia, it was mostly rice and rubber toys.

Back in Crawford, Texas, President Bush assembled his economic team. He took a moment, once again, to brief the press on Liberia. Everyone wanted to know what would happen to Charles Taylor, now exiled in Calabar, Nigeria.

The President directed attention instead to the task at hand in Monrovia. "They can work that out how they deal with Taylor," he said. "One, I'm glad he's gone, but my focus now is on making sure that humanitarian relief gets to the people who are suffering in Liberia. Obviously, one place we've got to make sure is secure and open is the port. So we're working with ECOMIL."

In Washington, at the Pentagon, Acting Assistant Secretary of Defense for Public Affairs Lawrence Di Rita held a joint briefing with Air Force Lieutenant General Norton Schwartz, Director of Operations, the Joint Staff, to spell out what was meant by "working with ECOMIL." "In Liberia," Schwartz said, "Joint Task Force Liberia planners are meeting with the Nigerian Force Commander and met today to work out details on how to facilitate ECOMIL force movement to certain key locations in Monrovia"

"We anticipate," he continued, "that the LURD forces will withdraw from the port area in Bushrod Island, based on negotiations between the ECOMIL Force Commander and the LURD leadership. And on that basis, if the ECOMIL Force Commander elects to move some of his forces to the port, then Marines will be embedded with those elements moving to the port as liaison. In addition, there will be a port assessment conducted by engineers, as well as SEALs surveilling the waterway for obstacles and so on. And there will be a land-based quick-reaction force to support the ECOMIL forces, both at the airport and the port."

"The objective," Di Rita added, reiterating the President's top line objective, "is to let the Nigerian forces continue with stabilizing key areas of the city that are needed for the reinstatement of humanitarian operations."

They were asked if they expected the QRF to be two hundred troops.

"That's a good guesstimate," Schwartz said. "The purpose," he added, was "to provide a reaction capability in the event that ECOMIL forces get in trouble. In the sense that the objective will be to stabilize the situation where ECOMIL feels that is not within their control, and, once stabilized, then ECOMIL forces will continue with their mission." And, he added, U.S. air power would cover ECOMIL as it moved on the Free Port, an aerial escort and "overwatch" with Harriers, Hueys, and Cobras. "Those assets," he noted, "which are organic to the expeditionary strike group are available to General Turner."

"This," he said, "was the first conversation between Brigadier General Okonkwo of the Nigerian army and Major General Turner. And the key point was an agreement that it was wise to move some portion of the ECOMIL forces to the port so that, consistent with the ECOMIL mission, they could secure the port and allow humanitarian assistance to flow in a more robust way." But, he said, "there appears to be respect for the ECOMIL force. That has been expressed in conversations that Okonkwo has had with LURD leaders in Monrovia. So we would expect this to proceed as planned."

The reunification of a city is a complex exercise from a security standpoint. Civilians will break across the lines at the first chance, but for those holding guns, choreography helps. The rebels agreed to hold a brief ceremony on the Gabriel Tucker Bridge at noon on Thursday to memorialize the handover of the Free Port and Bushrod Island to ECOMIL. President Blah gave his assent. The embassy halls filled with activity as West African and American officers laden with maps, binders, and briefing papers came and went from the conference room where the General Okonkwo, Major General Turner, the Ambassador, and their top military advisors plotted the ECOMIL deployment. Large topographical maps were draped over conference tables, Power Point presentations glowed on the walls, and they hashed out over the course of a long afternoon timelines of who would do what and when.

The idea was to hold the ceremony, then move to the port.

Colonel Tawiah admitted he was a bit apprehensive. They were using just one battalion to do the job. They were stretching NIBATT 1 from the airport, all the way up to Bushrod Island, and even deploying somebody at the Saint Paul River. Generally speaking, it wasn't good military thinking, but it was a risk they took. General Turner let them know he wouldn't be committing troops to come in alongside them. But, General Turner told them, he would give them all the assistance that they required. He would send engineers into the Free Port to help ECOMIL set up checkpoints and defensive fortifications, there would be a significant air presence and the QRF would be on standby.

The Colonel had always known somehow that U.S. troops would not deploy jointly with ECOMIL. They would be on call to assist if ECOMIL were hung up somewhere. He didn't expect more than that. He even told the Americans that, whether they supported ECOMIL from the ship or from the ground, it didn't matter to him. He did not, for one minute, think it was America's responsibility to intervene in Liberia. It was a West African responsibility to help a brother in need. Yes, the United States had historical links with Liberia, he said, and yes, one of the points Charles Taylor made in his last speech was that the United States hadn't helped Liberia much in the past. In all the years since Liberia was created, Taylor had said, America could have done more for Liberia. But, Colonel Tawiah thought, the Liberians had not helped themselves.

Lieutenant Colonel Del Colliano, for his part, had increasing confidence in where things were headed. In the first few days ECOMIL arrived, he and the other liaison officers traveled everywhere with General Okonkwo. The general had always been very cordial and on occasion he solicited Del Colliano's opinion. He never asked what should be done, but he knew that Del Colliano was the link to General Turner and the Joint Task Force. "Can we get helicopters here?" he would ask, because ECOMIL did not have air assets.

And so Del Colliano and Shinners and the others helped ECOMIL assemble a timeline and synchronization plan for the deployment to Bushrod and now looked on as the two generals and an ambassador finalized it. Del Colliano was impressed with General Okonkwo's leadership. He was an intuitive and common sense type of leader, and he had a good sense of humor. ECOMIL was not a U.S. military force. They didn't do business like us, he thought. They didn't battle track like the U.S. did and were not so spun about having the minute to minute information that U.S. troops depended on. It was understandable, since they did not have the same satellite and internet communication. Their methods were different, but deceptively effective. At the end of the day, Del Colliano reflected, although it was not done the American way, they seemed to get where they were going.

Finally the plan was done; everyone was satisfied.

Secretary Powell called the Ambassador.

"John," he said, "I understand you are going to do a ceremony."

"Yes sir," the Ambassador replied.

"On the bridge, at the front lines."

"Yes sir."

"Is it really necessary?"

"Well, we made an agreement."

"I understand that."

"They are very procedural people here."

"I see…"

"I'm not sure we can get them to leave the port if we don't do this."

The Secretary did not say no.

Around ten o'clock in the evening the Ambassador spoke with his wife. It was a bit on the late side given that he had an early start the next day, but it was not like it was going to be easy for him to sleep. The conversation ran on, as they sometimes did, and he knew he once again held up her carpool. He needed to hear her voice more than anything. Afterward, he had trouble sleeping. He ran through the plan in his head and his discussion with the Secretary. He wondered if he had been right to insist on the ceremony. It was a risk. He was also gravely concerned that someone might try to move against President Blah, which would throw everything off. Eventually he went down to the kitchen in his bathrobe, pulled a stool up to the counter, and poured himself the last glass of Buitenverwachting Christine that he swore would not be looted.

That settled him enough.

44

HISTORY ON THE BRIDGE

On game day, at the Royal Hotel, General Okonkwo woke up at five o'clock in the morning. It was a day, he thought, everybody was looking forward to. He was comfortable that proper arrangements had been made and Joint Task Force Liberia had lent its support. He listened to the BBC on the radio in his bedroom, dressed and went down to his morning briefing with his senior staff and the American liaison officers. They reviewed the movement to the Free Port. Everything was in order. He went out to his car.

Days history is made are less often cinematic than they are dim, overcast, marked with fire and smoke and the grey hue of uncertainty. On the morning the siege of Monrovia was to be lifted, the dawn skies along the Liberian coast were colorless, formless, and dark. The Ambassador found himself sitting on a hard bucket seat in the small departure lounge in an empty terminal staring at the tracking lines on a small wall-mounted television, as the wire antenna tried to capture and hold the fuzzy, split screen images of CNN International. The air-conditioner left the windows misted and beads of condensation on the thin plywood ceiling panels. Mildew hung in the air.

At the first sound of rotors, he jumped to the door and rushed into the tropical heat. His glasses fogged. ECOMIL troops, Liberian military and members of the Forward Coordination Element stood in small clusters on the tarmac. Colonel Sandusky marched to and fro off to the side with a satellite phone stuck to her ear. Nearby, "Koo Koo" Dennis turned out. Koo Koo was one of Charles Taylor's most feared commanders, not in the least because of his name. Gangly, rail thin, and standing well over six-feet tall, Koo Koo had a grizzled countenance framed by white muttonchops. In jeans and a flannel shirt, seemingly too hot for the climate, he strode across the tarmac with a pistol strapped across his thigh. Last he had been seen, he was fighting MODEL in the southeast, so the Ambassador took his presence as a sign Buchanan was quiet for now.

Members of the press, mostly camera crews and photographers, chatted and smoked by the main terminal. CNN commandeered the rolling staircase and set a camera atop it to frame establishing shots of the airfield. Fewer print reporters were around as many had left after Charles Taylor flew out. The reunification of Monrovia by West African peacekeepers just did not have the same cache for their editors, and, as most of them saw it, U.S. troops were too late to be of any use.

Only, the city was still split and the victory not yet won.

Well, Lieutenant Colonel Del Colliano thought, it was either going to be a big day for this country or it was going to be the worst day yet. In the distance, Cobra attack helicopters skipped along the tree line. Glancing around, Del Colliano spotted Koo Koo Dennis' men on the tarmac with a technical vehicle, a pickup with an anti-aircraft gun mounted in back. He recognized the car from the presidential motorcade. Elsewhere, Liberian soldiers with rocket-propelled grenade launchers loitered on the fringes.

"This isn't good," he said to himself.

The Liberian soldiers were like everybody else, just there to witness the spectacle of U.S. troops, but the helicopters had no way to know that. Their job was to clear the path for the troop transports. They would not want to see non-American, non-ECOMIL weapons anywhere near the runway. One misunderstanding, Del Colliano knew, one guy inadvertently aiming at a helicopter, and it would be bad situation. The Cobras circled the perimeter like angry wasps, black against the white sky. Del Colliano alerted Colonel Sandusky and she hustled to catch up with Koo Koo Dennis, who had wandered off.

Del Colliano strolled over to the technical. The anti-aircraft gun was casually tilted skyward. The fighters in the truck, young men with sloppy cargo pants and dirty tee shirts, rubbed their eyes in the heat and looked bewildered at the approach of an American officer. By now the Cobras had probably spotted the gun. Precision fire from the helicopters could easily take it out on their next pass. "Hey guys what's going on?" Del Colliano said with a smile. They looked at the ground and mumbled greetings. "You need to aim your guns down," he said, firmly. Floundering, the men did not seem to understand him.

"Okay," he said, "let's just get out of the vehicle."

The soldiers scrambled out and shuffled off a few yards with sheepish grins. Koo Koo Dennis showed up the next moment and ordered them to drive the truck away from airport. "It's not good for this to be here now," he barked. That took care of it.

The Ambassador found General Okonkwo and together they walked to a spot fifty yards from the terminal, close to where the international flights landed. Heat lifted the smells: asphalt, jet fuel, and diesel. The sky roared like a sluice had been opened somewhere, and parallel columns of CH-46 and CH-53 twin rotor transport helicopters floated into view over the palms at the far edge of the airfield. Everywhere among the spectators lips were drawn back to reveal pearly whites. The Ambassador smiled, General Okonkwo smiled, maybe even Koo Koo Dennis smiled. Everyone was smiling.

Fergy took a call from European Command.

"Wave, Fergy," a voice said, "you're on the live feed."

He turned to the CNN cameras and made a peace sign.

Now the first column of gunmetal grey helicopters hovered over the landing strip and slowly, in perfect formation, descended. The proximity of U.S. troops proved too much for the press to resist and the photographers galloped into the elephant grasses that grew lush along the divides, high-stepping like circus clowns across the marshy turf, camera bags wrenching at their shoulders. Most reached the helicopters in time to catch the first low angle shots as the Marines jumped down, crouched in patches of standing water on the tarmac or disappeared into the green.

The Marines that materialized in the Liberian bush, the Ambassador thought proudly, were the product, in some part, of the pages upon pages of telegrams sent back to policymakers, and of hours of phone calls with Washington, and the Ambassador's countless strategy sessions where, sometimes, it seemed no one would ever listen. The multilateral diplomacy and even interagency process that made it happen were far bigger than one small embassy, but when he thought of how close they had come to shutting everything down and walking away, he was immensely proud at how far they had come. It was, he thought, a perfect deployment. U.S. Marines in battle gear passed before his eyes, framed against the coarse, layered greens of Liberian brush.

This was what the outer winds of peace looked like.

The massive helicopters spit out Marine after Marine until a low wall of equipment packs rose on the runway. Soon after, the helicopters lifted off and tilted away, their furious wind plastering the photographers' hats and hair against their scrunched up faces. Hoisting their kits onto their shoulders, the Marines pointed their weapons down and marched to the American hangar, a decades old cathedral of wooden beams and corrugated tin where they would bunk for the next few weeks. En route, Liberian people raced into the grass and, smiling and laughing in delight, extended their hands in thanks.

When he saw the helicopters and saw the American fighters, well, General Okonkwo thought, with that, anybody could be encouraged. Anybody who was there could see that the Americans came in a military fashion. That helped build some courage, to know that they had the support should anything happen. It gave him full confidence to move the ECOMIL forces out from the airport and over to Bushrod Island.

A CNN correspondent and cameraman jogged over to him and the Ambassador. The man asked them if they would say something for the cameras. General Okonkwo smiled modestly and stepped back. The Ambassador thought why not and was handed an earpiece, then forced to wait for a few minutes as they lined up the news desk.

When they were ready, he looked at the black circle of glass.

He talked about how the United States was there to support ECOMIL and how the port would be opened and bring relief to hundreds of thousands of people. "U.S. boots are on the ground," he exclaimed. "Anyone who doubted an American presence in Monrovia, well, that's all dispelled right now." It was the one point, he confessed, where he exceeded his brief. But he was ecstatic to see his guys turn up. They looked great. He was proud, extremely proud. Harrier jets and attack helicopters flew all over the place.

If anyone even farted wrong, he thought, they would be blown away.

As soon as the grip and grin was over and the U.S. Quick Reaction Force successfully deployed, a joint ECOMIL and embassy convoy hurtled back along the empty highway through the scrublands toward Monrovia and a date with General Cobra and Sekou Fofana at the Gabriel Tucker Bridge. Along the way they heard that an ECOMIL company had, inadvertently, already taken the port.

The story was that the unit drove to the bridge earlier that morning with one hundred and fifty men and a pair of armored vehicles. They insisted they did not get the message that they should stop and wait for the Force

Commander and the other ECOMIL troops. They simply drove across the water. When they reached Bushrod Island, nobody asked them anything, so they just headed over to the port.

At first, General Okonkwo was not happy to hear the report. The Nigerian troops had not followed the plan he had given them. They were supposed to rendezvous with him and the Ambassador at the Gabriel Tucker Bridge, then proceed with them together to meet Cobra and Fofana for the handover ceremony. Afterward, everyone would go to the port. "Did LURD release the port?" he asked finally.

"Yes," came the reply, "There's no problem at all."

"Well," the Force Commander said, "it's a surprise." He was bothered that the company put themselves at great risk. He gave the company commander a mild tongue-lashing but, since there was no problem in the end, he decided to let the matter drop. Colonel Tawiah said the soldiers should be thankful. "They called," he said, stroking his smooth chin in amazement, "to tell us they were already at the port, when the rest of ECOMIL was on its way the bridge. They didn't see the problem. Of course, if things had gone wrong, they all could have been slaughtered."

Even with an ECOMIL company pre-positioned at the Free Port, there were still mixed signals on the progress of the rebel withdrawal from Bushrod Island. Colonel Sandusky and Fergy, who left the airport as soon as the first Marines touched down, ran into mayhem when they did the advance for the Ambassador. Looters ran amok and gunfire was general over the island as the fighters tried to scare off the people desperate for sacks of grain or generator parts, or plastic slippers and shower caps or whatever else they could cull from wrecked shops or the port itself. Hundreds of well-armed fighters roamed about on foot or cruised up and down the main avenue in battlewagons. Nobody seemed to be going anywhere, Fergy noticed. "Colonel," he said, "there's just as many fighters over here as when we came over the first two times."

The Defense Attaché and the Operations Coordinator found themselves at the Cape Maritime Agency trying to track down Sekou Fofana. Harriers flew by, two hundred feet off the deck. All around him, Fergy saw rebel fighters hit the ground. Somewhere in the street shooting started. The Defense Attaché was on her mobile, not paying attention, so Fergy pulled her into the car. They spotted Fofana and stashed him in the back seat.

Fofana panicked. He insisted that the rebels needed more time and that they were not ready. Colonel Sandusky let him know in no uncertain terms that LURD could not back out on its promises now and their time on Bushrod was up. "We didn't have much time to pack," Fofana argued, "It was ten-thirty, then it was eleven, and then you Americans come with—WAAH!—helicopters and military jets, all flying the streets. Colonel Sandusky, you do not understand. What you do as a mature, civilized country, we, in LURD, are a bit default in that." The point called for elaboration.

"Why do I say that?" Fofana said, "Well, some things we aren't experienced in. So, when you Americans said something should be done, we thought 'Yeah, well, we could say yes. Then we could try to arrange it so that the answer could become yes, little by little.' But you Americans said it should be automatic. You said LURD should leave Bushrod Island by noon, and then you came before noon!" The Colonel just frowned.

Fergy drove to the center of the Gabriel Tucker Bridge.

He called Brad Lynn, who was with the Ambassador.

They were surrounded by rebel fighters, looking wild as ever.

It was only the second time in the siege that Fergy drew his gun.

Around midday, a convoy crested the hill on the ridge above the Gabriel Tucker Bridge. The sky was bright and the winds were still and, as you looked down and out over the bridge and the glinting river, the zinc roofs rippled across Bushrod Island like the scales of the back of some great, dusty crocodile. All of Monrovia, it seemed, turned out for the event. Tens of thousands of people hiked in from Congo Town, Sinkor and other outlying areas, or trudged over from the displaced camps at Greystone, or Newport High School, or the Masonic Temple, to be on hand for the opening of Bushrod Island.

For more than three weeks they had waited to cross the forbidding waters of the Mesurado to find loved ones or to reach the food stocks that were said to be plentiful on the far banks. Up front, the Ambassador's car sank into the crowd like a bug in tree sap until only the radio antenna and the gold rectangle of the roof and were visible. The convoy all but stopped. Out the window, people pressed against each other. They were the same people who, just two months ago, were forced from their camps with nothing more than their bedrolls and buckets, the same people who endured the endless hail of gunfire and the blasts of the mortars. They filled the black branches of the few trees on the slope and huddled on the hot tin roofs and clambered atop the hoods of cars and crammed themselves onto narrow balconies. *Lappas*, palm leaves, and handkerchiefs flapped in their hands and chants cascaded over everything, seeming to break across the windshield.

"We want peace, no more war."

So many of the faces were children. Happy hands slapped the windows. The smell of heat and people filled the car. Now and again the convoy crept past press cars, moored like boats on the sandbar at ebb tide. Photographers sat on the roofs, legs slung over the side, looking for their shots. Even the panoramic lenses could not quite capture the depth of the swells of the crowds. Suddenly, arms interlocked as a human chain formed on either side to give the convoy the space to inch forward.

At the base of the bridge, they came upon a lone ECOMIL armored personnel carrier, a raft of brilliant white steel that barricaded the road. Four of five peacekeepers with rifles drawn kept the crowds at bay. Others tossed ECOMIL baseball caps to the crowd, eliciting roars of joy. Harrier jets and helicopters blanketed the skies with a relentless drone that pressed down like a giant, invisible hand.

From the bridge, Fergy watched the crowds churn downhill. People jumped into the rough, dirty river to try to swim across. The currents were too strong and many could not make it. Limp and lifeless bodies were dragged back to shore by cooler heads. They could not even wait ten minutes, Fergy thought, to get to the food at the port.

It was military planner's nightmare. The convoy slid past the ECOMIL armored personnel carrier, crossed a short, eerily empty stretch of tread, then ran into a thicket of reporters and rebels and who knew who else. Caught up in the moment, the Ambassador jumped out and waded into the crowd. Brad Lynn hustled to catch up. Before long the Ambassador, General Okonkwo, and the embassy security detachments stood completely exposed on the bridge in the middle of the wide river, surrounded by a hoard of unidentified people, some with cameras some with guns, with no way out.

Colonel Sandusky was in the vortex, dragging Sekou Fofana by the arm to meet with the Ambassador. The plan, such as it was, called for Fofana, as the senior rebel political figure in the city, to shake hands with the Ambassador to consummate the political deal to cede the Free Port and Bushrod Island to ECOMIL. Likewise, General Okonkwo and General Cobra would shake hands to cement the military-to-military agreement. But Cobra was nowhere to be seen and Fofana was dismayed. Colonel Sandusky almost lost her cool. She jabbed a finger at him and said, "If you don't leave Bushrod Island, you'll be charged with war—" Then she caught herself.

Fergy lost sight of the Ambassador for a moment behind heads and baseball caps and television cameras. The air was full of the fumes of baking mud flats and pavement and sweat. Lowering his shoulder, he split a pair of heavyset men to catch a glimpse of the Ambassador just as he came face to face with Sekou Fofana. The Ambassador grinned. Fofana had the wild look of a teen-ager desperate to escape his chores.

Harrier jets blistered the ears with a low pass.

There they stood, ambassador, peacekeeper, and rebel, on the long bridge that passed over Providence Island, the narrow strip of land in the middle of the river where the freed American slaves first successfully settled more than a hundred and fifty years ago, the site where Liberia began. Amid the tumult of jets and helicopters and crowds, there was the sense that somehow, for an instant, the veils of time parted at the very spot that anchored Liberia against the vicissitudes of history.

A new moment flickered above the old, sodden ground.

The Ambassador and Sekou Fofana shook hands, firmly.

Fergy was nervous now. He had the Ambassador, the Force Commander, and Sekou Fofana all together. General Cobra was on the way. There were no representatives from the Liberian government. They were the perfect target. It was the dumbest thing they could have ever done. If government forces really wanted to wreak havoc, he realized too late, one mortar, one rocket-propelled grenade and they could have killed a lot of people. Even sniper shots. You would have no idea where they came from.

He reached out to Brad Lynn and grabbed his arm.

"Get the Ambassador the fuck out of here," he yelled.

Bumped and jostled by the crush, the Ambassador was hustled back to his car. Behind him, General Okonkwo's placid profile towered above the crush of reporters. His head was tilted slightly in the curious way someone at an art exhibit contemplates a new installation. He looked calm as ever, serene, as if he really could be at a gallery. In the distance, General Cobra emerged from Via Town wearing a scarlet bandana and gold-rimmed shades, flanked by a gang of volatile gunmen. They walked straight up to General Okonkwo. There was not much to be said.

Okonkwo and Cobra looked at each other and clasped hands.

The agreement was complete. ECOMIL would now control the port, Bushrod Island, and the rest of the capital. Relief and food aid could once more flow to the Liberian people. After two and a half months and three rebel attacks, the siege was over and Monrovia reunified. "I looked at the helicopters overhead," Cobra said later, "and the thousands of people on the riverbank. You can see, as a rational man, that you won't be able to fight, even though you have the skills. Still, if Ambassador Blaney had not been on the ground, it would have been hard. We were not going to trust the Africans, especially the Nigerians and the Ghanaians. But, because of the Americans, when we were reassured that you had actually ordered your men there, that the Americans were part of everything, well, then we agreed. It's not a matter of respect, it's the history."

The next few hours on Bushrod Island was a military operation. ECOMIL units secured the port and the entire island as the LURD rebels withdraw. Bulky grey CH-53s dropped wire gabions into place to create barricades. They hovered over the sandlots and shanties of Via Town, kicking up phoenixes of dust and whipping black plastic bags into the air like fruit bats flushed from a cave. As they rode back to the embassy, the Ambassador saw a hundred thousand faces glitter in the glancing light. They transformed the muddy ridge of Cape Mesurado and the dilapidated homes on the slopes into an enormous amphitheater, like the grandest coliseums of antiquity. As the car reached the foot of the bridge, it was once again consumed by the rabble. Cheers and songs rose to a fevered crescendo. They all knew the car. Everyone wanted to know if it was done, the Ambassador could see. They wanted to know if truly they had freed Bushrod Island and reunified the city. His first impulse was to jump out and raise his hands in victory, but that was impossible. His security guys would have had a fit. So he just gave the "thumbs up" through the window.

Everyone went wild.

The convoy could only move in fits and starts. Almost as if the ridge above had collapsed, the crowds slid past the window in an inexorable surge toward the water's edge and base of the Gabriel Tucker Bridge. ECOMIL troops tried to beat back the crowds with canes but soon relented. Thousands upon thousands of men, women, and children raced across the scorching blacktop toward Bushrod Island. The Ambassador called Washington on his mobile phone. The Lonestar voice said, "You have one minute of credit left." Washington was on high alert: "What's happening in Monrovia?!"

"Well," he laughed, "it's not a ballet, but there's movement!"

45

A SORT OF HOMECOMING

Bushrod Island was pandemonium. Lieutenant Colonel Del Colliano found himself in a Suburban in the middle of the bridge surrounded by the faces of people he didn't recognize. General Okonkwo was nowhere to be seen and he had lost track of Colonel Sandusky and Fergy. There were no Liberian government troops or militia. General Cobra was long gone. He could only see one ECOMIL vehicle, a helpless white metal raft in a sea of people. He had no way to assess the risks.

By then, thousands of people had run onto the bridge. They frothed across in both directions. Beneath the wheels of his car, Del Colliano felt the stringers bounce and sway in a kind of rhythm. He rapped his hands on the steering wheel and spontaneously decided to step out. The familiar chant swept over him like gusts of hot wind, "We want peace, no more war!" He was mobbed. Women threw their arms around his neck and men slapped him on the back. Everyone wanted to shake his hand. Someone thrust a roll of bread at him. Dry-mouthed, he chewed as he walked. Hundreds of hands touched him, grabbed him, patted him. He never felt in danger. Everyone wanted to know his name. Over and over he shouted "John!" Always he heard, "Thank you John!" "Thank you, John, for coming!" "Thank you, thank you, thank you!"

Looting on the island reached a frenzy. To Declan Walsh, it looked like last-minute Christmas shopping. Everyone obviously wanted to get everything they could. Flatbeds driven by rebels sagged precipitously on their axles from the mountains of furniture and appliances roped on. Men and women bent double with sacks of wheat and rice on their heads and backs. "It was done so openly," Declan marveled. "In a non-traumatized society, you imagine stealing is something you don't parade. But here people stole in front of your eyes and openly carted it away. Rice bags, tinned goods, whatever they could find. But at least there was no shooting, except maybe in the air." He made his way to the port with a few other journalists. A team of men operated a forklift while another team pried open freight containers with crowbars. It reminded Declan of vultures on a carcass, ripping apart the metal frame and plunging into the dark cavities of the containers to find their loot. He and the others managed to get right into the heart of the port just by waving and looking like they knew what they were doing. "Maybe," Declan admitted, "the guys thought we were Americans or something."

Back in his car, Del Colliano drove cautiously onto Bushrod. ECOMIL troops were everywhere now, but still greatly outnumbered by the crowds. As a force they were just too thin to make an impact. They urged the rebels to take their newfound possessions and just leave. Meanwhile, civilians plundered every warehouse they could break into. Del Colliano ran across Sekou Fofana in an alleyway. Several men and women cowered against a wall as Fofana shot up bags of rice and flour with a Kalashnikov. When the clip was spent, he dropped the rifle and picked up a bamboo stick and beat a woman. He beat her savagely for ten, fifteen, twenty seconds until the stick broke over her back. ECOMIL soldiers appeared and stopped him. "It was outrageous," Del Colliano reflected.

"That just showed you the rebels' brutality."

Fofana had a different perspective. He said he was annoyed. He said the rebels were being "classified as looters" in the eyes of the international community, in front of the peacekeepers. The civilians stole what they could knowing that their actions would be attributed to LURD. He said he believed many would even blame the chaos on Bushrod Island on the rebel attack on Monrovia, which had turned everything upside down. "So," he said, "I took a stick and knocked a person there and the peacekeepers came and said: 'Don't do that.' So I left it. I got in my car and moved."

General Okonkwo, Colonal Tawiah, and a small security detail walked through the streets to disrupt looting and prod the rebels to leave once and for all. Colonel Sandusky, Lieutenant Colonel Del Colliano, and Fergy finally caught up to them. The rest of the ECOMIL troops were nowhere in sight. It was just General Okonkwo and four or five vehicles. He alone was the ECOMIL peacekeeping force. General Okonkwo, Fergy saw, did his best, but on the rebel side, there was just no command and control. Nobody was there. They basically just picked up their shit, Fergy thought, and left Sekou Fofana to clean up the mess. Truckloads of rebels with weapons kept heading in the wrong direction, too, sometimes back towards central Monrovia.

General Okonkwo was, Del Colliano observed, a down to the roots kind of leader, and he got involved on the ground and directed his force. He did not plan the same as the United States military. His plan was basically to bring some armored vehicles around at noon. But you could see, Del Colliano thought, he had great experience with these types of rebel forces. He had a sense that he could go onto Bushrod Island unarmed, walk with his aides right down the street, and start getting everyone under control.

For his part, General Okonkwo was confident the rebels would leave eventually, even though it was chaotic. He said later, with an inverted smile, "They had looted so much! They wanted to enjoy what they took, to sell it. So now everybody was just looking for a car." But whenever he came across rebels he said, "Look, you're supposed to be leaving, because of the time, and you agreed before. If you do not, I can't guarantee anyone's safety. You must allow ECOMIL to deploy. You have to leave."

Slowly, rebel cars got pointed in the right direction. Time and again, General Okonkwo personally broke up altercations and ECOMIL officers even snatched rifles away from the rebels. When others saw that, it spurred them to head north, to leave the island for the Po River. But, whenever General Okonkwo came across child soldiers, he knelt and told them that they had to stop fighting and go back to school. Some replied that they would go back to school, so long as their "boss" told them it was all right. "Well," he explained, "your boss must, because you cannot continue to carry arms."

Fergy watched in disbelief as child fighters, or at least children who had been handed rifles, emerged from every nook and cranny. Even after all the time he had spent in country he was not prepared for the sheer numbers. They wandered around, lost, confused, until older rebels lifted them onto crowded trucks. He and Colonel Sandusky came across two small boys, armed, who ran down the road towards the Gabriel Tucker Bridge. One of them looked about ten years old and wore a white jacket.

Fergy intercepted him.

"You need to leave Monrovia, you have a gun."

Without saying a word, without hesitation, the child handed his Kalashnikov to someone nearby. He looked over at Fergy again, water rising in his eyes. It broke Fergy's heart. He nodded and waved the boy on. The kid clearly did not want any part of the war. He did not know any better. But he was done, Fergy realized.

All that little boy wanted to do was go home.

Songbirds disappeared when there was fighting. Jenkins had not heard them for weeks. When he walked outside and heard the warbles in the trees, he knew that the siege had been lifted. He went and found his friend Ledgerhood Rennie, the manager of Radio Veritas, the Catholic station. Veritas had been off the air for a while after they ran out of fuel for the generators and the radio tower was struck with a mortar. Rennie was headed across town to talk to some members of the foreign press and Jenkins went with him. The excitement was down at the river, so the streets were calm. For long stretches of the drive to Sinkor all they saw were dogs. Spent shell casings clogged the gutters and here and there they saw stripped and abandoned cars. Looted shops stood naked before the elements, doors busted open, and whatever was not taken lay smashed on the floor.

At the Royal, they were surprised to find a lively scene, bustling with military advisors and television crews. At the embassy, Jenkins had been getting by for the better part of three months on either military rations or rice, potatoes, and canned tuna, and now he could pull up a comfortable chair with a carved seatback, pat down the creases in the table cloth, spend a few minutes with a laminated menu, and order a proper bowl of jollof rice. His countrymen were still suffering, far too many displaced, too far from home, but for a few moments his phone was mercifully silent. Images from the past few months flipped through his mind like a slideshow gone haywire. He thought about the panic the day Taylor was indicted and the chaotic evacuations when the rebels first attacked. He thought about the Greystone massacres and the bodies at the gates and the gardener and the guards they had lost. He thought about his family and his fears that the embassy might close altogether. It was a great day for the country. He was exhausted.

He dared to let himself think that he would see his mother again soon. He thought back to the day thirteen years ago when he arrived from Kakata with a sack of food to find an empty house, his aunty and uncle gone, maybe dead. He had been out of his mind with grief and made the snap decision to travel overland through rebel territory to Guinea. The trip was a blur, but he made it to his mother and father. After a time, they got word that his aunty and uncle also escaped. He was overcome with joy and relief.

In Ghana they reunited. His aunty and uncle rented an apartment in the upscale neighborhood of Dzorwulu and Jenkins was able to finish his studies, first through the Institute of Management Studies, then at the University of Ghana. The story of his aunty's escape was never far from his mind as he weighed the choice to live in exile or go back to Liberia. The day he had left for Kakata, firefights were intense in the neighborhood and the family heard that a Ghanaian cargo ship that steamed into the Free Port to drop off supplies would leave with room to spare. His aunty, uncle, and cousins rushed down to piers where crowds massed at the water's edge. The family scrambled aboard and found a spot on the overcrowded deck. When there was no more room, people still tried to board, and sailors knocked them off the ladders as the ship pulled out to sea. Bodies fell, flailing into the water, their shouts lost against the foghorn.

The trip took three days. People were sick, and hungry, and thirsty, and the crew sold them water to drink by the glass, for five American dollars a pop. When they finally reached Ghana, the local Red Cross was on hand to receive and process them. They were offered rice and bread. People broke into dry tears, they had not eaten in so long. Some families slept that night in the port, in empty shipping containers. In the morning it was on to a refugee camp and days and months of waiting for news that things were better back home. The news never really came and his family did not trust that the election of Charles Taylor in 1997 was really the start of a new and better phase for the country. For a long time Jenkins carried the guilt that his decision to come back to Liberia had not worked out as he had hoped. He realized too late that he had been looking for an imaginary Liberia, the Liberia of his youth, and that country was irretrievably lost.

Now, he finally let himself hope for something new.

Jenkins left the Royal and made his way back to the house in Gardnersville, where he met his little brother. He was grateful and relieved to find him alive and in good health and the house, miraculously, still standing. Others were far less fortunate. The old neighborhood had the dejected air of a familiar place where things have been rearranged. When he asked after people, he heard that this person had been shot, that person killed by shrapnel, or the people who lived over there had run away and not been seen again. In a trench near the wall of his house he came across the bloated bodies of his dogs and he dropped to his knees, broken. Militia shot them just before Charles Taylor left, he was told, in retribution for his "conniving" with the Americans to bring the Papay down. He went and got a shovel to bury them in the yard. They were such lovely dogs.

They knew "sit," "lie down," and "here."

46

A QUESTION OF DIPLOMACY

Sometimes you hear that someone had "a moment." There was no moment. The day that Monrovia was reunified, a software bug at a power station in Ohio caused one of the largest blackouts in history, knocking out power for huge swaths of the northeastern and midwestern United States. Media coverage of Liberia ended when Charles Taylor left the country, but any chance that U.S. viewers might have heard of the diplomatic win in West Africa was snuffed out with the light.

When Fergy returned to the embassy at days' end, he pushed his way through the crush of men and women in battledress uniforms in the Defense Attaché suite, waved off all the questions, and sank into his chair, exhausted. He scrolled dejectedly down the list of tasks on his computer screen. Between SETAF, the ARG-MEU, ECOMIL, the Quick Reaction Force and the demands of the Front Office, Colonel Sandusky and his own agency, he had no hope of rest anytime soon. And he knew when the Ambassador next gathered the team there would be a new litany of concerns. A peace treaty was still not signed. The Ambassador would of course call the U.S. representatives in Accra and urge them to strike while the iron was hot, to press the parties as hard as they could to forge a deal before the chance was lost, but it would still take a while. ECOMIL only controlled Monrovia, and just barely, while rebels held onto most of the rest of the country. President Blah had flown to Ghana to help move the needle on the peace talks, but rumors of a coup persisted, as did questions of who really controlled the rump government forces. And the terms of Charles Taylor's stay in Nigeria were not made public, so, Fergy knew, there was always a chance he could just hop on a plane and come back.

There was more. Aid ships were two days away and a cholera epidemic spreading. ECOMIL still waited for more troops. In Buchanan, MODEL held captive hundreds of men, women, and children in a church compound. The Liberian national budget was all of fifty million dollars, and no other countries had yet pledged any assistance for the transition. There was no funding for disarmament, demobilization, rehabilitation, and reintegration of the combatants, if they ever agreed to put down their weapons. Economic reconstruction was a long way off and national elections depended on a peace agreement.

It all meant that Fergy had no idea what really had just happened, or where they went from here. Had they just saved Liberia? Was that even possible? They had reunified the city, a dictator had been forced from power, but he wondered if Liberia really could change. He was not a diplomat. He was not paid to think long-term. He could see the Ambassador had a vision for what Liberia could be, but from where Fergy sat, at that moment, it seemed nearly impossible to put the pieces of a country that broken back together. He was still a doer, so deep down he knew it was weariness he felt more than pessimism, but what was his own fatigue compared to those huddled at Greystone, or that of the fighters wandering aimlessly on the river banks with nothing left to fight for?

At the corner of his desk, poking out from under a stack of reports, in a black plastic tray, he spied the manila folder with his retirement papers. He had talked it over with Stacie. He was still in his thirties, young enough for a second career. What that meant he could not say. In some ways it was easier just do keep doing what he did. The Defense Intelligence Agency seemed to want him back and the Air Force could probably find a slot for him. But he was not sure how much more he had left to give. The landline was ringing, people were knocking at the door, and the noise of the office was giving him a headache. He reached for the folder, spread the retirement forms out on the desk, and began to read, pressing his finger to the paper so he would not lose the line.

On August 18, 2003, in Accra, Ghana, a week after Charles Taylor left Liberia and four days after ECOMIL secured the Free Port and greater Monrovia, General Abdulsalami Abubakar, the mediator, convened Liberian stakeholders for the signing a Comprehensive Peace Agreement, or CPA, an accord to end the civil war once and for all. The CPA stipulated a national transitional government that would take over from President Blah in short order and guide the country to national elections. It did not, at first, reflect the power dynamics on the ground, where fighters were slow to cede any more territory to the peacekeepers. It relied instead on the good faith of all parties and the good works of ECOMIL, supported by Joint Task Force Liberia. It worked well enough.

Twenty-four, then forty-eight, then seventy-two hours after the capital was reunified, Fergy noticed that Bushrod Island started to feel less and less like enemy territory. He shuttled the Colonel between meetings with the ECOMIL, the government, and the rebels, who had opened a liaison office near New Kru Town. Relief agencies moved in and distributed supplies, then a World Food Program ship docked and offloaded much needed stocks of rice, maize, and bulgar wheat. The most desperate Liberians could eat again and, for everyone else, local markets started up again, flush with looted grains, biscuits, and other foodstuffs sold out of wheel-barrows. Fruit and vegetables reappeared on the curbs and fishermen took their small boats out to sea. The telegram offices reopened and families once more had cash to spend. Overhead, U.S. jets and gunships patrolled the skies and, in the distance, on silver washes of ocean, the Iwo Jima and its sister ships slowly turned in the great shafts of light that broke through the storm clouds.

International Committee of the Red Cross Deputy Head of Delegation Jordi Raich observed that Liberia was a country of deadlines, and Fergy could not disagree. Liberians were always waiting for the next one, as though once it had passed everything would be fine. In between, Raich said, it was either chaos or celebration. Liberians had waited for a peace conference, then a cease-fire, then an assessment. They waited for Charles Taylor to step down. They waited for a peacekeeping operation, then the end of the siege, and then the aid from the Free Port. Now came a new series of deadlines. The United Nations Security Council authorized an integrated peacekeeping and humanitarian mission to replace ECOMIL and Joint Task Force Liberia on October 1. The national transitional government was slated to stand up two weeks later, on October 14, for a period of two years. So now everyone waited for October.

About a month after ECOMIL first deployed, Fergy drove the Political Officer out to the Free Port to meet General Okonkwo, on behalf of the Ambassador, to discuss ECOMIL's views on a disarmament program. From a desk in an otherwise unfurnished office in an empty building, General Okonkwo tilted back in his wooden chair and put his hands on his belt. Even with the time that had passed, he said, Liberians still reached out to congratulate the peacekeepers for securing Monrovia despite their tiny force. He allowed himself a smile. "Ambassador Blaney," he remarked, "was of great help. His support made us talk to the rebels and that made things easy. Our own experiences helped a lot too, because most of us have been in Liberia before." But, he reflected, even members of the United Nations Mission in Sierra Leone, where the first battalion of Nigerian peacekeepers had been stationed before they came to Liberia, asked him how ECOMIL had been able to pull it off. Given Liberia's long, violent history, and its previous bad experiences with peacekeepers, they found it hard to believe that ECOMIL had secured the airport, the sea port, and greater Monrovia with only one battalion and without firing a single shot. "I told them," General Okonkwo said, "it wasn't an issue of fight, fight, fight."

He reached up and straightened his beret.

"It was," he said, "an issue of diplomacy."

EPILOGUE

Let's be clear: Liberians ended the Liberian civil war. At the peace talks, Liberian negotiators from the government, the rebel groups, local political parties, and civil society hashed out a framework for a transition to peace and for future governance of the country. Women peace activists, many of whom had spent years networking and advocating for an end to the violence, were documented to have played a role moving the process to conclusion. Yet all wars end as they begin, in messy and unexpected ways, and for many months after Charles Taylor's exile and the reunification of Monrovia it seemed as if the war might return at any moment. Even with a signed peace accord and international peacekeepers on the ground, rebels held much of the country and irregular forces still had their weapons. There were times when those with guns and those who paid them had trouble letting go.

"Peace is not a light switch," Ambassador Blaney often said, "it's more of a rheostat." Violence flared every so often, whether a firefight on Somalia Drive or a riot at a cantonment after disarmament started, but after each incident, and they could only be called incidents in retrospect, the new era came into sharper focus. In the immediate aftermath of a war everything seems so consequential, but time has a way of sorting all and in the sediments left behind only the most obvious markers of change stand out, and even those, in many cases, become the skeletons of words in reports with no emotional resonance, not notable enough to make it into the histories. So the markers of change piled up until Liberia became something other than a place at war.

Peace costs money to consolidate, to ward off those who would profit at its expense. Liberia had nothing in the coffers to fund disarmament, demobilization, rehabilitation, and reintegration of the armed factions, let alone national reconstruction. The United States Congress, under the leadership of Senator John Warner, who visited Liberia while the ARG-MEU was still deployed, the only congressman to do so, carved out of an 87 billion dollar Iraq supplemental bill two hundred million dollars for post-conflict stabilization in Liberia, not coincidentally the exact amount that Ambassador Blaney and Ed Birgells requested in the midst of the conflict, and the United States added another 245 million in assessed contributions to fund a United Nations mission. ECOMIL and the U.S. troops sent to support them soon gave way to a full-blown United Nations peacekeeping operation, the largest in the world at the time and for years afterward.

President Moses Blah then made good on his word that he would do right by the country when, after only a few months in office, he stepped down and transferred his authority to Gyude Bryant, a local businessman selected through the peace process to be the Chairman of the National Transitional Government of Liberia, a custodian government that managed the country until national elections could be conducted.

On January 16, 2006, roughly two and a half years after the war ended, Ellen Johnson-Sirleaf was sworn in as Liberia's president, the first elected female president in African history. The Harvard-educated economist had won a peaceful, free, and fair national election, and First Lady Laura Bush and Secretary of State Condoleezza Rice both attended the inauguration in Monrovia. The election changed the narrative of the country in the international press and Liberians flooded back from exile. Refugee camps emptied and more successful diaspora returned with cash to invest and renovate ruined family properties. The country was still poor, but not at war. President George W. Bush even made a trip to Monrovia before he left office, and video of him dancing to Liberian beats became an early viral sensation at the dawn of the social media era.

Charles Taylor returned to Liberia after all, but only for the purpose to be arrested and flown off to prison. Nigerian President Obasanjo stated publicly that he would place the former Liberian president in the custody of an elected Liberian government, if requested. Johnson-Sirleaf's government finally made the request and on March 29, 2006, the Nigerians returned Taylor to Robertsfield, where the United Nations Mission in Liberia arrested him on arrival and whisked him to detention facilities in Freetown, Sierra Leone, to await trial. He was then transferred to the Hague, where he was convicted on eleven counts of aiding and abetting war crimes and crimes against humanity committed in Sierra Leone. He was sentenced to fifty years in prison, and serves his time in a maximum-security facility in England. He was never charged with any crimes in Liberia.

As for the rebels and the militia, some of their political leaders joined the interim government, while their fighters turned over their weapons to the United Nations as part of a nationwide demobilization, disarmament, rehabilitation, and reintegration program. Liberia eventually put together a Truth and Reconciliation Commission, but otherwise the sins of the past were left in the past and everyone tried to move on. Fortune did not favor most of the ex-fighters in the new Liberia. Even General Cobra, though free to do as he pleased with no threat from state security, passed away a few years afterward with little to show for the role he played in launching the new era, forgotten to the wider world.

In Liberia, one can argue whether the U.S. policy to force Taylor from office was the best approach, but inarguably it catalyzed change. Many underlying conflicts and tensions within Liberian society are still not fully resolved, even years later, but the country averted the kind of perpetual war that many other nations have experienced. The inflection point came at a unique historical moment, just after the United States had destroyed the Iraqi army and overthrown Saddam Hussein, and just before the rise of al-Qaeda in Iraq, the reemergence of the Taliban, and the intensification of resistance to American leadership in the world. At the time, Russia was still consolidating its post-Soviet Union approach, and China had only just acceded to the World Trade Organization and was not quite yet ready to assert itself as a superpower. New global threats like the Islamic State did not exist and United States unilateralism was at its high-water mark. Though the events took place just over a decade ago, social networking and advanced mobile communications barely existed. Charles Taylor and his government were therefore isolated in every meaningful respect and up against a superpower that had just shown what it would do to its enemies.

Within a few years, the world changed. Today, new forms of extremism mean that the kind of frontline diplomacy that won the day in Liberia might not be possible without a higher body count. Improvised explosive devices and direct assaults on diplomatic facilities or peacekeeping missions are constant threats. New dynamics between the great powers make consensus much harder to achieve on issues like sanctions, which were used to devastating effect against the Taylor administration, and the networking technology now available means that governments and rebels alike have incredibly effective means to marshal and direct support to their causes. Any of these variables could have radically changed the outcome in Liberia, but did not. Peace was made.

Diplomacy is the art of avoiding conflict, but diplomacy in war is something a bit different. Diplomacy in war is alchemy that involves risk, timing, and a keen feel for context. No two wars are the same and all solutions must be tailored. But a common denominator is that, to be effective, diplomats and peacekeepers must not be drawn into a given conflict, or must separate themselves from it. Years on, what stands out about the Liberia story is that, when the moment was ripe, when Liberian and international interests finally aligned, diplomats and peacekeepers won the trust of the combatants, served as intermediaries, and enabled fighters from all sides to walk away from the war.

In the face of violence, disease, and other threats, the easy thing to do is to close an embassy or consulate and walk away. From a bureaucratic perspective, it is the safe call. The United States has shuttered embassies with regularity of late. But, in today's world, problems still metastasize. Diplomats, and the agencies they work in concert with, are the bell-weathers and first responders to crisis. If they are not there to take calculated risks and find solutions, dangers inevitably hit closer to home.

Late the evening of September 25, 2014, a man walked into the emergency room at Texas Health Presbyterian Hospital in Dallas, Texas, complaining of abdominal pain, dizziness, nausea, and a headache. He had a low fever. He was given acetaminophen and underwent a CT scan that did not reveal anything remarkable, then released well before daybreak with a prescription for antibiotics. Two days later he returned, this time with diarrhea, and doctors learned that he had recently come from Liberia. Tests were run. Eight days later, the man became the first person to die from Ebola in the United States and the case touched off a political firestorm. Liberia was back in the news for all the wrong reasons.

The 2014 Ebola outbreak in West Africa, centered in Guinea, Sierra Leone, and Liberia, was the largest Ebola outbreak in history. It killed more than 11,000 people, more than 4,800 in Liberia alone. In Liberia, a new country team at U.S. Embassy Monrovia, led by Ambassador Deborah Malac, coordinated closely with President Johnson-Sirleaf's government to bring resources to bear. President Barack Obama eventually deployed a 3,000 person military contingent to help with bolster civilian relief efforts. It was not until September 3, 2015, well more than a year after the first case was reported, that the World Health Organization was able to declare Liberia free of human transmission of the virus. Now imagine, for a moment, if there had been no Liberian state to coordinate international assistance, or if the country was still in chaos. Imagine if Ebola had broken out when two hundred thousand displaced were still encamped in and around the city, in muddy tents. How far beyond Liberia's borders would it have spread?

The place in the collective memory of the international diplomat and peacekeeper is a curious one. With rare exceptions, they are little acknowledged in the narratives of the countries to which they deploy and they are not celebrated much in their own country's histories. The bootprints of men like General Okonkwo fade like wet tracks on hot tarmac and hardly anyone hears of the courage of the Marines and local guards that protected a chancery as a country collapsed around them. Ted Collins, Sue Ann Sandusky, Robert Ferguson, and Jenkins Vangehn never became household names, but without them Liberia would have been a very different place.

After it was all over and the political transition well underway, Ambassador Blaney flew home. Liberia had been clear win for the Bush administration—a dictator brought to justice, a war ended with only the lightest military touch—but, since it divided the administration internally, it was an orphaned success. Still, Blaney half expected that there might be a reporter or two on hand when he landed, or several officials from the State Department, but by then Liberia was already back to near obscurity, so it was Robin alone at the arrival gate waiting for him, her beautiful features flush with emotion and eyes aquiver with tears. They embraced and stood there for a long time as the other passengers streamed by with their luggage carts, looking distractedly for family.

"Welcome home, Mr. Ambassador," she said.

ACKNOWLEDGEMENTS

The journey of every book starts with someone who believes in the story, and the first one who believed was my dear friend and colleague Amanda Pilz, who co-authored the earliest iterations. While service to our country in the wars in Iraq, Afghanistan and Pakistan, and other places, eventually pulled her away from the project, I have tried to stay true to the spirit of our early collaboration. She is an exceptional writer and the countless hours she dedicated to the book, writing, talking through structure with me, and parsing the interviews, helped me refine my craft and form the basis for a book that, I hope, will reflect well on all who have contributed to it. For this and more she has my deepest appreciation.

This book also would be radically different without the close collaboration of Ambassador John Blaney. It is a true honor that he entrusted me to tell his story through these pages, and his leadership, courage, friendship and mentorship, both in Liberia and over many years now, continue to inspire me. Likewise, you don't always get to work with heroes, and I consider myself fortunate to have had the chance to serve side by side with Robert Ferguson. His bravery under fire, his frankness and willingness to share his memories and perceptions of a very intense time form the core of this book. He will forever have my greatest respect for the things he accomplished in Liberia, and for opening up so that others can get a real sense of what happened. About Jenkins Vangehn the same word can be applied: hero. His dedication to his country and to our team were unparalleled, and his contributions to this work provide insights into the deeply personal side of a civil war that is often overlooked in the history books. That he has mad football skills is only a bonus.

Ted Collins I also must mention in this group for his fortitude and unerring judgment. He made the toughest of calls, kept us safe as possible, and then continued throughout his career to take on some of the toughest assignments in the Foreign Service. An incredible friend and colleague. Finally, I must thank Sue Anne Sandusky, who did not actively participate in the creation of this book, but through her drive and tireless work showed in the course of a remarkable career what the very best Foreign Area Officers can accomplish.

Most authors of non-fiction, I suspect, rue the material that cannot make the final edit. In this case the people who provided interviews, listed in full in the pages to follow, created a tapestry of stories and perspectives worthy of a far longer work, or several different works. While I truly regret that for reasons of structure, pace, focus and length that I could not given each and every voice its due measure, I have attempted to imbue this story with the spirit of their experiences. Each contribution is deeply valued and, I hope, in some way reflected in this recreation of time and place. I do want to give particular mention to the voices of my African friends and colleagues here. While I hope that they will find the time to tell their stories more fully, I also hope that they will find fair the representation of their perspectives through the prism of a story of an embassy. General Okonkwo, Colonel Tawiah, John T. Richardson, Jonathan Taylor, Lewis Brown, Daniel Chea, Benoni Urey, Sekou Conneh, Joe Gbala and Sekou Fofana all were incredibly candid and forthcoming, and added an invaluable dimension to this story. The late Moses Blah and the late Aliya Seah Sheriff were also brutally honest about the horror of this war, its ends and its consequences.

Finding an agent and publisher is always an uphill climb. In this regard I was fortunate to have the support of Dr. Chester Crocker, who from the start saw value in the narrative. There is no better call for an author to receive than from an agent who tells you that a publisher wants your book. Tony Outhwaite, who made that call to me, has forever earned thanks and appreciation for his faith, persistence and hard work in helping this book make it to print. Megan Trank earns the same as the editor who took the chance, and for her steadfast support and guidance. Eric Kampmann I cannot thank enough for the opportunity, as well as his teams at Beaufort Books and Midpoint Trade, especially including Laura Robinson and Michael Short, whose enthusiasm has made this process fun. Sebastian Junger from the start has been an important booster and is a model of creative generosity. I also thank David

Eizenman, for his calm, sage advice at a critical moment, Mary Bisbee-Beek
for help with publicity and Michael Jacobsohn for the ethics guidance.

Of course there would be no story if we had closed the embassy, and so
I also take a moment to acknowledge the bravery of the Marines who saw us
through: Jonathan Aldridge, Jason Scramlin, Mike Muniz, Jordan Weeks,
Anthony Adams, Daniel Brown and Brian Stovall. I hope in some small way
that this book conveys the true importance to foreign affairs of the Marine
Security Guard program. Captain Roger Coldiron and Greg Kuni and
Robert Lynch were terrific in leading the HAST and FAST respectively at a
most critical time. General Turner, John Del Colliano, Mike Shinners and
the entire ARG-MEU team (Kevin Owens!), as well as our various Special
Operations Forces, did an incredible job and I hope this book spurs more of
their stories. Hersh Hernandez, his deputy Tony Lopez, Kaetu Smith and
the full Inter-Con staff also deserve singular credit for protecting the embassy.
And of course I hope this book highlights the vital support and contributions
of each and every local staff member of U.S. Embassy Monrovia, from our
drivers to our administrative and facilities support teams, and at embassies the
world over, who make all the difference and without whose efforts embassies
simply could not operate.

Finally, I have always benefited from the best friends and mentors a person
can have, far too many to mention here, but I would be remiss if I did not
acknowledge at least a few. The late Peter Lewis for his enduring inspiration.
Antonia Merzon, Maria Merzon and Salvatore Zizza, without whose support
I could not have attended Yale: they set me up for success. Patrizia Ascani,
who encouraged me from the start. Patrizia's timely order of medicines for
JFK saved many lives, by the way. Anna Taruschio, who provided timely
advice, and Josh Swiller, who contributed a writer's insights to the journey of
this book. Terrance Johnson I thank for carrying the torch, and Marc Lerner
and Nina Rifkind for just about everything. I thank Abe and Dara Musher-
Eizenman for the family. Darragh, Rafael and Bear-the-Dog for all the love
and adventures and lastly, Peter Paradiso and Kathleen McCann, my parents,
for literature and for love.

Ambassador John W. Blaney and the U.S. Embassy Monrovia Marine Security Guard Detachment, June to August 2003. They kept the Embassy safe. Left to right, back row: Bryan Stovall, Jr.; Jonathan Aldridge; Jason Scramlin; Ambassador John W. Blaney; Michael Muniz; Jordan Weeks. Front row, left to right: Daniel Brown and Anthony Adams.

INTERVIEWS

(TITLES AND AFFILIATIONS IN 2003)

US GOVERNMENT/EMBASSY/MILITARY
Walter Kansteiner US Assistant Secretary of State for African Affairs
John William Blaney III US Ambassador to Liberia
Christopher Datta*Charge D'Affaires
Senior Master Sergeant Robert Ferguson ("Fergy") Operations Coordinator
Edward Collins ("Ted") Regional Security Officer (RSO)
Brad Lynn*Assistant Regional Security Officer (A/RSO)
Edward Birgells*USAID Mission Director
Jenkins Vangehn Political Assistant
James A. Jimmy ("JJ") Driver, Defense Attaché's Office
Lieutenant Colonel (Ret.) Horacio Hernandez Inter-Con Security Systems
Captain Roger Coldiron HAST
Major Philip Spangler HAST/Civil Affairs
Lieutenant Colonel John Del Colliano Executive Officer 26th MEU
Major Michael Shinners JTF-Liberia
Jason Scramlin*Marine Security Guard
Anthony Adams*Marine Security Guard

GOVERNMENT OF THE REPUBLIC OF LIBERIA
Moses Blah President/Vice President of Liberia
Jonathan Taylor Minister of State for Presidential Affairs
Lewis Brown Minister of State Without Portfolio
John T. Richardson ("JT") National Security Advisor
Daniel Chea Minister of Defense
Benoni Urey Commissioner For Maritime Affairs

LIBERIANS UNITED FOR RECONCILIATION AND DEMOCRACY (LURD)

Sekou Conneh Chairman
Joe Gbala Secretary General
Alhaji Sekou Fofana Deputy Secretary General for Civil Administration
Aliya Seyah Sheriff ("Cobra") Acting Chief of Staff
Ophoree Diah ("Iron Jacket") Acting Deputy Chief of Staff

ECOMIL

Brigadier General Festus Okonkwo ECOMIL Force Commander
Colonel Theophilus Tawiah ECOMIL Chief of Staff
Colonel (Ret.) Michael Larmas Smith US Advisor to ECOMIL

DIPLOMATIC MISSIONS

David Parker European Commission (EC) Aid Coordinator
Jean Chahine ("2JJ") EC Water Project
Ziad Sankari Consul, Embassy of Lebanon
Mario Giro Delegate, Community of Sant'Egidio

HUMANITARIAN ORGANIZATIONS

Frederique Bardou Action Contra La Faim Mission Director
Jordi Raich Curcó ICRC Deputy Head of Delegation
Kim Johansen ICRC Senior Logistician
Magnus Wolf-Murray Merlin Head of Delegation
Alain Kassa MSF Belgium Head of Mission
Juanita Angulo MSF Belgium Surgeon
S. Segbeh Nyamphor Campaign for Promotion of Democracy (CPD)
Thompson Togbah Campaign for Promotion of Democracy (CPD)
Blamo Sieh National Human Rights Center

JOURNALISTS

Tim Hetherington Gabriel Films
Somini Sangupta New York Times
Karl Vick Washington Post
Declan Walsh The Irish Times/The Independent

OTHERS

Robert Khourey ("Bob") Sabanoh Printing Press
Francis Gallo Student
*Provided answers to specific questions vice a full-length interview

REFERENCES

The Liberian civil war generated an incredible amount of printed work, including news reports, academic essays and analysis, and comprehensive reports issued by international organizations and local and international non-governmental organizations. Testimonials from the Liberian Truth and Reconciliation Commission, as well as transcripts from the proceedings of the Special Court for Sierra Leone, provide a compelling record of the conflict. There have also been multiple documentary films produced and, particularly for June-August 2003, the period covered by this book, a rich video and photographic history exists. Many informal or self-published memoirs from Liberians describing the conflict can also be found online. The bibliography below provides a list of the better known, recently published works on Liberia that helped inform and inspire this book.

LIBERIA BIBLIOGRAPHY

Berkeley, Bill. *The Graves Are Not Yet Full: Race, Tribe and Power in the Heart of Africa.* New York: Basic Books, 2002.

Brabazon, James. *My Friend the Mercenary.* Edinburgh: Canongate Books, 2010.

Ciment, James. *Another America: The Story of Liberia and the Former Slaves Who Ruled It.* New York: Hill and Wang, 2013.

Cooper, Helene. *The House at Sugar Beach: In Search of a Lost African Childhood.* New York: Simon & Schuster, 2009.

Dwyer, Johnny. *American Warlord: A True Story.* New York: Alfred A. Knopf, 2015.

Ellis, Stephen. *The Mask of Anarchy Updated Edition: The Destruction of Liberia and the Religious Dimension of an African Civil War.* New York: NYU Press, 2006.

Gbowee, Leymah and Carol Mithers. *Mighty Be Our Powers: How Sisterhood, Prayer and Sex Changed a Nation at War.* New York: Beast Books, 2011.

Greene, Barbara. *Too Late to Turn Back: Barbara and Graham Greene in Liberia.* New York: Penguin Books, 1991.

Greene, Graham. Journey Without Maps. New York: Penguin Classics, 2006.

Hetherington, Tim. *Long Story Bit by Bit: Liberia Retold.* New York: Umbrage Editions, 2009.

Hondros, Chris. *Testament.* New York: powerHouse Books, 2013.

Huffman, Alan. *Mississippi in Africa: The Saga of the Slaves of Prospect Hill Plantation and Their Legacy in Liberia.* New York: Gotham, 2004.

Huffman, Alan. *Here I Am: The Story of Tim Hetherington, War Photographer.* New York: Grove Press, 2013.

Johnson Sirleaf, Ellen. *This Child Will Be Great: Memoir of a Remarkable Life by Africa's First Woman President.* New York: Harper Perennial, 2010.

Kamara-Umunna and Emily Holland. *And Still Peace Did Not Come: A Memoir of Reconciliation.* New York: Hyperion, 2011.

Pham, John-Peter. *Liberia: Portrait of a Failed State.* New York: Reed Press, 2004.

Powers, William D. *Blue Clay People: Seasons on Africa's Fragile Edge.* New York: Bloomsbury, 2008.

Waugh, Colin. *Charles Taylor and Liberia: Ambition and Atrocity in Africa's Lone Star State.* New York: Zed Books, 2011.

LIBERIA FILMOGRAPHY

Firestone and the Warlord. (2014) (PBS)
Pray the Devil Back to Hell. (2008) (Fork Films)
Which Way Is The Front Line From Here? The Life and Time of Tim Hetherington. (2013) (HBO)
Liberia: An Uncivil War. (2004) (Gabriel Films)

NOTES

PART ONE: THE FIRST ATTACK

ONE: THE INDICTMENT

Material for this section was primarily drawn from the author's interviews with Robert Ferguson, James Arthur Jimmy and Jenkins Vangehn.

"Some people believe that President Taylor is the problem. If President Taylor removes himself, fellow Liberians, will that bring peace? If so, I will remove myself." See e.g., "Pray the Devil Back to Hell," Produced by Abigail Disney and Directed by Gini Reticker, Fork Films (2008).

"Liberian President Charles Taylor," he said, "has just been indicted for war crimes by a United Nations-backed court in Sierra Leone." BBC broadcast the story. For the corresponding article see: "Arrest warrant for Liberia leader," http://news.bbc.co.uk/2/hi/africa/2961390.stm BBC News, June 4, 2003.

"Everyone started to run." Material for this passage was primarily drawn from the author's interviews with Robert Ferguson, Jenkins Vangehn, Robert Khourey, Blamo Sieh, Thompson Togba, S. Segbeh Nyamphor and Jean Chahine.

TWO: THE RETURN

Material for this section was primarily drawn from the author's interviews with John Blaney, Christopher Datta, Robert Ferguson, Ted Collins, Jenkins Vangehn, Blamo Sieh, Thompson Togba, S. Segbeh Nyamphor and Jean Chahine.

"Military vibrations." Yeaten's radio pronouncement was recollected by Christopher Datta, Ted Collins and Jenkins Vangehn. Moses Blah also noted Yeaten's use of the phrase during Charles Taylor's trial. See, e.g., http://www.ijmonitor.org/2008/05/former-vp-moses-blah-discusses-beheading-of-ruf-commander-in-chief-and-other-events/.

THREE: THE ATTACK

Material for this section was primarily drawn from the author's interviews with Christopher Datta, Ted Collins, Robert Ferguson and James Arthur Jimmy.

"This particular time, as in every organization, there are weaklings..." See, e.g., "Coup Attempt Foiled," GhanaWeb, June 5, 2003, (via Reuters). http://www.ghanaweb.com/GhanaHomePage/NewsArchive/Coup-Attempt-Foiled-37370

"In Liberia, missing and dead were synonymous." On July 16, 2003, President Charles Taylor confirmed to the Liberian parliament that John Yormie and Isaac Vaye were dead but gave no explanation. See "Liberian Ministers Were Killed," BBC News, July 16, 2003. http://news.bbc.co.uk/2/hi/africa/3070157.stm.

"If we think we're looking at evacuations, we can ask European Command to send a survey and assessment team, what they call an ESAT... They'll likely bring Navy SEALs with them." In 2003, three separate U.S. Unified Commands had responsibility for U.S. military operations in Africa. The United States European Command (EUCOM) covered West Africa. In 2007, the Pentagon stood up the Africa Command (AFRICOM), headquartered in Stuttgart, Germany, to oversee operations, including the operations of Special Operations Forces, for all of Africa save Egypt. Today, AFRICOM, not EUCOM, would respond to a crisis in Liberia, and one must refer to AFRICOM to determine what capabilities it could bring to bear in a given crisis. Fleet Anti-terrorism Security Teams continue to provide augmented security for embassies facing crisis around the world. See, e.g., Church, Chris, "FAST Training With the U.S. Marines," Star and Stripes, October 5, 2015. http://www.stripes.com/news/marine-corps/fast-training-with-the-us-marine-corps-1.370861.

FOUR: THE EVACUATION

Material for this section was primarily drawn from the author's interviews with John Blaney, Christopher Datta, Ted Collins, Robert Ferguson, David Parker, Jenkins Vangehn, Jason Scramlin, Anthony Adams, John Richardson, Horacio Hernandez, and Jean Chahine.

"In any event, Datta knew better than to give the Liberian president a photo opportunity, and the ESAT and SEALs had flown in at the earliest waking hour." On June 9, President Bush notified the U.S. Congress by letter of the insertion of a 35-member "[assessment] and evacuation and standby response" team into Liberia. The full text of his letter can be found at: http://www.presidency.ucsb.edu/ws/index.php?pid=64982.

PART TWO: PRESSURE

ONE: THE AMBASSADOR TO HELL

Material for this section was primarily drawn from the author's interviews with John Blaney.

TWO: THE OSTRICH AND THE RAT

Material for this section was primarily drawn from the author's interviews with John Blaney, Ted Collins, Lewis Brown, Benoni Urey, and John Richardson.

"I want to prevent catastrophe in Liberia." See, e.g., "Taylor Calls War Crimes Charges a 'Plot', Warns African Peers," Emmanuel Goujon, Agence-France Presse, June 12, 2013.

"No white boy from Washington can come into Africa and indict a sitting African President." See, e.g., "Troops to Leave Liberia's Streets," CNN International, June 12, 2003. http://edition.cnn.com/2003/WORLD/africa/06/12/liberia.taylor/.

THREE: THE AFTERMATH

Material for this section was primarily drawn from the author's interviews with Robert Ferguson and on the author's own recollections. "Political Officer" refers to the author.

FOUR: THE AFRICANS

Material for this section was primarily drawn from the author's interviews with John Blaney.

FIVE: THE KEARSARGE

Material for this section was primarily drawn from the author's interviews with John Blaney, Ted Collins and Horacio Hernandez.

"At the request of the U.S. Ambassador to Liberia…" See e.g., "USS Kearsarge Joins Operation Shining Express," Commander, U.S. Atlantic Fleet Public Affairs, June 13, 2003. http://www.navy.mil/submit/display.asp?story_id=7997.

SIX: THE VICE PRESIDENT

Material for this section was primarily drawn from the author's interview with Moses Blah. The text is largely derived from the author's interview with Mr. Blah, though it should be noted he repeated many elements of the story publicly, and consistently, for the Liberian Truth and Reconciliation Commission and at Charles Taylor's trial.

SEVEN: THE CEASEFIRE

Material for this section was primarily drawn from the author's interviews with John Blaney and Jenkins Vangehn.

"Anyone who thinks I will resign within a month is holding onto, at best, a dream." See, e.g., "Taylor insists on completing tenure 6 January 2004," Panapress, June 20, 2003.

The full text of the June 17 Ceasefire Agreement can be found at: http://www.usip.org/publications/peace-agreements-liberia.

PART THREE: THE SECOND ATTACK

ONE: THE MEZZE HOUSE

Material for this section was primarily drawn from the author's interviews with Robert Ferguson.

TWO: THE SECOND ATTACK

Material for this section was primarily drawn from the author's interviews with John Blaney, Ted Collins, Robert Ferguson, and Anthony Adams.

The U.S. State Department's Office of the Inspector General has posted a number of reports on security at specific embassies that provide general information on Emergency Action Plans and Emergency Action Committees. For a report related to Afghanistan, as an exemplar, see i.e., https://oig.state.gov/system/files/212779.pdf.

THREE: THE DEAD

Material for this section was primarily drawn from the author's interviews with Jenkins Vangehn, Robert Ferguson, Magnus Wolf-Murray, Blamo Sieh and Anthony Adams.

FOUR: THE DEMAND

Material for this section was primarily drawn from the author's interviews with John Blaney, Ted Collins, Jonathan Taylor and Benoni Urey.

"Inexplicably Fox News reported…" See "U.S. Could Send Troops to Liberia," Fox News, July 3, 2003. http://www.foxnews.com/story/2003/07/03/us-could-send-troops-to-liberia.html. The story also cites an unnamed senior defense official as stating that a FAST team was on standby.

A text of President George W. Bush's remarks to the U.S.-Africa Business Summit can be found at http://georgewbush-whitehouse.archives.gov/news/releases/2003/06/20030626-2.html.

The text of the Government of Liberia's response to President Bush's call that President Taylor step down is noted in Dwyer, Johnny, "American Warlord: A True Story," (Alfred A. Knopf, New York, 2015), footnote 5, referencing "U.S. ambassador to Liberia to U.S. secretary of state, June 27, 2003, U.S. Department of State, Document E550, National Security Archive, George Washington University.

FIVE: THE DISPLACED

Material for this section was primarily drawn from the author's interviews with Jenkins Vangehn, Jordi Raich Curco, Alain Kassa, and David Parker.

SIX: WE LOVE YOU GEORGE BUSH

Material for this section was primarily drawn from the author's interviews with John Blaney, Ted Collins and Jenkins Vangehn.

"United Nations Secretary General Kofi Annan called publicly for the United Nations Security Council to authorize the United States to lead a peacekeeping operation." See Lynch, Colum, "Annan Requests U.S. Peacekeepers in Liberia," Washington Post, July 2, 2003.

"Astonishingly, U.S. peacekeepers became an option." See, i.e. "U.S. prepares military options," CNN International.com/World, July 4, 2003. http://edition.cnn.com/2003/WORLD/africa/07/03/us.liberia/index.html

"CNN White House Correspondent John King reported…" See, "U.S. may send 500-1000 troops to Liberia," CNN International.com/WORLD, July 2, 2003. http://edition.cnn.com/2003/WORLD/africa/07/02/us.liberia/index.html?iref=mpstoryview

"Yet divisions within the Cabinet percolated in the press." See, e.g., "U.S. is pressed to weigh sending troops to Liberia," Mathews, Mark, The Baltimore Sun, July 1, 2003. http://articles.baltimoresun.com/2003-07-01/news/0307010128_1_liberia-peacekeeping-west-african.

"Rumsfeld," the Associated Press noted, "also doubts…" See, i.e., Fox News, "Bush Administration Ponders Liberian Peace Force," July 1, 2003 (via Associated Press). http://www.foxnews.com/story/2003/07/01/bush-administration-ponders-liberian-peace-force.html.

"I'm not ruling it out." The full text of Ari Fleischer's remarks can be found at: http://www.presidency.ucsb.edu/ws/?pid=61118. (Via UC Santa Barbara's American Presidency Project).

PART FOUR: THE HAST

ONE: THE PRESS

Material for this section was primarily drawn from the author's interviews with John Blaney, Ted
 Collins, Robert Ferguson and Somini Sengupta. Karl Vick's quote is from an email exchange
 with the author.

"The Pentagon, it stated, was assembling a survey team..." See "Humanitarian Assistance Team to Depart
 for Liberia Today," U.S. European Command, July 6, 2003. http://www.eucom.mil/media-library/
 article/21853/Humanitarian-Assistance-Team-depart-Liberia-today (cached).

TWO: THE NIGERIAN OFFER

Material for this section was primarily drawn from the author's interviews with John Blaney and Jenkins
 Vangehn.

"He has extended and invitation and we have accepted an invitation." See, i.e., "Liberia's Taylor
 accepts asylum offer," CNN International.com/World http://edition.cnn.com/2003/WORLD/
 africa/07/06/liberia.taylor/.

THREE: THE HAST

Material for this section was primarily drawn from the author's interviews with John Blaney, Daniel Chea,
 Roger Coldiron, Phil Spangler, Ed Birgells, Robert Ferguson, David Parker and Somini Sengupta.

"Look it's been a long ride and we're here to see what we can do." See, e.g., Sengupta, Somini, "U.S.
 Soldiers Arrive in Liberia for Humanitarian Mission," New York Times, July 7, 2003. (The quote
 given is "We are here to inspect and see what we can do.") http://www.nytimes.com/2003/07/07/
 international/africa/07CND-LIBE.html

The CNN "American Morning Interview" between John Blaney and Bill Hemmer can be found at:
 http://edition.cnn.com/TRANSCRIPTS/0307/07/ltm.18.html.

"We had a good discussion about Liberia." The full text of President Bush's remarks can be found at
 http://2001-2009.state.gov/p/af/rls/rm/22275.htm.

FOUR: THE REPORT

Material for this section was primarily drawn from the author's interviews with John Blaney, Roger
 Coldiron, Phil Spangler, Ted Collins, and Somini Sengupta.

"Our assessment team in Monrovia has about finished its work..." The full text of Colin Powell's remarks
 can be found at: http://2001-2009.state.gov/secretary/former/powell/remarks/2003/22350.htm.

"What about Liberia?" The full text of President Bush's remarks to the press can be found at: http://www.
 presidency.ucsb.edu/ws/index.php?pid=550 (Via UC Santa Barbara's American Presidency Project).

"A couple weeks later, the Los Angeles Times broke the story." Farley, Maggie, Ann Simmons and Paul
 Richter, "Team in Liberia Sought Fast Aid," Los Angeles Times, August 17, 2003. http://articles.
 latimes.com/2003/aug/17/world/fg-intervene17.

FIVE: A TENSE CEASEFIRE

Material for this section was primarily drawn from the author's interviews with John Blaney, Ted Collins,
 Robert Ferguson, Sekou Damate Conneh, Sekou Fofana, Ed Birgells, and David Parker.

The LURD press release can be found at: http://www.theperspective.org/lurdthreats.html.

SIX: THE PRAYER RALLY
Material for this section was primarily drawn from the author's interviews with John Blaney, Jenkins Vangehn, Blamo Sieh, Kim Johansen, Jordi Raich Curco, Declan Walsh and Somini Sengupta.
"My decision to step down." See, e.g., Murphy, Jarrett, "Liberia's Taylor Forecasts Chaos," CBS News, July 19, 2003. http://www.cbsnews.com/news/liberias-taylor-forecasts-chaos/.

PART FIVE: THE THIRD ATTACK

ONE: THE THIRD ATTACK
Material for this section was primarily drawn from the author's interviews with John Blaney, Ted Collins, Brad Lynn, Robert Ferguson, Somini Sengupta, Daniel Chea, Anthony Adams.
"Liberia was hot, and not in a good way." Tensions between the State Department and the Defense Department continued to spill into the press. See e.g., Marquis, Christopher and Thom Shanker, "Pentagon Leaders Warn of Dangers for U.S. in Liberia," New York Times, July 24, 2003. http://www.nytimes.com/2003/07/25/international/africa/25LIBE.html See, also, "Turmoil in Liberia," PBS NewsHour, July 25, 2003. http://www.pbs.org/newshour/bb/africa-july-dec03-liberia_7-25/.
"Meeting of the minds." A full text of President Bush's and Secretary-General Kofi Annan's remarks can be found at: http://georgewbush-whitehouse.archives.gov/news/releases/2003/07/20030714-3.html.

TWO: THE ALAMO MEETING
Material for this section was primarily drawn from the author's interviews with John Blaney and Ted Collins.

THREE: BROKEN GLASSES
Material for this section was primarily drawn from the author's interviews with John Blaney, John Richardson, Ted Collins, Robert Ferguson, Jenkins Vangehn, and Magnus Wolf-Murray.
"At the request of U.S. ambassador," See, i.e., Rhem, Kathleen, "21 Marines Sent Into Liberia at Ambassador's Request," American Forces Press Services, July 21, 2003. http://archive.defense.gov/news/newsarticle.aspx?id=28695.
"More ships headed to Liberia too." See, e.g., CNN International.com/World "Bush orders troops to positions off Liberia," June 25, 2003. http://edition.cnn.com/2003/US/07/25/us.liberia/
"We can tell you," he intoned, "we are still very much inside the compound of the U.S. embassy, the heavily fortified compound." See, "Fighting Erupts Again in Capital of Liberia," CNN.com Transcripts http://edition.cnn.com/TRANSCRIPTS/0307/22/ltm.11.html.

FOUR: NEAR MISSES
Material for this section was primarily drawn from the author's interviews with John Blaney, John Richardson, Daniel Chea, Ted Collins, and Robert Ferguson.
"We're concerned about our people in Liberia." The full text of President Bush's remarks can be found at: http://georgewbush-whitehouse.archives.gov/news/releases/2003/07/20030721.html.

"You know, mortar fire comes from a long distance away..." The full text of Phillip Reeker's remarks can be found at: http://iipdigital.usembassy.gov/st/english/texttrans/2003/07/20030722082934 ifas0.5738336.html#axzz40X1rbaZC.

FIVE: ENDURANCE

Material for this section was primarily drawn from the author's interviews with John Blaney, Ted Collins, Jenkins Vangehn, Horaciao Hernandez, Kaetu Smith and Magnus Wolf-Murray.

The email exchange cited is shared with the permission of John Blaney and Robin Suppe-Blaney.

SIX: RECONSTRUCTION

John Blaney, Ted Collins, Phil Spangler, Ed Birgells, Ziad Sankari.

See, e.g., CNN International.com/World, "Port becomes focus of Liberian war," July, 24, 2003. http://allafrica.com/stories/200307240870.html.

"Complete cessation of hostilities." See e.g., "No ECOWAS force in Liberia till cease-fire returns – Obasanjo," Panapress, July 21, 2003. http://www.panapress.com/No-ECOWAS-force-in-Liberia-till-cease-fire-returns---Obasanjo--12-486654-100-lang3-index.html.

"Appropriate military capabilities." The White House press statement can be found at: http://iipdigital.usembassy.gov/st/english/texttrans/2003/07/20030725114651yeroc0.2745478.html#axzz40X1rbaZC.

"The prospect of U.S. engagement kept Liberia current and questions popped up at odd moments." The transcript of the joint press conference between President Bush and Prime Minister Abbas can be found at: http://2001-2009.state.gov/p/nea/rls/rm/22795.htm.

"The President's order triggered a cascade of plans and actions." Phillip Spangler provided the author and overview of how Joint Task Forces are assembled and their operational significance. For the disposition of forces in Joint Task Force Liberia and other details related to the deployment, including the deployment of the Forward Command Element, see, e.g., Collins, Lt. Col. Thomas W., "Joint Efforts Prevent Humanitarian Disaster in Liberia," Army Magazine, February, 2004.

"The news from the peace talks was not encouraging." See, e.g., "Mediators: It's too early to agree on a peace document," GhanaWeb, July, 23, 2003. http://www.ghanaweb.com/GhanaHomePage/NewsArchive/Mediators-It-s-too-early-to-agree-on-peace-document-39696.

SEVEN: NO MONKEY NO DOG

Material for this section was primarily drawn from the author's interviews Robert Ferguson, Jenkins Vangehn, Robert Khourey, Jean Chahine, Declan Walsh, Emmanuel Goujon, Somini Sengupta, Magnus Wolf-Murray, Jordi Raich Curco, Blamo Sieh and Francis Gallo.

EIGHT: THE PRESS CONFERENCE

Material for this section was primarily drawn from the author's interviews with John Blaney, Sekou Conneh and Daniel Chea. "Political Officer" refers to the author.

"The LURD needs to accept this proposal..." See, e.g., "U.S. urges rebels to withdraw from capital," Washington Times, July 27, 2003. http://www.washingtontimes.com/news/2003/jul/27/20030727-104305-9036r/?page=all

"The new demarcation line…" See, e.g., "Peacekeepers could reach Liberia on Wednesday," CNN International.com/World, July 28, 2003. http://edition.cnn.com/2003/WORLD/africa/07/27/liberia.fighting/

"We agree to fall back, but we want peacekeepers to come." See, e.g., Zavis, Alexandra, "U.S. Urges Rebels to Retreat," The Washington Post, July 28, 2003. www.washingtonpost.com/archive/politics/2003/07/28/us-urges-liberian-rebels-to-retreat/af07d011-59f8-4d48-b58a-f383baa35558/

"The information about the ceasefire…" See, e.g., "Liberian Rebels Declare Ceasefire," The Guardian, July 29, 2003. http://www.theguardian.com/world/2003/jul/29/westafrica

NINE: MODEL

Material for this section was primarily drawn from the author's interviews with John Blaney, Daniel Chea, Benoni Urey, Jenkins Vangehn, Blamo Sieh, Jordi Raich Curco, Emmanuel Goujon, John Del Colliano and Mike Shinners. "Political Officer" refers to the author.

"Once I'm stripped away from my supporters…" See, "Q&A: Nobody Understands Me," Newsweek, August 29, 2003. http://www.newsweek.com/qampa-nobody-understands-me-139639

TEN: THE FORCE COMMANDER'S RECCE

Material for this section was primarily drawn from the author's interviews with John Blaney, Jonathan Taylor, Festus Okonkwo, Theophilus Tawiah, Ted Collins, Brad Lynn, Jenkins Vangehn, Sekou Fofana, Karl Vick and Robert Ferguson. "Political Officer" refers to the author.

"On Thursday, July 31 in Accra…" The Extrordinary Summit of ECOWAS Heads of State and Government on the Situation in Liberia Final Communique can be found at: http://www.ecowas.int/wp-content/uploads/2015/02/2003-July-Extra.pdf.

"On Friday, August 1…" The United Nations Security Council press release announcing the resolution authorizing a peacekeeping force can be found here: http://www.un.org/press/en/2003/sc7836.doc.htm.

"The Multinational Force is a crucial short-term bridge to our goal of placing United Nations peacekeepers on the ground in Liberia as soon as possible." A full text of Ambassador Negroponte's remarks can be found at: http://2001-2009.state.gov/p/io/rls/rm/2003/22990.htm.

"We Will Wait." See, e.g., Sengupta, Somini "African Envoys Try in Vain to See Liberian," New York Times, August 2, 2003. http://www.nytimes.com/2003/08/02/world/african-envoys-try-in-vain-to-see-liberian.html.

PART SIX: FRONTLINE DIPLOMACY

ONE: THE CROSSING

Material for this section was primarily drawn from the author's interviews with John Blaney, Ted Collins, Somini Sengupta, Declan Walsh, Jenkins Vangehn, Kaetu Smith, Emmanuel Goujon, Richard Butler, Sekou Fofana and Robert Ferguson. "Political Officer" refers to the author.

"On Monday, August 4…" See, e.g., Murphy, Jarrett, "Peacekeepers Cheered in Liberia," CBS News, August 4, 2003. "http://www.cbsnews.com/news/peacekeepers-cheered-in-liberia/

"I will move on him, I will attack him militarily." Sengupta, Somini, "The Haves and the Have-Nots Reside on Both Sides of the Liberian Capital," New York Times, August 6, 2003. http://www.nytimes.com/2003/08/06/world/the-haves-and-have-nots-reside-on-both-sides-of-liberian-capital.html?pagewanted=all.

"Divided by a series of bridges," Ibid.

"It was the Forward Coordination Element." See, e.g., Kniazkov, Maxim, "US Military Liaison Team to Be Dispatched to Liberia," Associated Press, August 6, 2003. http://reliefweb.int/report/liberia/us-military-liaison-team-be-dispatched-liberia.

"U.S. Sending Six to Ten Troops to Liberia," Associated Press, August 6, 2003.

TWO: AMBASSADOR, PEACEKEEPER, REBEL

Material for this section was primarily drawn from the author's interviews with John Blaney, Daniel Chea, Festus Okonkwo, Brad Lynn, Ophoree Diah, Robert Ferguson, Sekou Fofana, Aliya Seyah Sheriff and Theophilus Tawiah.

THREE: A PIECE OF PAPER

Material for this section was primarily drawn from the author's interviews with John Blaney, Festus Okonkwo, Daniel Chea, and Ted Collins. "Political Officer" refers to the author.

"Unilateral Cease-fire and Disengagement Declaration." The author drafted the document but is not in possession of a copy.

FOUR: THE PRESENCE PATROLS

Material for this section was primarily drawn from the author's interviews with John Blaney, Festus Okonkwo, Jenkins Vangehn, and Somini Sengupta.

FIVE: THE ARMS SHIPMENT

Material for this section was primarily drawn from the author's interviews with John Blaney, Ted Collins, Festus Okonkwo, Theophilus Tawiah and Daniel Chea.

SIX: THE DELIVERY

Material for this section was primarily drawn from the author's interviews with Robert Ferguson, Aliya Seyah Sheriff and Theophilus Tawiah. "Political Officer" refers to the author.

SEVEN: THE NEGOTIATION

Material for this section was primarily drawn from the author's interviews with John Blaney, Jonathan Taylor, Benoni Urey, Declan Walsh, Daniel Chea, Festus Okonkwo, Brad Lynn, Ophoree Diah, Robert Ferguson, Sekou Fofana, Aliya Seyah Sheriff, Theophilus Tawiah and John Del Colliano.

PART SEVEN

ONE: GOD WILLING, I WILL BE BACK

Material for this section was primarily drawn from the author's interviews with John Blaney, Moses Blah, Daniel Chea, Lewis Brown, John Richardson, Ophoree Diah, Robert Ferguson, Declan Walsh, Sekou Fofana, Jenkins Vangehn and Theophilus Tawiah. "Political Officer" refers to the author.

"His tone was sober, a touch weary." President Taylor's farewell speech can be viewed in full in the "extras" section of the docuramafilms DVD released in 2008 for "Liberia: An Uncivil War" Directed and Produced by Jonathan Stack, Gabriel Films (in association with California Newsreel), 2004.

TWO: THE AGREEMENT

Material for this section was primarily drawn from the author's interviews with John Blaney, Sekou Damate Conneh, Festus Okonkwo, Aliya Seyah Sheriff, Sekou Fofana, Ophoree Diah, Robert Ferguson, Michael Smith, Theophilus Tawiah and John Del Colliano. "Political Officer" refers to the author.

"First, I want to make a comment about some foreign policy." President Bush's remarks can be found at: http://www.presidency.ucsb.edu/ws/?pid=477. (Via UC Santa Barbara's American Presidency Project).

THREE: THE FREE PORT OF MONROVIA

Material for this section was primarily drawn from the author's interviews with John Blaney, Jordi Raich Curco, Alain Kassa, Declan Walsh, Festus Okonkwo, Sekou Fofana, John Del Colliano, Mike Shinners and Theophilus Tawiah.

"Civilians, literally like thousands of them…" See "Liberians Looting Monrovia Port," CNN.com, Transcripts, August 13, 2003. http://edition.cnn.com/TRANSCRIPTS/0308/13/bn.01.html.

"We are totally in control of the situation." See, e.g., "Liberia Looting," Associated Press, August 13, 2003. http://www.aparchive.com/metadata/youtube/d99a0683f9c30343b5de014968c6acb4.

He took a moment, once again, to brief the press on Liberia. President Bush's remarks can be found at: http://www.presidency.ucsb.edu/ws/?pid=62987 (Via UC Santa Barbara's American Presidency Project).

The Lawrence Di Rita and Norton Schwartz press briefing can be found at: http://www.c-span.org/video/?177791-1/defense-department-briefing.

FOUR: HISTORY ON THE BRIDGE

Material for this section was primarily drawn from the author's interviews with John Blaney, Festus Okonkwo, Aliya Seyah Sheriff, Sekou Fofana, Robert Ferguson, Declan Walsh and Theophilus Tawiah.

FIVE: A SORT OF HOMECOMING

Material for this section was primarily drawn from the author's interviews with John Blaney, Festus Okonkwo, Robert Ferguson, Declan Walsh, Theophilus Tawiah, Jenkins Vangehn and John Del Colliano.

SIX: A QUESTION OF DIPLOMACY

Material for this section was primarily drawn from the author's interviews with John Blaney, Festus Okonkwo, Jordi Raich Curco.

"The CPA stipulated…" The full text of the Comprehensive Peace Agreement can be found at: http://www.usip.org/sites/default/files/file/resources/collections/peace_agreements/liberia_08182003.pdf.

"The United Nations authorized…" For an overview of the United Nations peacekeeping mission in Liberia, see, e.g., http://www.un.org/en/peacekeeping/missions/unmil/background.shtml.

INDEX

"White Flower" mansion, 22
Taylor, Jonathan, 121
    to lay groundwork for exile, 248
Terry McKnight, Captain USS Kearsarge, 80–81
"tripwires," 108–9
Truth and Reconciliation Commission, 345
Tubman, Winston, former Liberian president,
    156
Turner, Thomas, head, "Joint Task Force" for
    Liberia, 216–17, 243, 311
turnover ceremony. *See also* ECOWAS Mission
    in Liberia (ECOMIL)
    chaos at Gabriel Tucker Bridge, 329–30

"Unilateral Ceasefire and Disengagement
    Declaration," 277–78
    Cobra to sign, 287–88
    signature and timetable for unification of
        capital, 309–12, 314–15
United Nations, arms embargo, 8
United Nations Mission in Sierra Leone
    (UNAMSIL), 70
United Nations, Security Council
    lumber, ban on sale, 25
    peacekeeping force authorized, 246, 344
United States
    Blaney denies U.S. coup involvement, 62
    citizens encouraged to leave Liberia, 16
United States Agency for International
    Development (USAID), 32
    assessment of projects, 165–66
    Phebe hospital destroyed, 166
    Salala clinic, 165–66
United States citizens, evacuation of, 38–41
United States Marine Security Guard. *See*
    Adams, Anthony
Urey, Benoni, 59, 86
    on end of Taylor regime, 293
    opinion of Taylor, 236
USAID. *See* United States Agency for
    International Development (USAID)
U.S. European Command (ESAT), 34, 37, 54
    Ambassador's gratitude for work, 93
    evacuation of U.S. citizens, 45–46
    evacuation plans for Embassy personnel,
        71–72

"Joint Task Force" for Liberia, 216
USS Kearsarge, 71, 80–81, 92–93

Vangehn, Jenkins, 8, 42, 89–91, 112, 125–26
    contact LURD field officer Alhaji Sekou
        Fofana, 239–40
    danger in working for Embassy, 91–92
    hope for future, 336–38
    memories of past siege, 224
    MODEL rebels near taking Buchanan, 234
    reports on conditions, family sent to Ghana,
        171–72
    thoughts on Taylor exit, 304–5
Vaye, Isaac, 30
Veritas, Catholic radio station, 8
Vick, Karl, 133
Voice of America, 29

Wald, Charles "Chuck," EUCOM Deputy
    Commander, 78
Walsh, Declan, 174
    description of Monrovia during third attack,
        221–22
    looting and chaos after turnover, 333–34
    Marines at LURD headquarters, 315
    at Waterside and Bushrod Island, 257–59
Warner, John, U.S. senator, 344
water supply, 222–23
weapon sale, plane at Robertsfield, 284
Weeks, Jordan, Marine Security Guard, 99, 102
Welsh, Paul, BBC reporter, 174
Wolf-Murray, Magnus, 112
    Greystone walkways sandbagged, 213
    third attack, offices hit, 198
Wong, Joseph, 25

Yeaten, Benjamin, head, Anti-Terrorist Unit
    (ATU), 18–19, 82–84
    press conference at Iron Gate, 182
Yormie, John, 30